PONTIFICAL INSTITUTE OF MEDIAEVAL STUDIES

STUDIES AND TEXTS
3

THE
ESTATES
OF
RAMSEY ABBEY

TORONTO
1957

PONTIFICAL INSTITUTE OF MEDIAEVAL STUDIES

STUDIES AND TEXTS

3

THE
ESTATES
OF
RAMSEY ABBEY

A STUDY IN ECONOMIC GROWTH AND ORGANIZATION

J. AMBROSE RAFTIS
Professor of Mediaeval History, Pontifical Institute of Mediaeval Studies

With a Preface by
M. M. POSTAN

Pontifical Institute of Mediaeval Studies
Toronto, 1957

TABLE OF CONTENTS

M<small>APS</small>

PREFACE

D<small>R.</small> Raftis's study fills a very important gap in the literature of mediaeval economic history. It is economic in the rare and exacting sense of the adjective. For in spite of their ostensible pre-occupation with mediaeval economy historians of mediaeval agriculture and trade have until recently shared none of the pre-occupations of theoretical economists or economic administrators. Their interests have been largely juridical and administrative and sometimes technological, and their topics largely those of manorial management, legal status of tenants and, to a less extent, the technique of field systems. The present generation of economic historians is probably the first to approach mediaeval economy with the same questions which have hitherto been considered proper to the study of modern economy: the growth and decline of economic activity, the qualities and mobilities of economic resources, and more especially the course of investment, the movements of population, the fluctuations of output and the changes in the distribution of national product.

Dr. Raftis's book links up with these new interests, but does it with a difference. In so far as historians have looked at the economic problems of the Middle Ages, they have seen it almost entirely as one of trends, i.e. broad changes over long periods of time. This pre-occupation with trends is to some extent accidental: no more than a personal preference on the part of the historians who have so far dealt with the economic problem of the Middle Ages. To some extent their interest in trends also reflects the present-day concern of economists and statesmen with economic growth of societies. But the main reason why they occupy themselves with trends is that there has been an urgent need to fill an obvious and dangerous gap in mediaeval study. In the absence of any critical appreciation of the general direction of mediaeval development, historians were prone to fit their studies into a scheme of economic chronology rooted in nothing more than an ancient and uncritically accepted tradition. It is therefore not surprising that, in their endeavours to reform the mediaeval chronology, students should have concentrated on secular changes to the exclusion of other and briefer economic movements.

It is at this point that Dr. Raftis's study attaches itself to the newer tendencies of mediaeval study and puts them right at the same time. His main concern is with the economic fluctuations of shorter range, which students of economic development have hitherto neglected. This neglect now stands corrected. As Dr. Raftis shows, recurrent oscillations were superimposed upon the flow of economic activity in the twelfth and thirteenth century and its ebb in the fourteenth and fifteenth centuries. Some of these were eddies and ripples due to no other cause than the vagary of harvests; others may have occurred in response to more deeply seated economic forces. But whatever the cause, they disturbed and complicated, though never obscured, the swelling and receding tides of secular change.

In one other respect Dr. Raftis's study corrects the impression which the literature on mediaeval trends may give the unwary reader. The student reading the few existing essays on mediaeval expansion and contraction may carry away the impression that the break in the trend occurred everywhere at the same time, i.e. in the middle or at the earliest in the second or third decades of the fourteenth century. Dr. Raftis shows that on the estates of the Ramsey Abbey (and so far as we know also on most other estates on the borders of the great fens) the break occurred somewhat earlier, probably the end of the thirteenth century. Thereby Dr. Raftis's study helps to bring home how intensely local the particulars of agrarian history are bound to be. The very nature of mediaeval trends made it impossible for them to synchronise over the country as a whole. The influences behind them were those of population, soil and settlement, and they could not possibly have combined everywhere in the same manner and at the same point of time.

The reader will also discover in Dr. Raftis's study many other new facts and fresh ideas. It is because both he and his advisers knew or suspected that the Ramsey evidence was capable of revealing much that was hitherto unknown or misunderstood, that they have decided to go over the ground already covered in Miss Neilson's early study of the same estates. That study was in every way a pioneering effort, inspired by the teaching and example of Vinogradoff and reflecting the pre-occupations of mediaeval economic historians at the beginning of the present century. But in spite of her clearly defined interests Miss Neilson was able to disclose a wealth of information in Ramsey documents which she was not herself prepared to exploit. And this disclosure was bound to tempt the next generations of historians to take a second crop from the field she cleaned and tilled. How much in taking it Dr. Raftis benefited from Miss Neilson's earlier labours will be obvious to all the readers of this book.

M. M. Postan,
Peterhouse, Cambridge.

INTRODUCTION

DOCUMENTS relating to the mediaeval manors of Ramsey Abbey have long been familiar to students of the agrarian history of England. One of the earliest products of the Vinogradoff school was Nellie Neilson's survey of the economic conditions on these manors, a study largely dependent upon the charters then recently printed in the Rolls Series; T. W. Page based much of his argumentation for the 'Black Death controversy' upon some manorial account series from Ramsey; and more recently such studies as Professor Postan's investigation of twelfth-century commutation, or the thirteenth-century studies of Professor Kosminsky, have illustrated the continued utility of Ramsey sources. But on the whole, such studies have not been attempts at a systematic exploitation of the vast sources for the history of Ramsey properties. It is the very abundance of these un-explored materials and the importance of Ramsey evidence for the writing of the mediaeval economic history of England over the past two generations that have prompted the present effort to make these materials more fully available for the student of economic history.

Since the object of our investigation has been the economic history of Ramsey manors, many important aspects of the abbey history, in particular legal questions and those of abbey administration, have not received a system-atic treatment. The reader will find in appropriate places throughout the study a description of the various sources employed, and a glance at the List of Tables and Appendices entered at the beginning of this volume will reveal the bulk of the data extracted from Ramsey sources. We shall only mention briefly here some important considerations that have determined the pattern of our investigation.

With those gradual refinements in the discipline of mediaeval economic history, which have brought more and more to the fore an emphasis upon regional and local differences, and upon the existence of local variations in economic evolution, a heavier burden of proof has been thrown upon the more widely representative as well as the more chronologically cohesive treatment of economic data. For such purposes, the data of economic life must be sufficiently copious to allow the separation of general trend from local variation; and they must be comparative to permit the delineation of movement and change over both the short and long run period. The follow-ing study has attempted to meet these requirements, first, by an investiga-tion of Ramsey estates as a group, and secondly, by an extensive tabulation of the data of extents and account rolls. Without a composite group of estates, it would have been impossible to draw together, even in a too often tentative manner, the various threads of productivity and price changes, or of demesne exploitation and the employment of villeins. In particular, the hundreds of manorial account rolls that illustrate, for example, the annual adjustment of commutation from the late thirteenth century, or the manifold permutations and combinations of rent and labour services ordained to mitigate the secular decline in effective demand for land in the fourteenth century, provide in the investigation of almost every problem instances for which the data from one manor will vary from the overall trend of the group.

Despite the advantages of such an approach, it must be recognized at once that the limitations of even this larger mediaeval collection have been many with regard to various problems and periods in the economic history of Ramsey Abbey estates. While the corporate nature of abbey holdings provided some picture of the early organization of the abbey as a consumer and of its administrative superstructure, it has only been possible to sift from the chronicler's story a few impressions of agrarian organization proper in the pre-conquest era. For the twelfth century, extents make it possible to reconstruct tenemental conditions; and, in addition, a comparative picture of prices and rents for several generations of the post-conquest century has been drawn from numerous charters. But for many important problems of this period the Ramsey sources were too scattered to stand alone, and the more detailed parallels from other monastic collections have been brought into the description. Nor will the reader find a complete analysis of the account rolls as administrative tools of the abbey. Owing to the paucity of surviving administrative directives from the abbey we have been content to unfold the evidence of the account rolls themselves. However, the surprising degree to which this simple inductive method revealed changes in organizational policy was not the least pleasant reward for its investigation.

The dependence of a study upon several score statistical tables has raised difficult problems of presentation. In order to avoid tedious interruption of the text by page upon page of statistical tabulation, chapters five to seven present a simple summary of the statistics of demesne livestock, of the data relevant to corn production and livery, and of wages and prices on the manor. In the same fashion, the arrangement of much material as appendices to chapters eight and nine has been rendered possible by the employment of sample tables in the text. But, whatever may be the facility in reading gained by these methods, it will be clear from the text that both statistical chapters and appendices remain essential to the discussion.

The debts of acknowledgement contracted by this transatlantic investigation are indeed many. The staffs of the British Museum and of the Public Record Office must be especially thanked for the regular and extra facilities placed at my disposal to expedite the investigation of numerous manorial records. Grateful acknowledgement is offered to the various members of the history department of the University of Cambridge and to my colleagues at the University of Toronto, in particular Dr. Karl Helleiner and Rev. Michael Sheehan, C.S.B., for readings and criticism of the text. Fresh from his own studies of Ely records, Mr. Edward Miller, of St. John's College, Cambridge, became more than the usual guide in first introducing me to Ramsey Abbey

materials.   To Rev. J. C. Wey, C.S.B., editor of this series, is owed a heavy
debt of gratitude for giving unstintingly of his time and experience in the
difficult tasks of editing and proof reading.   But above all I must thank Mr.
M. M. Postan, professor of economic history at the University of Cambridge,
for his encouragement and guidance throughout much of this investigation;
my encounter with the stimulating and imaginative approach of one equally a
master in mediaeval and modern economic history has been a unique experience.   The Preface to this volume places me further in debt to his generos-
ity.   But for the form of the following study, with the defects that remain
from my grappling with problems of growth and organization, I must accept
the sole responsibility.

J. A. R.

Pontifical Institute of Mediaeval Studies,
Toronto.

November 21, 1957.

LIST OF TABLES AND APPENDICES

CHAPTER TEN

APPENDICES

LIST OF ABBREVIATIONS

Add. Ch.   *Additional Charters* (British Museum)

A. H. E. S.   *Annales d'histoire économique et sociale*

B. M.   British Museum

Cam. Ec. H.   *Cambridge Economic History of Europe* (I, ed. J. H. Clapham and Eileen Power, 1941; II, ed. M. M. Postan and E. E. Rich, 1952)

Carts.   *Cartularium Monasterii de Rameseia*, 3 vols., ed. W. H. Hart and P. A. Lyons (Rolls Series, 79, 1884-1893)

Chronicon   *Chronicon Abbatiæ Rameseiensis*, ed. W. D. Macray (Rolls Series, 83, 1886)

D. B.   *Domesday Book*, 4 vols. (London, 1783-1816)

Ec. H. R.   *Economic History Review*

E. H. R.   *English Historical Review*

P. R. O.   Public Record Office

R. S.   Rolls Series

Trans. R. H. S.   *Transactions of the Royal Historical Society*

V. C. H.   *Victoria County History*

The conventional abbreviations for English counties (as Hunts. for Huntingdonshire) have been freely used.

LIST OF ABBOTS OF RAMSEY

Aednoth	993-1006
Wulfsy	1006-1016
Withman	*ca.* 1016-*ca.* 1020
Ethelstan	*ca.* 1020-1043
Alfwin	1044-*ca.* 1079
Ailsi	*ca.* 1080-1087
Herbert Losinga	1087-1091
Aldwin	1091-1102; 1107-1111
Bernard	1102-1107
Reginald	1114-1130
Walter	1133-1161
William	1161-1177; 1178-1179
Robert Trianel	1180-1200
Eudo	1200-1201
Robert of Reding	1202-1206
Richard	1214-1216
Hugh Foliot	1216-1231
Ranulph	1231-1253
William Accolt	1253-1254
Hugh of Sulgrave	1255-1268
William of Godmanchester	1268-1285
John of Sawtrey	1286-1316
Simon Eye	1316-1342
Robert of Nassyngton	1342-1349
Robert of Shenyngton	1349-1378
Edmund of Ellington	1378-1396
Thomas Butterwyk	1396-1419
John Tychemersch	1419-1434
John Crowland	1434-1436
John Stow	1436-1468
William Witlesey	1468-1473
John Warboys	1473-1489
John Huntyngdon	1489-1506
Henry Stukeley	1506-1507
John Warboys	1507-1539

CHAPTER I

THE FIRST CENTURY

ONE of the most important constructive movements to come to the fore, after the subsidence of the barbarian invasions which prevailed throughout so much of the Anglo-Saxon era, was the monastic revival of the tenth century. The simple conception of social functions that divided men of that time into those who work, fight, and pray, guaranteed a weighty position to the ecclesiastical institution. Where the monasteries were concerned this social function was, in turn, translated into vast territorial grants, on one hand by the impressive needs of important establishments, and, on the other, by the amazing sollicitude of their Anglo-Saxon patrons to supply a landed endowment for every facet of monastic needs. This became almost literally an equation of monastic influence with a large segment of the English countryside — an equation best seen in the *banleuca* liberties — and it meant that such a religious institution could never remain remote from English social and economic developments. Long before the knights of William the Conqueror introduced the fiefs which were to mould, and to be moulded by, the legal, social, and economic evolution of the centuries, the Benedictine monastery was leaving its imprint upon the formation of agrarian life.

The crowning memorial to the work of St. Oswald in the tenth-century monastic revival, was his foundation at Ramsey. On a wooded island in that region of the then flooded fens called Ramsey Mere, this bishop of Worcester discovered those conditions which were lacking to his earlier choice of Westbury-on-Trym. Henceforth he was to lavish his special attention upon Ramsey, and make of it the matrix of other monastic foundations. These efforts were duly rewarded when the abbey became within a short time a seat of learning, the foster home of bishops, and, by the time of the Domesday Inquest, the fourth wealthiest monastery in the land.

The conditions which made the Ramsey site attractive to St. Oswald were not only the privacy and protection afforded by the island, but the acquisition of cultivable lands to the south through the co-operation of the ealdorman Aethelwin. As a result, the history of Ramsey Abbey and its estates emerges for the greater part with the early history of the county of Huntingdonshire. The county boundaries were to embrace the major concentration of abbey properties: along with scattered holdings in the west and southern portions of the county, these properties of the abbey came to occupy nearly the whole of the eastern of the four hundreds. The monastery also has a remarkable parallel with the county in chronology of foundation. For the foundation of Ramsey Abbey around 970[1] was not a revival similar

---

[1] Records for the foundation of Ramsey generally give the year as 969, but some evidence points to the following year. J. A. ROBINSON has given a summary of

to that appearing in the neighbouring fen monasteries but a completely new venture; and for its part, the county name of Huntingdon only appears for the first time in 1011.[2] Nevertheless, Ramsey Abbey was given properties to the south and west of the island because they were already productive. So while it will be appropriate to restrict our remarks to the territory now forming the county of Huntingdon, this study of the abbey's estates must commence with a review of topographical details and a general perspective of ancient and early Anglo-Saxon settlement.

I

The county of Huntingdon today is of an irregular shape lying between the Nene river, which forms roughly the northern boundary from Elton to Peterborough, and the Ouse river that cuts across its south-eastern corner. It is the third smallest county in England with an area of approximately 234,000 acres.[3] A geological structure of Oxford clay underlies the greater part of the county although this is usually covered with a deep crust of boulder clay interspersed in some areas with chalk. The whole county is low lying, sloping from a height of approximately 250 feet between Covington and Catworth in the west to 163 feet at Elton in the north and to the fen area of an average 10 to 12 feet above Ordnance Datum in the east.

This fen area is a deposit of gravel, light clay and peat upon older geological formations, and in Huntingdon it is rather more peaty at the surfaces than in other fen counties. The fens occupy today nearly 80,000[4] acres in Huntingdonshire. Of course drainage has changed considerably the topography and even the geology of this zone. Ramsey 'Island' has for long been no longer an island, though the adjacent Ramsey Mere and Uggmere were drained as recently as 1840. A branch of the Ouse, the Old West Water, that once extended from Earith to Ramsey Mere thence joining the Nene via Whittlesey Mere, has been dried up for centuries. The last extensive marsh to be drained was Whittlesey Mere in 1851-2.[5] The subsequent shrinkage of the peaty ground there, to the extent of about four and one half inches *per annum* during the first nine years, is a strong warning to the agricultural historian of the physical transformation wrought by fen drainage.[6]

---

this problem of dating in 'St. Oswald and the Church of Worcester', *British Academy Supplemental Paper*, No. V (1919), pp. 36-37.

The Ramsey *Chronicon*, and the *Vita Sancti Oswaldi auctore anonymo* (Historians of the Church of York, ed. J. Raine, R. S. 71, 1879), pp. 399 ff., form the main sources for the life of St. Oswald.

[2] *The Place-Names of Bedfordshire and Huntingdonshire*, ed. A. Mawer and F. M. Stenton (Cambridge, 1926), p. xviii.

[3] V. C. H., Hunts., I (1926), p. 31. The next few paragraphs owe much to the excellent preliminary chapters of vol. I,

V. C. H., Hunts., and to the *Report of the Land Utilization Survey of Britain* (London, 1941), Part 75, by D. W. Fryer.

[4] *Report of the Land Utilization Survey of Britain*, p. 435.

[5] Wood Walton and Holme Fen are still partially unreclaimed.

[6] In the study 'Extinct Waterways of Fens', *Geographical Journal*, LXXXIII (1934), G. Fowler gives another interesting example of a topographical change at Willingham, Cambs.: a former marsh bottom has now become an elevated area by shrinkage of the peat formations around it (pp. 32-3).

Boulder clays were suitable for forest growths,[7] and the reconstruction of early forest areas indicates heavily wooded uplands in Huntingdon.[8] Archæological evidence suggests that prehistoric man failed to attack these forests. Instead he settled in the gravel river valleys which were probably more extensive in ancient times[9] than today.[10] It is noteworthy too that the rich fishing resources of the fens attracted early man to settle along its edge as well as in the valley formed by the Nene and Ouse and their tributaries.[11]

Beyond the great pottery industry of the Nene Valley, the economic life of the Romano-British period does not seem to have been significant. The construction of Ermine Street brought the Huntingdon region into active contact with the rest of Britain and the town of Godmanchester appeared at the juncture of this street with other roads from Cambridge and the Midlands. But Godmanchester apparently did not share in the bustling life of the northerly town of Castor on the Nene, and agricultural activity that grew up along Ermine Street, and indeed even in the old valleys,[12] was slight.[13] Coin hoards suggest that the inhabitants at this period were a poor people scattered over the traditionally cultivated river valleys.[14] Only in the late period of Roman occupation are there interesting indications that the people were beginning to hew wedges into the wooded uplands at Broughton, Wyton, Woodhurst, Wood Walton, and Wistow.[15] Increased occupation of the fen islands in the third and fourth centuries gives further evidence of this late activity.[16]

But the fact that only two indigenous sites can be located[17] suggests that the Britons disappeared from the area before the end of the 6th century.[18] The fen rivers left this region very accessible to the ravages of Anglo-Saxon bands; and some settlement would eventually be expected from the invaders passing up these avenues to the midlands. Four very ancient names in Huntingdon — Gidding, Yelling, Lymage, and Wintringham — are hints to the existence of these upland settlements of pre-700 at the latest.[19] On the other hand, the almost entire lack of Anglo-Saxon heathen relics[20] in the county implies that such pre-Christian settlement in this district must have been exiguous. Certainly the movements of the late Romano-British period

[7] H. A. WILCOX, *Woodlands and Marshlands of England*, p. 12.

[8] *Ibid.*, Map A.

[9] Archaeological finds on the former gravel river banks are frequently now covered with many feet of clay, cf. V. C. H., Hunts., I, *passim*.

[10] *Ibid.*, p. 13: Considerable tracts of Valley Gravel border the Ouse from St. Neots to Huntingdon, Godmanchester, St. Ives, Fenny Stanton, and Holywell. A broad tract extends from Bluntisham to Somersham marking a former course of the river ... FRYER, *op. cit.*, gives the Ouse Valley and Fen Gravels as about 50,000 acres (p. 439).

[11] V. C. H. Hunts., I, p. 193: Prehistoric Map; and p. 214: Tribal Groups of Early Iron Age (map).

[12] Map of Roman Britain, Ordnance Survey, 1928.

[13] V. C. H., Hunts., I, p. 221.

[14] *Ibid.*, p. 222; and H. A. WILCOX, *op. cit.*, Map B.

[15] V. C. H., Hunts., I, p. 223.

[16] *Ibid.*, p. 255 and ff. Air photography finds have been interpreted as showing that the fens were cultivated in Roman times in contrast to earlier or mediæval times. See the *Fenland Survey Exhibition*, Fenland Research Committee (Cambridge, 1934), pp. 28 ff.

[17] V. C. H., Hunts., I, p. 223.

[18] *The Place-Names of Bedfordshire and Huntingdonshire*, p. xviii.

[19] *Ibid.*, p. xvii.

[20] Cyril Fox, *The Personality of Britain* (Cardiff, 1947), p. 35: The Map of Anglo-Saxon Burial Places 450-650; and, by the same author, *Archæology of the Cambridge Region* (Cambridge, 1923), pp. 217-218.

into the fen islands were not continued. The pagan,[21] and even early Christian Anglo-Saxon[22] avoided the 'evil fens'. Furthermore, evidence for settlement along the valleys of the Ouse and Nene themselves in this early period is not very extensive.[23]

The fact that the particular area now represented by Huntingdonshire failed to attract such early monastic outposts as those at Ely, Croyland, and Peterborough, may have been due to the unsettled political frontier that made the southern fen border a scene of tribal warfare between the East and Middle Angles.[24] In addition, when the Mercians began the first big Anglo-Saxon onslaught on the forests[25] they concentrated in the west and central midlands. That position beyond the pale of existing civilization, given to Bruneswald in late Anglo-Saxon literature[26] must have meant, too, that this forest on the eastern side of the Northampton escarpment somewhat isolated Huntingdon from the developments in the Mercian midlands. Indeed the divisions of the Tribal Hidage that are associated with Huntingdon[27] appear to centre on the old river valleys in the smaller numbers appropriate to less developed regions. The 300 families of the Sweord Ora could be easily scattered along the old course of the Nene and the northern boundary of the present county divisions; the 1,200 families of the Herefinna would more likely be found scattered along the easily cultivable banks of some 30 miles of the Ouse river together with its tributaries, rather than limited to the area of the modern Hurstingstone hundred.

But there is no justification for assuming that the unsettled character of the Huntingdon uplands of Romano-British days remained down through the eighth and ninth centuries to the time of the Ramsey Abbey foundation. Huntingdonshire presented no real natural barriers to the Anglo-Saxon settler:[28] the boulder clay forest was not as impenetrable as the growths upon wealden clay or the Gault,[29] and the tongues of forest running down between the valleys of the Nene and Ouse with their tributary streams would frequently be less than 3 or 4 miles in width.[30] Generations of peace must have produced

[21] H. C. DARBY, 'The Fenland Frontier in Anglo-Saxon England', *Antiquity*, VIII (1934), 188.

[22] *Memorials of St. Guthlac*, ed. W. de G. Birch (Wisbech, 1881).

[23] V. C. H., Hunts., I, pp. 271 ff., and R. G. COLLINGWOOD and J. N. L. MYRES, *Roman Britain and the English Settlement* (Oxford, 1937), pp. 383-393 for questions of the above paragraph generally.

[24] H. C. DARBY, 'The Fenland Frontier in Anglo-Saxon England', pp. 194 ff., and Cyril Fox, *Archæology of the Cambridge Region*, pp. 285-295.

[25] COLLINGWOOD and MYRES, *op. cit.*, p. 410.

[26] F. M. STENTON, *Anglo-Saxon England* (Oxford, 1950), p. 281-2.

[27] *The Place-Names of Beds. and Hunts.*, p. xix, where Sweord Ora is considered to have represented the Sword Point peninsula of northwest Huntingdon, while Herefinna is suggested as an early form of Hurs-

tingstone (cf. Hurstingstone Hundred).

[28] Of the approximately 234,000 acres in Huntingdonshire today, 86,522 are under permanent pasture, 140,000 are devoted to arable land, and only some 5,000 acres are woodlands (V. C. H., Hunts., I, p. 31). FRYER, *op. cit.*, gives the arable as 57.3 per cent in 1938.

[29] H. A. WILCOX, *op. cit.*, p. 12.

[30] The manorial nomenclature on the upland penetrating the fen region between the Ouse and Nene in Huntingdon has remained specifically indicative of its former wooded features: following a contour height where a rather sharp drop from the 100 foot level towards the 50 foot level occurs, at the extreme east is found Wood End; proceeding westwards on the southern side of the contour is Woodhurst, then directly north of Huntingdon town is Sapley (cf. Sapley forest); proceeding west from Wood End on the northern side of the

considerable penetration of these wooded rises.[31] And the fact that later
Scandinavian invasions of the ninth century left little trace upon local nomenclature[32] cannot be taken as evidence of no settlement;[33] indeed there is a
suggestion in the Ramsey chronicle that in the later Danish invasions the
newcomers were frequently repelled or absorbed by the very extent of the
existing Anglo-Saxon settlements. In the course of his history of land
benefactions, the Ramsey chronicler devotes a long detailed section[34] to the
manner in which the Anglo-Saxon ostracized the Danish invaders in the early
11th century. An unnamed Danish lord of the vill of Therfield in Hertford,
and another Dane holding Shillington in Bedfordshire, were so isolated and
threatened by hostile natives that they sold cheaply and evacuated the area
for fear of their lives. Even as far north as Elton, just below Peterborough in
the Danelaw, the invaders' position was so insecure that a Dane called
Turkillus was tricked into a bet while drunk, and thereby deprived of the Elton
estate by the Anglo-Saxons, while his misfortune was mocked and ridiculed
by the latter.

The accounts given of the Ramsey foundation bear out very strongly
this impression of a well-established agrarian economy in the Huntingdonshire
of the late 10th century. The chronicler singles out only Ramsey island as a
region newly cleared and cultivated at the foundation. To his picture must
be added that of the primitive aspect of the fens in the late 10th century,
and we may likely suppose a heavily wooded area in the mainland immediately
facing the island, from the fact that Aethelwin kept a hunting lodge on Ramsey
island. But the Ramsey foundation was not a primary formative influence
like the twelfth-century Cistercian plantations, which so often tended to
mould the agrarian pattern in northern England or eastern Germany. Nor is
there any indication that the abbey at this stage sponsored the settlement of
new vills, such as were to develop by the twelfth century in Huntingdon.
The vills were so clearly established, named, hidaged, and sufficiently well
defined to the Anglo-Saxon landlord of the time that transfers did not necessi-
tate the elaborate descriptive detail of newly staked-out regions.[35] As will be
seen below, Huntingdon was a territory so adequately occupied that purchase,
sale, and exchange even at the risk of competitive suits, had to complete the
property nucleus founded upon hereditary lands.[36] The fact that the chroni-

---

contour are Warboys (Warbois), Old
Hurst, Upwood, and Wood Walton.
Efforts to give more precision to the history
of forest exploitation by tracing the shape of
parish extensions into the upland from this
100 foot contour fringe of manors do reveal
a significant 'tangle of lanes and paths',
but their chronology remains obscure.

[31] Cyril Fox, *Archæology of the Cambridge
Region*, p. 307: The four hundred years of
the Christian Anglo-Saxon period . . . was
on the whole one of progress . . . ; and p.
312: . . . and we may justifiably picture the
processes of expansion of the arable in the
I–IV centuries as identical with those
operating in the VII–XI centuries.

[32] Eilert EKWELL, 'The Scandinavian Settlement', in H. C. Darby (ed.), *A Historical
Geography of England to 1800* (Cambridge,
1936), p. 153.

[33] *Ibid.*, p. 160.

[34] *Chronicon*, pp. 135 ff. For another interesting reference to the purchase of lands
from the Danes by Saxons, see the publi-
cations of the *Bedford Historical Society*,
Vol. 5, pp. 42-4.

[35] *The Place-Names of Beds. and Hunts.*, p. xix.

[36] The chronicler mentions specifically the
clearing of Ramsey island for cultivation,
and the fact that its famous trees gave the
huge beams still to be seen in the abbey
church in his time.

cler can almost give his account by the transcription of legal documents has
deprived us of the informal and personal materials that we should require
for an intimate knowledge of the foundation. Nevertheless, by the very
magnitude of the arrangements necessary for the endowment of the abbey,
there cannot fail to be exposed an important cross-section of the social and
economic structure of the time.

II

The first generation of Ramsey's history was dominated by the activities
of the two founders, Oswald, Bishop of Worcester, and Aethelwin the ealdorman of East Anglia. These two men visited the abbey at least once a year
from the time of the consecration of the church in 974 until their deaths in
992. Indeed St. Oswald kept a direct governing hand over his precious new
community, and the chronicler, who must be the main source for this pre-
conquest history, states that an abbot was appointed only some 24 years after
the foundation.[37] Aethelwin in turn was the patriarchal benefactor, nursing
the fledgling's growth, and at his last meeting not finding it unfitting to
designate the first abbot for election.[38]

From the *Chronicon* come the charters of land grants that earned for this
collection the more exact alternative title of *Liber Benefactorum*. Although it
is of twelfth-century vintage, the compilation of the *Chronicon* from the
Anglo-Saxon charters has been readily ascertained.[39] More recent scientific
investigation has drawn attention to the manipulation of some original charter
forms, in particular the royal writs of privilege and liberties, but the genuineness
of the main substance of the materials in even these more suspect charters
remains very probable.[40] Despite the almost complete lack of that detail
about the structure of land holdings and the obligations of tenure found in
the continental *Polyptyques* and *Censiers* for this earlier mediæval period,[41] —
a gap that has been augmented by the chronicler's unfortunate neglect of
economic data through the reduction of many Anglo-Saxon charters to mere
notitiæ records of grant, benefactor, and recipient — these charter materials
may be fitted into a mosaic of the property structure instrumental to the
birth of a large tenth-century Benedictine community.

The grants over the first forty years to the new abbey were governed by
an explicit concern for securing abbatial consumption needs from lands

[37] *Chronicon*, p. 109.
[38] An advice not followed, however, for the
monks elected their steward Aednoth as
abbot, and Aethelwin's appointee Germanus
was finally made abbot of Cholsey in
Berkshire.
[39] Editor's introduction to *Chronicon*, especially pp. xxii-xxiii.
[40] F. E. HARMER, *Anglo-Saxon Writs* (Manchester, 1951), pp. 245-269.
[41] E. g., the classical studies of the *Polyptyque
d'Irminon*, abbé of Saint-Germain-des-Prés
(811-832), by B. E. C. GUÉRARD (Paris,
1844), especially vol. I; and a study of the
estates of Prüm, *ca.* 895, by C.-E. PERRIN
in A.H.E.S., VI (1934); for the low countries
F. L. GANSHOF, 'Manorial Organization
in the Low Countries, in the Seventh,
Eighth and Ninth Centuries', Trans. R. H.
S., XXI, 4th series (1949), pp. 29-59; for
the royal estates in particular, A. DOPSCH,
Wirtschaftsentwicklung der Karolingerzeit
(Weimar, 1911), I, no. 3, 'Die Königliche
Grundherrschaft'.

and rents. First and foremost in this respect was the establishment of the abbey location and the consolidation of the surrounding territory by the immediate and unconditional land grants of the co-founders. Ealdorman Aethelwin granted[42] the island of Ramsey with the surrounding waters, the adjoining mainland territory of Upwood with its adjunct at Raveley, and ten hides at Stukeley. From his hereditary holdings in west Huntingdon, the vill of Brington and the ten hides of Weston were bequeathed. Some balance for the monastic diet was assured from the gift of his fen properties: Hilgay and the surrounding waters with the berewick at Snorehill and one half of the fisheries in the area, five hides in Walsoken and one half of the contingent fishery in Welles.

The amount of donation deemed necessary by the founders bears impressive witness to that pivotal position of the monastery in the Anglo-Saxon socio-religious conception.[43] Oswald and Aethelwin seem to have been directly or indirectly concerned in the transfer of some fifteen complete vills involving over one hundred hides of land. In order to supplement the resources from their own hereditary lands, therefore, purchase, exchange, and wider communal support were employed to meet the foundation dowry. This became only one demand segment in an intensive land market. For, over the short period of one-half dozen years (966-972), contemporaries of St. Oswald were adding foundations at St. Neot's, Thorney, Croyland, Peterborough, and Ely, which combined with Ramsey to form that 'encirclement movement' by the great Benedictine abbeys which was to remain the dominant institutional feature of the fen region over mediæval times. Of some 83 vills listed in Domesday for Huntingdon, for example, nearly fifty per cent appear to have changed hands in the late tenth-century revival.[44]

Aethelwin purchased a meadow and mill at Houghton for the abbey; part of a ten hide hereditary holding at Toft was completed by property exchange for donation to the abbey. Ten hides at Gidding and Wedeton which he held 'by right of purchase' were also bestowed by the ealdorman, and forty hides at Hatfield were exchanged for thirty at Hemmingford at a sacrifice for greater 'fertility and proximity'. St. Oswald apparently had no hereditary

[42] All the land exchanges recorded during the life of Oswald and Aethelwin and the early eleventh century cited below are from Chronicon, Pars Secunda, pp. 47 ff., unless otherwise stated.
The names of the vills are given in modern spelling, where possible. In order to distinguish between the manor and the market village this study retains throughout the mediæval name of Slepe for the former; St. Ives refers to the village only. The abbey manor of Weston is the modern Old Weston.
[43] For a comprehensive picture of the important point of the relationship of Benedictine monasteries to the society of their time see the early chapters of Dom David KNOWLES, The Monastic Order in England (Cambridge, 1941), especially pp. 7-9, 16-17.

621-2. The chronicler's own apologia upon the spiritual and social regenerative effect of the monasteries comes on pp. 34-5 of the Ramsey Chronicon.
[44] Ely gained Bluntisham, Colne, and Somersham vills in one corner of Hurstingstone Hundred; in Toseland Hundred, St. Neot's vill went to the monastery of that name and Stoughton to the Bishop of Lincoln (though at first held by Ramsey); Ely also held Spaldwick, Barham, and four hides in Little Catworth in Leightonstone Hundred; in the fourth Hunts. Hundred of Norman cross, Peterborough gained Alwalton, Fletton, and Orton Waterville; Thorney Abbey held Farcet, Haddon, Water Neton, Woodston, Yaxley, and most of Stibbington while Whittlesey Mere was divided among Peterborough, Thorney, and Ramsey.

lands in the region for grant.   But he bought Niddingworth from King Edgar, and received Wistow in an exchange with the same king *quia ecclesiæ Ramesensi vicinior magis accessu competens erat et recessu*.   Oswald likewise purchased five hides in Burwell to complete the abbey control over all that vill.   For King Edgar, by the prayers and urgings of St. Oswald, had already granted five hides at Burwell *in necessarios incœpti ædificii sumptus*.   The same king gave the church and three hides at Godmanchester, and one hide at Stukeley. Dunstan supported the foundation and completed a solid block of land from the abbey to the Ouse by a gift of the estate of Warboys.   Edward the Martyr widened this block by donating two hides in Broughton, and King Aethelred later added nine more hides in the same vill so that Ramsey held nearly all of Hurstingstone hundred.   The three small vills of Ely in the south-east corner, and royal demesne at King's Ripton, Great Stukeley, and Hartford in the west were the only large sections of land not belonging to the abbey in this hundred. As will be noted below, there were strong legal reasons favouring conveyance by purchase rather than by the hereditary grant over this period.   But, at the same time, enough ready money seems to have been available so that, from the very first years of its creation, the abbey administration too, under its steward Aednoth, had been able to invest in property.   In Henny Hill, *Fratres . . . plurimas ibidem terras tam in campo arabili quam in villæ mansis multi aeris pretio comparaverunt*;[45] lands were bought in Snailswell *viginti librarum pretio*; and two hides in Stapleford (later exchanged for more suitable property at Swaffham), were purchased for one hundred silver shillings.

This avoidance by the abbey of a long period of gradual property accumulation is of course a tribute to the zeal and wealth of her patrons.   But it is also important to notice that the rapidity of the foundation draws attention to a much neglected feature of Anglo-Saxon life, the extensive employment of money in exchange.   Taken together with the cost of redemption of seized lands,[46] and the rounding out of demesne for the sake of legal security,[47] these purchases must have required considerable disbursements.   The specialized needs of a new monastic community in the Anglo-Saxon society would serve further to foster the use of money.

While there are no figures for the expenditure by the abbey itself some notion of volume in these considerable funds necessary for the initial capital expenditure on an abbey may be gained from the collateral allocations of benefactors.   Anglo-Saxons were fond of lavishing money upon adornments[48] and the devoted supporters of the abbey showed themselves to be unstinting in the standards they set for the first stone church.   Alfwara gave 5 gold marks for gilding vestments; Aethelwin supplied most of the altar hangings *ad decus ecclesiæ amplis et solidis argenti laminis*; King Edgar spent 20 pounds upon bells for the twin stone towers, while Aethelwin in turn guaranteed musical accom-

---

[45] *Chronicon*, p. 51.
[46] E. g., Wammaford, *Chronicon*, p. 54: numerata pecunia redemerunt.
[47] *Ibid.*, p. 52: in Stukeley, dato . . . competenti pretio, aliam hidam integram in

eadem villa justo emptionis titulo possederunt.
[48] Dorothy WHITELOCK, *The Beginnings of English Society* (London, 1952), pp. 95-6, for a general discussion of this question.

paniment for services at a cost of 30 pounds.[49]   Other items of similar interest
were the two *ciphi* worth 12 marks, *filacterium unum habens pretium duodecim
marcarum*, a gold cross worth four and one half marks.   These were costly
furnishings indeed when St. Oswald seems to have obtained the vill of Niddingworth for two crucifixes.[50]

The above figures permit some appreciation of the complementary
expenditure that would be necessary by the abbey in order to acquire and
maintain parallel standards in other buildings and furnishings, but it is
equally important to remember that monastic life called for liturgical expenses
of considerable amount and unusual requirements.   As Solomon 'sacrificed
to the Lord two and twenty thousand oxen, and a hundred and twenty thousand sheep' for peace offerings, so the monasteries performed regularly a vast
liturgical office of expiation.[51]   It is in this sense that the bequests *in pretium
sepulturæ et salutis*, and *pro ejus anima in ellemosynam liberam*[52] are indices of
the expense of religious ceremony as well as real contractual agreements.[53]
Only with the rolls of anniversary rents and such relevant obedientiary calendars as sacristan rolls in the 13th century is it possible to acquire a more
unified picture of the hundreds of pounds thus expended annually upon
incense, wax, vestments, shrines, wine, and the ceremonial clothing of the
monks.

Some gifts of money, such as the bequest of six marks by Aelfric,[54] would
have helped provide the capital for investment, domestic, and liturgical
expense at this early period.   But the revenues from regular property rents
would have to form the more likely source of a ready cash surplus.   It is

[49] Aethelwin was certainly the *pater munificus* of the early days.   When one of the towers cracked from the settling of the foundation in the fen subsoil a large part of the edifice had to be entirely pulled down and reconstructed.   But in these words the chronicler has Aethelwin allay the treasurer's worries: Ego vero de opibus quas hactenus ad crumenas corrogavi sufficientiam vobis omnem ad expensas munificus ministrabo.

[50] *Chronicon*, pp. 48-9: Emerat igitur a rege Aedgaro villam quæ Nidingworth dicitur, competentis pretii mutatione, multis scilicet et pretiosis reliquiis, quae in duabus crucibus de sexies viginti marcarum auri pondere fabricatis continebantur.   The calculation of land values is only rarely possible: in the Burwell purchase of 5 hides for 80 gold mancuses (taking each as worth 30 silver pence), and the hides of Stapleford for 100 shillings, there are given, *ceteris paribus*, values of 40 to 50 shillings per hide.   The area of most property purchases is too indeterminate, however, for any attempt at evaluation.   For other examples, citing land values in the early eleventh century at 2 pounds per hide, see Marjory HOLLINGS, *The Red Book of Worcester* (Worcester, 4 vols., 1934-50), IV, p. xxi.

[51] The tenth-century *Regularis Concordia*, as well as Lanfranc's *Constitutions*, brings out

well the full devotion of the monastic day to divine services and the elaborate seasonal liturgy of the monastery.

[52] *Chronicon*, p. 67: Et ego Aernketel volo quod in pretium sepulturæ meæ et animæ salutem proveniant ecclesiæ Ramesensi XV libræ de argento et auro et catallis quæ die defunctionis meæ apud me contigerit inveniri.

[53] H. B. HAZELTINE points out the contractual aspect of spiritual benefits in A. J. RoBERTSON, *Anglo-Saxon Charters* (Cambridge 1939), Introduction, p. xx.

[54] Dorothy WHITELOCK, *Anglo-Saxon Wills* (Cambridge, 1930), p. 75.   Some wills belonging to the peers of the founders of Ramsey Abbey attest to the monetary potential of this source.   Bishop Theodred, *ibid.*, pp. 3 ff., bequeathed 200 gold marks as heriot, as well as 2 silver cups, 50 gold marks, 5 pounds to every bishop, 5 gold marks to the archbishop, 20 pounds for distribution to estates, and 5 pounds to Glastonbury; and Ealdorman Aethelmaar, *ibid.*, pp. 25 ff., left four armlets worth 300 mancuses of gold as heriot, 500 gold mancuses, 20 pounds in pence, and 36 pounds in 16 small gifts.   Religious institutions were the main beneficiaries of both the bishops and laymen.

impossible to make any precise quantitative estimate of revenues from the small number of rental details that have been preserved. The chronicler austerely relates, for instance, that the vill of Stour was donated *cum dominio et firma*, without adding amounts. Information on monastic *feorms* from the late Anglo-Saxon period makes it quite clear that most of the produce consumed by the monks was received in kind. There are indeed many rents and donations in kind in the very charters of foundation: the 60,000 eels rent from the fisheries of Welles, the food rents to be paid from Hickling estate on the feast of St. Benedict,[55] the supplies for the rental of part of Burwell,[56] the vestments and the crucifixes given by Alfwara. But many of the rents which are mentioned indicate monetary transactions: Burwell rents are to meet construction expenses, the vill of Brancaster in Norfolk was to buy clothing for the monks, one gold mark was to be expended between the monastery and refectory; 'Offertun' estate was *ad fabum, salem, et mel fratribus procurandi*; and again two pounds rent were allocated *singulis annis ad vestitum*.

With the more precise information available from the late eleventh-century records, it is possible to see a common practice whereby the funds for the regular purchase of such important items as clothing and the sacristan's requisites in the Black Monk establishments were received in cash rents. The charters of Ramsey do not reveal how the chamberlain of the abbey financed his purchase of clothing, but in the *Liber Niger*[57] of her neighbour Peterborough, for example, we find that Fisherton pays 20 pounds *ad vestitum monachorum*, whereas most of the manors of this abbey are paying some food *feorm*. The most detailed survey for the chamberlain's revenues over this period, that of Abingdon,[58] shows the same dependence upon cash rents. Some of the earliest forms in which the sacristan's revenues are indicated are the abbots' allocations for anniversaries. Around the time of the conquest Abbot Baldwin of Bury St. Edmunds granted 20s. in this fashion for the king and 20s. for himself.[59] Certainly from the late eleventh century the abbots of Ramsey[60] resorted to this common practice of subsidizing obedientiary revenues by small money rents from churches, mills, and other properties.

There is, unfortunately, too little information upon the structure of the Anglo-Saxon *feorm*, that payment of agrarian produce to king or lord which was the usual burden borne by the vills of the time. But there is some indication that the requirements of capital at the abbeys during this period, before the high farming economy of monasteries, encouraged an increasing commutation even of such food rents. From the time of the Conquest, for example, we have no certain information that the manors of the abbot's *camera* at

---

[55] This document has been cited by F. M. STENTON, *Types of Manorial Structure in the Northern Danelaw* (Oxford, 1910), p. 38, as the earliest extant example of detailed food rents.

[56] *Chronicon*, p. 175: ... et singulis annis de consuetudine hospitium ei et cuncta hospiti necessaria firmata utrimque pactione procuravit.

[57] Camden Society (1849), ed. Thomas Stapleton, p. 164.

[58] *Chronicon Monasterii de Abingdon*, ed. Joseph Stevenson, (R. S., 1858), II, pp. 299 ff. Although this evidence was collected in the time of Henry II, it refers back to the customs of Edward (T.R.E.).

[59] ROBERTSON, *Anglo-Saxon Wills*, pp. 197 ff.

[60] See *infra*, Ch. IV, section I, *passim*.

Ramsey or elsewhere were usually receiving liveries in kind, whereas the evidence for such liveries to the cellarers is abundant. Abbot Faricius of Abingdon found in the early 12th century that the tithes due from the abbey's men had been long since commuted to a money rent.[61] Furthermore, by the time of the conquest, the percentage of cash payments due in even the cellarers *feorms* was very considerable.[62] And for a monastery like Canterbury, where the evidence upon parochial taxes is obviously of much greater antiquity than the conquest, the petty cash dues from the villagers accumulate to surprising proportions.[63] Many of the rental arrangements from the very foundation of Ramsey were probably determined by this need for ready money. This may help to explain the advice of St. Oswald to the monks of Ramsey that they rent the vill of Risby for life *pro certa annui censi pensitatione*. And it is not unreasonable to assume that the early rent combination called *censa et firma*, like that from Bodekesham to Ramsey Abbey, indicate the payment of substantial cash amounts along with the food liveries.[64]

While these records reveal an extensive use of money from the tenth century, and the manner by which monastic needs fostered exchange, such evidence must not be taken to imply an immediate administration of their estates by the monastery. The *Regularis Concordia*, concerned though it was with a detailed explanation of the monastic routine, frowned upon external interests: "The brethren shall not gad about visiting the properties of the monastery unless either great necessity or reasonable discretion require it."[65] There are a few references in the Ramsey documents concerning the devolution of property control to individual monks, who, as they bore no obedientiary title, were unlikely to have had any special administrative claim to lands. Bishop Aetheric's gift of Bodekesham is farmed to the monk Alricus, *firmarii vice custodiendam, . . . dedit exinde Ramesensi ecclesiæ censum et firmam constitutam.*[66] Another monk Mokerus, held the lands of 'Langeton, Wipsinton Mertona, and Wathingworth' that his father had given to Ramsey: *Idem quoque Mokerus, de permissione abbatis jam dictas terras vice firmarii tenens, statutum ex eis censum singulis annis persolvit.*[67] However, as elsewhere in the late Anglo-Saxon monasteries,[68] such disposition of monastic properties does not appear to have become very prevalent. The monk could inherit and possess,[69] and so great was the danger of lawsuit with bequests to the abbey that it was probably a legal precaution for a monk relative like Mokerus to hold power of attorney over familial bequests. Another practice that fostered

[61] *Chronicon Monasterii de Abingdon*, II, pp. 321-2.
[62] E.g., the *Liber Niger* of Peterborough, p. 167.
[63] *The Domesday Monachorum of Christ Church, Canterbury*, ed. D. C. Douglas (London, 1944), pp. 77-9.
[64] There are indeed very early Anglo-Saxon charters allowing for the payment of rents in money or food, e.g., *Cartularium Saxonicum*, ed. W. de G. Birch (3 vols., London, 1885-1893), I, p. 361 (no. 790); II, pp. 115-116 (no. 863).
[65] Ed. Thomas Symons, Nelson Series (London, 1953), p. 8.
[66] *Chronicon*, pp. 144-145.
[67] *Ibid.*, p. 154.
[68] Dom David KNOWLES, *op. cit.*, p. 81; and M. GIBBS, *Early Charters of St. Paul's Cathedral* (Camden Society, 1939), p. xxi.
[69] Émile LESNE, *Histoire de la Propriété Ecclésiastique en France*, I (Paris, 1910), p. 109.

the allocation of estates or their revenues to individual monks was the common custom[70] of child oblation to the monastery. The parents of such children frequently granted revenues to the monastery for their support. It is probably noteworthy that in the clearest example of such a grant from the charters of Ramsey, along with the assurance of private means of support, the parents of the young Aethelricus were careful to subordinate this arrangement to the regular abbey discipline:

> Quum autem in dominio eam habuerint, duas libras singulis annis Aethelrico monacho filio nostro inde ad vestitum procurabunt, quatenus idem Aethelricus, hujus respectu beneficii, humilis et devotus Deo sit, abbati quoque et fratribus suis tractabilis.[71]

As the rule of St. Benedict provided, Ramsey monks would have found it necessary to appoint a monk steward or cellarer at a very early stage in order to assist the abbot in the dispensation of material things at the abbey. However, since the endowments were of well established vills, and apparently in most cases, as has been seen above, their revenues were allocated immediately to monastic needs, the cellarer's function in the first decades would be simply to receive and dispose of these revenues. Most of the grants were of considerable estates formerly held by the king or an important lord, so they would be already well organized to supply the large quantities of produce consumed by the monks and their servants. In what is probably the first detailed *feorm* for which we have extant evidence, that with the gift of Hickling and Kinoulton to Ramsey Abbey, — *X mittas de brasio, et V de grut, et X mittas farinæ triticæ, et VIII pernas, et XVI caseos, et duas vaccas pingues ... in capite vero quadragesimæ VIII isicios* — the donor has obviously pre-arranged the food rents that will go to the abbey from these properties. As Professor Stenton has argued, "there was little room for the interference of the bailiffs of the theyn or abbot in the matter of its incidence or collection."[72] In fact, the obedientiaries who in a later period were to have immediate jurisdiction over vast sections of the monastic lands, fail to appear in our records of public life over the Anglo-Saxon period. Neither the cellarer, nor other monastic officials were named as such among the many witnesses to charters in the late 10th and early 11th centuries. Nor is there any recognition of the administrative personnel of the abbey in the lawsuits or various tenurial arrangements of the time.

These observations simply emphasize that the tenth-century Benedictine foundation was far from having in its early decades that competent administrative superstructure, and those conventual liberties, which were to appear in later centuries. Much remained to be done by Oswald and Aethelwin after

---

[70] KNOWLES, *op. cit.*, pp. 418-420.
[71] *Chronicon*, p. 174. This quotation also suggests another element in the allocation of rents to the abbey, that is, the maintenance of the school. The Ramsey school was one of the most renowned of England, in its early generations at least. The

Chronicon cites (p. 267) a charter from a later period (1149) in which the expense of educating a son at the abbey is one of the items involved in the rent of land to the abbey.
[72] F. M. STENTON, *Types of Manorial Structure in the Northern Danelaw*, p. 38.

the settlement of the monks at Ramsey and the allocation of lands and revenues for their sustenance.   The pious phraseology of the Anglo-Saxon charter, and the zeal of the chronicler to expound the *opera* of the founders, cannot conceal the fact that the foundation and endowments projected a group of monks into temporal affairs for which they were largely unprepared, and into a temporal society fraught with legal and political insecurities.   We may begin the study of the little information that is available from Ramsey documents on these questions with one of the most striking examples of legal insecurity, that of the problems of conveyance.   Then some illustrations will be found from the *Chronicon* as to how the increased holdings of the abbey brought a corresponding dependence upon lay tenants for the administration of these lands.

It is again and again emphasized in the Ramsey charters that the rapid accumulation of properties for the abbey incurred the rivalry of other patrons, or the downright ire of those relatives of the patrons who did not look so dispassionately upon the allocation of large portions of their patrimony to monastic uses.   This threat of lawsuit was so real that immediate transfer, or even more, purchase and exchange, became the most favoured methods of conveyance for endowment.   Both Aethelwin and Oswald made this a policy:

> Accordingly, the worthy duke bestowed on the church many and magnificent gifts in lands, revenues, fisheries, meadows and mills, not from those (properties) which appeared to have come to him by hereditary right, lest his successors should seize this opportunity to have them reclaimed from the church, but from those he had acquired in full freedom at open purchase, either by public exchange, or at home by the transfer of his own money.[73]

Most of the early grants were sufficiently immediate and unconditional to escape litigation.   The bequest of 'the other half' of the fishery of Welles appears to have been the sole example of a *post obitum* conveyance in all of Aethelwin's gifts.   However, even in the earliest purchase and exchange policy of land settlement there was not complete success.   St. Oswald, for instance, had to ensure his purchase of lands at Burwell by an additional exchange of properties, and Aethelwin's Hemmingford exchange was challenged.

It was in the second generation, when the abbey had become an accepted beneficiary, that property grants entered more and more into family wills.   An example from one of the main legal contests will serve as witness to the founders' wisdom in avoiding these hereditary titles as well as being illustrative of the superiority of the nuncupative transaction over the charter in the judicial processes of the time.[74]   The wealthy Aethelstanus Mannessone left the demesne and men, waters and fisheries of Chatteris to Ramsey, together with some land at Wald.   To his wife and family he bequeathed lands in Knapwell, Over, Holywell, 'Hettenleia, Cottenham, Grantendene', Potton, and fisheries

---

[73] *Chronicon*, p. 44.   The chronicler also makes precise the sources of St. Oswald's gifts, *ibid.*, p. 44: Sanctus quoque Oswaldus ... quasdam terras, quas a rege Edgaro vel prece adquisierat, vel mani-festæ commutationis sive legitimæ emptionis quæstu obtinuerat, munificentia liberali adjecit.

[74] H. D. HAZELTINE, in DOROTHY WHITELOCK, *Anglo-Saxon Wills*, Introduction.

at Welles.   In another group of lands — Clopham, Graveley, and Elsworth —
the testator left his wife a part interest: ... *quattuor scilicet has terras in vita
sua possidendas, post mortem vero ejus ut remanerent Sancto Benedicto, pro sua
utriusque salute.*[75]

The wife of Aethelstanus made a claim for all of Elsworth, however, on the
basis of a *viva voce* agreement:

> After the death of this same Aethelstanus, his wife, at the suggestion of
> her relatives, completely dishonoured this agreement, claiming a certain
> devised contract had been settled between herself and her husband while
> he was still alive.   On this basis the woman requested the monks of
> Ramsey to hand over to her the free possession of the land of Elsworth
> so that whatever disposition she should make of this property should be
> confirmed and held permanent both during her life and after her death.

This unwritten contract prevailed and Ramsey Abbey only gained as compensation a more definite claim upon a further joint bequest of Slepe, which had
been left to the daughter Alfwenna:

> ... after her death this same land was to come into the possession of
> Ramsey; however, if she should have an heir during her life, this heir
> should have the land; afterwards it was to remain to the church of
> Ramsey for his soul and those of his forebears.

At this point a more definite title was arranged, whereby: *Terra de Slepe
post dies prædictæ Alfwennæ filiæ ejus tota simul Ramesensi ecclesiæ remaneret,
sive haberet liberos sive non.*   But even this was thwarted by Oswald a relative
of Mannessone's wife, and ten hides of Slepe were thereby seized.   Finally,
when a third party's claim against Oswald's son for another property arose,
the abbey was content to settle its insecure title to 18 hides at Barnwell upon
the new claimant in return for Oswald's demission of Slepe.[76]

During the more violent social disturbances it took more than exchange
or purchase to guarantee land titles.   The very acquisition and maintenance
of property often turned upon political humours.   Only the powerful influence
of Aethelwin [77] kept the monastic holdings intact during the resurgence of
opposition upon the death of King Edgar.[78]   Since the monastic chronicles
like that of Ramsey were immediately concerned with the series of losses
initiated by the Conquest, and were perhaps unwilling to temper their detesta-
tion of the Bastard or to weaken their claims to liberties from the time of
King Edward by reference to the encroachments of Anglo-Saxon kings, they
fail to emphasize the fact that the divestment of monastic lands did not begin
with the conquest.[79]   After death removed the protective hand of Aethelwin,

---

[75] *Chronicon*, pp. 59 ff.
[76] *Chronicon*, pp. 76 ff.
[77] This appears to have been a double-edged
power since the monks of Ely complained
that they were victimized by Aethelwin to
the advantage of Ramsey.   See Edward
MILLER, *The Abbey and Bishopric of Ely*
(Cambridge, 1951), p. 21.

[78] D. J. V. FISHER, 'The Anti-Monastic
Reaction in the Reign of Edward the
Martyr', *Cambridge Historical Journal*, X
(1950-2), 254-270.
[79] The collection of charters by Hemming,
which summarizes the losses from dynastic
changes from the end of the tenth century,
is a welcome exception to this general rule.

the abbey lost Swaffham, and probably Risby and Worlingworth. The
protection of the highest legal authority thus became a real and continuous
need in the murky days of Danish invasions and aristocratic feuds, when the
abbey had been endowed by only one of many and changing circles of episcopal
and aristocratic influence.[80]   Consequently that simple 'familiarity' of
temporal and spiritual institutions in Anglo-Saxon society [81] had real security
ramifications in the economic sphere.[82]   When Hardicnute granted East
Hemmingford and five hides in Gilling, or Edward the Confessor gave Ringstead, Wimbotsham with one hundred and 'another hundred', and the fair
of Downham, these were valuable accretions to monastic resources.   But of
equal importance was the fact that the king was now a 'real' patron of St.
Benet's of Ramsey and the royal wrath threatened anyone who dared unlaw-
fully to disturb the monastic properties.   After the two founders, the royal
charters of confirmation form the main topic of the chronicler's genealogical
pæan.   This necessity of royal patronage could be one reason for the large
gaps in the Chronicler's history of Ramsey properties; for it is only obliquely,
through the grant of Ramsey's vills of Risby and Worlingworth to Bury St.
Edmund's by Edward the Confessor,[83] for instance, that a coercive side of
Anglo-Saxon royal protection may be suggested.[84]

The system of leaseholds which appears on the Anglo-Saxon monastic
estates was, like the conveyance, strongly conditioned by the needs of the
abbey for lands and their revenues, and by problems of security.   It seems
fairly clear that a policy of farming or leasing most of the monastic estates
was practiced universally for a long time after the tenth-century revival.[85]
The necessity for the monks to devolve responsibilities which the limited
administrative scope of the monastic officials and the obligations of the cloister
made it impossible for them to undertake personally would be in itself a
sufficient reason for the extensive leasing of properties.   Moreover, the
rigidity of revenues implied by a system of leaseholds was not alien to the
spirit of monastic administration.   The *Regularis Concordia*, in keeping with
the rule of St. Benedict, decreed that the victuals consumed by each monk

---

See *Hemmingi Chartularium Ecclesiæ Wigorniensis*, ed. T. Hearne (Oxford, 1723),
I. pp. 248 ff.

[80] This strained social climate carried over
early into inter-monastic litigation. See
the 1053 settlement of an early boundary
dispute between Ramsey and Thorney,
Chronicon, p. 166.

[81] H. BÖHMER, *Kirche und Staat in England
und in der Normandie* (Leipzig, 1899), p. 56,
discusses this association as a genesis of the
feudal encroachment on ecclesiastical properties.

[82] *Regularis Concordia*, p. 7: On the other
hand, they commanded that the sovereign
power of the King and Queen — and that
only — should ever be besought with
confident petition, both for the safe-
guarding of holy places and for the increase
of the goods of the Church.

[83] A. J. ROBERTSON, *Anglo-Saxon Charters*,
pp. 443-4.

[84] A good example of royal control over the
disposition of the properties, even of powerful men, may be seen in the grant to
Abingdon by King Ethelred, of lands in
various counties, as compensation for
property grants to this abbey by King
Edgar that had been seized after his death
(*English Historical Documents*, I, ed.
Dorothy Whitelock, London, 1955, pp.
537 ff.).

[85] See *infra*, Ch. III, for a fuller discussion
upon this point; and J. E. A. JOLIFFE,
'Alod and Fee', *Cambridge Historical Journal*, V (1935-7), 225-235, for a discussion on
the insecurity of Anglo-Saxon tenure and
the need of long term rentals.

were to be determined specifically by 'weight, measure, and number'.   Most of the tenth-century founders likely took the example of St. Ethelwold, who followed this rule to the letter by fixing a statutory quota of monks for Abingdon, Ely, and Peterborough; and on the basis of this quota he catalogued the regular produce that should be received from the monastic lands.[86]

In this question of the lease, the tenth-century monastery of England was not developing something new to the monks of western Europe.   The rapid increase in church properties, together with the inalienability of church lands over the period of advancing feudal pressure had made the monastery, and the ecclesiastical bodies generally, prominent in the development of new forms of tenure.   Most notably, the long term lease, usually for one life, had come into prominence on the continent when the *precarium*[87] was being introduced as the method of lay tenancy on church property.[88]   The life lease seems to have had equally ancient roots in Anglo-Saxon England.[89]

For the whole Anglo-Saxon period St. Oswald has left the most prolific number of these leases.   In fact, he had the peculiar practice of frequently lengthening the lease to three lives, — a practice which has been suggested as the cause of much loss of land by the 11th century.[90]   But it seems more likely that Oswald's rental arrangements were actually offered as an antidote to what has been considered their weakness.   From his period of training at Fleury, one of the intellectual cross-roads on the continent, Oswald must have become well acquainted with the dangerous transcendence of lay control due to the decline of central political authority — a feudal trend that attracted not only competition for church lands but also brought the loss of monastic revenues to the Carolingian *Abbayes laïques* and the Teutonic *Eigenkirche*. On all sides the simple economic obligation was taking on legal, military and political overtones.   There is no evidence that rents in the Anglo-Saxon leases were paid in recognition of a title to homage and dependence.   However, since the leasing of monastic lands was necessary, the rent would tend to take on extra-economic functions.   Above all, the difficulties in establishment of titles to ownership that have been already mentioned, and of establishing proof of seisin during the constant social and political disturbances, meant that the rent must also be a security lien.   Hence, the advice of St. Oswald to the monks of Ramsey that they rent the vill of Risby for life *pro certa annui*

---

[86] *Chronicon* of Abingdon, *op. cit.*, II, pp. 277-279. While many passages in this *Chronicon* concerning Ethelwold are suspect (see KNOWLES, *op. cit.*, p. 716), the remarks concerning the organization of revenues are probably trustworthy. See further on this topic, *infra*, Chapter III, Section II.

[87] Joseph CALMETTE, *Le Monde féodal*, Clio Series, IV, (Paris, 1951), pp. 158 ff.   The *precarium* was a contract covering the lease of substantial properties by religious bodies and widely prevalent in Carolingian times. See Cam. Ec. H., I, pp. 233-4.

[88] Alfons DOPSCH, *Wirtschaftsentwicklung der Karolingerzeit*, I, pp. 190 ff.

[89] F. E. HARMER, *Select English Historical Documents of the Ninth and Tenth Centuries* (Cambridge, 1914), p. 112. It may also be noted that whereas fines for land grants from the kings were usually for perpetual privileges, the abbots or bishops commonly required the fine for the perpetual or long lease alone. See *Cartularium Saxonicum*, esp. III, pp. 549 ff.

[90] J. M. KEMBLE (ed.), *Codex Diplomaticus Aevi Saxonici* (London, 1839-1848), I, p. xxxiv, and references there given to Hemming's cartularies.

censi pensitatione,[91] was more than an effort to stabilize the revenues of the abbey. The value of a money rent which may almost be called a traditional livery cannot be minimized in times so dependent upon the oral contract. Right down through Domesday and into the twelfth century the reception of a determined farm or rent remained an important proof of title to property.

The wide use of the land charter gave to the long lease increasing functions in the shifting of burdens on monastic land. A hundred years before the foundation at Ramsey, the bishop of Worcester was able to commute secular services on his lands for a four-life lease of property at Daylesford.[92] St. Oswald, too, was interested in more than security. That unique charter[93] preserving the letter of Oswald to King Edgar, which set forth the nature of his leasehold tenures, probably means that in the tenth-century reconstruction Oswald was looked upon as the pace setter and exemplar in administration. The first part of the letter does emphasize the security value of the charter and of the three-life lease. But the main burden of the document demonstrates how Oswald is using the lease to establish a system of administration. From the leases St. Oswald builds up a system of works to maintain his bridges, fences, the important riding services, etc., and he tells the king:

> . . . insuper ad multas alias indigentiæ causas, quibus opus est domino antistiti sepe frunisci sive ad suum servitium sive ad regale explendum, semper illius archiductoris dominatui et voluntati qui episcopatui presidet propter beneficium quod illis prestitum est cum omni humilitate et subjectione subditi fiant secundum ipsius voluntatem et terrarum quas quisque possidet quantitatem . . .

These principles can be found exemplified in the extant records of St. Oswald. Many of Oswald's charters are leases of property concerned with the settlement of such officials as 'knights' and 'sergeants' on some lands, or with the rewarding of an acquaintance for a service.[94] An example of the latter type of lease may probably be seen from the Ramsey charter where the abbey agreed to let the vill of Stowe to a *cognatus* of Oswald *sub gratuita conditione* for a one life term. However, the main Ramsey materials are bound to be a disappointment as records of Oswald's administration, for the leases of such lands as Risby and Stowe have only slipped into the *Chronicon* because the former was lost to the abbey before, the latter after, the Conquest. While the influence of Oswald's administrative system upon the growth of administration over Ramsey properties could not but be very great, the charters of the *Chronicon* have been selected too carefully only with the *Liber Benefactorum* in mind to have preserved any representative data upon leases except in so far as these were related to an original grant of lands to the abbey. Such data naturally pertain to the leasing policy of Ramsey's benefactors rather than of the abbey itself. However, these are interesting in as much as they suggest

---

[91] And the charter continues: quamdiu autem fidem fratribus de statuto censo annuatim solvendo integram servaret, eandem terram quietu possideret, . . . (*Chronicon*, p. 81).

[92] *English Historical Documents*, I, no. 95, p. 491.
[93] *Cartularium Saxonicum*, III, pp. 382-4.
[94] A. J. ROBERTSON, *Anglo-Saxon Charters*, numbers LXIV, and LXV.

that servants or officials seem generally to have been rewarded by the tenure of land, and these non-ecclesiastical holdings at least, do not have the static appearance of the mid-eleventh-century *Rectitudines Singularum Personarum*. For example, Aethelwin's sister-in-law reserved the life occupancy of one of her estates to the chaplain; Alfwara reserved a hide of land for her servant's lifetime, and Godwin ensured the life holdings of three servants, including a steward and goldsmith.

Some of the alumni of the abbey school and Ramsey monks raised to episcopal honours gave new impetus to the growth of the abbey's property in the 11th century. After the death of Oswald, Ramsey provided three prelates in succession to the see of Dorchester, Aednoth I, Aetheric, and Aednoth II. From the fen monastery also came Aelfward the first abbot of Evesham, who in time became bishop of London (1035-44), and two abbots of Worcester monasteries. Aetheric, a former student at the abbey was particularly generous as bishop of Dorchester. From him came the entire vills of Therfield, Shillington, and Elton, which were purchased or extracted from Danes, as well as Westmill, 'Offertun', Hemington. Girton, Longstowe, lands at Barnwell, three hides in Broughton and three hides in 'Bodekesham'. His successor in the see of Worcester, Aednoth, made the generous grants of Over, Barton, and Knapwell vills to his former monastic home.

It was to handle this, the most rapid expansion of properties since the foundation donation, that the *precaria remuneratoria* appear to have been introduced for the first time on the abbey's estates. By this rental form the lessee held a vill or number of vills for life under the guarantee that designated lands of his own would accrue to the lessor along with the return of the latter's own lands upon the holder's demise. This *precarium* lease is a definite departure from other rental forms, even the life lease, for, there was in the *precarium* lease terms no annual payment to the abbey. Hence the use of the *precarium* would seem to imply that the abbey revenue needs were stabilized or well secured. In effect this lease was tantamount to a long term sinking fund for investment in land. Conversely, the *precaria remuneratoria* offered an economic advantage to the holder. In earlier grants of land to the abbey the reservations of life interests for relations or servants of the grantor were frequently made, but the bulk of the property went immediately to the abbey. Now the spiritual benefits, as *in pretium sepulturæ et salutis*, were preserved in these agreements,[95] in conjunction with the inducements of the yearly returns from these properties to be gained by the lessee during his lifetime. The *precarium remuneratorium* was thus at the same time a long term gain to the abbey while it ministered to immediate land demands of the lay lord.

Under this *precarium* lease Westmill was held by Osgardus for life by the *post obitum* promise of Offord. At the death of Osgardus, Westmill went to one Sexius upon the promise of Walton in bequest. In similar fashion a life lease

---

[95] Paul VINOGRADOFF, *English Society in the Eleventh Century* (Oxford, 1908), p. 229, where the author does not seem to have allowed for the 'spiritual benefits' term in a discussion of the *precaria remuneratoria* entailment.

was obtained on East Hemmingford and the five hides of Gilling for the promise of lands at 'Abbitune, Uuggele, Weldingford, and Burnstede'.[96] When Cranfield came to the abbey it was let out to Count Radulphus for life on the promise of Charlton and 'Brunstanthorp' at its redemption. On the continent the *post obitum* bequest in the *precaria remuneratoria* leases has been found to represent a rent of one third the value of the properties held from the abbey,[97] although the actuarial details for such calculations must remain unsatisfactory. In any case, the chronicler's rough designations make it impossible to estimate the values involved in these Ramsey agreements.

III

In summary, the early territorial development of Ramsey Abbey did not look to the fens. Rather, the growth of the monastic properties described a large fanlike sweep inland from the island at the vertex, through a solid block of uplands and gravel flats which form most of the north-west corner of the county of Huntingdon, above the river Ouse, to spread out more discretively in southern Huntingdon and upon the clays of west Cambridgeshire and to end upon a wide periphery touching from Hertford and Suffolk to the Wash in Norfolk. More disinterested *post obitum* gifts and bequests that succeeded the founders' bounty, together with the extensive grants of former monastic pupils and the parents of Ramsey monks had caused this wider spread of the abbey properties. The chronicler's account cannot be taken as complete.[98] For instance, the vills of Shouldham[99] and Sempringham[100] had been granted to Ramsey Abbey, but with the Conquest these conveyances were disrupted. Several of the property *remuneratoria*[101] in the *precaria* contracts as well as many of the lands whose rentals had been mentioned by the chronicler,[102] succumbed to the same disturbance. On the other hand the movement of properties in the late Anglo-Saxon period is very confused: the vills of Hadley and Potton were at one time given to Ramsey,[103] but afterwards appear as holdings of Ely;[104] Knapwell was in the hands of Ely before the Conquest,[105] but belongs to Ramsey in Domesday Book. Thus, a whole chapter of ex-

---

[96] These were probably vills in Northampton, the 'Abbitune' being Abington of today and the 'Weldingford' perhaps the modern Welford. The vills of 'Offertun', 'Bodekesham', and 'Westmill' mentioned several times in this chapter, were located in Holland according to the chronicler. The other vills whose names have been left in the *Chronicon* form in this chapter do not seem to have been identified by the Place-Name Society; these latter vill names usually involve generic meanings which might apply to several modern villages of East Anglia and the eastern midlands.

[97] *Polyptyque de l'abbé Irminon*, p. 577. This may be estimated as a ten years purchase on a thirty year life basis; for a more general picture of such rents from the Capitularies, see DOPSCH, *op. cit.*, I, p. 188.

[98] And it also involved occasional discrepancies in information: e.g., the mention of two hides from King Edward the Martyr on p. 74 and the same gift as three hides on p. 194.

[99] Dorothy WHITELOCK, *Anglo-Saxon Wills*, p. 80.

[100] *Ibid.*, p. 94.

[101] *Chronicon*, p. 146.

[102] *Ibid.*, pp. 144, 153.

[103] *Ibid.*, p. 60.

[104] Dorothy WHITELOCK, *Anglo-Saxon Wills*, 133-4.

[105] *Ibid.*, p. 190.

TABLE I
THE AGRARIAN HOLDINGS OF RAMSEY ABBEY IN DOMESDAY BOOK[1]

Complete Vills			Other Large Holdings		
Abbots Ripton	(Hunts.)	10 h.[2]	Stukeley	(Hunts.)	7 h.
Wistow	,,	9 h.	Broughton	,,	4 h.
Upwood	,,	10 h.	Yelling	,,	5 h.
Holywell	,,	9 h.	Hemmingford		
Slepe	,,	20 h.	Abbots	,,	18 h.
Houghton	,,	7 h.	Offord	,,	4 h.
Wyton	,,	7 h.	Weston	,,	10 h.
Bythorn	,,	4 h.	Sawtrey	,,	7½ h. 1 v.
Brington	,,	4 h.	Lutton	,,	2 h.
Warboys	,,	10 h.	Elsworth	(Cambs.)	9 h. 1 v.
Hemmingford			Burwell	,,	10 h. 1 v.
Grey	,,	5 h.	Girton	,,	8 h. 2 v.
Dillington	,,	6 h.	Over	,,	10 h. 3 v.
Ellington	,,	10 h.	Chatteris	,,	3 h. ½ v.
Elton	,,	10 h.	Longstowe	,,	2 h.
Graveley	(Cambs.)	5 h.	Barford	(Beds.)	5 h.
Knapwell	,,	5 h.	Holywell	,,	3 h.
Therfield	(Herts.)	10 h.	Whiston and Dodding-		
Lawshall	(Suffolk)	8 car.	ton	(Northants.)	3 h.
Cranfield	(Beds.)	10 h.	Barnwell	,,	6 h.
Barton	,,	11 h.	Hemington	,,	2 h.
Pegsdon	,,	10 h.	Hilgay	(Norfolk)	2 car.
Shillington	,,	10 h.	Wimbotsham	,,	2 car.
Brancaster	(Norfolk)	10 car.	Ringstead	,,	2 car.

Small Holdings [3]					
Gidding	(Hunts.)	1 h.	Lutton	(Northants.)	½ h.
Bourn	(Cambs.)	1 h.	Brayfield	,,	1 t.
Fen Drayton	,,	3 v.	Cornington		
Wyboston	(Beds.)	1 v.	(Quarrington, Lincs.)		1 car.
Clifton	,,	1 h.	Threekingham,	,,	1 car.
Stondon	,,	1 h.	Snorehill	(Norfolk)	1 car.
Hale	(Northants.)	1½ v.	Walsoken	,,	1 car.

[1] Ramsey also had valuable fisheries — those of Hunts. being worth 10 pounds in 1066; and the abbey had 32 'burgesses' in Huntingdon, and one toft in Northampton towns.

[2] Throughout the various tables of this study the following symbols are employed h. = hide; v. = virgate; car. = carrucate (ploughland); t. = toft; cot. (*or* c.) = cotland; cr. = croft; a. = acre.

[3] The area of other smallholds (Cranwell, Dereham, Fordham, Outwell, Boxworth, and Burnham) is not available for this period; and some properties noted in the Lincoln-shire Domesday, but not appearing again for Ramsey, are not listed above.

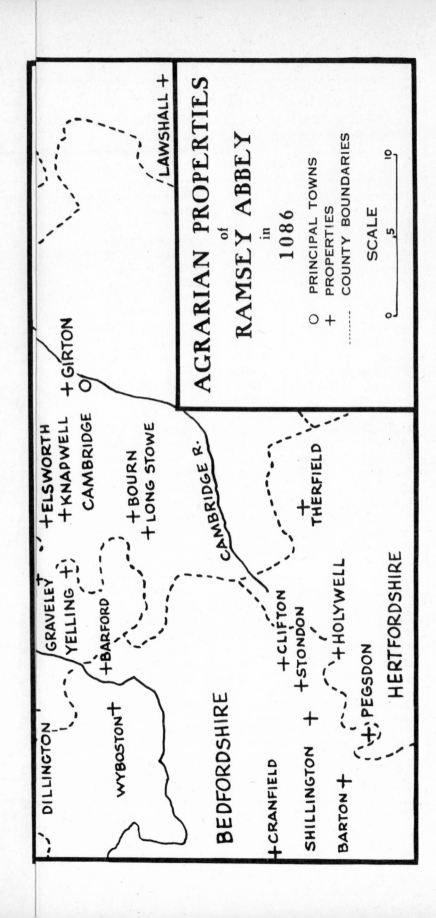

AGRARIAN PROPERTIES
of
RAMSEY ABBEY
in
1086

O PRINCIPAL TOWNS
+ PROPERTIES
---- COUNTY BOUNDARIES

SCALE

0   5   10

LAWSHALL +

+ GIRTON
O

+ ELSWORTH
+ KNAPWELL
CAMBRIDGE

+ BOURN
+ LONG STOWE

CAMBRIDGE R.

+
THERFIELD

GRAVELEY +
YELLING +
+ BARFORD

+ CLIFTON
+ STONDON
+ HOLYWELL

+ PEGSDON

HERTFORDSHIRE

DILLINGTON
WYBOSTON +

BEDFORDSHIRE

+ CRANFIELD
SHILLINGTON +
BARTON +

changes,[106] redemptions,[107] and condonations[108] trailing back into Anglo-Saxon times seems to be largely hidden so that there may be much merit in accepting William's inquest as the proper *status questionis* of that time. In substance, of course, the inquest does corroborate the chronicler's story of property acquisitions.

The long list of properties pertaining to Ramsey Abbey enumerated in 1086 (Table I, above) is a fitting epitaph to that first century of growth. Beyond burghal tenures, there were 68 holdings. Approximately 25 of these holdings were substantial vills averaging 10 hides and held entirely by the abbey; in some 10 other equally substantial vills Ramsey held most of the land. This Domesday map marked the end of an era of geographical expansion. It was the substantially complete ground plan upon which may be traced movements in agrarian history for the next four and one half centuries so that the list of properties compiled by Cromwell's inquisitors tallies remarkably with that of his eleventh-century predecessor.

---

[106] Ramsey exchanged Marholm for the Peterborough property of Lutton sometime around 1053. See F. E. HARMER, *Anglo-Saxon Writs*, p. 264.

[107] E. g., the return of the 'seized' Bichamdich by the influence of Edward the Confessor in 1053.

[108] See *infra*, Ch. II, Section I.

CHAPTER II

TWELFTH-CENTURY TENURIAL SETTLEMENT

ALTHOUGH Ramsey lay in the region of one of the most desperate last ditch stands made by the Anglo-Saxon guerilla bands against the Conqueror, the abbey escaped lightly from the heavy penalties that issued upon this violent reaction to the new order. Ely and Peterborough became centres of revolt, suffered heavy losses in the consequence, and were virtually turned into armed camps by corrective settlements of Norman knights, and another neighbour, the Abbot of Croyland, was deposed for suspected conspiracy. But Ramsey somehow astutely avoided becoming embroiled in these disturbances. The continuity of her organization is reflected in the appointment of Anglo-Saxon abbots until the twelfth century, in the fact that the military burden imposed by the Conqueror was extraordinarily light, and that the properties acquired by William's followers were surprisingly few. Among the *clamores* of the Huntingdonshire Domesday,[1] only the abbey manors of Yelling, Hemmingford, and Sawtrey were docketed as 'seized' by William's followers, although that powerful Norman, Eustace the sheriff, had gained twenty-three manors in Huntingdon. There was more trouble in countering the losses of men to new lordships in East Anglia,[2] though even here the actual losses of property were not very significant. The Domesday accounts of property values offer a further corroboration of Ramsey's good fortune. The Ely demesne values of 1086 were still recovering from an approximate loss of 25 per cent suffered by the Cambridgeshire and Hertfordshire properties of that abbey, since the days of King Edward. By 1086 many Northamptonshire estates had failed to make any progress against the disastrous waste of that county reported in the Geld Roll. But Ramsey land values remained practically stable between *in tempore Regis Edwardi* and 1086.

Perhaps because of this unexceptionable adjustment to the Conquest the late eleventh-century charters for Ramsey are as disparate as those of Anglo-Saxon provenance. But, as the following chapter will show, the burden of conversion to the feudal order had to be met sooner or later. The extant records of this adjustment began to increase in numbers during the last decade of the eleventh century and to assume substantial proportions under

---

[1] V. C. H., Hunts., I, 354-5. This admirable edition by F. M. Stenton (*ibid.*, pp. 315-336) has discussed fully the basic picture of geld distribution and holdings by tenants-in-chief. J. H. ROUND (V. C. H. Northants., I, 271) also solved several problems of identification for the Ramsey Domesday. The V.C.H. edition of Domesday has been used throughout this study. Huntingdon is one of the few counties to have its judicial pleas, or *clamores*, so clearly summarized in D. B.

[2] V.C.H., Norfolk, I. In Hilgay William de Warrene took 8 men from Ramsey customary tenants and 44 acres of land; in Ringstead 9 sokemen were taken by Radfrid, 7 by William Scoliies and de Warrene, 3 by the king's manor of Titchwell, 4 by William de Noiers, 5 by R. Bigot.

Henry I. While these documents are of considerable general use, they represent only a very slight advance over the Anglo-Saxon records as detailed sources of information. It is the Domesday evidence which permits the first real penetration of the social and agrarian structure of Ramsey estates. As generations of scholars now bear witness, the abbreviated nature of this report leaves the investigator more often than not with many challenging enigmas. But, on the other hand, the breadth of its information provides a framework for the interpretation of the otherwise isolated charters. Above all, Domesday Book presents statistics vital for detailed comparison with the general estate surveys which form the main sources for twelfth-century agrarian history.[3]

The Anglo-Norman socio-economic structure becomes revealed through these extents and charters as a complicated distribution upon land of all burdens public or private, military, judicial, or simply administrative. In this fashion the post-conquest tenure of land involved much more than an economic instrument. The economic terms of the tenure, in turn, took on an institutional stability necessary for judicial and administrative functions. In the following section this post-conquest land settlement is outlined as the formation of a tenurial structure. As a consequence, it will be possible after this stage in our investigation to set to one side the study of many superior tenures and quasi-legal and political relationships, which were to remain fairly stable for generations and even for centuries, so that the economic history of such lands remained outside the detailed developments traceable for other Ramsey estates. More attention may then be concentrated upon those elements of economic history which changed generation by generation, or even year by year, throughout the mediæval period under study.

I

The pacific submission of Ramsey to the new order did not mean that the abbey escaped the imposition of feudal lordship by the Norman kings. A full-blooded royal *dominium*[4] over Ramsey Abbey is revealed in the series of charters proclaiming surety for abbatial liberties, privileges,[5] properties,[6] property claims,[7] property increases,[8] or alienations,[9] as well as confirmation

---

[3] The available Ramsey extents are listed in Appendix A *infra*. The well-known pioneer work by F. M. Stenton and D. C. Douglas, especially in the collation of 12th-century charters and Domesday, has earned the gratitude of all students of the manor in the 12th century.

[4] This power of feudal jurisdiction must be distinguished from the more restricted tenurial *dominicatum* or *dominicum*, that is, the demesne. The term demesne has been used in this study only in reference to that part of the manor co-operatively cultivated by hired labour and villein services for the lord or his lessee.

[5] *Chronicon*, p. 200, and *passim*.

[6] E. g., ... manuteneatis et protegas sicut meas dominicas ... (*Chronicon*, 293).

[7] *Chronicon*, 213 ff.

[8] ... concessisse omnes terras illas quas perquisivit postquam fuit abbas quæ non erant in dominio abbathiæ die qua recepit abbathiam ... (*Chronicon*, p. 225).

[9] *Carts.*, I, 234: Præcipio et defendo, ne abbas de Rameseia, videlicet Aldwin, ullo modo tribuat alicui homini aliquam terram de dominio suo, vel de terris de dominico victu monachorum suorum, sine licentia mea et consilio.

in office of the abbot himself.[10]   As tenant-in-chief the abbot bore the obligation of supplying knight services.   Even into the lower feudal and social strata
of knight, freeman, and peasant, a like influence of the royal arm prevailed,
and was maintained.[11]

It was, above all, through the settlement of military obligations on abbey
lands that the Norman Conquest left its most enduring mark on the economic
organization of Ramsey.   Although William the Conqueror placed upon
Ramsey Abbey the remarkably light burden of only four knights from this the
fourth wealthiest ecclesiastical landholder in England, the Norman warriors
who ultimately settled upon these monastic lands proved to be much more
numerous.   Already in Domesday Book, in addition to the 'two knights of
the abbot' holding three hides of Stukeley, and the 'two knights of the abbey'
upon the one hide of Bourn, Barford was held in 'fee' of the abbey, 'two
knights' held three and one-half virgates of Bythorn, and 'two knights' held
one hide of Ellington.

Despite this early Norman plantation, the knight fee proper does not
seem to have been established at Ramsey in the eleventh century.   For
example, we learn from a charter of 1080 that the above-mentioned Barford was
only leased for life, to be held by the service of one-half knight by Eudo, the
royal sheriff.[12]   And there is no indication from the wording of the Domesday
text that those tenants designated as 'knights' held partly in return for
military services or even by a military tenure at all.   Indeed, as we shall see
below, many of these tenures proved revocable under Henry I.   In any case,
the smaller holdings of this group could not have maintained the expenses of
their tenants as fully armed knights.   Some of these Ramsey lands were
likely providing for the serjeants, the servants and companions of the knights.[13]
At the opposite extreme, there were many 'knights' holding lands in Domesday
that were not fees, in origin, at least; such were properties held by powerful
sheriffs and royal administrators who in 1066 and over later decades had
utilized the coercive opportunities of their positions to seize extensive lands.

[10] E. g., *Carts.*, I, 238: Sciatis me dedisse
Bernardo monacho de Sancto Albano
abbatiam de Ramesia.

[11] *Chronicon*, p. 232: Precipio quod facias
abbati de Ramesia domino tuo servitium et
auxilium . . . *Ibid.*, p. 229: Precipio quod
cito et justi reddatis abbati domino vestro
quicquid ei debetis de censo et firma et
debitis et placitis . . . *Ibid.*, p. 297:
Præcipio quod abbas de Ramesia teneat
terras et homines suos ita bene et in pace . . .

[12] *Chronicon*, p. 232; and see also the life lease
of Dillington *pro suo servitio*, probably
about 1091, *Chronicon*, p. 234.   Miss H. M.
CHEW, *Ecclesiastical Tenants-in-Chief*,
(Oxford, 1932), pp. 123-4, has followed
W. O. AULT (*Private Jurisdiction in
England*, New Haven, 1923) in insisting that
fees were eventually established on Ramsey
estates.   But Ault's evidence points to the
establishment of fees as perpetual tenures
only from the reign of Henry I; and the

significance of this late enfeoffment has not
been discussed by either writer.   Despite
Professor GALBRAITH's important note
drawing attention to life-grants for military
service in the 11th century ('An Episcopal
Land-Grant of 1085,' E. H. R., XLIV, 1929,
371-2), this tenure still awaits definitive
treatment by the historians of English
feudalism.

[13] An extremely good example of these various
services and men expected with the
enfeoffment of one knight may be seen in a
charter of Bury St. Edmund's from the time
of William I (*Eng. Hist. Doc.*, II, ed. D. C.
Douglas and G. A. Greenaway, London,
1953, p. 896, no. 220).   Apparently the
enfeofee, Peter, is to serve with three or
four companions in answer to the national
levy; but when the abbot is supplying his
own retainer to the king, Peter shall equip
one knight for service at home or abroad.

While the Norman tenants-in-chief were gradually replacing the native secular and ecclesiastical aristocracy, hordes of lesser Normans too, must have been pressing to acquire property by the payment of rents, services, or simply by seizure. Hence, the actual feudalization of Anglo-Saxon lands could have much wider ramifications than the establishment of a military quota, according as there were fluctuations in the friendly relations between king and tenant-in-chief, and according as the royal favourites and knights were ingenious in extending their property through the medium of the military service. The civil disturbances for two generations after the Conquest, and difficulties in adapting Norman law to old English customs, prolonged, in turn, the above elements in the first settlement of the Norman army in England.

The movement of these various forces is especially important in the history of Ramsey Abbey estates where the vague 1086 disposition of military tenants was to remain peculiarly indicative of future developments in this form of tenure. That is to say, more and more lands were let for military service, without any clear plan of retiring the obligations to fees; and even when this process was halted in the early 12th century, no clearcut re-allocation of the military fees seems to have been possible. Remnants of this lack of rationalization of the military burden at Ramsey may probably still be seen in the *servitia debita* of the *Carta Baronum*. For this abbey alone, there is found listed in the *Carta* only the hides and virgates owing service through a common pooling of efforts, rather than, as for other tenants-in-chief, the specific amount of service, as indicated in the number of fees. The charters of the abbey reflect this vague condition when they speak of some freemen who owe no service proper, but are obliged to help with the expenses of the knights.[14] It will be seen in the next few pages that this failure to isolate the *servitia debita* by the creation of fees in the rapidly-changing society of the late eleventh century was a costly mistake. The military tenure at Ramsey grew out of all proportion to the obligations of the abbey by becoming the instrument of a broad and indefinite social evolution.

Since there is no evidence that the abbots of Ramsey failed to co-operate with the Conqueror, that first movement of knights who were not of the abbey on to the abbey lands, which we have seen in Domesday Book, was probably endured to maintain royal favour and to placate the royal agents. It had not at all been unusual in earlier times to cede lands to royal *ministri* for 'love of the king',[15] and now there was all the more reason to court royal favour. For, even when he co-operated voluntarily with the new regime, the Anglo-Saxon abbot was a decidedly passive party to the Norman settlement. He had not participated as a feudal baron in the campaign, so he could not expect to

---

[14] Abbot William of Ramsey (1161-1179), *Carts.*, III, 220, concludes a list of his military tenants with: Praeter hos, habemus franchelenos, quorum quidam unam hidam, alii plus, alii minus, tenent, quorum servitium nominatum nescimus, nisi quod per hidas alios milites adjuvant ad servitium Regis faciendum.

[15] We learn from the *clamores* of the Hunts. Domesday, for example, that the Abbot of Ramsey had given one hide of Hemmingford to Aluuin the fowler, T. R. E., 'for love of the king.'

gain the rewards accorded to an ecclesiastical peer from across the channel, like an Odo of Bayeux. The Anglo-Saxon abbeys failed to enjoy the predilection of the Normans, especially when the abbot was still an Anglo-Saxon. During former times the abbey might acquire property as the aftermath of social or political disturbances. We have seen in the preceding chapter, for instance, the gifts to Ramsey by Bishop Aetheric to the loss of retreating Danes. But the Norman warriors had their own ecclesiastical attachments, and were naturally more interested at this period in the endowment of new orders, or in the establishment of English cells from their native communities.[16]

The invaders held the more positive legal and social position and were pushing their advantage. The Norman knight was a companion-in-arms of the king. He had fought under the royal standard at Hastings and had been promised great rewards to undertake the hazardous channel crossing. The Conqueror and his successors must have felt it difficult not to connive at much free-lance land grabbing by his fellow victors. Indeed, by feudal custom the warrior had a right to his reward in lands and booty.[17] And we have many writs of the Anglo-Norman kings making it clear that the royal grants are definitive. Furthermore, the Norman knights had a legal entrée as successors to Anglo-Saxon thegns and warriors who held land from the abbey, and very often, it would appear that the latter had held by a vague or disputed title. Therefore, despite the relative tranquillity of the first impact of the conquest upon Ramsey, it is not suprising to find that the abbey was eventually to suffer from this aftermath of the conquest. The expansion of powerful lay neighbours by the disputed 'seizure' became an outstanding element in the settlement of knights upon abbey lands. This aristocratic party, far more than the royal assessment of knights, determined the course and the degree to which the military tenure developed at Ramsey.

Only a few years after the published *clamores* of Domesday, noted above, the accession of William II was ushered in with a royal charter supporting abbey claims against fresh seizures in Isham, the one-half hide of Sawtrey which Walter de Belmeys 'now holds by force', one-half carrucate in Threekingham, one-half hide in Bythorn seized by Humfredus, the royal larderer, and the additional seizures of Brampton, Hurst, Ringstead, Holme, and Longstowe. The disorders of the reign of Rufus would certainly not have created an atmosphere conducive to the legal retirement of these claims, and in fact, they dragged on into the twelfth century. His temporary extension of the abbey burden to ten knights may indeed have given new incentive to feudal encroachments.[18] But it is difficult to trace the effects of such an increase in military assessment since the royal influence upon the contractual relations between knight and tenant-in-chief had been indirect, even from the first arrangement of military service.[19] The charters of the first decades of the

---

[16] For a general summary of this point, see KNOWLES, *The Monastic Order in England*, esp. pp. 128 ff.

[17] Marc BLOCH, *La Société féodale* (*Les Classes et le gouvernement des hommes*, Paris, 1949), pp. 20-23.

[18] *Chronicon*, p. 212; *Carts.*, I, p. 235.

[19] The *Inquisitio Eliensis* makes it possible to trace these relations through many writs for that abbey. But the principle would be the same for Ramsey. As Mr. Miller concludes: It is not a question of the king

twelfth century censure Abbot Aldwin,[20] rather than the Norman kings, for permitting, or submitting to, encroachments on abbey lands in the previous decades. In any case, the feudal obligations of Ramsey were again reduced to four knights, apparently during the reign of Rufus,[21] so that royal pressure was not sustained from this quarter.

It is in the rapacious administration of the royal servants, and the licence permitted these officials before the reforms of Henry I,[22] that the main influences must be sought for the dispersion of Ramsey lands. The increasing number of extant charters from around 1090 makes it possible to trace the pressure by this group. As already noted, they were not isolated by an early arrangement of military fees; nor was their influence confined to small holdings and to less important peripheral manors. By the twelfth century royal officials were threatening the very heart of the abbey's dowry. After 1100 we meet a large group of the royal curia who have established interests on Ramsey lands. William Nicholas, the royal chaplain, and William, the royal *dispensator*, were holding respectively Stukeley and Ellington. Roger Foliot was attempting to extend his *dominium* over Broughton manor. The Pecke family was gradually gaining hereditary possession of Over. Stowe and Girton were recovered from Paganus Peverel shortly after 1100 with the help of King Henry. But after another decade the abbot was again trying to recover Girton and Needingham from the Le Moignes. Probably descendants of William, baron and sheriff of Somerset under William I, this family obtained a strong foothold in the eastern midlands from the time of William II. The abbot also lost control of his wealthiest manors in Bedford, Pegsdon to William, the royal chamberlain, and Cranfield to Radulphus Bassett, an important royal justice appointed early in the reign of Henry I. Paganus Peverel is a representative of that group of powerful companions of William I and William II who were shorn of much of their influence by Henry I; William Pecke and Radulphus Bassett, on the other hand, were new magnates, members of a social group on the ascendancy with the support of Henry I.[23]

The rapid extension of military tenure on Ramsey lands from the time of Domesday Book came by means of the holdings of these officials. It was natural, in many respects, that these powerful officials should supply knights. They would be accompanied by knights on their administrative perambulations; they kept a small personal army, and perhaps a castle; they led large numbers of knights into battle on the king's command. Accordingly it would

---

ordering the enfeoffment of mesne tenants. Picot and Guy were ordered to serve, not the abbey to enfeoff them (*The Abbey and Bishopric of Ely*, p. 67).
In similar fashion, it was the abbot who took the steps against the tenant for his failure to provide military service, although he may often have needed royal aid in the process as this writ of Henry I concerning Burnham illustrates: Præcipio ut facias Rainaldo Abbati de Rameseia servitium terræ quam tenes de eo. Quod nisi feceris ipse

recognoscat terram et inde non me intromittam. *Chronicon*, pp. 231-2.
[20] *Chronicon*, p. 220, no. 211, and p. 228, no. 222.
[21] *Chronicon*, p. 212, no. 191.
[22] See W. A. MORRIS, *The Mediæval English Sheriff to 1300* (Manchester, 1927), especially pp. 70-71, for other and more bold examples of the plundering of ecclesiastical property at this time.
[23] *Ibid.*, Ch. IV, for changes in the royal officialdom.

be simple and convenient for a powerful official to extend his property by offering the military services of some of his retinue.   The Ramsey fee would be all the more attractive to the Norman aspirant because of the lightness of the obligatory military burden, with the additional fact that these four knights had only to be supplied in turn by the leading tenants[24] while the expenses were assessed upon all military tenures in common.[25]

The place of the abbot himself in this expansion of military tenures at Ramsey is difficult to assess, for beyond his placatory gestures to the king, or whatever supernumerary margin of services he might think necessary, as a non-combatant baron he would have little military use for knights.[26]   Over the hundred years after the Conquest there is only the one really detailed transaction, that concerned with the grant of Walton to Abbot Walter by Albreda de Selhee,[27] which shows an abbot of Ramsey dealing in land for military service.   This contract actually serves to illustrate the attraction of military service to the mesne lord as a tenurial obligation, for Abbot Walter was willing to supply two knights to Walter de Bolbeck in whose honour Walton lay, in order to secure his grant from Albreda:

> Et de hoc pacto Walterus abbas fecit eum securum per duos milites quos abbas posuit in suo loco, Houerinnum, scilicet, et Henricum de Wichentone, et si aliquis eorum moriatur alium ponat in loco suo abbas per electionem domini Walteri de Bolebech aut hæredis sui; et si alius abbas venerit, iterum faciet dominum Walterum de Bolbeck securum, vel hæredem suum, de hoc eodem pacto per alios duos milites in electione Walteri vel hæredis sui si alios habere voluerit.

Nor are there any obvious economic reasons that would make the military tenures appeal especially to the abbot of Ramsey.   As the arrangement appears in the *Carta*, the abbot could apparently tax all the freemen for expenses related to the military service no matter how many actual fees there happened to be.   The fees on Ramsey land in excess of those recognized

[24] At least such was the system as it appears in the earliest public records on this matter. See CHEW, *Ecclesiastical Tenants-in-Chief*, p. 122 ff. Since Miss Chew has dwelt thoroughly upon the military obligations of Ramsey we shall refer freely to her study throughout this section for greater detail upon several problems.

[25] *Red Book of the Exchequer*, ed. H. Hall, R. S., I, (1897), p. 371: Homines faciunt IIII milites in communi ad servitium domini Regis. Ita quod tota terra Abbatiæ communicata est cum eis per hidas ad prædictum servitium faciendum; et hoc eodem modo fecerunt tempore ejusdem Regis Henrici. Post mortem autem ejusdem Regis Henrici nullus miles in tota Abbatia de novo feodatus est. Quidam autem de dominio Ecclesiæ post mortem Regis Henrici aliquid tenent. Et tota terra Abbatiæ ita communicata cum militibus prædictis, quod omnes milites prædicti communicati sunt cum dominio

Abbatiæ in omnibus quæ ad necessitatem Ecclesiæ pertinent.
A thirteenth century charter, summarized in *Carts.*, I, p. 91, no. 241, mentions : ... trecentæ et sexaginta hidæ faciunt servitium quatuor militum per positionem militum et libere tenentium de curia ejusdem abbatis et successorum suorum.

[26] The non-military character of the abbot's household is probably reflected in the witnesses to his charters; over the late 11th and early 12th century everybody from powerful neighbouring magnates to the abbey cooks and carpenters appears as witness at Ramsey, but the *miles* is very rare.

[27] *Carts.*, I, 153-8. In his account of Abbot Walter the chronicler states (*Chronicon*, p. 336): Abbas iste multis laboribus et expensis magnaque sui corporis anxietate, Graveleiam, Bradenache, Crauleiam, Elingtone, ad dominium ecclesiæ Ramesensis revocavit; Waltone vero de novo adquisivit.

for military purposes thus held no clear title that would serve the financial purposes commonly attributed to such 'extra' fees at other abbeys.[28]   Substantial profits could, no doubt, accrue from such feudal incidents as aids, recognitions, wardships, and escheats.   But it is doubtful whether the abbot's baronial authority was always sufficient for the collection of these dues.[29] And, in any case, such profits would be irregular, and to a large extent static insofar as the abbey was concerned.   In contrast, as will be seen, most of the properties of Ramsey were increasing in value over the early Anglo-Norman days, and might be expected to be farmed at even higher rates, like the numerous royal manors of the Hampshire Domesday.   For such purposes there were the various age-old rental instruments at hand if direct exploitation was not feasible.   In short, there would appear to be little economic rationale in the enfeoffment of knights.

The Ramsey charters bear out this lack of attraction for knights' fees. As has been noted above, the abbey tenaciously held to its growing list of claims against usurpation of property from the time of the Conquest.   Doubtless the reforms in royal administration from the middle of the reign of Henry I[30] established that peace and order essential for the settlement of many lawsuits.   But above all the appointment of Abbot Reginald in 1114 brought to the fore one of those energetic administrators whom Norman society seemed to produce so abundantly.   Reginald's name stands out in the annals of the abbey as the builder of one of the most magnificent Norman abbey churches in England.   The economic foundation for this building programme was made possible by a policy of checking feudal encroachment, by the recovery of property from the feudal intruders, and by a clearing up of the disputed claims that had been accumulating for two generations.

There are dozens of charters bearing tribute to this activity of Reginald. In this general programme of property redemption, it is clear that he had singled out the properties leased for knight services as a special objective of his attack; in this fashion the three virgates of Bythorn, some 'new fees' of Hurst, Barford, Burnham, lands in Holywell (Hunts.), and Lutton were recovered.   That such tenures could be revoked at all shows again   that many of these holdings by military service were not considered hereditary fees

---

[28] CHEW, op. cit., table, pp. 32-3, and discussion pp. 138 ff.   However, even where a large number of fees were 'recognized for financial purposes', it is not clear how much of a 'profit system' the tenant-in-chief could make out of such fees.   The mesne tenants could get royal protection against excessive taxation: as we see in the writ forbidding the exaction of more from tenants than the tenant-in-chief himself pays to the king (Red Book of the Exchequer, R. S., I, p. cxvii, no. 184).   It is still useful to recall Maitland's suggestion that the king never really resigned his direct claim to secular services even from land in frankalmoigne; and the new taxes were like scutage, where there was 'an element of royal and

national taxation which is incompatible with purely feudal principles' (POLLOCK and MAITLAND, History of English Law, 2nd ed., Cambridge, 1923, I, p. 274, and Book II, Ch. I, passim).

[29] E. g., Chronicon, p. 232, no. 237, where Ramsey had to call upon a royal writ in order to enforce service.   This was also a common problem at her neighbours Ely and Bury St. Edmunds in the twelfth century, and indeed generally in England.   For the importance of this factor in the early development of scutage from ecclesiastical tenants-in-chef, see CHEW, op. cit., pp. 45-6.

[30] W. A. MORRIS, The Mediæval English Sheriff to 1300, Ch. IV, especially pp. 79 ff.

by the king.   For Henry I was not simply to be moved by a claim to title by military service.   For example, Radulphus Bassett was ordered to give up Cranfield, which he had unjustly taken from the abbey, . . . *et non remaneat pro transfretatione tua*.   The surviving writs that do uphold disputed tenure by knight service frequently point to the convenience of some temporary rewards for royal officials rather than to the interest of the permanent feudal discipline. In this manner William Nicholson, the royal chaplain, was allowed to retain Stukeley for life by the (military) service that such an amount of Ramsey land paid, but the land must revert to the perpetual use of the abbey at his decease. The royal official holding Ellington was treated in the same fashion.   There may be much of the serjeanty tenure in such nominal knight fees.   On the other hand, it has already been noted that this type of lease did not originate in the time of Henry I.   The first post-conquest fees at Ramsey for which we have charters, like that of Eudo, the royal *dapifer* in 1080,[31] were life tenures only.   Only with the final agreements from the time of Abbot Reginald was the hereditary principle fully enforced for Ramsey military tenures.

In reaching agreements with the powerful knights who had got a foothold under Aldwin, Abbot Reginald never seems to have granted knights' fees when he had a strong legal title to the property in question.   However, the most formidable hindrance to the reduction of military tenures were the counter claims that these tenants had acquired over some Ramsey land or other in the confusion of previous decades.   Indeed, the majority of the substantial military tenures on the abbey's land had to be renewed in return for the guarantee of title to some other property, or for the quitting of a debt.   There are charters involving such 'compromise leases' for Whiston, Burnham, Depedale, Hurst, one-half hide of Sawtrey, Fordham, Lutton, Gidding, Raveley, Stowe and Bluntisham.[32]   The compromise formula may have enjoyed a peculiar popularity because of the scope it gave to feudal seisin. The exchange transmitted in compromise supplied perpetual real evidence both to the surrender of a claim and to the maintenance of a title.   This would be especially useful for the re-organization of tenures by Norman followers who

---

[31] *Chronicon*, p. 207; see also pp. 234 and 257.

[32] *Chronicon*, p. 244 (Whiston): . . . Idem vero Henricus omnem calumniam Ramesiensi ecclesiæ clamat quietam . . .
Ibid., p. 252 (Hyrst): . . . Ipse autem Rogerus dedit abbati e contra viginti marcas argenti, et evenit homo ejus liges de hoc quod tenet de eo, et clamavit abbati octo virgatas terræ solutas et quietas apud Hurst de novo feudo et Ingel(ranni) hagam apud Huntedone.
Ibid., p. 262: . . . Reinaldus abbas totusque Ramesiensis conventus in capitulo nostro concedimus Gileberto Widonis filio tam sibi quam hæredibus suis Stowe et quicquid habemus in Bluntesham et unam hidam terræ in Hyrst, cum ea libertate et cum eo servitio quod prædictis pertinet terris; Gilebertus vero omnem calumniam clamat quietam, nominatim de Ringstede et de tribus virgatis terræ in Elesworthe et de soca in Huntedone et de omni alia re.
Ibid., pp. 260-261: . . . concedimus Herveo Monacho quicquid habemus in Ludintona et quicquid habemus in Giddinge præter eam partem quam habet Henricus archidiaconus.   Concedimus quoque Herveo Monacho apud Reveleium terram Edwini; præter hoc, unam virgatam terræ in Upwode et suum hospicium apud Ramesiam. Concedimus etiam prædicto Herveo Monacho Saltreiam in feoudum ad firmam pro quatuor libris per singulos annos, tali pacto quod tam ipse quam hæres suus qui eam post eum habebit totam terram sancti Benedicti pro posse suo in omnibus defendat placitis et ubicumque opus fuerit.   Idem vero Herveus omnem omnino calumniam clamat quietam in omnibus rebus ecclesiæ Ramesensi pertinentibus, excepta Bradenach quam tenet Willelmus de Hoctone . . .

Table II

PROPERTIES OWING MILITARY SERVICE IN 1135

Estate	Assessment	Fee
Holywell (Beds.).....	3½ H(ides)	1
Barford............	5 H.	1
Stowe, Hurst, etc.....	5½ H.	1
Yelling............	5 H.	1 (or ½)
Gravenhurst........	5½ H.	1
Hemmingford G......	5 H.	1
Barnwell, etc........	6½ H.	1
Whiston...........	3½ (or 4) H. ⎫	1
Doddington........	1 H. ⎭	
Isham............	1½ H. ⎫	
Dillington..........	6 H. ⎪	
(Long) Stowe........	1½ (or 2½) H. ⎬	1
Hemington.........	3½ H. ⎭	
Cranwell...........	4 (or 5) H.	1
Stukeley & Hurst....	4½ H.	½
?	2½ H.	½
?	3 H.	1
Clifton............	1 H.	
Sawtrey...........	7½ H.	
Gidding...........	1 H.	
Offord............	4 H.	
Graveley..........	1 H.	
Upwood...........	1½ H.	
Broughton.........	1. H.	
Barton............	2 H.	
Hemmingford A......	2 H.	
Ellington..........	2 H., 3 V(irgates)	
Houghton.........	6 V.	

Note: By supplementing the *Red Book of the Exchequer* with two twelfth-century
monastic surveys (*Carts.*, III, 48-9, & 218-220) most of the holdings in knights fee
can be located. The exchequer account apparently listed some half-dozen
tenants in addition to the charter list of names. Most of these names have been
cross-checked with extents to add to the greater completion of the above list.
It may be noted that Sawtrey paid forty shillings as well as one knight. Where
the assessment of some holdings was in dispute the two claims have been included
in the above figures (see Whiston, Longstowe, and Cranwell).

had already received some confirmation in their holding by the king. The earliest trials by charter show that compromise was devised out of 'a prudent regard for the king's seal.'[33] The suasion behind the *servitium debitum*, the rights of succession to Anglo-Saxon tenants claimed by Norman warriors, these and many other elements of the previous generations were finally resolved in the compromise leases. In general the abbey had least success in recovering the lands with the longest seisin, like Hemmingford Grey, Yelling, or Isham, which could boast more than a generation of tenancy in defence of their title.

With the summary of the abbey's military tenants given in the *Carta Baronum* may be seen the final list of the rewards that the conquering Norman warrior carved out from the estates of Ramsey Abbey under the permanent title of military service. Over the next two centuries this tenurial settlement was to remain relatively fixed. Even setting aside the fact that military expenses were borne by freemen on Ramsey estates, it is remarkable that the proportion of fees to 'knights owed to the king' is about three to one in comparison with abbatial honours like those of Tavistock or Abingdon that had carved the fees out of their property immediately after the Conquest. No increase in military costs by this period could account or this disproportionate increase in the fees for Ramsey. Probably the history of the settlement of knights at Ramsey serves as a proof for the wisdom of those lords who immediately translated their military obligations into hereditary fees after the conquest.[34] At a time when royal officials freely exploited the country under the aegis of the feudal prerogatives of the king, and when the expenses of the mounted warrior were fast increasing, it was a wise policy to isolate the feudal obligations by the creation of permanent fees.[35] The preceding table shows ninety hides and nine virgates held by knight service. Roughly twenty-five per cent of the Domesday assessment for Ramsey estates was allocated to the supply of four knights! It was a tribute to the success of Abbot Reginald's policy that these burdens tended to be settled upon the smaller and more remote of the abbot's manors. Apparently some of the largest and most valuable of his manors, like Shillington and Cranfield, eventually carried no fees or portions of fees at all; at others, like Barton and Broughton, the hidage devoted to knight fees was reduced to a small percentage.

The preceding pages have shown the process by which were gradually defined the military tenures dedicated by Ramsey Abbey to its obligations as a feudal landlord. But at the same time Ramsey was an ecclesiastical body, and over its already long history extensive properties had been bestowed solely for the maintenance of its peculiarly abbatial functions. The monastic tenure of land in Anglo-Saxon England seems to have developed those qualities found in its continental counterparts.[36] These were in the main that of the

[33] M. M. BIGELOW, *History of Procedure in England*, (London, 1880), pp. 67-8.
[34] There is of course no differential in the value of these properties in D. B. to justify such variations.
[35] In this context it should be noted that the chroniclers entered this early post-conquest 'separation' of lands that were to bear the military burdens among the good works of the abbots; e.g., *Chronicon Monasterii de Abingdon*, II, pp. 3-4.
[36] Émile LESNE, *Histoire de la Propriété ecclésiastique en France*, I, *passim*.

corporative notion of a moral person, with the consequent undying tenure; the important identification of the abbey and its patron, with bequests to 'God and St. Benedict of Ramsey,' for example; and the broad exemptions from civil obligations as well as the liberties that the abbey lands enjoyed. As noted in the previous chapter, the effectual use of these liberties depended in Anglo-Saxon times to a great extent upon the personal favour and protection of earls and kings. But the vague Anglo-Saxon institutional relations were unsuited to the feudal regime where the Norman king as the suzerain held all property. In the decades after the conquest various implications of this feudal domination became only too clear, and the abbatial tenure had to work out its independent rôle in the structure of feudal services.

The eventual compromise involved a concession to the personal bond of feudalism on one hand, and to the independent moral person of the abbey on the other. The abbot as tenant-in-chief took more explicitly upon himself the feudal obligations of the abbey; the convent, in turn, became identified with the undying corporative body. Anglo-Saxon traditions had not left the abbey wholly unprepared for this development. Many, and perhaps all, of the major monasteries had been developing important administrative divisions between the rents, especially the food rents, allocated to the peculiar needs of the convent, and those more general revenues of the monastery received by the abbot. In Ramsey we may trace early forms of this division even in tenth-century foundation bequests. Probably before the year 1000, one-half of a long boat was willed to the community, the other half to the abbot.[37] More often, however, the bequest leaves a property to the abbey, but designates that certain rents are to go to the abbot or to the convent.[38] Such specification of grants was but a natural consequence of the donors' solicitude for the particular needs of the abbey. In making these grants the benefactors would be able to be governed by a detailed knowledge of monastic needs, for the *Regularis Concordia*, in keeping with the counsel of St. Benedict, ruled that the victuals consumed by each monk were to be determined specifically by 'weight, measure, and number.'[39] Most of the tenth-century monasteries likely took the example of St. Ethelwold, who had followed this rule to the letter by fixing the statutory quota of monks for Abingdon, Ely, and Peterborough; and on the basis of this quota he catalogued the regular produce that should be received from the monastic lands.[40] Probably Ethelwold left it to the donors of monastic lands to supply this produce, for it was only by the time of Abbot Leofsige at Ely (1029-35) that there first appears a specific list of manors, and their weekly obligations, in supplying the produce needs of the monastery.[41] This food farm system, as it has become known to historians, was well devel-

[37] WHITELOCK, *Anglo-Saxon Wills*, p. 30.
[38] See the grants cited *supra* in Ch. 1, Section II. In accordance with the rule of St. Benedict, these revenues would likely be administered by the manager of the monasteries' material affairs, the cellarer. Aednoth junior seems to have held such a position at Ramsey over the late 10th century.
[39] Nelson edition, p. 8.
[40] *Chronicon Monasterii de Abingdon*, II, 277-9.
[41] MILLER, *The Abbey and Bishopric of Ely*, p. 38.

oped at many other monasteries before the Conquest,[42] although the first evidence for its existence at Ramsey only comes at the end of the 11th century. This was a natural movement for administrative efficiency since it provided for stability in the basic sustenance requirements of the monks. At the same time the well-ordered reception of rents would make administrative devolution more feasible without jeopardizing the spirit of poverty, or removing the monk for long periods from the community. And henceforth more monks were likely appointed to dispense various revenues, that is, in the language of the records, to be appointed obedientiaries.[43]

It is only to be expected that rents which were necessary for the very food and clothing of the monks would give a special force to the monastic title over these lands. There seems to be little doubt that the recording of food rents in Anglo-Saxon documents added a special 'sustenance title' to the charter of king or monastery. The same tradition was carried over into the Anglo-Norman period. Professor Galbraith[44] has noted that the Domesday phrase *de victu monachorum*, or its variants like *ad vestitum* or *ad victum*, were never used to mean that the property was not *in dominio*; but such terms *were* used for a real reason in that they provided an additional title to the property. Apparently only in five instances, out of approximately fifty uses of the phrase in the Domesday of ecclesiastical tenants-in-chief, is a general title given for the lands allocated to conventual food rents.[45] The remaining entries show that the food rent title has been invoked as special proof that the property was held *in dominio*; hence it was employed for holdings of which the title was actually *sub judice* or liable to dispute. Such were usually smaller holdings, precarious because the property had been sublet,[46] or isolated from the main monastic holdings.[47]

---

[42] E. g., Worcester, Hemming's *Chartularium Ecclesiæ Wigorniensis*, fol. 45d; Bury St. Edmund's, Robertson, *Anglo-Saxon Charters*, pp. 195-6; *Domesday Monachorum of Christ Church, Canterbury*, ed. Douglas, pp. 88 ff.

[43] It would be an oversimplification to regard this development as a disciplinary reform directed against any deleterious effects that the management of many estates might be having upon the life of the monastic community. The *Regularis Concordia* gave no scope for 'living out' on manors, nor indeed for their direct administration: Villarum autem circuitus, nisi necessitas magna compulerit et necessariæ rationis discretio hoc dictaverit, vagando nequaquam frequentent (p. 8, Nelson ed.); and we have noted that the rule was apparently well kept in this regard (*supra*, ch. I, esp. n. 68). Nor, on the other hand, would the appointment of obedientiaries necessarily present a challenge to monastic discipline from the late eleventh century. The system of farming manors prevalent at the period (*infra*, ch. 3) obviated a detailed supervision by the central body.

[44] 'An Episcopal Land-Grant of 1086', p. 363.

[45] D. B., I, p. 41 (Winchester): Hæ Terræ Infra Scriptæ Sunt de victu Monachorum Wint'; and see also p. 65.
I, p. 77: H' Nove' Descripta Maner' Sunt de Victu Monachorum Scireburn.
I, p. 101: Hæ quattuor Villæ Sunt de Victu Canonicorum (Exeter).
II, p. 8: Terræ S'ctæ Trinitatis de Cantorberia ad victu monachorum.
II, p. 216: Terræ Sancti benedicti de holmo ad victu monachorum.

[46] D. B., I, e.g., Berkshire, Terra Ecclesiæ Abbedoniens, p. 59: De hac terra hujus maneris tenet Uluui. 3 hidas que fuerunt de dominicum victu monachorum.
P. 59, d., Berkshire, Terra Abbatiæ S. Petri Wintoniens: Ipsa abbatia tenuit Sotwelle in dominio de victu monachorum T.R.E. Modo ten' Hugo de Port de Abb'e in feudo.
P. 68, d., Wiltshire, Terra Ecclesiæ Ambresberiensis: Ipsa ecclesia tenebat II hidas T.R.E. & post tenuit R.R. Willi. & sunt de victu moniāliu'm. Has ten' com' moriton' injuste.
Wiltshire, Worcester, 173, d.: Dodd' tenet (Seggesbarue) & e' de victu monachorum. Eldred' dirationcinat' est a Britrico filio eius.

The royal writs concerning recovery of monastic lands indicate that the Anglo-Norman kings continued to respect this special title. At least from the time of William II there was employed a writ with the form, 'I am unwilling that in any manner should be lost what pertains to the food and clothing of the monks'.[48] These writs became especially necessary from the arbitrary nature of the first Norman settlement. At Ramsey, for example, two of the above-mentioned five properties held by the 'knights' of Domesday had ordinarily supplied food rents for the convent. The royal writs served as a check to such overambitious Normans, and as aids to the previously discussed land recoveries at Ramsey. The principle behind these writs does not appear to be novel, since by them the conventual needs were simply used to corroborate rather than to establish the monastic title to the property concerned. A payment so traditional and intrinsic to the monastic life as the farm (feorm), would always form a sound basis upon which to establish proof of title. Nevertheless, the royal interest in the definition of this proof extended no further in the late eleventh century; for example, William II only wished his sheriff to investigate whether 'the land of Isham rendered a farm to the monks of St. Benedict in the time of my father, and if it is discovered that it did, it (this land) is to be in the abbot's demesne.'[49]

But the position of conventual revenues had yet to be defined against the powers of the royal overlord himself. Under William II's minister, Ranulf Flamand, an attempt was made to exact full feudal jurisdiction over the ecclesiastical tenants-in-chief, that is to control monastic properties during vacancies in the office of abbot, and to exact the payment of a relief by the abbot upon the latter's reception of his office.[50] The latter charge does not seem to have become an institution, apparently because of the precautions being taken against simony in the spirit of the Hildebrandine reform. But vacancy control became a plague under Rufus, and as many as eleven houses were said to be still held in his hands at the time of his death. Ramsey was to be especially afflicted with vacancy charges over the twelfth century. Despite Henry's promises to correct the abuses of his predecessors, Ramsey suffered over the first five years of his reign by vacancy and the appointment of a royal nominee as abbot, and again from a vacancy of nearly two years upon the death of abbot Aldwin (1111). Henry was even prepared to leave a conventual manor in the hands of his curial administrator despite the writs by which he forbade the practice to others. In this fashion Ellington was to be retained for

---

Or see p. 173 d., Cnihtewic, and Hineltun; 175 d., Bradeway; 181 d., Hamme, Herefordshire; 191, Escelforde, Cambridgeshire; 222, Eldewingle, Northants; II, 201, Flecwest, Norfolk.

[47] E. g., Wiltshire, Worcester, I, 173: Ad hoc manerium (Breodun) iacent III hidas ad Teotintune & una hida ad Mitune & sunt de victu monachorum.
Ibid., Ad supradicta M (Blochelei) iacet I hida ad I acu'be. ptin' ad victu monachorum.
[48] *Carts.*, I, p. 234 (no. CL); *Chronicon*, p.

210 (no. 187), p. 213 (no. 195), p. 214 (no. 197). William I only confirmed the general 'liberties and privileges' of the monastery, e.g., *Chronicon*, p. 200.
[49] *Chronicon*, p. 206 (no. 178). A similar document was issued for Ely lands in the time of William I. See H. W. C. DAVIS, *Regesta Regum Anglo-Normannorum*, I (Oxford, 1913), p. 72, no. 276.
[50] See KNOWLES, *The Monastic Order in England*, pp. 612-613, for a good summary of this attempt to control the monasteries under William II.

life by William the royal *dispensator*, and only then returned *ad victum monachorum Rameseiæ*.

In the correction and stabilization of feudal organizations under Henry I, the convent finally acquired protection against such encroachments when a new legal force was given to the divisions of revenues. While there is an extraordinary lack of specialization in the use of terminology at this time,[51] Henry I may be seen drawing an ever more clear line between those lands *ad opus* to the 'church' or 'abbey', as against the lands *ad usum monachorum* or *ad elemosinam ecclesiæ*.[52] The 'use' or 'alms' became a broader category expressive of the traditional title by food and clothing.[53] Towards the end of Abbot Reginald's term of office (1116-1130), in a charter addressed to the magnates of the realm, Henry confirmed the lands taken into the abbey's *dominium* during Reginald's term of office and clearly distinguished the two basic services to which they were to be allocated:

> ... ita quod unam partem istarum terrarum ponat ad operationem ecclesiæ suæ et aliam partem ponat ad eleemosinam ecclesiæ suæ; et partem illam quam ad operationem ecclesiæ posuerit ex quo parata fuerit ecclesia ponat eam ad supradictam eleemosinam ecclesiæ.[54]

Other charters in the Ramsey collection suggest that this division was made earlier in the reign of Henry I, and at the same time give us more detail upon the actual division of property. An important document explains that Abbot Aldwin drew up the statute which was confirmed later by Gilbert Capellanus on the part of Henry I:

> In primis statuit et ad celerarium, pro victu prædictorum monachorum, et hospitum, assignavit diversa maneria, que vocantur firmas monachorum sicut superius plenius annotantur.[55]

Probably contemporary with this document is a charter given a few pages later in the Cartularies[56] where it is noted that the convent have Burwell, Elsworth with Knapwell, Slepe, Houghton, Warboys, Abbots Ripton, Weston, Elton, each as a full farm, Graveley, and Holywell each as one-half farms, and Therfield, Wistow, and Upwood each as three-quarter farms. Then follows the valuable document which shows in detail for the first time in our extant records that the *opus* to be borne by the abbey, in contradistinction to the

[51] On this point, see F. M. STENTON, *The First Century of English Feudalism, passim.*

[52] E. g., *Chronicon*, p. 207, no. 179; p. 215, nos.199 & 200; p. 234, no. 240; p. 240-1, no. 255.

[53] A good example may be seen in the issue by Henry I of a specific charter: Præcipio quod totus proprius victus et vestitus abbatis et monachorum de Ramesia et quicquid homines sui poterunt affidare esse ad proprium usum ipsorum sit quietum ab omni theloneo et consuetudine et passagio ... (*Chronicon*, p. 283, no.331),

despite the general privilege: Præcipio quod omnes monachi et omnes homines sancti Benedicti de Ramesia sint quieti ab omni theloneo et consuetudine ubicunque vadant vel vendant vel conducant aliquid ad opus monachorum Sancti Benedicti (*Chronicon*, p. 278-9, no. 318).

[54] *Chronicon*, p. 225, no. 217.

[55] *Carts.*, III, p. 163: Hoc est statutum quod statuit piæ memoriæ, dominus Aldwinus ...; quod post eum Gilbertus Capellanus, ex parte Regis Henrici, confirmavit.

[56] *Ibid.*, p. 168.

properties *in elemosinam* to the convent, was the forensic burdens placed on
the abbot's manors:

> Suthlingdeon, Cramfeld, Barton, Brancester, Ringstede, Holm, Depedale,
> Wimbodesham, Dunham, Walsocne, Helyngeia, Chateriz, Broctona,
> Hemingford, Elington, Riptona Regis, Salptreia, visum francii plegii,
> terra de Hirst.
>
> Hæc omnia maneria assignata sunt cameræ domini Abbatis, cui
> incumbit defendere ecclesiam in omnibus placitis undecunque emer-
> gentibus, tam in foro laicali, quam ecclesiastico, in omnibus officinis
> ecclesiæ nostræ spectantibus.[57]

This distinction between the two services within Ramsey Abbey seems
to have become accepted from the time of Henry I. In a charter of 1187
concerning the rental of Over to Godfrey Pecke, Henry II refers to the formula
employed by Henry I : ... *quia audivi coram me per cartam Regis Henrici
avi mei quod exitus illius terræ debet poni in operatione illius ecclesiæ Rameseia et
in elemosinis ejusdem ecclesiæ.*[58] Archbishop Theobald (1142-7) of Canterbury
refutes a claim of Robert Foliot to Graveley, one of the manors in the above
list of cellarer's farms, which was to be held *sicut dominium mensæ monachorum.*[59]
By the *divisio* the convent acquired a real possessory title. Henceforth, these
manors are the convent's, or the cellarer's, or some other obedientiary's
manors.[60] They will be recognized as such by as distant an authority as the
papal charters of confirmation. Or again, as late as the 14th century the
Quo Warranto records will speak of the abbot's manors as *spectant ad baroniam*,
of the others as *spectant ad conventum.*[61]

This division of properties remained the conventual charter of economic
liberties for centuries. For example, the interference with conventual manors
by Abbot William later in the 12th century, or by King John with the beginning
of the 13th, were definitely regarded as illegal and extortionist. All Ramsey
properties continued to be held *in capite* by the abbot; but the *divisio* challenges
Maitland's *dictum* that 'freedom from secular jurisdiction rather than freedom
from secular service has been the focus of frankalmoign'.[62] Except for a few
small holdings and the freeholds owing support towards the expenses of
knights, the military tenants were located on the abbot's manors. It is
generally recognized that centrifugal tendencies of feudalism were to have

---

[57] *Ibid.*, pp. 169-170. Although the above
documents on the *divisio* cannot be dated
before the reign of Stephen because of the
inclusion of the manor of King's Ripton
granted to Ramsey by that king, and hence
likely pertain to the post-civil war reconstruction period, still due to Henry's
confirmation of Abbot Aldwin's *divisio* and
the fact that we have found Henry referring to this *divisio* himself (above, note 54),
it is unlikely that the formulæ of these
charters have changed from the time of
Henry I.
[58] *Chronicon*, p. 300.
[59] *Ibid.*, p. 306, no.379. The old formula

might still be employed however, as we see
in the Pipe Roll entry for 1207, where
Master Hubert renders his account for
Ramsey revenues in custody 'praeter
hoc quod pertinet ad victum et vestitum
monachorum' (*Carts.*, III, p. 11, no. DXVI).
[60] E.g., during the 12th century properties
were donated *in dominium elemosinarii*
(*Chronicon*, p. 304); or ... quum autem
obierit vel vitam mutaverit, eadem ecclesia
ad dispositionem elemosinarii Ramesiæ
libere revertetur. (*Chronicon*, p. 315).
[61] *Carts.*, I, pp. 267-281.
[62] POLLOCK and MAITLAND, *History of English
Law*, 2nd ed., I, p. 246.

immense consequences for the internal administration of English monasteries from the early 12th century, above all in the separation of the abbot from the convent, and in the diffusion of obedientiary affairs.[63]　But the effect of this policy upon the economic organization of the Black Monk estates has received little attention.　For Ramsey we shall have to let the feudal tendencies of the 12th century run their course before it will be possible to investigate the light that the materials for this period will throw upon the problem.

When we attempt to trace in detail the tenurial structure that appears beneath or along with the military fees on Ramsey estates, the picture becomes increasingly complicated.　There remains no possibility of a simple formulation of all tenures along feudal lines, since the Norman system of enfeoffment failed to be circumscribed by a literal application of the principle of tenure by service.　The very early commutation of military obligations permitted a flexible system of supplying the expenses of the *servitium debitum* itself, such as has been described for Ramsey.　But, in addition, the fee was adapted to non-military relationships.　For example, a liberal extension of the 'fief' to the designation of a simple money rent as a 'fee farm' became a common policy of the king and barons during Anglo-Norman times.[64]　The fee in such cases was a legal fiction, implying more the acceptance of existing modes of tenure rather than the imposition of obligations in vassalage.[65]　On Ramsey estates, in turn, many of the obligations in military service were mixed in with simple money rents which became part of the terms in a lease.　This admixture of service and rent also added multiformity to the tenure as it descended the baronial structure.　The service to court as well as the peasant *opera* dues, were usually payable in a complementary or alternative relation with a money rent.

At least part of this flexibility was due also to more traditional complexities.　The Norman entered upon his holding not only by the imposition of a tenure initiated by the Conquest, but under the title of successor.　For Ramsey Abbey, as elsewhere,[66] the lands seized at the conquest had often been held previously by some of the Anglo-Saxon rentals we have noted in the preceding chapter so that the Norman claimed the title of succession as conqueror of the Anglo-Saxon tenant,[67] and the seizure may be seen, technically at least, as a continuation of the ancient problem of conveyance rather

---

[63] KNOWLES, *The Monastic Order in England*, especially p. 404, and pp. 433-434.

[64] One of these advanced applications of the fee to money payments has been studied by Byce D. LYON in 'The Money Fief under the English Kings, 1066-1485', E.H.R., LXVI (1951), 161-193.

[65] A charter from the *Historia Monasteria de Abingdon*, II, *ca.* 1100, sets out some of the possible tenurial alternatives to the military fee proper at this time: . . . ., et servitium unius militis facere debet in omni loco ubi cæteri homines ecclesiæ faciunt servitium militum, et nulli unquam debet illam terram vendere, vel vadimonizare, vel in feudo dare, sive in feudo firma.　See also,

GLANVILLE, *Laws and Customs of the Kingdom of England*, tr. John Beames (London, 1812), pp. 59-60.

[66] E.g., V. C. H., Berkshire, I, p. 298.

[67] Ramsey has provided a classical description of this replacement, V. C. H., Hunts., I, p. 354: They bear witness that Aluuin's land of Gellinge and Emmingford belonged to Saint Benedict and that it was granted to Aluuin for the term of his life on this condition, that after his death it ought to return to the church and Bocstede with it. But this same Aluuin was killed in the battle of Hastings, and the abbot took back his lands until Alberic de Ver disseised them.

than a repudiation of the Anglo-Saxon contract. Where the name of the pre-conquest tenant has not been preserved, the Anglo-Norman charter terminology provides no easy solution to the problem of tracing this movement of lands, for the *clamores* of Domesday proclaim against a 'seized' property, but with the same phrase royal writs order the abbot to be 're-seized' of his property. In any case, viewed in the light of their legal structure, Abbot Reginald's charters of land redemption had come to stress three problems of his time: the necessity of confirmation by the king of those leases issued previous to his reign, the value of reasserting a lease of the abbot's predecessor in the reigning abbot's name, and the importance of clarifying life tenancy conditions in these new charters for the eradication of hereditary claims to Ramsey lands.

The charters that have survived from the late 11th century also show that the Anglo-Saxon rental terms can still be traced in the later period, and that the military service was incorporated in a more traditional contract. For example, Eudo, the royal *dapifer*, is granted the Ramsey land in Barford in 1080 as one knight's fee with the familiar *precaria remuneratoria* stipulation that this estate together with his own adjacent land be returned to the abbey upon his demise;[68] a life rental agreement upon Over manor was arranged in 1088 under terms common one hundred years earlier; and in Dillington the yearly money rent now complements a fee: *Reliquas vero tres libras, quas Radulphus inde debet, habeat ipsemet pro suo servitio.*

The early twelfth-century charters of Ramsey offer no indication that the extraordinary extension of the military fee on its lands was due to the attraction of these complementary money rents. On the contrary, Abbot Reginald was equally concerned to regain control of abbey lands by the redemption or curtailment of any non-military tenures which threatened to become perpetual alienations. The small invasion (*invasiones*) of the abbey domain by local men, like the assart at Cranfield taken by Aelric of that village, or the grove of Knapwell seized by Godfredus, were apparently easily recovered by the witness of the local men.[69] More often, however, the redemption involved a costly settlement. Ramsey paid ten marks to Antony of Huntingdon for the church of Shillington despite the fact that an episcopal inquest had found that Antony had no rights in the church;[70] twenty shillings was paid to Gilbert Ingulph for land at Over, although it was established at the monastic inquest that Gilbert never had any *utilitatis de terra illa.*[71] The chronicler explains

---

[68] Something of a *remuneratoria* clause may be found in leases towards the close of Abbot Reginald's term of office. E.g., *Chronicon*, p. 245-6, no. 264: ... juravit Wlgetus se fidelem fore Ramesiensi ecclesiæ in omnibus pro posse suo propter nostram terram de Maringes, quam si prædictus abbas cum suo conventu concessit habere pro dimidia marca argenti per unumquemque annum dum iste viverit Wlgetus; ... post obitum suum pro salute suæ animæ dedit ecclesiæ Ramesiæ de sua propria terra, decem acras.

The grant in such leases is now assuming, however, more the nature of a fine. It is not the accumulated rent of the Anglo-Saxon *precaria remuneratoria.* This can be seen very clearly in the terms of the lease of Over in 1088, *Chronicon*, p. 232, where it is stated that one hundred shillings of land *or* one gold mark were to accrue to the abbey upon reversion of the property.

[69] *Chronicon*, p. 253, nos. 275 and 276.

[70] *Ibid.*, p. 247.

[71] *Ibid.*, p. 242, no. 258.

that these fines are paid to gain surety against further litigation. An unusual agreement was made at the redemption of one-half hide of Bythorn.[72] The abbey paid a fine of one hundred shillings, but added a clause permitting the other party to re-institute a claim for the land within six years. According to the evidence that does survive for this period, the most common method of settlement was by some exchange of property. As with the military tenure, exchange or purchase would be the only alternative when the tenant had a real seisin. Still by exchange Reginald would be able to restrict the intrusion of lay lords into conventual manors. Such would seem to be the purpose behind the agreement with Hugo of Holywell.[73] Hugo gave up his fee in Holywell, one of the conventual vills, in exchange for a plot on the market place of St. Ives, a turbary and other appurtenances in that village. Abbot Reginald also conceded sixty shillings to Hugo, some cloth to his wife, and twelve pence to their child. In trying to prevent the breakup of some of his own larger estates, the abbot had sometimes to be content with curtailing the *dominium* of others, without being able to redeem all his former lands. Thus Reginald renewed the forty shilling fee farm of William, son of Gosfridus, in return for the latter's quit claim over all appurtenances in the marsh;[74] and a royal writ restricted Roger Foliot's fee to one hide in Broughton, the remainder of his holdings to be in the abbot's *dominium*.[75]

Again, in these arrangements, it was the powerful magnates and the royal officers who provoked the most costly settlements. Unless the royal writ could be invoked to prove that the property had paid a *feorm* to the convent, or had been seized in a very recent disturbance, only rarely did Abbot Reginald regain control of his lands simply by an insistence upon the one life term of the contracts submitted by his abbatial predecessor Aldwin. More often considerable monies went into the fines for redemption or compromise of permanent leases: Ramsey paid out £10. to regain Lutton, 20 marks and 2 palfreys for Crawley, more than 13 marks for Pegsdon, 100 silver marks to William de Houghton for a quit claim to his hereditary hold on Bradenach (in Therfield).

On the other hand, the fine was the touchstone of a hereditary lease. In exchanges of property involving the settlement of military tenures, Abbot Reginald had himself required the fine with hereditary fees: 20 marks came to Ramsey from the Hurst group of estates in this fashion, and 40 marks with the concession of Hemington and a number of smallholds. Far back into Anglo-Saxon times the substantial fine had signified the price of a long tenure.[76] But the Anglo-Norman hereditary lease was perpetual, not just a lease for two, three, or even four lives. Abbot Reginald probably realized the significance of this virtual alienation of lands, and was consequently prepared to go to great lengths in order to recover a perpetual lease. It is impossible to trace the legal history of these quitclaims in order to discover

[72] *Ibid.*, pp. 256-7.
[73] *Ibid.*, pp. 246-7.
[74] *Ibid.*, p. 251.
[75] *Ibid.*, p. 231, no. 233.

[76] See especially the last fifty pages of Vol. II, *Cartularium Saxonicum*, for many charters of this type.

whether the fine itself induced the tenant to return the lease to the abbey or whether it was in fact a purchase; but the substantial size of some of the above-mentioned fines dispensed by the abbot does at least suggest that we are faced here with primarily an economic transaction in the recovery of valid titles to perpetual freehold.

There is some evidence for the positive augmentation of abbey lands at this time, exclusive of the claim settlements. The remaining 'third' of the Lothwere fishery was sold to Reginald for a sum to be paid out of back debts in eels and *redditus* owed to the abbey. The considerable manor at Crawley which now appears among the Ramsey properties for the first time may have been an outright purchase, although we have only the vague statement in a *divisio*[77] of the district from the time of Henry I to the effect that Crawley 'had been of the fee of William de Houghton'. Lands and churches of Hugo of Worcester in Elton and Warboys, and of Richard Vetula in Houghton and Wyton were confirmed to Ramsey Abbey by a charter of Henry I, 'to be held as the abbey holds its other lands';[78] but there is no record of how the abbey obtained seisin of these properties.

On the whole, however, the charters give no clear indication that the abbey was the recipient of substantial land bequests in the late eleventh and early twelfth centuries. Nor is there any positive evidence from this period of an extension to the abbatial *dominium* by actual purchase, such as had been common under the Anglo-Saxons and was to re-appear as a significant policy in the 13th century. The best proof of this may be seen in a royal charter,[79] issued late in Abbot Reginald's term of office, in order to confirm to the abbey those lands now held which were not in domain upon Reginald's entrance to office. The charter speaks of Reginald's gains as *perquisivit* — obviously with that early twelfth-century meaning of 'restored'[80] — for, where the complementary charters of seisin are extant, they exclusively pertain to such 're-claimed' lands as those in Graveley, Over, Holywell, or Bythorn, noted above. The fact that important acquisitions, like Bradenach, are not mentioned in this charter, offers further support to our previous suggestion that these 'claims' were in reality purchases of land. But, on the other hand, the charter cannot be taken as completely definitive, for the list of properties trails off into the confirmation of 'all other lands'. In addition, properties like Bradenach, which was still held by William de Houghton late in Reginald's term of office, may not have yet been regained when this royal charter was issued.[81]

An investigation of the non-military services that were important conditions in the formation of the Anglo-Norman tenurial structure is confronted with the problem that no complete lists are extant of the *ministeriales* of the barons, that might correspond with the *Carta Baronum*, the *Feudarium*

---

[77] *Chronicon*, p. 255.
[78] *Ibid.*, pp. 281-2.
[79] *Ibid.*, p. 225: ... Sciatis me Reinaldo abbati de Ramesia concessisse omnes terras illas quas perquisivit postquam fuit abbas quæ non erant in dominio abbathiæ die qua recepit abbathiam, ...
[80] *Medieval Latin Word-List*, ed. Baxter, Johnson, *et al.*, p. 306.
[81] *Chronicon*, p. 261, no.289.

of Bury St. Edmund's, or the *Descriptio Militum* of Peterborough. Even for the tenures of the royal serjeants,[82] the information in the late eleventh and during the twelfth centuries is confused and scanty. It was only with the public records of the thirteenth century that this tenure became clearly treated. On the other hand, many of these thirteenth-century serjeanty tenures are traceable to early Anglo-Norman times, so that their early importance should not be misjudged through lack of evidence. It is equally unlikely that the grant of lands to important abbey servants, a policy found so useful in the time of St. Oswald, should have been eclipsed by the conquest. Despite the great developments in the internal organization of the monastery, the commitment to public affairs required by the feudal position of the abbot must have called for greater dependance upon lay officials, especially the steward.[83]

But the cartularies of Ramsey, like the collections of other abbeys, throw remarkably little light upon serjeanty tenures. During the confused reign of Rufus, families like the Le Moignes may have gained their initial foothold upon the abbey lands as stewards or chamberlains to Abbot Aldwin, in addition to their various serjeanty services to the king. However, a hereditary lease like that granted by Abbot Reginald to Hervey Le Moigne, which included Lutton, Gidding, Raveley, and additional smallholds, was occasioned by a quitclaim on Ramsey lands rather than the need of service, and merely entailed the usual freehold obligations. . . *pro posse suo in omnibus defendat placitis et ubicumque opus fuerit.* At the same time, the Ramsey documents do give some information on serjeanty tenures, and this is not least valuable as an explanation of why we are so ill-informed upon service tenures for this period. Primarily, the main officials seem to have been informal assistants of the abbot, and, quite often, relatives. Something of a reward for stewardship may be seen in the 'grant' of Pegsdon to Abbot Reginald's nephew Ebroinus for the latter's services in regaining this substantial property from the royal chamberlain;[84] and indeed as witness to another charter, we find *Ebroinus dapifer.*[85] Probably we should take this to mean that the property was farmed to Ebroinus for life, since Pegsdon certainly remained in the abbot's domain and was never let in perpetuity.

As early as 1106, Henry I was re-organizing the management of his lands in order to reduce the control of powerful ministers, and after decades of *invasiones*, the abbey too must have been chary about giving her neighbouring magnates further title for claims to abbey estates. Hence, it becomes probable that in addition to the haphazard family compact in the abbot's management, few records have been preserved, because the baronial serjeants, like their

---

[82] The following remarks upon royal serjeants are summarized from E. KIMBALL, *Serjeanty Tenure in Mediæval England* (New Haven, 1936), Ch. I, especially pp. 3 and 9.

[83] E.g., charter of Westminster Abbey between 1085 and 1100 (J. A. ROBINSON, *Gilbert Crispin, Abbot of Westminster*, Cambridge, 1911, p. 30) has preserved the royal confirmation to Hugh de Coleham of hereditary office of steward: . . . , videlicet, ut ipse Hugo totius prædictæ abbatiæ sit dapifer et sub abbate procurator, et heredes sui post eum, . . .

[84] *Chronicon*, pp. 253-4.

[85] *Ibid.*, p. 258, no. 283.

royal counterparts, were rewarded with only the temporary farm or custody of abbey lands. In contrast, during and after the civil war when so many of the monasteries suffered from mal-administration, the ministers were able to obtain a more permanent seisin upon abbey lands. The seneschal of Ramsey, brother of Abbot William, was granted a carrucate of land at Cranfield; and a freehold in King's Ripton was alienated to the son of this steward.[86] A number of leases have been preserved for Bury St. Edmund's for this period, and we find hereditary leases to the abbot's butlers, stewards, and so forth.[87] On the other hand, a reforming abbot like Samson of Bury, kept his manors in his own hands as much as possible; and the inquisitions of Ramsey estates in the late 12th century castigate William for the above alienations.

II

From a discussion of the superior tenures established on Ramsey estates after the Conquest for military service, money rent, and obligations in serjeanty, we may pass to the consideration of a lower order less influenced by the external coercion of king or magnate. The Benedictine abbot was already an important lord in Anglo-Saxon times, so to a great extent the conquest brought only confirmation of his rights over 'lands and men'.[88] More specifically, these confirmations enabled the abbey to retain such traditional Anglo-Saxon modes of jurisdiction as sac and soc, toll and team, infangthief, and so forth.[89] However, as an emergent baron under the Anglo-Norman feudalism, the abbot of Ramsey would also have to follow the pattern set by his royal overlord, and to emulate his lay peers, in the constitution of his own domainal rights.

Important changes may be particularly noted in the abbot's jurisdiction over traditional freemen, that is, the thegns and sokemen. The description of this transition given in the *Dialogue of the Exchequer*[90] is useful for the integration of monastic evidence from the post-conquest period. Freemen lost their lands by fighting against the Conqueror, the *Dialogue* tells us:

> . . . careful investigation was made as to the identity of those who had contended against the king in war and had saved themselves by flight. To all such, and even to the heirs of those who had fallen in battle, all hope of recovering the lands, estates and revenues, which they had previously possessed, was precluded; . . .

It is not apparent that the Anglo-Saxon abbeys benefited always, or even often from this dispossession. As noted above in this chapter this right of

[86] *Carts.*, III, 223-4.
[87] *Feudal Documents of Bury St. Edmunds*, ed. D. C. Douglas (London, 1931), charters 148, 150, 155, 156, 164.
[88] One of the clearest expressions of such a confirmation is given in the following charter of W. II for Bury St. Edmunds, although in some form or other all the great abbeys received a similar grant: That the abbot of St. Edmunds have all his lands and men as well as he had them on the day when the king lately came into England (*Regesta Regum Anglo-Normannorum*, I, p. 76, no.291).
[89] E.g., *Carts.*, I, 233.
[90] The excerpts in the following pages have been taken from *English Historical Documents*, II, p. 524.

conquest gave the Norman warrior a strong claim to abbey lands that had been leased to the thegns and other warriors.[91]   But it was not only upon those who had fought in battle and their relatives that the penalty of dispossession fell.   The *Dialogue* makes it clear that the Anglo-Saxon warriors were punished as a class:

> Those indeed who had been summoned to war, but had not yet joined the host, or had taken no part in the battle through preoccupation with their domestic affairs or some other indispensable business, contrived in course of time to obtain lands for themselves, according as by their devoted service they gained the favour of their lords, and this without hope of hereditary possession, but solely at their lords' pleasure.

Since the abbots were important landlords, they would be affected by this dependence of the disinherited.   Some valuable evidence has been preserved to show how the thegns, the backbone of the Anglo-Saxon militia, suffered the penalty of defeated warriors.   In a writ concerning the disputed Ramsey property of Isham,[92] William II declared: If in fact this is discovered to have been thegnland, whoever holds it of the abbey may retain it, and let him recognize that if he wishes, the abbot may have it in demesne.   A writ from William I to Archbishop Lanfranc concerning the lands of Ely,[93] makes it clear that this policy towards thegnlands commenced with the conquest: Those who hold thegnlands, which beyond doubt ought to be held of the church, must make the best terms they can with the church; otherwise it is to have back their lands.   Since the writs of this nature are rare, we may note another writ issued by William I to Ely reiterating this dependence of the thegn upon the will of the abbot for his tenure: . . . the abbot is to be seized of those thegnlands which pertained to the abbey on the day of Edward's death, if the tenants cannot come to an agreement with him.[94]

It is not altogether clear whether the destruction of thegn freeholds was universal, dependent upon a general grant of such freeholds to every lord, or whether the dispossession of freeholders was contingent upon the military opposition received from that district.   William II's confirmation to Canterbury of jurisdiction over 'all their own men and over the free tenants whom he has given to them',[95] seems to imply a limited jurisdiction over the freemen of the district.   On the other hand, those holding freeholds contested by the abbot of Ely had to prove under William I that 'they hold by gift from the king';[96] there is here no allusion to hereditary titles.   In general, the

---

[91] A good general account of this problem for the monasteries is given by the chronicle of Abingdon, II, p. 3., and a charter of W. I. to Bury St. Edmund's shows how the Normans claimed such lands for themselves: . . . , and I give you to know that I will that Abbot Baldwin hand to me the land that those men possessed who stood in battle against me and were slain there, who belonged to St. Edmund's soc (*Regesta Regum Anglo-Normannorum*, I, p. 119, App. no.VI, Calendar 40).

[92] *Carts.*, I, 234, CXLVII: Si vero teinlanda tunc fuisse invenietur, qui eam tenet de abbate, teneat, et recognoscat, quod, si voluerit, eam abbas in dominio habeat.

[93] *Regesta Regum Anglo-Normannorum*, I, p. 43, no. 155.

[94] *Ibid.*, p. 72, no. 276.

[95] *Ibid.*, p. 81, no. 311.

[96] *Ibid.*, p. 43, no. 156.

jurisdiction over thegnholdings given to the abbots in the above writs, and the mass induction of former freemen into lords' domains that can be seen in Domesday Book, show that the odds were highly against these lesser men over the actual troubled post-conquest period. An example of this induction relevant to our study may be found at the Ramsey manor of Ringstead in East Anglia, where powerful Normans had 'taken' as their men thirty-one of the formerly privileged class of sokemen in that manor. All this goes far to confirm the account of the *Dialogue* which pictures dispossessed freemen after the conquest preparing, in despair, to leave the country.

But it would be more than our records suggest to take the misfortune of freemen in the conquest crisis as typical of the condition of this class over the Anglo-Norman period. To begin with, we must recognize feudalism as primarily an alternative legal structure rather than a depression of lower orders; the interposition of a lord between tenant and king only becomes synonymous with a depression and servitude of the tenant in later common law theories. In addition, the Anglo-Saxons were probably not totally unfamiliar with the new order of things. There was something of a lordship in the abbot of Ramsey's soc jurisdiction, for example. And at Ringstead in the Domesday plea, it was apparent that Ramsey wished to recover her own soc jurisdiction over the thirty-one men, not to impose villein status. The Anglo-Saxon abbot had some jurisdiction over thegns too, a condition probably implied in the above reference to 'those thegnlands which pertained to the abbey on the day of Edward's death'. Indeed, the sole important reference to sokemen in the Domesday of Ramsey estates indicates a pre-conquest extension of the abbot's jurisdiction. Among the postscript of pleas in Huntingdon, the inquisitors 'say that five hides of Broughton was land of sokemen *in tempore Regis Edwardi* but that king gave their land and soke to St. Benedict of Ramsey for a service that Abbot Aldwin performed for him in Saxony; and afterwards (the abbey) always kept it'. In short, the increase of monastic lordship by the conquest was not a radical innovation.

By the same token, the submission of freemen to the jurisdiction of a lord was not uncommon, nor necessarily derogative to freehold status. The violence of the conquest period was exceptional and had to be checked to preserve the social order of the time. Even the pro-Norman author of the *Dialogue* makes it quite clear from his text that, rather than lose these men, new forms of hereditary tenure were introduced:

> ... since they had become hateful in the sight of all men and been despoiled of their property, they would be compelled to cross over to foreign parts.   At length council was taken on these matters, and it was decreed that whatsoever, by virtue of their merits and the interposition of a legal convenant, they had been able to obtain from their lords, the same should be conceded to them by inviolable right.   Nevertheless, they might claim nothing for themselves by right of hereditary succession from the time of the conquest of their nation.   Indeed, with what prudent consideration this provision was made is manifest, especially since they would thus be bound, in order to consult their own advantage, *to strive thereafter* by every means to purchase the goodwill of their lords *by devoted services.*

There is no question here of a reduction to villeinage, since the villein could be kept on his land by other means than a hereditary title to land. The need for 'devoted services' is the *pièce justificative* of the arrangement.

Hence the post-conquest settlement ultimately involved a compromise, and a veritable continuance of the grant of hereditary lands for services or for a charter. Whether lesser men were able to employ these means to acquire a higher state in life is not clear. Freehold status had been obtainable under the Anglo-Saxon laws with the acquisition of a holding of a certain size. An important document of Bury St. Edmunds states specifically the continuance of this privilege after the Conquest.[97] While there is no such charter extant for Ramsey, there was a real possibility for movement to a higher level in the 12th century. As will be noted below, over the mid-12th century large amounts of land were lost from the villeinage on Ramsey estates by being 'freed' for money rents or court services; when the abbot of Ramsey began to attempt a recovery of such lands in the early thirteenth century villeins as well as freemen were found to have purchased charters for non-free lands.[98] The early twelfth-century information for Ramsey estates does, at least, confirm the existence of a substantial freehold class. Extents for these manors indicate that by far the most common reason for the spread of hereditary freeholds into the large manorial structure was for service to courts.[99] By the time of Henry I, it was common for two to four hides on a manor to be held for the duty *sequitur comitatum et hundredum*, or some variant as *ad hundredum*. These tenants, generally called *liberi feudati*,[100] were well established by the time of the first extents, so the creation of such a tenurial group was unlikely to have been a post-conquest innovation.[101] Ramsey Abbey had immense jurisdiction in the

---

[97] Upon these holdings the important note of Miss HARMER (*Anglo-Saxon Writs*, p. 476) deserves to be quoted in full: H. W. C. Davis pointed out (*Regesta*, I, p. xxix) that there is evidence that the right and duty of attending the shire or hundred court, rather than the manorial court, might be contingent on the tenure of a holding of a certain size. A writ of Wm. II, (DAVIS, *Regesta*, I, p. 135, no. 393, charter no. LXIV, and D. C. DOUGLAS, *Feudal Documents of Bury St. Edmunds*, charter no. 16) addressed to all the king's judges (judicibus), sheriffs and officials (ministris) of England, contains this precept: 'defendo etiam ut non cogatis homines Sancti ire ad schiras vel ad hundreda nisi illos qui tantum terre habent (Douglas, tenent) unde digni fuissent tempore regis Edwardi ire ad schiras vel ad hundreda'. To this evidence might be added that of the Domesday entry concerning Fersfield in Norfolk (D.B. ii, 130 b) 'In Fervelle iacet soca et saca T.R.E. de omnibus qui minus habent quam XXX acras. De illis qui habent XXX acras iacet soca et saca in hundredo,' i.e. those persons with less than 30 acres were required to attend the manorial court of Fersfield, those with more, the court of the hundred.

[98] See, *infra*, Chapter IV, Section I.

[99] Again something like the thirty acre rule of Bury St. Edmunds may have been in use for Ramsey, for the virgate on Ramsey estates was usually around thirty acres, and almost invariably court service is due from holdings of more than a virgate in size. D. C. DOUGLAS has remarked for Bury (*Feudal Documents from the Abbey of Bury St. Edmunds*, London, 1932, p. clviii): Just as hidage is the typical payment of the free peasant, so is suit to the hundred court throughout the twelfth century in the Liberty of St. Edmunds his typical jurisdictional obligation . . . These lists supply strong support from a document of early date for Maitland's view that these suits became tenurial in arrangement.

[100] *Carts.*, III, 257, 274, 283, 305, 307, 308. 'Feudalism' is used throughout this study with the general meaning of the *feudati* in Ramsey charters, that is, the holding of land for services other than those of the villein.

[101] Only five hides of Broughton and the five hides of Hemmingford are mentioned as sokeland in the Hunts. Domesday of Ramsey, but the *clamores* suggest that small freeholdings were common, e.g.,

courts of Huntingdon: an honour court at Broughton, franchisal court for the Ramsey banlieu, hundred court jurisdiction over each of her manors, and the manorial courts.[102]   Through this court system not only was criminal and civil law enforced, but much of the routine ordering of rural society was administered.   Hence the meeting of courts was frequent, and since the jurors rather than a judge administered justice, the need for 'suit to court' was very pressing. The baronial administration had its 'tenurial cost', therefore, as well as its profits from courts and from entry fines to land of the *liberi feudati*.   A thirteenth-century extent can state clearly the economic position of these tenures in a manner more familiar to the military fee: *Et non reddit per annum pro una virgata aliquem censum Abbati, quia est una de quattuor virgatis, quæ defendunt totam villatam de secta comitatus et hundredi per annum.*[103]   In the following table some holdings for suit to court have been collected to show these 'costs' of baronial administration:

'concerning the two hides by Ralf son of Osmund in Hemmingford they say one of them belonged to the demesne of the church of Ramsey in king Edward's day, and that Ralf holds it against the abbot's will; concerning the other hide, they say Godric held it of the abbot, but when the abbot was in Denmark, Osmund, Ralf's father, seized it from Aluuin the fowler, to whom the abbot had given it for love of the king.'

Eustace claimed by succession five hides in Broughton, two and one-half hides in Slepe, one hide in Houghton, which had probably been small freeholds.   In addition to these claims there was one hide held of the abbot in Holywell by one man; four hides in Slepe by three men of the abbot; the two and one-half hides of Lutton; the five hides of Yelling; one hide of Gidding held by Lunen.   In short, if holdings by 'knights' are considered in the same category, it was more unusual in the Ramsey Domesday for a hide or two not to be parcelled out to a freeholder in every manor.

[102] W. O. AULT, *Court Rolls of the Abbey of Ramsey and of the Honour of Clare*, (New Haven, 1928).

[103] *Carts.*, I, 438.

An entry for Cranfield suggests that personal liberty came with this service to the shire and hundred: Johannes filius Adæ tenet dimidiam hidam. Pro qua pater ejus, in diebus Henrici Regis, sequebatur comitatum et hundredum, et fuit *liber* a servitio. Et ipse idem Johannes modo tenet. (*Carts.*, III, 301). The extents are for the most part, however, concerned with services rather than the status of men; so we must be content to trace in more detail the freeing from services. Two entries from the extent of Burwell may serve as a starting point: Gaufridus, pater Michaelis Clerici, habuit duas virgatas de libero feudo, pro quibus sequebatur comitatum

et hundredum. Et quietusfuit. Sed secundum testimonium proborum hominum, antiquitus reddebat terra illa quinque solidos ad censum (*Carts.*, III, p. 308). Or on page 309 of the same extent: Radulphus filius Ricardi tenet tres virgatas, libere. Pro quibus sequebatur comitatum et hundredum. Unde, secundum testimonium proborum hominum, pater ejus reddebat quadraginta denarios; et ipse Radulphus nihil dat pro eis.

The *censum* in detailed explanations throughout these extents is a payment for the commutation of villein services, hence, in the first example from Burwell at least, the two virgates were likely former villein holdings. A more important key to this transition is probably provided by the *liberi feudati* owing some ploughing services. In the detailed explanations of commutation the tenant usually retains some ploughing services besides the *censum* payment. E.g. (*Carts.*, III, 243): Si non operatur, dat duos solidos per annum, et arat qualibet die Veneris, et quietus erit a cæteris consuetudinibus præter preces; . . . Or for Warboys (III, 254): Et si non operatur, dat sex solidos per annum; et arat qualibet septimana una die; etc. . . . sed non operatur in septimana, . . . See also p. 256, twice. Now, many lands held for service to shire and hundred courts have also retained some of the *censum*, and plough services along with it. E.g. *ibid.*, III, 278: Thurkillus de Wittona tenuit antiquitus duas virgatas, pro quinque solidos. Et sequebatur comitatum et hundredum, et arabat omni die Veneris. Et modo tenuit Reinaldus eandem terram pro eodem servitio. Wlfricu tenuit tunc duas virgatas pro quinque solidis, et sequebatur comitatum et hundredum, et arabat. See also Eaduuardus, pater Jordani, p. 258; Suetwinus, p. 273; same page, Robertus; etc.

TABLE III

PROPERTIES ALIENATED FOR BARONIAL ADMINISTRATION

BY 1135

Stukeley....................................	5 h. (A)
Hemmingford Abbots......................	6½ v.
Shillington & Pegsdon....................	5 h. (A)
Brancaster...............................	1 *terra*
Ringstead................................	the demesne
Broughton................................	3 v. (B)
Cranfield.................................	2 h., 1 v.
Barton...................................	2 h. (A)
Lawshall..................................	½ h., 1 v.
Upwood...................................	1 h., 2½ v.
Burwell...................................	5 v.
Weston...................................	2 h.
Bythorn..................................	1½ v.
Elton.....................................	8 v.
Graveley..................................	4 v. (A)
Houghton & Wyton......................	4 v. (B)

A. Both suit to court and obligations to the support of military service are mentioned for these lands.

B. Including some properties also owing minor money rents and services.

Note: The length of this list corresponds with the extant evidence for the time of King Henry I, and consequently cannot pretend to be a complete summary of this type of tenure.

While suit to court by the *liberi feudati* remained the predominant obligation of freehold grants until the mid-12th century, there is no evidence to suggest that the payment of regular money rents, for smaller units of land at least, was not within the economic order of the day. Reclaimed properties, like the one-half hide of Bythorn, were immediately let out on money terms. Small holdings previously held on the same terms, like the hide in Broughton or the *terra* in Brancaster, were renewed by Abbot Reginald. There are many charters attesting to new rentals by the same abbot: 'the land of Vincent the monk' for four shillings per year, 'the land of Maurice the monk' for five shillings, one-half hide in Burwell for ten shillings, one hide in Burwell for twenty shillings, one virgate in Girton.

From the twelfth-century extents can be gained something of the completed picture of the small holdings alienated in these hereditary leases.   The
prevalence of these rents under Abbot Reginald whose decease only shortly
preceded the death of Henry I is strikingly brought out in the data of the
extents that pertain to the early twelfth century (below, Table IV).   The
'ancients' interviewed for information upon conditions in *tempore Henrici* did
not dispute the money renting of this era; rather they complained frequently
that lands which *antiquitus reddebant censum* are now freed from rents,[104] or
they noted that the rent 'might have been more'.[105]   Since we have practically
no charter evidence for these small money rentals, distinct from some instances
when services are at stake, it is impossible to explain their appearance in such
numbers.   The unusually large entry fine of five marks for the hereditary
lease of one virgate in Girton suggests one stimulus to this type of rental.[106]

TABLE IV

PROPERTIES AT MONEY RENT IN 1135

CHARTER EVIDENCE	ADDITIONAL EVIDENCE FROM THE 12TH-C. EXTENTS	
	Abbot's Manors	Convent's Manors
St. Ives (cr., etc.)	Ellington (3½ v., 2 cr.)	Wistow (3½ v.)
Burnham, Depedale	Shillington & Pegsdon (1 h., 1 v., 60 a.)	Holywell (3½ v.)
Raveley	Girton (1 v., 7½ a.)	Burwell (1 h., 3 v.)
Lutton	Depedale (48 a., *terra*, marsh)	Brington (1 cot.)
Burwell (1½ h.)	Brancaster (40 a., *terra*)	Knapwell (½ v.)
Stowe (demesne)	Ringstead (1 car. & small holdings)	Graveley (1 v.)
Ringstead	Hemmingford Abb. (5 v., 6 cr.)	Elton (5½ v.)
Over	Lawshall (3 v.)	Stukeley (2½ v.)
Broughton (1 h.)	Cranfield (1 v.)	Houghton &
Maringe		Wyton (9 v., 1 cot.)
Barnwell, *et al.*		
Unspecified holdings		
Whiston		

Note: There is some repetition of Table II here as some properties (e.g. Barnwell *et al.*)
          gave both military *debita* and money rent. Col. II & III are from incidental
          references in these extents and must be considered in relation to the indica-
          tions that much greater amounts of land were at money rent (v. *infra*, Chapter
          III, Section II).

[104] *Carts.*, III, 308, 312.
[105] *Ibid.*, extents, *passim.*
[106] *Chronicon*, p. 251. Despite the large
       amount of spurious material in this
       collection, Ingulph's description of the

farm of many Croyland properties for a
substantial fine in order to meet the
immediate necessities of the monastery
after the disastrous fire of 1091, still
remains one of the most useful examples

But more often the fine is less spectacular; and the size of the money rents themselves, by comparison with the value of *opera* and customary rents for instance, does not seem to offer a great financial attraction. There is the further difficulty in investigating the hereditary small holding leases that the money rent often remains mixed up with some suit to court or even an obligation of work on the demesne; and many of these lands are let to friends, relatives, and servants, so that the cost of service still blurs the rental contract.

Indeed, if the *liberi feudati* with their established title to land and important civil functions were in many ways successors to the Anglo-Saxon thegns, a successor in the post-conquest period may also be found for that amorphous Anglo-Saxon group called the geneats — a class whose dues varied from rents, to labour services on the demesne, but whose main obligation was some serjeanty function. Our sources for information upon such base serjeanties at Ramsey Abbey are more complete than those for the superior tenures of this category. As witnesses to a series of documents under Abbot Reginald, and following such important men as Hervey and Berengarius Le Moigne, Ebroinus, or Gilbert son of Wido, may be found Gilbert the chaplain, Herbert the constable, Durand the cook, Arnold the chamberlain, Walter the ostler, Hugh the interpreter, John the mason, Fulk Asketell the steward, Richard the cook, Godwin the cordwainer, Harold the brewer, Richard the baker, Robert and Richard masons, Osbern the glazier, Warenne the vintner, Herbert the marshall, Richard the chamberlain, Ingelran the forester.[107] These are evidently the *famuli*, or servants at the abbey. The fuller complement of abbey servants may be seen in a document probably of the late 12th or early 13th century, which outlines in detail the payments to be received by eighty servants.[108] The list begins with the chaplain, and it includes men and women engaged in a wide variety of domestic activities.[109] The remuneration of these ser-

---

of this financial expedient. See *Ingulph's Chronicle of the Abbey of Croyland*, tr. H. T. Riley, Bohn's Antiquary Library edition (London, 1854), pp. 203 ff.

[107] *Chronicon*, pp. 260-63.

[108] *Carts.*, III, 236-41. Some of the trades of the above witnesses are not mentioned; but the later account rolls show that many *famuli* concerned with construction or unusual crafts were not hired regularly but only for 'task' or piece work. More important officers probably held by grant of a freehold, and would not be mentioned in this list of 'wage-labour'; see references to freehold grants for serjeants at Bury St. Edmunds, *supra*, n. 87. In this Ramsey document of *Carts.*, III, 236-41, the name *famulus* is only applied to servants of the master craftsmen.

[109] Chaplain,* master porter* and servant, two stewards,* two servants for the church, a washerwoman and servant for the church, two servants in the infirmary, refectorian, washerwoman for the refectory, two master cooks for the monks, scullion, hostler for the kitchen, servant for windows of the infirmary, cook for the hall, cellarer's porter, two woodmen (*lignarii*) for the kitchen, a woodman for the hall,* *wacca*,* ostler* (*stabularius*), two master bakers, two boilers (*buletores*), two sweepers in the bakery (*rosarii*), two master brewers, five sweepers in the brewery, two master tailors, three servants in the laundry, seven fishermen and seven servants, a carpenter and servant, reeve, pigman, two cattlemen, mason, the wool merchant with his horse and servant, the winnower with his horse, two carpenters of the church, the cellarer's carpenter, two gardiners, two orchardkeepers, a master and six servants in the vineyard, forester, park-keeper, miller, keeper of the granaries, oxherds, seven almsmen in the guesthouse, fifteen paupers. The servants starred above ate in the hall. The custodian of the granary and the oxherds were paid out of the granaries by amounts not indicated in this document; and the chaplain is only said to be paid by the sacristan.

vants was composed of food received in the hall or as a certain number of loaves, and a wage (*merces*), either in the form of a cash sum or of acres on various manors.

Unfortunately this *famuli* list is probably too late to show the movements of this group to land on Ramsey estates in the late 11th and early 12th centuries,[110] and in addition it does not specify whether the servants received in acres a small plot for their own uses, or merely the produce of so many 'sown acres' on the lord's demesne. From mid-thirteenth-century extents it can be clearly seen that the abbey servants were by that time at least receiving sown acres rather than plots of their own.[111] On the other hand, these 'acre' allocations of the thirteenth-century extents do not correspond with the manorial allocations to *famuli* in the earlier document, so that no direct comparison between the two periods is possible. Certainly, where the opportunity presented itself, the twelfth-century *famulus* extended himself upon abbey lands. Over the civil war disturbances, Alfgaro the chamberlain obtained four acres within the abbey gates from the cellarer's lands, and four without.[112] Herbert the reeve, who obtained a virgate of freehold at Brancaster, may have been the reeve from the abbey.[113] In any case, beyond the money wages of more than four pounds mentioned in the *famuli* list, and the fortnightly livery of 2,000 loaves of bread, these servants received 141 acres in eighteen manors.

While many of the *famuli* at the abbey, like Gilbert the chaplain, were undoubtedly freemen, the manorial *famuli* were of a lesser dignity. A recent study has collected materials representing a wide geographical area to illustrate a movement of the Anglo-Saxon slaves and house-servants on to small parcels of land in a manner parallel to the creation of knights' fees.[114] The detailed information from thirteenth-century account rolls reveals such substantial *famuli* labour forces on each of the Ramsey manors. While the slaves of Domesday disappeared at Ramsey, as elsewhere, the twelfth-century extents for these manors are too late and abbreviated to supply data upon the actual transition. We shall have to wait for the later period of Ramsey history to obtain comprehensive data on the manorial *famuli*.[115] Nevertheless, it is clear that the hired labour force appeared at an early period and was paid by small holdings. The extent of Elsworth (*ca.* 1135), for example, states that of the nine cotlands that remain (from a total of thirty-three), the farmer shall

---

[110] Some carpenters had seized one hide and two virgates of land from Ely after the Conquest (*Regesta, op. cit.*, p. 43, no. 156). The early twelfth century extents for Ramsey's neighbour Peterborough, show servants settling around the town: In Burgo ... Et præter hoc. X. servientes qui deserviunt terram per sergentariam, et si non essent servientes, redderent de consuetudine. I. marcham argenti (*Liber Niger*, p. 161).

[111] *Carts.*, I, 319: ... percipiunt apud Wardeboys acras inbladas; ... Cocus etiam conventus et pistor percipiunt quattuor acras frumenti in pejoribus culturis manerii, et quattuor acras avenæ; ... *Carts.*, I, 351: Isti subscripti percipiunt acras inbladas apud Upwode, ..., carpentarius, cementarius, et carrectarius Rameseiæ in eisdem campis tres acras frumenti, et tres acras avenæ.

[112] *Carts.*, II, 272.

[113] *Ibid.*, 223.

[114] M. M. Postan, 'The Famulus', *Economic History Review Supplement*, no. 2 (Cambridge, 1954).

[115] See *infra*, Ch. VII.

allocate them for four oxherds, two haywards, one swineherd, one shepherd, and one watchman.[116] This dependence of manorial servants upon the contract with the farmer of the manor rather than solely upon custom, probably means that more flexibility was permitted to the *famuli* tenure than to the regular villein holdings. Despite the quota of stock and cultivation exigent for the 'farmed manor', there were annual fluctuations from crop failures and epidemics, that must have allowed for considerable variations in the staff requirements. On the other hand, the smallholds would have to be occupied by someone, and when they were villein lands, they could revert to tenure by services to the demesne when the *famulus* was not required. We find such an arrangement explicitly provided for in the extent of Warboys where the two 'acremen', who hold their *acremonelandæ* for service to the demesne plough, were to hold for the same service as a cotter when the plough work was not performed.[117]

III

In the post-conquest tenurial pattern on Ramsey estates two forms occur, the tenure by service, and the tenure for a rent payment. It would be altogether to misconstrue the historical setting of the time to consider the tenure by service as simply a more primitive and inflexible antecedent of, or alternative to, the rent payment. The tenure by service had a much wider content. Personal service was still the bond of society, and, until law and government took more articulate and specialized forms, the personal element was essential. The granting of many and varied tenures by service aided the evolution to higher forms; so that it is not surprising to find from the early crude feudal equation of land portions and services that the burden of military and judicial administration should lead to a dissipation of baronial property analogous to that dwindling of the ancient demesne of the royal overlord.[118]

---

[116] *Carts.*, III, p. 300. At Knapwell (*ibid.*, pp. 300-301), the farmer 'made' three ploughmen, one shepherd, one hayward, one watchman, one swineherd, and one smith, from eleven cotlands, the remaining three cotlands being devoted to general services. The three cotlands at Brington were 'to make' ploughmen, or to be put at money rent if the farmer so wished (*ibid.*, p. 311). The extent for Upwood only mentions (*ibid.*, p. 271) that there are six cotlands whose tenants 'follow the ploughs of the demesne'. One example is particularly illuminating upon the means by which the *famulus* could get plough services for his own lands: at Warboys 'William Acreman holds one acremanland, and serves the plough of the abbot; and ought, once every twenty days, to have the plough of the abbot'. Another interesting type of service may be found at Graveley where Hugo *facit ferrura aratrorum curiæ pro omni servitio.*

[117] *Ibid.*, p. 257.
[118] See R. S. HOYT, *The Royal Demesne in English Constitutional History, 1066-1272*, pp. 85 ff.; and Edward MILLER, *The Abbey and Bishopric of Ely*, p. 2: The great estate, in short, had functions and powers which were derived, not from private right, but from the exigencies of public administration.

G. J. TURNER (*Brevia Placitata*, Selden Society, 66, 1947) has some remarks that are helpful for the interpretation of Ramsey materials, although he does not seem to have brought the *Dialogue* into this context. See *Brevia Placitata*, p. lviii: Thus we have good reason for thinking that in the early days of the Norman kings the great mass of civil litigation took place in the county and seigneurial courts and especially in the county courts.

And again, *ibid.*, p. lxxv: But it must be remembered that at the time of Domesday Book, outside the northern and eastern

The tenurial echelon that ranged from the freehold and knight fee through the laylord and abbot baron to the king marked, too, a socio-economic framework constructed upon the foundation of land; and the very pervasiveness of this framework gave a tremendous rigidity — a rigidity necessary to social stability.

At the same time, the ensuing rigidity of the hereditary tenures for services was not a backward step for the tenant. So long as society was built upon the principle of personal obligations to a lord, it was less satisfactory for the vassal to leave himself open to the increasing needs of his lord by adjustable tenurial obligations. Ramsey Abbey herself paid dearly for this indefinite dependence by her delay in establishing knight fees to cover military obligations to the king. The tenure of thegns and other Anglo-Saxon freemen who had formed the backbone of the anti-Norman army was left completely at the mercy of the king and his tenants-in-chief after the conquest. But in the reaction, the freemen and even the villeins of the Ramsey manors unanimously strove to obtain hereditary tenures for suit to court or other determined services in the early twelfth century. Even the settlement of slaves on the land may be considered as part of the same movement, for the establishment of a petty serjeanty tenure opened the way to the freeing of these least free from some disabilities of personal dependence. This fixing of the obligation on land would permit a shifting of the burdens of personal obligation, whether on the highest levels, as in the rotation of the four knights at Ramsey, or on the level of the humble *famulus* who could hold villein land for driving the lord's plough; and in due course this flexibility made commutation feasible.

On the other hand, it would be incorrect to consider the formation of the Anglo-Norman feudal society as the universal note of the twelfth-century economy. Cast in the form of 'orders of men', fiefs, and services, the post-conquest records often obscure the flexibility of economic actions that brought commutation of the military services by the early twelfth century, or threatened to absorb the lord's demesne by the time of Henry II. Above all, as has been seen, the spread of a system of money rents on Ramsey estates did not wait upon the commutation of services. The Normans inherited and adapted the considerable rentals of this type employed by the Anglo-Saxons. But especially for the small freehold was there an accepted pattern of hereditary leases for a money rent. As will be seen in the following chapter, it was the rent for a money payment rather than service which became the principle of agrarian evolution on these estates in the twelfth century.

The student of Ramsey estates is fortunate in the survivals of rent data that pertain to this early period. These data have been collected in Table V in order to illustrate something of the chronology of changes in manorial returns. In the Domesday are found *valets* for the manors of Hunts. in 1086 and *in tempore Regis Edwardi*; most of the remaining Ramsey manors have

---

counties, free manorial tenants were scarce. For long after the Conquest there were few lords of manors who could hold a court baron if they wished to do so. Even in the north and east the free tenants of the twelfth century were mostly sokemen and customary tenants, whose tenements were probably transferred by surrender and admittance, and not by a charter of feoffment.

been given the further intermediate value for *tunc* or 'when received'. In the Norfolk Domesday, however, the values *in tempore Regis Edwardi* are missing. The money values for the food rents in Abbot Aldwin's charter permit the construction of a group of manorial rents for the decade after Domesday, probably *ca.* 1095 (Table V, Col. IV). Next, the first series of evidence, from the extents *ca.* 1135, gives a few rental items (Col. V). Most remarkable is the preservation of a document entitled the *Redditus Annui* of Ramsey Abbey,[119] and containing one figure (for Ellington) expressed as in the 'time of Abbot Reginald'. Probably then these *Redditus* referred to the returns for some year before the civil war, so it is here given the date *ca.* 1140 (Table V, Col. VI). The rents given for the actual time of the taking of the inquisition fall under the dating of *ca.* 1160 for the extents (Table V, Col. VII). Nearer the end of the century are placed the values for the new food and money rent liveries (Table V, Col. VIII), with the corn values estimates at a perhaps cautious double of their earlier figure (though the farm price for Abbots Ripton, 1201, Col. IX, roughly corroborates this estimation). Finally, occasional rents were obtainable from the charters of leases and from vacancy rolls at the end of the twelfth century (Cols. IX and X).

[119] This has been printed by Hearne and Dugdale; the only extant manuscript seems to be that in B. M., Harleian 5071.   A discussion of the dating of the food rent documents will be found in Appendix B, *infra*.

TABLE V

VALUES OF RAMSEY ABBEY ESTATES

Estate	Domesday Book			IV 1095	V 1135
	I T.R.E.	II Tunc	III Modo		
Stukeley	£ 6	—	£ 6	—	£ 7
Girton	£ 8	£ 6	£ 4	—	—
Over	£10	£ 6	£ 8	£ 6	—
Ripton (A.)	£ 8	—	£ 8	£ 8·6	—
Broughton	£ 9	—	£10	£ 8·6	—
Wistow	£ 9	—	£ 8	£ 8·6	—
Upwood	£10	—	£ 9	£ 8·6	—
Holywell	£ 8	—	£ 8	£ 8·6	—
Slepe	£20	—	£18	£17	—
Houghton	£ 8	—	£ 8	} £17	} £10+farm
Wyton	£ 7	—	£ 7		
Warboys	£12	—	£12	£17	—
Sawtrey	£ 4	—	£ 4	—	—
Elton	£14	—	£16	£17	£10+farm
Hemmingford Abbots	£11	—	£10	£ 8·6	—
Hemmingford Grey	£ 3	—	£ 3	—	—
Bythorn	£ 4	—	£ 5·10	} £17	£21 or farm
Brington	£ 4	—	£ 4		
Weston	£10	—	£10		
Ellington	£10	—	£10	£ 8·6	—
Cranfield	£12	£ 9	£ 9	£ 8·6	£15 }
Crawley	—	—	—	—	—
Barton	£12	£10	—	—	—
Pegsdon	£12	£10	£10	—	} £29
Shillington	£12	£12	£12	—	
Therfield	£12	£10	£11	£17	— }
Bradenach	—	—	—	—	—
Hilgay	—	80s.	70s.	—	—
Yelling	£ 4	—	£ 4	—	—
Snorehill	—	—	10s.	—	—
Wimbotsham	—	£ 4	£ 3	—	—

TABLE V

VALUES OF RAMSEY ABBEY ESTATES

VI 1140	VII 1160	VIII 1170	IX 1201	X 1212	Estate
£ 7	£ 8	—	(100s.)	—	Stukeley
£10	£10	—	£12	£20	Girton
£7	—	—	£ 8	—	Over
£11	—	£37·15·6	£40	—	Ripton (A.)
£18	—	—	£23	—	Broughton
£ 9	—	£25·1·4	—	—	Wistow
£10	—	£25·1·4	—	—	Upwood
—	—	£18	—	—	Holywell
—	—	£37·15·6	—	—	Slepe
£60{	—	£37·15·6	}£10+farm{	—	Houghton
	—	—		—	Wyton
£17	—	—	—	—	Warboys
£ 7	—	—	(40s.)	—	Sawtrey
£30	—	£37·15·6	£10+farm	—	Elton
£15	—	—	£22·14	—	Hemmingford Abbots
—	—	—	—	—	Hemmingford Grey
£21{	—	£37·15·6	{ —	—	Bythorn
	—			—	Brington
	—			—	Weston
£ 9	—	—	£12	—	Ellington
£25{	—	—	}£34{	—	Cranfield
	—	—		—	Crawley
£15	—	—	£26	—	Barton
£40{	—	—	}£80{	—	Pegsdon
	—	—		—	Shillington
£27{	—	}£37·15·6	{ —	—	Therfield
	—		—	—	Bradenach
£10	£10	—	}£16{	£30{	Hilgay
£ 6	—	—			Yelling
—	—	—	—	—	Snorehill
£14	—	—	£16	—	Wimbotsham

TABLE V *(Cont'd.)*

VALUES OF RAMSEY ABBEY ESTATES

Estate	Domesday Book			IV 1095	V 1135
	I T.R.E.	II Tunc	III Modo		
Brancaster	—	—	£10	—	—
Ringstead	—	£ 6	£ 5·10	£ 8	—
Holme	—	—	—	—	—
Graveley	£ 8	£ 6	£ 6	£ 8·6	—
Elsworth	£20	£14	£16	£17	—
Knapwell	£ 8	£ 6	£ 6	£ 8·6	—
Burwell	£20	£16	£16	£17	—
Lawshall	—	£ 8	£12	—	—
Chatteris	£ 4	£ 1	£ 3	—	—
Walsoken	—	—	20s.	—	—

While this table lists, for the most part, only those large manors not perpetually leased by the abbey, the contrast between fixed returns from some manors and rapidly increasing revenues from the majority of the manors here listed is clearly discernible. The substantial manor of Over, leased in the time of the Conqueror, was to pay a constant return for more than a hundred years. Other manors — Sawtrey, Girton, Yelling, the Barnwell group — were leased sometime after Domesday and consequently seem to have absorbed some increase acquired since that date; but once leased they too gave only a fixed income to the abbey. The manors alienated by Abbot Walter (1133-61) over the troubled mid-century — Barford for ten pounds, Middleho for three pounds of wax, Offord — also belong in this fixed rent category. And finally, those numerous perpetual leases, large or small, indicated in the previous tables in this chapter demonstrate more completely the accumulated properties in this category.

There was, of course, some degree of variation in the hereditary rents from the reception of entry fines, dues, and commutation of services. Except for the substantial military aid of £48. 11s. 6d. still debited to Ramsey in that isolated Pipe Roll of 31 Henry I, the regular scutage of only four pounds or eight marks could not have been much of a burden on the abbey fees, or an opportunity for profit to the lord. The extraordinary feudal due offered, in all probability, a more profitable item to the overlord. The charter by which the relief tax was assessed has been handed down in the Ramsey collection, to

TABLE V (Cont'd.)

VALUES OF RAMSEY ABBEY ESTATES

VI 1140	VII 1160	VIII 1170	IX 1201	X 1212	Estate
£24	—	—	£60	—	Brancaster
£15	—	} £18	—	—	Ringstead
—	—		—	—	Holme
£10	—	} £37·15·6	—	—	Graveley
£30	—		—	—	Elsworth
£12	—	—	—	—	Knapwell
£30	—	£37·15·6	£10+farm	—	Burwell
£24	—	—	£30	£50	Lawshall
£ 8	—	—	£12	—	Chatteris
£ 5	—	—	£20	—	Walsoken

show the disposition of the hundred shillings per fee.[120]   Generally, however, the costs of collection and the tendency for succession dues and extraordinary levies to become customary would minimize their importance in an era of rising agricultural revenues.   The knight fees themselves should not be thought to get off too lightly, however, since the abbey could pass on royal exactions.   Something of what these obligations might become may be seen in the payments by knights entered on the vacancy rolls under King John, although this period cannot be taken as normal.   In addition to the regular scutage, they paid thirty pounds in 1201 *ne transfretent*, in 1201 the four fees obligation paid one hundred marks as a fine, for the next year the same group paid one hundred and seventy-two pounds, six shillings, and four pence as an aid.

The abbots also had the right to extraordinary taxes upon those freemen who owed otherwise simply the suit to court, and (or) a fixed money rent.   An

[120] *Carts.*, III, 47-8: Modus qualiter relevium liberorum tenentium domini Abbatis Rameseiæ debet solvi et exigi de feodis militum, ... ; scilicet quod quatuor hidæ faciunt feodum integrum, quatuor virgatæ hidam et (   ) acræ faciunt virgatam; ... Feodum integrum solvit ad relevium centum solidos.   Una hida, quæ est quarta pars feodi, viginti et quinque solidos. Una virgata terræ, quæ est quarta pars

hidæ, sex solidos, et tres denarios. Apparently this became a generally established rent for relief, cf. A. L. POOLE, *Obligations of Society in the Twelfth and Thirteenth Centuries* (Oxford, 1946), pp. 94-5.

An early fourteenth century roll (*Add. Ch.*, 34517) seems to show the abbot's chamberlain passing this relief on in its entirety to the royal sheriff.

undated charter shows that the 'recognition' fees for these freeholders were
extensive:

> Memorandum, quod est consuetudo in Nortffolca, ut invenitur in rotulis,
> tempore Hugonis Abbatis de Sulgrave, quod quilibet liber homo de
> homagio domini Abbatis dupplicabit redditum suum, pro recognitione
> domini Abbatis, post quamlibet vacationem.[121]

But the freemen were gradually ensured by the royal courts against excessive
or new charges by the overlord: near the mid-century, some freemen on
Ramsey holdings were able to gain protection against an effort by the abbot
to increase their hereditary rents.[122]

While it might be dangerous to minimize the overlord's power of exaction
during the post-conquest mutations of customary social privileges and
economic obligations, it appears reasonable to conclude that despite the signs
of rising returns to agricultual production, the abbots' ability to recoup a
proportionate increase of revenues from his knight fees and freemen was severely
curtailed by a system of perpetual leases and the hardening of the feudal and
customary institutions.   The regular revenues — the rents — were fixed, and
even most of the incidental returns were customary.   This was the evil of
alienation that is castigated in twelfth-century monastic records.   Alienation
was not, as it is to-day, the transfer of radical ownership; it was a loss of control
over revenues.   Abbot Reginald's revocation of knight fees and hereditary
leases was a reaction against this trend, but, as has been seen in the first
section of this chapter, this reaction had a limited success.   The problem
became endemic.   Every Ramsey abbot from the middle of the twelfth
century to the thirteenth was indicted for alienations.   The problem, indeed,
was nation-wide and drew the reproval of the popes.   By the early thirteenth
century, control of alienations loomed prominently on the agenda for reform
in monastic administration.[123]   Opposed by the centrifugal tendencies of feudalism, and the notion of rents as customary payments, the lesson was a long
time in the learning; but once acquired, it remained a governing factor in the
control and acquisition of monastic lands for at least one hundred and fifty
years.

---

[121] *Carts.*, III, 49. This custom likely extended back to Anglo-Saxon times. See *Die Gesetze der Angelsachsen*, ed. F. Liebermann (3 vols., Halle, 1903-16), I, p. 507.

[122] *Chronicon*, p. 290: (T. H. II.) '... Præcipio ... teneas plenum rectum Geraldo de Sancto Ivone de dimidia virgata terræ quam clamat de te tenere in Athelingtone per liberum servitium :.. pro duobus solidis annuatim inde reddendo pro omni servitio ... ne amplius inde clamorem ...' 'Præcipio tibi quod sine dilatione plenum rectum teneas Ricardo de Sancto Ivone de dimidia hida terræ in Haliwelle, quam tu ei diffortias, quam clamat tenere de te per liberum servitium sequendi schiram et hundredum, ...'

[123] See *infra*, Ch. IV, Section I.

CHAPTER III

RENT MOVEMENTS IN THE TWELFTH CENTURY

THE explanation for that striking increase in the revenues from many Ramsey manors, which can be seen in Table V of the previous chapter, must be reconstructed piecemeal, since twelfth-century sources are isolated, and comprehensive statements upon administrative policy are totally lacking. A beginning may be made with the investigation of some primary economic data, that is to say, movements in prices, productivity, and cultivable areas which are fundamental to the economic organization of this period.

I

Prices relevant to the estates of Ramsey Abbey in the twelfth century can be collected from food rent statutes and manorial extents. Neither source may be taken as direct evidence of market value; but as comparative materials they do provide a significant index to the change in evaluations over this century.

One food rent document belongs to the late eleventh or early twelfth century, the other to the late twelfth.[1] In the later document, unfortunately, only livestock produce are evaluated, though in the earlier set every item of food, corn, and livestock is given a monetary equivalence. In addition, the *treia* measure for butter, or the *sextoria* for honey in 1095 do not permit of comparison with the *discus* and *bolla* for these respective items at the later period. These price data were applicable to eighteen manors in 1095, and to thirteen manors in the later date, taken here for convenience as *ca.* 1195.

TABLE VI

FARM PRODUCE VALUES

Manors (numbers)	Cheese (per pond')	Bacon (per pond')	Suckling Pigs (each)	Lambs (each)	Date
18	3s.	5s.	6d.	1d.	*ca.* 1095
13	8s.	10s.	40d.	3.86d.	*ca.* 1195

[1] *Carts.*, III, pp. 230-234; *Carts.*, III, pp. 163-5. For the dating of these documents see Appendix B, *infra*.

From the manorial extents can be collected in turn the prices of the demesne 'capital' — that is the stock of oxen, horses, sheep, and cattle. The comparative data in these extents provide a fairly broad impression of price movements from the time of Henry I to the end of the century.

TABLE VII

PRICES OF DEMESNE STOCK

Manors	Oxen (each)	Horses (each)	Sheep (each)	Cows (each)	Date
Stukeley	3s.	3s.	—	—	ca. 1135
Wimbotsham	3s.	3s.	—	—	ca. 1135
Lawshall	3s.	3s.	—	3s.	ca. 1135
Brington	3s.	3s.	—	3s.	ca. 1135
Weston	3s.	3s.	—	3s.	ca. 1135
Bythorn	3s.	3s.	—	—	ca. 1135
Girton	3s.	3s.	4d.	—	ca. 1135
Brancaster	3s.	3s.4d.	6d.	—	ca. 1135
Ringstead	2s.8d.	4s.	—	—	ca. 1135
Holme	2s.8d.	4s.	—	—	ca. 1135
Houghton & Wyton	3s.6d.	4s.	—	—	ca. 1135
Elton	3s.4d.	—	—	40d.	ca. 1135
Hemmingford Abbots	4s.	4s.	4d.	—	ca. 1135
Shillington	4s.	4s.	—	—	ca. 1135
Pegsdon	4s.	4s.	—	—	ca. 1135
Weston	3s.6d.	—	—	—	ca. 1160
Wyton & Houghton	3s.6d.	4s.	—	—	ca. 1160
Wimbotsham	3s.	3s.	—	—	ca. 1160
Girton	3s.4d.	3s.4d.	—	—	ca. 1160
Brancaster	3s.	3s.4d.	11d.	3s.	ca. 1160
Elton	4s.	4s.	—	40d.	ca. 1160
Hemmingford Abbots	4s.	4s.	4d.	—	ca. 1160
Shillington	4s.	4s.	—	—	ca. 1160
Pegsdon	4s.	4s.	—	—	ca. 1160
Hemmingford Grey	4s.	4s.	7d.+	—	ca. 1195
Elsworth	4s.	4s.	—	—	ca. 1195
Knapwell	4s.	4s.	—	—	ca. 1160

Table VI, including as it does 'dressed' farm produce or *peroptimæ* stock, the young pig, and lamb, would not be expected to correspond exactly with the Table VII livestock prices that are issued only for the work animals and mature stock of concern to the demesne capital evaluation. However, for those items for which a comparison is possible — the lamb and sheep, the cow and 'carcass' (not tabulated), — the dual set of later twelfth-century prices are roughly corroborative. In the changes of these produce prices themselves from the late 11th century (Table VI) there has been an all-round rapid rise with a doubling in price for bacon, a steeper rise for cheese, and almost a quadrupling for lambs. The fact that bacon prices double only clashes with evidence for the item classified as *frescing* which is subject to a phenomenal rise of six times the 1095 value, and suggests a cautionary allowance for price variation here due to alteration in definition of the product over the intervening period.[2] Whatever may have been the exact range of the price movements from the late Anglo-Saxon period,[3] these food rents do show a rapid increase in value, which, as the movements in demesne stock prices will indicate, must have occurred before the second quarter of the twelfth century. An interesting contrast is found in the cow or 'carcass', valued at two shillings from the earliest food rent lists, and still listed at this value in the late thirteenth century although the cow was worth about nine shillings on Ramsey estates by this time. Since the cow was worth considerably more than two shillings even by the time of the surveys under Henry I, we have here apparently an example of commutation from an earlier period.

As an overall picture of the level of stock prices and the degree of their change during the reign of Henry II the extent data follow the pattern that A. L. Poole found for the royal manors in the Pipe Roll evidence.[4] That is, the earlier price of a horse or ox for plough service was usually 3 shillings, this changing at a later date to 4 shillings. The prices for sheep and cows from Ramsey materials are more exiguous and do not show a pattern of increase, if there was such over the mid-twelfth-century period. The sheep seems to have been usually valued at fourpence, the cow at three shillings.

It is difficult to attach a precise chronological framework to the price changes for the stocking of manors. Ramsey had some plough animals worth four shillings *ca.* 1135, but many manors still had such animals worth three shillings in the time of King Henry II. The royal manors showed the same type of variation: the four shillings per plough beast often appeared in 1166, but three shillings was frequent enough in 1198 and 1199! The stickiness in adjustment of stock valuations to prevalent prices which permitted such diversities in one area as have been found for Ramsey manors would be due to the rate of adjustment of the manorial farms.[5] In the same fashion, an

[2] The term *hoggastre* offers an important example of such a change in definition over this period. See A. L. POOLE, 'Livestock Prices in the Twelfth Century', *E.H.R.*, LV (1940), 295.

[3] Some prices from Anglo-Saxon times corroborate these lower levels of the early food rent statute, e.g. the six pence for the hog at Thorney Abbey in the early 11th century (A. J. ROBERTSON, *Charters, op. cit.*, 254); the sheep with its young lamb was 5 pence under Aethelstan, the cow 20d., the hog 8d. But the few prices that can be found for this early period are often very erratic. See F. W. MAITLAND, *Domesday Book and Beyond*, (Cambridge, 1897), p. 44, note 2; and it is not always clear when the Anglo-Saxon shilling ceased to be used as a unit of account.

[4] *Op. cit.*, pp. 284-295.

[5] See Section II, this chapter, for illustration of this point.

artificial common 'price' could be effected throughout the country by an evaluation actively applied to all the manors of one lord, like the adjustment to one value on over one hundred royal manors in 1194.[6] Despite these limitations the twelfth-century stock valuations do contain elements which seem to reflect price adjustments. There are in the earlier manorial extents lower values than the three shilling level for plough animals (e.g. thirty-two pence, for oxen at Ringstead and Holme) which may be supporting evidence for that movement from an earlier and lower price level which is suggested in the tables of food rents;[7] and there is an indication of how the adjustment moved through later intermediate price stages (three shillings, four pence for oxen in Elton and Girton, three shillings, six pence for oxen in Houghton, Wyton and Weston, forty pence for horses in Brancaster and Girton). These examples merely show that some *real* variations apparently did occur — variations which an omnibus study of twelfth-century price data for all England should be able to delineate more precisely.

Since there are no actual sales or purchase data available for Ramsey livestock in the 12th century which might be comparable with these extent evaluations, and in any case the rough dating of the extents leaves a further problem of imprecision, the deductions from these materials must remain of a general nature: the food rent evaluations suggest a sharp price rise in the time of King Henry I; there appears to have been no pressure to increase the values of livestock over the mid-century; where stocking evaluations were adjusted towards the last quarter of the century (e.g. Girton, Elton) there was an upward movement.

Unfortunately the changes in prices for corn cannot be traced in the same manner. That corn was not evaluated in the late twelfth-century food rent

TABLE VIII

MILL VALUES

Manor	Domesday	*ca.* 1135
Hemmingford Abbots.............	10s.8d.	30s.
Elton.........................	40s.	100s.
Houghton & Wyton..............	32s.	100s.
Barton........................	2s.	30s. (2)

[6] 'Livestock Prices in the Twelfth Century', p. 285.
[7] This lower price level for the early 12th century is also supported by statistics from the neighbouring abbey of Peterborough.

The *Liber Niger* (*ca.* 1125) has values of 24d., 32d., and 33d. for cows, 24d. for oxen (see pp. 158, 160, 166, *Chronicon Petroburgense*, Camden Society, 1849).

statutes does not mean that there was no change in price for this agrarian product. It was in fact not valued for the next 200 years in such statutes, or in the account roll liveries, despite the clearly discernible rise in the price of corn during the 13th century, for there was never any question of a monetary substitution or equivalence. Certainly if mill rents are taken as criteria, corn prices must have risen at this time. In the fifty years after Domesday the rent of the mills for Hemmingford Abbots, Elton, Houghton, and Wyton, nearly tripled; although to what degree this may have been also due to an increase in milling turnover cannot be estimated.

It will be appropriate to turn next to some indices of real productivity increase that accompanied this rise in prices. First, for the lord's demesne there is a frequent picture of increase in productive capacity both as regards ploughs and villein labour. In 12 out of 18 manors for which there are comparative data, the number of ploughs had increased by one in the time of Henry I, over the Domesday figures. When equality in ploughlands and ploughs in Domesday is taken as the accepted quota,[8] or ratio of plough capital, these increases can only be seen as replacements for under-capitalization on the three manors of Upwood, Wistow, and Girton in 1086. The twelfth-century extents do not give evidence of variations in the technical size of ploughs[9] that might be suggested as responsible for the increase in numbers. The use of villein ploughs apart, therefore, this growth in numbers of ploughs represented increases of twenty to thirty per cent in ploughing potential on at least nine manors in the two generations after Domesday.

Whether or no the actual demesne production was increased to a corresponding degree is less clear.[10] The increases in grain livery by the new food rent adjustments of the twelfth century were only trivial, although this is probably a reflection of stable consumption requirements. In the productive organization itself many combinations were possible. With the many hereditary leases of small holdings from the Conquest to 1135 there may have been a cancellation of plough services from those lands formerly *ad opera*. That these should fail to be mentioned is not surprising, for, even if the memory of the ancients extended back to these changes, the twelfth-century extents are quite clearly concerned only with the reduction of lands *ad opera from* the time of Henry I. Another hypothesis might be that the settlement of additional *famuli* labour upon the manor was accompanied by an increase in the demesne 'plough capital', a corresponding fall in demand for villein services, and the continuation of demesne production at much the same level. This may have released villein ploughs for the cultivation of new holdings. In any case on Ramsey manors, where the Domesday proportion of ploughs on the villeinage to those on the demesne averaged about five to one,

[8] There is much less equality between the villeins' ploughs and ploughlands. Generally the villeins' ploughlands were under-capitalized, if such equality is taken as standard capitalization. See *infra*, Table IX.

[9] The eight animal team seems to have been usual. See Appendix C, *infra*.

[10] For strong evidence of very substantial decline in demesne production over this early twelfth-century period, see M. M. POSTAN, 'Glastonbury Estates in the Twelfth Century', *Ec. H. R.*, Second Series. VI, (1953), 360-1.

even a substantial increase in demesne might be easily absorbed, or at least could be spread proportionately thinner in its repercussions upon the villein organization.

Estate	Domesday Book		T. Henry I Ploughs	T. Henry II Ploughs
	Ploughland	Ploughs		
Stukeley.............	2	2	3	2
Houghton............	2	2	3	3
Elton...............	4	4	5	4
Hemmingford Abbots..	?	2	3	3
Bythorn.............	1	1	2	?
Brington............	1	1	2	?
Weston.............	2	2	3	3
Ellington...........	2	2	2	1
Shillington..........	2	2	3	?
Ringstead...........	?	2	3	?
Girton.............	3	1	2	3
Elsworth............	4	3	3	?
Graveley............	2(½)	2	2	2
Cranfield...........	2	2	2	?
Brancaster..........	?	3	3	2
Broughton..........	?	4	(4)	4
Wistow.............	3	2	(3)	3
Upwood............	3	2	(4)	4

TABLE IX

DEMESNE PLOUGHS

If the villeins and borders mentioned with their ploughs in Domesday may be assumed to be landholders, then by the period of the extents of the second half of the twelfth century there is found a phenomenal increase in their numbers by frequently as much as forty to fifty per cent. As all conceivable permutations of money rents and services are found in the tenurial terms it is not possible to calculate that there was a net increase in work on the demesne after allowances are made for new putting out at money rent and non-productive services. There is here at least another index of productive potential upon the manor at large, however, if not upon the demesne. In those manors where the peasant name is given, the following increases in the numbers of landholders occur: Hemmingford Abbots 31 to 47, the Brancaster group 59 to 80, Elton 28 to 38, Knapwell 24 to 34, Hilgay and Snorehill 19

to 35, Ringstead and Holme 48 to 70, Graveley 20 to 37, Holywell 29 to 52,
Cranfield 20 to 58, Welles 16 to 46, Warboys 47 to 112.   As it was, moreover,
the custom in these extents to list separately properties held by different
persons even when the personal names are omitted, a more extensive column
(B) may be constructed on this basis for comparison with Domesday figures
(Table X, *infra*).   A third column is added from the thirteenth-century inquisitions.   When due qualifications have been made,[11] the thirteenth-
century data show that the increase in landholders was maintained.   Although
this later increase is less significant in many cases, it should be remarked that

Table X

PROPERTY HOLDERS ON RAMSEY MANORS

Manor	A 1086	B T. Henry II	C ca. 1250
Hemmingford Abbots............	31	47	96
Warboys......................	47	112	138
Holywell.....................	29	52	62
Cranfield....................	20	58	124
Elton........................	28	48	?
Ripton (Abbots)...............	33	?	87
Broughton....................	30	?	59
Wistow.......................	32	?	88
Upwood.......................	34	?	64
Brington.....................	14	16	32
Bythorn......................	17	23	?
Weston.......................	21	33	55
Barton.......................	33	?	76
Shillington & Pegsdon............	82	?	116
Brancaster, etc.................	59	80	89
Hilgay & Snorehill.............	19	35	?
Ringstead & Holme..............	48	70	101 *
Welles (Outwell)...............	16	46	?
Knapwell.....................	24	34	?
Graveley.....................	20	37	?

* The tax roll for Ringstead and Holme in 1315 (*Rawlinson Ms.* 333, fol. 64) lists 189
tenants in Ringstead and over 30 in Holme.

[11] The most important limitation is the lack of
reference to subtenants of freeholders in the
12th century; and, with a different type of
extent, if not rental system, prevailing
in the thirteenth century, the listing of
tenants may have been more complete at
the later period.

the time gap between the twelfth and thirteenth-century inquisitions is often
much less than that represented by the first two columns.

There is no ready picture of the extension into new arable and pastoral
land area that accompanied these movements in productivity and holdings.
While we must keep in mind that the handling of Domesday data turns easily
to a theorising from the want of a real nexus between fiscal terminology and
the simple data of manorial organization, there are a number of observations
on land development to be derived from Ramsey documents over this period
that may provide at least secondary approximations of twelfth-century
movements. In retrospect from Domesday, it is interesting to suggest that
if the acre as the basic unit of land measurement remained fairly constant[12]
within a radius of some dozen miles around St. Ives, then the ratios of the acre
to virgate and of the virgate to the hide may illustrate the settlement pro-
gression of the district. In the easily cultivable, earlier settled, and semi-
pastoral gravel valleys the *terra unius familiæ* could be less than the virgate
in the wooded and heavy clay uplands, and this may be one reason why the
manors containing a large proportion of the Ouse valley developed virgates in
general smaller than the upland virgate.

TABLE XI

ACRES PER VIRGATE IN SOME RAMSEY MANORS (12th C.)

I Along Gravel Flats		II Predominantly Upland	
Manor	Acres per virgate	Manor	Acres per virgate
Hemmingford.........	16	Wistow........	30
Holywell.............	18	Warboys.......	30
Slepe................	16	Bythorn.......	44
Houghton............	18	Brington.......	34
Wyton...............	18	Weston........	28
Graveley.............	20	Elsworth.......	30
Ripton (Abbots)........	15½	Knapwell......	40
Upwood..............	20	Broughton......	32

By the time of latest hidage assessments however, upland cultivation
would have to a considerable degree approached that of the valleys so that the

---

[12] This district seems to have had no great
variations as far as can be discovered from
later surveys, e.g. *Royal Commission on*
Weights and Measures, Vol. VII (1820),
s.v. "customary acre".

geld burden became now more justly re-distributed by an inverse ratio of hide and virgate to virgate and acre:

TABLE XII

VIRGATES PER HIDE IN SOME RAMSEY MANORS (12th C.)

Along Gravel Flats		Predominantly Upland	
Manor	Virgates per hide	Manor	Virgates per hide
Hemmingford..........	6	Wistow........	4
Holywell..............	5	Warboys.......	4
Slepe.................	5	Bythorn.......	4
Houghton.............	6	Brington.......	4
Wyton................	5	Weston........	4
Graveley..............	7	Elsworth.......	4
Abbots Ripton.........	4	Knapwell......	4
Upwood..............	4	Broughton......	6½

Note: These tables present simply a hypothesis of the agricultural development in this area.   Besides the possible evidence for beneficial hidation (e.g., Broughton was until late largely a royal manor), there remains the complication that some gravel lands, such as Slepe and Holywell, preserved large tracts of forest down into the time of the Conquest.   Or A. Ripton and Upwood, manors which showed a very slow development until late in the twelfth century, may not have received any hidage amelioration.   In short, the great variations in the rate of development of even adjacent manors in the twelfth century warn against any precise chronological use of these tables.

The increase of landholders by a subdivision of previously cultivated areas continuing generation after generation would be one further stage in the intensification of land settlement.   There is some suggestion of this in the numerous subdivisions of the *ad opus* virgate into semi-virgates awkwardly performing one-half the services of a virgate (Warboys, Elsworth, Knapwell, Graveley), or into the still smaller units of cotlands upon which the *famuli* were sometimes settled.   But the manor was not settled simply by an increasing intensity of occupation; so it is necessary to attempt some estimations of net additions to manorial agricultural areas.

Moving back from the 'known' of manorial organization in the twelfth-century extents to that, in contrast, 'unknown' of the Domesday tenurial structure, there may be found first, a common denominator provided by the Ramsey fiscal hidage of Domesday which remained relatively unchanged throughout the Middle Ages.   Next, the total virgate units derived from the fiscal proportions of virgate to hide from the first surviving report, that of the late twelfth century,[13] may also be pushed back to seek a numerical comparison with the virgate units of the extents which were real villein tenurial units.   For it seems very probable that at some date the number of fiscal virgates for Ramsey manors was about the same as that of the actual virgate holdings.   This may have been due to the necessary homogeneity among units organized to supply identical work on the desmesne.   On the other hand, there was no necessary economic identity between fiscal units and these villein tenements.   This can be seen by the 'new lands' of the twelfth century which were not heavily obligated with services to the lord's demesne.   The Cranfield extent illustrates that the abbey was giving virgate or semi-virgate assessment to assarts varying in acreage and in money rents.   To compare such extent tenures with hidage denominations is therefore, to compare baronial assessment with geld assessment; but, just as the fiscal virgatage became fixed, so too the villein unit with its customary obligations apparently remained fixed from an early period.   These factors provide us with a possible foundation upon which to add the net increase of holdings from the late eleventh, or early twelfth century.

TABLE XIII

SOME EARLY TWELFTH-CENTURY TENEMENTS

Manors	Fiscal Virga-tage	Actual Villein Holdings
Stukeley..............	28	28 v(illeins)
Wistow..............	36	37 v., 8 c(otters)
Warboys..............	40	38 v., 13 c., 24½ t(ofts)
Bythorn..............	12	12½ v., 11 c.
Brington..............	12	12 v., 9 c.
Knapwell..............	8	8½ v., 16 c.
Elton................	60	50 v., 16 t.
Cranfield..............	32	38 v.
Graveley..............	32	32½ v., 3½ c.
Upwood..............	40	42½ v., 6 c.
Weston..............	32	31 v., 3 c.
Ellington..............	48	45½ v., 3 c., plus (?)
Houghton & Wyton......	77	61 v., 21 c., 13½ t., 7 cr.
Elsworth..............	18	28½ v., 24½ c.

[13] *Carts.*, III, 220.

For some manors the period in which the number of fiscal virgates corresponded with the villein holdings seems to have been near 1086, for, when the cotland is taken as one quarter of a virgate,[14] and the villein's holding as one virgate, there were in Stukeley at that time 16 fiscal and 16 occupied virgates, in Knapwell 8 and 8, in Bythorn 12 and 12, and other near approximations such as the eleven villeins and three *bovarii* on 12 fiscal virgates in Brington. For most of the Ramsey manors, however, the number of virgates from a fiscal calculus on the basis of the twelfth-century multiple of hides and virgates exceeds an enumeration of Domesday tenurial units, so for these manors 'fiscal virgatage' division found by the twelfth century was probably established later than 1086. That this division came in most cases before 1135 is arguable from the fact that the actual tenures by that time generally exceeded the number of fiscal virgates; there is also, of course, a suggestion that the virgate assessment remained fixed from this time in the picture from the extents of a rigid demesne and villeinage organization prevailing down through the twelfth century from the time of Henry the Senior. From these considerations the total manorial assessment might be compared with the total tenemental holdings (see Table XIII, above).

The most that can be suggested by this inferential picture from the above Ramsey evidence is that those actual villein holdings in excess of the fiscal virgate quota in the extents of 1135 may represent net additions to the manorial area by assart, drainage of fen, or from waste, since the time these fiscal allocations were made. Such additions are clearly recorded in the extent of Cranfield, and in general, there is a veritable boom in holdings paying only money rent and not designated 'withdrawn from demesne or villeinage' in 1135 that might be set out as a supporting coincidence to the above table. Still it has been already noted that no precision or completeness may be expected from the extent information before 1135, for the investigations are concerned primarily with changes after that date.[15] But, in addition, no Ramsey investigation which pictures solely the tenurial map would show the net accretions to the manors — and this for two reasons: first, the telltale 'assart' designation seems to signify only one category of new land, and secondly, expansion was generally effected by the individual peasant and his family, and was consequently not listed in the descriptions of demesne organization appearing in the extents, but must rather be surmised from the addition of tenements to the manor.

To consider the first point further: the Ramsey manors faced two frontiers — the forest and the fen; and the utilization of Ramsey lands required continual attention lest they were to suffer a rapid retrogression into waste. This problem of land utilization meant, as it means today[16] that the heavy

---

[14] *Carts.*, III, *passim*, and 3 or 4 cotlands to the virgate was a common division found in the later mediaeval account rolls.

[15] Again the Cranfield extent seems to have been written merely by a happy accident before the new assarts were assessed and thereby to lose their assart identity. In this context it may be further noted how the assarts of Graveley acquired in the early twelfth century (*Chronicon*, p. 225), are no longer mentioned in the 1135 extent of that manor.

[16] See D. W. FRYER, *Land Utilization in Britain*, pp. 442-3.

uplands required a 'working out' if they were not to turn cold, and the gravel valley fields needed attention every spring as they were frequently covered by the flooded river for several weeks. How many of the new landholders had simply redeemed these properties that had 'soured' over years of vacancy there is no means of reckoning. As was the case with the fen, the area of the wooded regions[17] on Ramsey properties was very extensive in Domesday. In Hurstingstone hundred there was the biggest concentration: Stukeley — four furlongs by two; Wistow — one league by one-half; Upwood — one-and-one-half leagues by one league; Holywell — one league by four furlongs; Slepe — one league by one-half league; Houghton — one league by one-half league; Warboys — one league by one-half league. These forests would be centred on the upland; by breaking the league and furlong down into acres, and by applying an average elliptical significance to Domesday 'length and width' data, the following map can be constructed to gain some realization of the proportion of the potential arable still covered by woods.[18] This wooded district figures more and more prominently in the agrarian picture from the early twelfth century. Manors and submanors gradually separate off; while all fringe manors show an addition of small holdings from the wood-land.

The unique amount of individual initiative in the early mediæval forest clearing of England has often been recognised.[19] Happily, the extent of Cranfield breaks right in upon a large assart movement by the peasantry. In Cranfield (Beds.) may be seen some 350 acres of assarts held in the second half of the twelfth century by about thirty peasants for money rents, with frequently a hidage due. Pegsdon and Crawley manors in the same county and with the same heavily-wooded terrain in the time of Domesday, also show considerable groups of small holdings under identical tenurial conditions, though if forest clearings, these must have been earlier as there is no assart designation in their twelfth-century extents. The tenurial pattern of Houghton and Wyton in Hunts. belongs to the same species. Beyond Cranfield, however, other notices of assarts for the early twelfth century are more incidental:[20] nine acres in Upwood, two acres of *incrementum* in Wistow,

---

[17] For a study of the Forest Law in this area, *Speculum*, III (1928), E. C. WRIGHT, 'Common Law in the Thirteenth Century English Royal Forest', 166-191, wherein Huntingdonshire is the main example. Also M. L. BAZELEY, 'The Extent of the English Forest in the Thirteenth Century', *Trans. R.H.S.*, XXIII (1941), 140-172.

[18] The considerable forest area of *Hartford* manor (one league by one-half league) is included in this map; but the east side of the hundred, with some forest lands at *Colne, Bluntisham,* and *Somersham* has not been brought into the calculation. In modern units the woodlands were approximately thirty square miles.

[19] E. g., Richard KŒBNER, Cam. Ec. H., I, pp. 77-8; or for scatterings of small assarts in the twelfth century, *Red Book of Wor-*

cester, manors of Bishop's Cleeve (p. 351), and of Wick (p. 58); *Boldon Buke* ed. W. Greenwell, Surtees Society, XXV (1852), *passim.*

The policy of the lord encouraging this initiative has been set out clearly in a letter to the Bishop of Worcester, 1179 (J. D. MANSI, *Conciliorum,* vol. 22, col. 380, Cap. VI. 'Idem Wigorniensi episcopo'): Illas vero terras, quæ de silvis extirpatæ, sunt arabiles factæ, eis hæreditario jure sub annuo censu poteris concedere tenendas, a quibus ipsas suorum vel parentum suorum labore constiterit fuisse extirpatas; nisi forte aliis possint ad majorem ecclesiæ utilitatem cum eodem honore et labore conferri.

[20] Most of the *assarts* mentioned in the extents seem to have gained this designation to

one-half hide of *essartis dominicis* in Cranfield, *unum essartum* in Ellington, sixty acres of assart from the demesne in Shillington, an assart worth five shillings in Pegsdon.[21]

The Pipe Roll evidence begins too late to tell how legal adaptation allowed these early encroachments in land governed by forest law, but probably the king was content to accept the *fait accompli* for a fine.[22] On the other hand much of the manorial evidence for Huntingdonshire, a county which came under the forest law, showed little increase by the small holding accretion paying money rents over the mid-twelfth century.[23] This points again to the lack of direct seigneurial interest in assarting since considerable amounts of the forest areas of Upwood and Warboys manors, at least, must have come within the banlieu, where the royal forest law did not prevail.[24] It was only with the fresh vigour of the late 12th and early 13th centuries, when the indictments of the late 12th century had stimulated reform, that the Huntingdon forest appears to have been attacked in many of these manors. A new note is struck when the abbey is found paying one hundred marks for liberty of woods;[25] and perhaps the abbey's efforts to extend the banlieu at this later date were part of this renewed interest.[26] The *Feet of Fines* also show sixteen acres of assart being rented from the abbey in Little Raveley in 1182; and under John,[27] Ramsey pays two hundred marks and four palfreys for sixty acres of new assarts *in riffleto suo de Hurst*. New lands were likely opened up over the next generations, for there appear frequent bits of evidence as, in the account roll of Ripton (Regis) for 1250 when an assart yielded 144 bushels of wheat, 104 bushels of barley, 340 bushels of mixed grain and 60 bushels of oats.

---

bring out some particular qualification as, *quæ numquam fuerunt ad opus* (Cranfield), *de dominicis* (Shillington & Pegsdon). As a consequence it would seem justifiable to classify the assarts of the twelfth-century extents as those 'exceptions' not yet integrated with the fiscal structure of the manor.

[21] The Ramsey charters would seem to point to the same conclusions that T. A. M. Bishop draws from the Yorkshire part of this central and eastern English plain: "There can be no doubt, for instance, that the terms toft and croft properly refer to terms of enclosure;... These names suggest that much of the land afterwards incorporated in open fields was originally cleared and cultivated by individuals." 'Assarting and the Growth of the Open Fields', *Ec. H. R.* (1935-6), pp. 13-29. The extent of Cranfield, *Carts.*, I, 455-6, mentions 1 cot., 1½ v., and 12 a. taken into demesne in the early 13th century; and the smallholds given in acre units had replaced the tofts and crofts by the mid-13th-century extents of Ramsey, as the most common unit of tenure; or at Barton, for instance, the extent states clearly that there were 46 virgates (11½ hides of four virgates): six virgates were in demesne,

eight free, and the remainder *ad opus* or *ad censum* at the discretion of the abbot and farmer. But beyond this there were eleven cotsettler holdings not yet hidaged !

[22] Cf. D. M. STENTON, *English Society in the Early Middle Ages* (London, 1951), p. 105; and Charles PETIT-DUTAILLIS, *Studies and Notes Supplementary to Stubbs' Constitutional History*, I & II (Manchester, 1915), pp. 154 ff.

[23] *Infra*, Ch. III, Section II.

[24] Ramsey Abbey *Inspeximus*, Add. Ch. 33651 & *Chronicon*.

[25] *Pipe Roll*, I Ric. I. Miss M. L. BAZELEY, *op. cit.*, seems to suggest that the payment of a heavy 'liberty' fine was a quasi-licence for assarting. Certainly the multitude of perambulations and Inquisitions of Hunts. among the 13th-century forest proceedings are too vague to imply that the royal administration had a direct relation with the detail of clearing.

[26] W. O. AULT, *Private Jurisdiction in England*, p. 108, note 106.

[27] *Pipe Roll*, 9 John. Since Ramsey lands were legally afforested from early in the reign of Henry III (*Carts.*, II, p. 300), later assarting cannot be traced through royal licences.

Small assarts were still being opened up at the end of the thirteenth century in Abbots Ripton (1307) and King's Ripton (1300).

While the direct management of manors in the 13th century may have caused the more careful elucidation of many tenements not enumerated in that sometimes abbreviated and static twelfth-century farming structure, yet the net expansion of small holdings held largely for money rent by 1250 should bear an interesting comparison with some more elaborate and complete samples obtainable from the twelfth-century extents. Most comparisons, like those given below in illustration, show that there was a net addition of lands in an order of magnitude sometimes not far inferior to the increase in numbers of tenants seen in the above Table X (Col. 2 and 3).

TABLE XIV

HOLDINGS 'NOT IN VILLEINAGE'

Manor	*ca.* 1160	*ca.* 1250
Warboys	{ 1½ v., 5 cot. { 12½ t., 1 meadow.	} 13 v., 1 a.
Broughton	10½ v.	{ 14 v., 10½ a., 1 rod, { 2 *terræ*, 3 cr., 1 *pytel*.
Holywell	8 v., 3 cr.	{ 18 v., 5 cot., 6 *culturæ*, { 3 manses, 12 cr., 1 *pytel*.[28]
Wistow	6½ v., 7 cr., 1 t.	{ 8 v., 6½ a., 2 furrows, 2 manses, 2 messuages, 1 *pytel*.

According to our surviving records there was even more activity on the fen frontier. In the west fenland manors of Ramsey the increase in landholders since 1086 corresponds to dozens of small plots of usually eight to twelve acres, paying money rents only, and not bound by the foldage or plough dues of the group of holdings which probably formed the earlier manorial compact. A recent study[29] of the Lincoln fens has shown how the peasant in this fen region, before the revolution in drainage by the Bedford Level, was wont by his individual efforts gradually to extend his pasture lands towards the sea by dyke and drainage. The twelfth-century tenurial structure in Hilgay and Snorehill, Brancaster (*cum* Depedale *et* Holme), Ringstead, Holme, and Welles points to an identical strategy against the sea.

---

[28] An entire new area was opened up as Holywell 'Fen' sometime in the 13th century, which may have been partly given over to smallholdings as well as to pasture for demesne stock.

[29] Joan THIRSK, *Fenland Farming in the Sixteenth Century*, University College of Leicester, Occasional Paper 3 (1953), p. 21.

The fortunate survival of a charter giving the new rents[30] for Welles manor makes it possible to gain more complete information upon this method of property expansion than may be acquired from the extents. This charter appears to be entirely devoted to new lands in the manor,[31] and these fell into two groups, the small 'close' for which no acreage data were given and the rent was nearly always according to 'sticks' of eels (a stick being worth a penny farthing), and the measured allotments within the 'first Fendike', that is, the oldest drained land. The latter holdings were paying twopence per acre, nearly twice as much as the rents from other measured lands mentioned in the charter, and totalled eighty-one acres, one-and-one-half rods. It is probable, then, that the numerous 'closes', which were frequently paying a rent *de novo*, are the more recent and less valuable individual encroachments upon the fen. One of the last clauses in the charter offers a confirmation of this by giving further information upon the lower rents of 'new lands': *Et sciendum, quod cum prædicti homines alias purpresturas fecerint, solvent de singulis acris annuatim unum denarium.*

Something of the cumulative effect of these new holdings may be seen in a comparison taken from the two series of extents. In the twelfth century Ringstead had in villeinage 555½ acres,[32] three crofts, one fold, three rods; by the thirteenth century this had become 698 acres, one rod, two *pytels* and one messuage. Holme demesne and villeinage was extended from approximately 458½ acres,[33] one rod and two crofts to 605½ acres, one-half virgate, two *pytels*, and two bits of marsh. The group of estates including Brancaster, Depedale, and Holme comprised one free *terra*, 1,215 acres, four *terræ*, three marshes, seven crofts, five folds, one rod, one manse, one field, in the twelfth century; whereas there were in the thirteenth century five free hides, a marsh, pasture and 2 crofts, and in villeinage 1,232 acres, 2 *pytels*, 2 marshes, and three crofts. There is nothing in the extents to disclose how this latter estate was extended largely by freeholders, whereas Ringstead and Holme had a more active growth in villein tenements.

In the tempo of their advance, as well as the predilection for money rents, the twelfth-century peasants spilling over into new lands form a unified complex with those other tenurial proliferations already seen above (Chapter II) for the early part of the century. Another side of the same activity was

---

[30] *Carts.*, II, 318-320, 'Rotulus de redditibus novis assisæ apud Welles'. I take this to be an extension into Cambridgeshire, towards modern Welney, rather than a portion of the Ramsey Manor at Outwell (Norfolk). The earliest references in Ramsey documents speak only of fisheries at Welles, but by the tax roll of the early fourteenth century (*Rawlinson Ms.* 333, fol. 64) Welles' (Welney) has so developed that it is assessed as a manor separate from Outwell.

[31] The complete manorial extent of the old properties at Outwell is given in *Carts.*, III, 296 ff.

[32] The two carucates included in this figure were estimated to be 100 acres each, i.e. the measure of demesne carucates for Ringstead.

[33] This twelfth-century figure may be slightly large as sixteen small holdings are interpolated from rent comparisons, etc., to be a perhaps generous ten acres each. The 12th-century extents for the fen manors are so dominated by references to lands rented from the demesne and villeinage that it is impossible to separate the total new lands. See MILLER, *The Abbey and Bishopric of Ely*, pp. 95 ff. and pp. 119-120, for other references to new lands in this area.

the encroachment on demesne and the decline in villeinage that will be seen in the next section to have characterized later generations of this century. It may be a tribute to the frequency of additions to arable or pasture, though a stumbling block to the investigator, that the 'assart' designation rapidly disappeared from currency. The opportunities for encroachment upon demesne and villeinage from the time of the civil war until the late twelfth century probably offered an easier alternative than the assarting or drainage of new lands, but again, the detailed concentration of the extents upon this period and with this problem, practically obliterates their contribution to the picture of net agricultural expansion.

II

An investigation of the manner in which these primary economic developments were translated into movements of manorial rents, must turn around the study of the farming system. This system, like the feudal 'system' of the time, followed no rigid pattern, but was rather the functional principle by which were rented revenue-bearing properties not under the immediate management of the lord's officials. In origin the farm was probably a natural instrument for a fairly stable economy and many uses of the farm from the eleventh century preserved a connotation of rigidity. The *feorm* of the Anglo-Saxon king from his various estates had been the backbone of royal sustenance, and the same term, or at least the same institution, transcribed into Latin as *firma*, became applied to the food and money rents allocated for monastic sustenance. From this consumption allocation the expression 'farm' necessarily took on more permanent or fixed time-unit aspects, as in the *firma unius noctis* for the royal household. Many early monastic farms were 'day' or 'night' farms too, perhaps as a repetition of the royal formula, although these units might have all been paid on one day to avoid transportation difficulties. The convent could not travel about from manor to manor eating up the *feorms* like the king, so it is not surprising to find very early a pattern of food rents laid out according to monastic needs. In the large Benedictine monasteries the expression persevered down through the Middle Ages — for Ramsey as the *firma unius ebdomadæ, duarum ebdomadarum*, and *lentefirma*. We have seen how these conventual farms remained for generations or even centuries without change, so much so, indeed, that they became the basis for conventual titles to land as well as revenues.[34]

The extensive references to royal farms in Domesday Book still reveal how useful the more primitive food farming system had been found for royal administration as late as *in tempore Regis Edwardi*. But this document also shows how the farm as a 'firm' or 'fixed' disposition of revenues was being applied in many ways as a principle of royal administration. The king's

---

[34] *Supra*, Ch. II, Section I. For some useful remarks on the farm as a fixed return, see M. M. Postan, 'The Rise of a Money Economy', *Ec. H. R.*, XIV (1944-45), 132-4.

sheriff, for example, was said to 'hold in farm' the various judicial fees and regal fines as well as profits from the royal demesne. This meant that the sheriff contracted for a fixed sum — the farm — to collect these revenues; his own reward would consist in that amount by which the actual collection exceeded the farm. The abbot of Ramsey, largely by virtue of his ancient privileges and liberties, partook also of the right to collect some of the royal revenues: he paid four marks farm to the royal sheriff for revenues of the Hundred Court of Hurstingstone,[35] he paid eight pounds farm for the manor of King's Ripton,[36] and five pounds for collecting licences and fines at the fair of St. Ives.

This shifting of the responsibilities of economic management to another by the farming system fitted in well with the career of a feudal lord who was by profession a warrior and held estates primarily to support his obligations of knighthood. But it was by the same token within the logic of monastic administration that this farming of manors should become a policy from the early days of monastic existence. To look after the obedientiary tasks of internal administration was feasible for a monk; but the time-consuming and on-the-spot employment requisite for demesne exploitation could be ill-adjusted to a day largely spent in spiritual exercises. A monastic community could not burthen the various manors with its presence from week to week, so, for consumption security, there resulted the regular commitments of fixed food rents. In addition, the demesne was a 'planned economy' organized meticulously upon the pre-determined components of villein service, plough teams and arable, livestock and pasture. It was possible, therefore, to arrange a contract governing the maintenance of the productive organization of the demesne and making a 'farm price' from the estimated annual value of the arable and pastoral produce together with various customary rents. Besides the possibility of its adjustment in relation to increases in prices and productivity, such a contract would give a stable floor to annual revenues against the omnipresent uncertainties of animal plague and crop failure.

Some evidence of these farm contracts has come down from Anglo-Saxon days,[37] and it has been observed that on Benedictine estates generally the farm system was "... ubiquitous throughout the eleventh and twelfth centuries; ..."[38] As the *firmarius* is mentioned in practically every extent, the twelfth-century disposition of the Ramsey estates also appears to have centred upon this method. From these extents it can be seen that the *firmarius* was a person distinct from the demesne overseer — the reeve — as both obtained mention in the same extent. Where the personal name is given he was a wealthy laylord or knight — Simon the Chamberlain in Hemmingford Grey, Adam the son of Henry the Archdeacon in Stukeley.[39] Probably the

---

[35] *Chronicon*, p. 226.
[36] *Ibid.*, p. 323.
[37] For Ramsey manors, see *supra*, Ch. I, Section II; for examples of extant Anglo-Saxon charters of farm agreements, see ROBERTSON, *Anglo-Saxon Charters*, p. 155.

[38] KNOWLES, *The Monastic Order in England*, p. 442.
[39] Robert of Girton held that manor at farm in the time of Abbot Reginald (*Chronicon*, pp. 250-251); while Wido, who had seized many Ramsey manors in the fen district, held Burwell at farm (*Chronicon*, p. 261).

Philip who had 'received' the demesne stock of Knapwell and Elworth was the important freeman of the district, Philip of Clervaux. The farmer is tied in with the manorial organization since he worked the demesne for his own profit: the villeins must come for the boon works of the farmer,[40] and are to perform other works at his command;[41] they are fed by the farmer when working for him;[42] they transport his produce,[43] especially when the farmer is delivering his food rents to the abbey;[44] their cash rents, like the fishsilver at Upwood or the aids at other manors, are delivered personally to him;[45] the farmer had special rights to produce from the mill for his sustenance.[46]

Such evidence, in showing how the farmer could come between the intimate interrelationships of the lord and his villeins, will be important for an understanding of the breakdown of the manorial economy in the twelfth century. So long as it was the farmer who was immediately concerned with the detailed deposition of the extents and farm payments, the manorial economy might change and develop for decades or even generations in relative independence of the lord. The extents also reveal, of course, some of the farmer's obligations to the lord of the manor, particularly in the maintenance of demesne stock. The replacement capital value of demesne stock was given in the extents (*supra*, Table VII); and this stock was specifically included in the payments to be made by the farmer: *Et cum isto instauramento reddebant tunc istæ duæ villæ quindecim libras;*[47] *Et reddebat, cum hoc instauramento . . .*[48]

It would appear that a pledge against undue exploitation or dilapidation of the soil was covered in the terms of another document, a written contract between the farmer and the lord of the manor. Many of these contracts exist for the twelfth century, most noteworthy perhaps being the records of St. Pauls.[49] No charters of these farm agreements have been found extant for Ramsey before the thirteenth century,[50] but in the transcript from such an agreement for a Bury St. Edmund's manor, these remarks follow upon the enumeration of ploughs and livestock: ". . . and the land of the demesne (will be) well sown with wheat, rye, and oats, that is, each grain in its own field at its proper time. And the land that ought to be at fallow, will be well fallowed and cultivated."[51] This general commitment would seem to take for granted an accepted cycle of cultivation. In any case, the given number of ploughs and the detailed itemization as well as allocation of villein services must have to all intents and purposes almost predetermined the range of the agrarian programme available to the *firmarius* — if he fulfilled the contract. The farm contracts issued by the Canons of St. Paul, as with the above-noted

[40] *Carts.*, III, 259, 262, 268, 300, 301, 308, 312.
[41] *Ibid.*, 274, 278, 289, 300, 309, 310, 311, 313.
[42] *Ibid.*, 269, 285, 289.
[43] *Ibid.*, 269, 274, 282, 310.
[44] *Ibid.*, 301, 306.
[45] *Ibid.*, 271, 282, 309, 311.
[46] *Ibid.*, 258, 310.
[47] *Ibid.*, p. 266, for the manors of Ringstead and Holme.
[48] *Ibid.*, for Elton and Stukeley.

[49] *The Domesday of St. Paul's*, ed. William Hale, Camden Society (1858), pp. 122 ff.
[50] *Carts.*, II, p. 244.
[51] *Registrum de Bury* (Cambridge University library), fol. 145, dorse. I am indebted to Professor Postan for drawing this charter to my attention. See also *Boldon Buke*, p. 19: Walter de Halctone tenet ad firmam, dominium cum instauramento iv carucarum et iv herciarum et, cum acris seminatis, *sicut in cyrografo continetur, . . .*

thirteenth-century agreement by Ramsey, were also concerned to enumerate in detail the stock of corn for which the farmer was responsible. The Ramsey document clearly shows, too, that at least in the thirteenth century, the lord was careful to retain his feudal and seigneurial incidents and jurisdiction.[52]

The combined information of the most detailed extents and farm contracts still leaves something wanting for the determination of the annual rent to be paid by the farmer. A third instrument, the *valor*, would seem to have been used to assess this value of the farm. The most detailed extant *valor* for a Ramsey manor is probably that of Whiston *ca.* 1270, itemizing and summarizing the total annual revenues from the manor.[53] The distinctive nature of this document stands out clearly against those other documents such as that of Barnwell evaluating the market price of the demesne stock which were to be purchased with the manor,[54] or the two series of Ramsey extents for the twelfth and thirteenth centuries which were not concerned at all with evaluating profits of the demesne. The fact that many elements in the *valor* changed with market prices would destroy their utility as more permanent records, and to this we may probably ascribe the remarkably few extant documents of this nature among charter collections. By the same token, where valuations had been inscribed along with the detailed inquisitions of manors, as in the well-known case for the manors of the bishop of Worcester, this information has been permitted to survive.[55]

By good fortune a Ramsey fragment has been discovered in that often surprising collection of *Rentals and Surveys* which appears to be a list of twelfth or early thirteenth-century *valors* for the abbot's manors.[56] These *valors* show clearly the remarkable calculus that would make possible the

---

[52] *Carts.*, II, p. 244: Habebunt (i.e. the farmers) etiam omnes proventus ipsius villæ, præter talliagia nostra, et præter auxilium vicecomitis, hundredi, et præter wardpenys et scutagium domini Regis, et præter exitum causarum illarum, . . .

[53] *Carts.*, I, 54-7.

[54] *Ibid.*, pp. 53-4.

[55] The term *valor* has been employed above because it expresses more precisely the nature of this document, and came into general use, at least at a later period. The *valor* would be used closely in conjunction with the extent, and indeed depended directly on the extent for valuation of *redditus*, *opera*, etc., so that it could be considered as a *Summa* of the extent. See *Summaria Extentæ*, for Tregof, Gloucester, in *Historia et Cartularium Monasterii Gloucestriæ*, ed. W. H. Hart, R. S., 3 vols. (1863-67), III, p. 271. While the *Red Book of Worcester* does have subdivisions entitled *Summa Valoris*, the general title is still *extenta*. The above-mentioned charter of Whiston manor was still called an *extenta*, as were similar valuations for the manors of Littleton and Linkholt of St. Peter's Gloucester at this time (*op. cit.*, III, 35 ff.).

[56] The only copy of this roll I have been able to find (SC 12:18/26) is written in a late fourteenth-century hand, but from internal evidence it would appear to be the transcription of a *valor* belonging to a much earlier period. The total value for each manor given in this document corresponds roughly with farm values for these manors in the late twelfth century. They are much less than fourteenth-century *valors* available from the account rolls (*infra*, Ch. IX, Appendix V), or much less than late thirteenth-century taxation assessments (*infra*, Table LV). Furthermore, the value of villein livery in this document corresponds more to late twelfth than to fourteenth-century prices (see especially the 1 s. per quarter for oats, and 3s. 4d. per quarter for wheat). Finally, from after the Black Death, Shillington, Cranfield, and Barton paid farms to the cellarer; Girton and Lawshall came into the chamberlain's hands sometime before the mid-thirteenth century. But these five manors are treated as held by the abbot in this *valor*. For these reasons we are inclined to date SC 12: 18/26 as of the late twelfth or early thirteenth century.

assessment of the farm value, an assessment pervading completely and rigidly the value of land as well as livestock, *opera* as well as customary rents, courts and land fines as well as dovecotes, mills, woods, and pasture. The *valor* of Barton is here presented in full in illustration:

> The abbot of Ramsey has one manor in the vill of Barton to which pertains two carucates of land; [57] each valued at XLs. per annum.　Total, £IIII.
> The same has from *redditus assisus* and tallage £XII. 18d. ob.
> The same has work of bondmen and cotters which is worth annually LXVs. VId.
> The same has in *redditus* from bondmen annually I q. VII b. wheat worth Vs.
> The same has in *redditus* from bondmen annually I q. of oats worth XIId.
> The same has a dovecote worth annually XIId.
> The same has in *redditus* from bondmen III ploughshares worth IIs. VId.
> The same has from *subbosco*, grass and pasture in value of IIIIs.
> The same has from the court, reliefs, fines, *gersumæ*, and other casuals each year Vs. VId.
> The abbot has VIII cows, the *exitus* of each being worth VI d. Total, IIIIs.
> The abbot has XVIII ewes, the *exitus* of each being worth IIIId. Total, VIs.
> The same has II watermills worth XXXs.
> The abbot has III sows, the *exitus* of each being worth IIIId. Total, XIId.
> The abbot has from the fruits of the orchards and vines annually, IIs. VId.
> The same has from ten hens @ 1d., 10d.
> Total — £22. 10s. 1d. ob.

The actual rent paid by the farmer for the whole manor would seem usually to have been one round sum, though it might also be indicated in terms of its various constituent elements such as food rents, *censa*, or *redditus*.　In some cases the conventual farm itself was adjusted to embody all manorial returns, as may be noted in that charter of Bury St. Edmunds cited above where the manor of Groton paid annually one farm to the cellarer, while in contrast, its sister manor in the same contract paid a twelve pound rent to the pittancer. Where the food rents were commutable, as at Ramsey, we find it clearly stated that the Bythorn, Brington, and Weston manorial group paid twenty-one pounds or one (conventual) farm.　Whatever may have been the precise criteria used in calculating the Domesday *valet*, the entire value of the manor was probably included, for a striking similarity is found between the food rent values of Abbot Aldwin's charter (*ca.* 1100) and the Domesday *valet*: the full

---

[57] On some monastic estates in the twelfth century the demesne lands were evaluated according to corn sown, e.g. *Boldon Buke*, p. 4: Dominium est ad firmam, cum instauramento IV carucarum de frumento et XVI celdras de avena, et VIII de ordeo, et pro II di (halves) carucis X marcis. There does not seem to have been any basic change in the system of valuation by the late thirteenth century. See *Red Book of Worcester*, 'Summa Valoris totius terre' and 'Ad Proficuum Gannagii',

passim. And see the *Chronicle of Jocelin of Brakelond*, ed. H. E. Butler (Nelson Series, 1949), p. 63: ". . . both of our manors and of his, and their reasonable *value*, at the rate at which they might be put to farm in a season when corn is sold at a moderate (*mediocriter*, perhaps better translated as *average*) price."
The discussion in this and the preceding paragraph may be followed more easily with the aid of Table V, *supra*.

farm was worth seventeen pounds, and most of the manors so allocated — Elton, Burwell, Elsworth, Slepe, Houghton and Wyton — vary only slightly from their Domesday valuations. Only the two manors of Warboys and Therfield, both seriously undercapitalized in Domesday, have increased by five and six pounds respectively, to meet their food rent specifications. Of the ten manors that were classified as 'one-half' farms worth eight pounds six shillings each, only Knapwell and Graveley vary as much as two pounds ten shillings from their 1086 values, five of the manors registering a variation of less than fifteen shillings. For Broughton, Upwood, Hemmingford, Ellington, Cranfield, the farm rent is less than in the 1086 *valet*. In short the range of adjustment to meet these food rents is thus much the same as the degree of variations between *in tempore Regis Edwardi* and 1086.

It is probable, then, that the cellarer's farm livery at the time of the conventual farm arrangement by Aldwin was approximately equal in value to the 'farm price' paid by the *firmarius* for the whole manor. Aldwin's statute of monastic farms shows this was indeed the case, especially in the clumsy adjustments necessary for the construction of a neat farm price from the gross consumption quotas: although each manor is assigned a specific fortnight or week throughout the year for the disposal of its food livery, the total seasonal gifts of fowl and produce[58] have to be delivered outside the regular farm at Christmas, Easter, and at the feast of St. Benedict, and without tally. In addition, the *firmarius* must make up the round[59] seventeen pounds by a payment of four shillings eleven pence, and the half farm of eight pounds six shillings by a payment of twenty-nine pence and one-half penny. The regimentation of eighteen manors into two equal conventual farm rent categories was for the sake of accounting convenience only.

While changes in the commutable value of food rents meant that even the conventual farm could move with changes in prices, a contrast of the food farm values of columns IV and VIII with other rent values in the above table of twelfth-century rents (Table V), shows that many other elements of variation were affecting the total farm price in the twelfth century. In order to understand how the farming system, which had so many traditionally rigid constituents and involved the lack of direct control over profits of agrarian production, could permit adjustments to an expanding economy, it is essential to realize first that farming by a monastic community like Ramsey was not usually an alienation or a perpetual lease. The wide employment of the term 'farm' makes a careful reading of the charters essential in this respect. The 'fee farm' payment, like the four pounds to be given by Hervey Le Moigne for Stukeley, was hereditary; the monetary complement of the

[58] *Carts.*, III, 232-3. The failure to include these items in the farm was probably due more to their seigneurial, rather than their economic, import. Nevertheless, for a full farm they would have been worth nearly ten shillings.

[59] These 'round' sums appear to be a useful identification of a farm price. See too, the farmed manors in Ramsey vacancy rolls 1201 ff. in contrast with the revenues from the manors directly exploited whose revenues are reported in the same rolls; or see the *Redditus Annui* values above, Table V, Col. VI; or note the farms of Peterborough manors in the *Liber Niger* of that abbey, *op. cit.*, pp. 166-7.

military fee, like the hundred shillings paid by Reginald Le Moigne with the one knight for Barnwell, would naturally acquire the perpetuity of the military tenure; and many components of the total manorial rent, like the customary payments (*redditus*) of the villeins or freemen, or in time the conventual farm at Ramsey, tended to become fixed.   But the farm of manors as such failed to become identified with the hereditary, or even with the life lease.   In the time of the increasing manorial returns of the late eleventh and early twelfth centuries, the farming of manors was in fact contrasted to and favoured over the perpetual lease in Ramsey documents.   It has been already seen in this period how the 'farm' was used as a title against hereditary seisin for regaining Stowe, and the abbey properties generally after the conquest.

Most of our evidence for this aspect of the farm contract is indirect. When, in the twelfth-century records, tenures were converted into hereditary leases, the perpetual terms were specifically laid out.   But the typical twelfth-century farm agreement, the non-perpetual leasing of whole manors, did not seem to have been judged as a matter of great significance in the collections of cartularies, except perhaps where manors were farmed for life.[60]   Something of the nature of the manorial farming still peers through the hereditary lease however.   Under Abbot Reginald the hereditary lease of one hide at Burwell was made to Wido for a rent that was to be paid into the farm of Burwell as long as the abbot and convent so wish, and with the understanding that Wido, who apparently now farms the manor may or may not have the manor at farm in the future.[61]   Even clearer is the example from Girton around the same time: Robert of Girton and his wife were given hereditary title to a virgate of land in that vill for five shillings annual rent, with the proviso that Robert who now holds the vill at farm shall not change the rent while he holds that vill, nor shall his successor to the virgate have to give more than five shillings to the farm of Girton.[62]

These vague references to the farm of the vill suggest that there was something basically informal and revocable about the typical farm lease. The revocable nature of leases for large farmed manors in the twelfth century may be explained, in all probability, by the traditional sustenance function of these properties.   The pantry of the monks depended upon the complete and regular reception of manorial food and money rents.   Hence it is not

---

[60] See the above-mentioned leases by the Canons of St. Paul, or the leases to the *ministeriales* of Bury (*Feudal Documents of of Bury St. Edmunds, passim*).

[61] *Chronicon*, p. 261: Notum esse volumus quod ego Reinaldus abbas totusque Ramesiensis conventus in capitulo nostro Ramesensi concessimus Widoni tam sibi quam hæredibus suis unam hidam terræ apud Burewellam, quamdiu abbas Ramesiensisque conventus voluerit, ad talem firmam qualem modo habet eam; et in ipsa firma per singulos annos pro supra dicta hida terræ reddat sibi tenenti firmam vel cuilibet tenenti eam firmam viginti solidos, . . .

[62] *Ibid.*, pp. 250-251: . . . concesserunt in suo Ramesensi capitulo Roberto de Grettona suæque uxori Beatrici in hæreditatem quandam virgatam terræ quam tunc temporis Emma habebat in villa de Grettona pro quinque solidis per singulos annos.   Ita tamen quod idem Robertus, qui tunc temporis prædictam villam habebat ad firmam, quamdiu eam tenebit non dabit inde plus sive minus quam ipse dabat prius; at ubi ipse eam sive vivens sive moriens dimiserit, qui supradictam terræ virgatam habebit pro ea quinque solidos dabit in firma de Grettona per singulos annos. And for an example from non-Ramsey charters, see B. A. LEES, *Records of the Templars* (Oxford, 1935), pp. 208-9.

surprising to find that the regular payment of the farm is a fundamental condition of the contract.[63] *A fortiori*, the farm lease of a manor would be revocable *ad voluntatem domini* if the stock were dissipated, or the fields neglected in the manor. In short, the lord was in a position to re-issue or readjust the farming contract with allowances for increases in manorial returns, perhaps by restocking the demesne for higher production, or by changing the evaluation of commutable food rents.[64]

The charters of Ramsey do not show evidence of frequent adjustments in these major points, but the flexibility of the farm system would be of regular importance for another factor, the addition of new smallholds at money rent. Already in Anglo-Saxon times we have been able to remark numerous accretions to the farm payment, usually under some such phrase as *firma et censa*. Round has noted an exceptionally clear example of this combination of money rents with the farm in the Domesday materials.[65] In the Ramsey estates of Houghton, Wyton, Elton, Cranfield, and especially the fen manors of Hilgay, Wimbotsham, Brancaster, and Ringstead and their attachments, a phenomenal

[63] See the leases of St. Paul in *The Domesday of St. Paul's*, p. 125 (Runewella): ... quod concedunt ei ... quam diu vixerit et bene firmam reddiderit, ...; or p. 128 (Keneswurda): ... quam diu vixerit et bene eis constitutis terminis firmam reddiderit; ...; or p. 135 (Ardele): ... quam diu eis inde bene servierit et firmam bene reddiderit; ..., as also Belchamp, p. 138. The early thirteenth-century reforms in monastic administration at Ramsey show this concern for regular liveries (*Carts.*, II, p. 205): A firmariis etiam sufficiens cautio recipiatur, quod firmam terminis statutis persolvent, et quod homines monasterii sibi subjectos injuste non gravabunt, et quod in nemoribus et aliis dominicis non facient vastum, nec sustinebunt fieri de redditibus spectantibus ad Camerarium et Elemosinarium. Provisum est, ut ipsi Camerarius et Elemosinarius recipiant suos redditus per manus firmariorum terminis statutis, sicut fieri solebat tempore Roberti Abbatis.

[64] When fluctuations in agricultural production are considered, this would seem to give the lessor very broad powers. I have indeed been unable to find any legal disputes controverting the termination of a farm contract, in a century in which the lawsuits over hereditary leases were frequent; to take the example from a reforming lord like Abbot Samson of Bury St. Edmunds: "When Michælmas came round, he took all his manors into his own hand, but with very few implements or stock" (*Chronicle of Jocelin de Brakelond*, p. 32); for evidence that all of these manors were at farm, *ibid.*, p. 1: Dabuntur ville abbatis et omnes hundredi ad firmam; ... The 'increases' of food rents by Abbot Baldwin of Bury in the late eleventh century, (ROBERTSON, *Anglo-Saxon Charters*, p. 440), seem to have all come at the same

time without a regard for termination of previous farming contracts; and the various 'confirmations' of Abbot Aldwin's Ramsey food rent arrangement (*Carts.*, III, p. 163) seem to bear no relation to an irrevocable *ad vitam* contract. It is interesting to note also that in the 13th-century organization of the treasury for the abbots and monks of St. Peter's, Gloucester, only the charters of those leases *ad terminum vitæ concessarum* were considered worthy of special concern (*Historia et Cartularium Monasterii Gloucestriæ*, III, p. 106). For a corresponding picture pointing out flexible farming of royal estates in the eleventh century in contrast to the thirteenth, see HOYT, *op. cit.*, p. 18; and J. G. TURNER, 'The Sheriff's Farm', *Trans. R. H. S.*, (1898), pp. 122 ff., where he has noted the variations that can be seen in the *Pipe Roll* evidence, esp. 2-8 H. II. Some short-term farm leases are also found in the Anglo-Saxon charters, e.g. ROBERTSON, *op. cit.*, p. 155: Lutton is farmed for three years; or for the twelfth century, *Feudal Documents of Bury St. Edmunds*, p. 135, no.145: the farming of a manor in 1160 for 12 years.

[65] *Domesday Studies*, ed. E. Dove, (London, 1888), I, p. 135: "In the case of Edesham, which is given as a specimen, the Exchequer Domesday merely states that the manor renders (*redit*) £46.16s.4d. (for the 26s.4d. of the Report is an error), whereas the Kentish Domesday gives us the two constituents of this total, stating that it is worth (*valet*) £30 *de firma* and *de gablo reddit* £16.16s.4d." For references to *censum et firmam* rent combinations from Ramsey lands in Anglo-Saxon times, see above, Ch. I, note 66, and text; Ch. 2, note 11.

increase in manorial rents by the mid-twelfth century corresponds with that proliferation of small holdings in wood, waste, and fen.   The extents suggest that such increases in *censa* from small rentals were just added to the conventual farm in those manors from which the latter was due:[66] for Houghton and Wyton combined the *summa censa* was ten pounds ten shillings and eleven pence in the inquisitors' calculus and the properties were farmed for ten pounds plus (conventual) farm; in Elton, the *summa censa præter ad opus* was six pounds with one hundred shillings for the mill and the manor was farmed for ten pounds plus (conventual) farm.   In conjunction with rents from small holdings, the increase in productivity from such additions as that of the plough teams (*supra*, Table IX, Col. 3) also helps to explain the reason for some rise in the *Redditus Annui* of all manors except Ellington and Warboys, as well as illustrating that a real adjustment had been made in capital value preliminary to movements in farm prices.   In addition, the monetary equivalence of the Bythorn, Weston, and Brington conventual farm in the extent was twenty-one pounds, rather than the 'full farm' value of seventeen pounds in the time of Aldwin's charter.   Such being the case, the various confirmations since the time of Abbot Aldwin might well have allowed for increases in produce prices of the livery as the small holding money rents were negligible for these three manors.   On the other hand, many of the manors sending the conventual food farm had increased little in value by the time of the *Redditus Annui*, so the four pounds increase for the farm of the Weston group was more likely due to the usual four pound tallage of the abbot.

Since the farming system allowed the maintenance of this control over increases in agricultural revenues it is easier to realize why Abbot Reginald would have favoured the farm system — as the extent organization demonstrates — over the hereditary lease.   The *Redditus Annui* of *ca.* 1140 (*supra* Table V, Col. V) serves, therefore, as a record for the appreciation of that vigorous reaction by Abbot Reginald to the losses of the late eleventh century. The increases in returns from Ramsey manors by 1140 were, in many cases, as much as one hundred per cent over the Domesday valuations.[67]   Occasionally this has been due of course to a large property acquisition.   The twelfth-century hidage shows that Ramsey now held the five hides of Broughton claimed by sokemen in Domesday — hence probably the increase from ten to eighteen pounds in the value of this manor.   Crawley and Bradenach were extensive submanors added to Cranfield and Therfield respectively in the early twelfth century (*supra*, Ch. II, Sect. I), so they would account for the proportionate rise in returns from these manors by 1140.   From the *Redditus Annui* also comes the picture of a considerable grouping of manors: Holywell with Slepe, Houghton and Wyton, Pegsdon with Shillington, Cranfield with Crawley, Therfield with Bradenach, Hilgay with Snorehill, Ringstead with Holme, Wimbotsham with Dunham, Brancaster with Burnham.   Some of

---

[66] The *incrementa* additions to the farms of royal manors have been noted by TURNER, *op. cit.*, pp. 122 ff.

[67] This increase was not singular to Ramsey manors, of course.   The changes in the values of the Northants. manors of Peterborough Abbey, T.R.E. to 1086, and 1086 to 1122, are equally great.

these combinations were perhaps based on the collection of the conventual farm — Holywell always went in with Slepe, for example. But it would be an administrative convenience, too, for the wealthy farmer to hold several manors from one district in his hands. These combinations were rendering round sums as *redditus* figures, and are quite obviously farmed manors. Abbot Reginald's acquisitions and consolidations apparently preceded a new farming and in every case these deliberate groupings are associated with the greatest rent increases. From this evidence it appears that so long as royal officials or powerful magnates did not keep the lands in their hands, the early twelfth-century farming system had sufficient flexibility to tap the increases in prices and productivity; and, moreover, re-organized farming of manors symbolized the most successful mode of increasing manorial returns in the early twelfth century. But this state of affluence in manorial revenues was not to remain for long.

III

Despite its great utility in the earlier monastic period, the farming system became ill-adapted to the development of the twelfth-century manorial economy. A number of points must be particularly noted for the understanding of this administrative crisis. Without a well-developed accounting system and a regular itinerary by the steward, the lord must have been largely dependent upon simple trust in the farmer's promises and the efficiency of the reeve in the maintenance of the demesne capital, the villeinage structure, and the works and services of the manor. Such problems of control would also tend to confirm the fixed farm payment, and the lease for a number of years, or for a lifetime, as the basic framework of the system. In addition, prior to the full scale machinery of the highly-developed agrarian exploitation of the thirteenth century, the initiative in management of estates belonging to the non-cathedral monasteries seems to have lain with the abbots. This was peculiarly unfortunate as abbots became occupied more and more with national affairs and separated from the life of the community. But the abbot was especially inept as an agrarian administrator when he became increasingly burdened with a heavy backlog of debts. The bankrupt exchequer would not be liable to expand manorial profits from the demesne by the investment in capital for the enlargement of arable or pasture, or for the increase in the numbers of teams and livestock. This was a very costly procedure,[68] and of a long run nature, as it implied the willingness to wait a number of years in order to recoup profits from the investment. The alternative would be to allow the stock to decrease or remain stable and to meet the needs of ready money by renting more service-bearing land in villeinage or even some of the demesne. Both the abbot and the farmers could thus co-operate in the

---

[68] E.g., J. G. TURNER, *op. cit.*, p. 133, where £13.12s.4d. was spent in one year on improvements in the manor of Bosham (Sussex); also *Red Book of the Exchequer*, or the 1222 extents in *The Domesday of St. Paul's.*

disintegration, or at least retardation, of the demesne economy; and such
was the story on Ramsey estates in the latter half of the twelfth century.
The actual extent regulations opened the way to this renting by permitting
virgates to be put *ad censum* at the discretion of the *firmarius* and abbot,[69] or
even by allowing other properties, like pasture,[70] to be rented at the discretion
of the *firmarius* alone.   No doubt such renting gave a useful flexibility to
the very real annual variation in work necessary on the demesne.   But from
some time in the reign of Abbot Walter (1133-1161) the alienation of portions
of the villeinage as well as of the demesne spread and became permanent.

The beginning of this decadence in manorial policy must likely be sought
in the Civil War.   Geoffrey de Mandeville made Ramsey Abbey the head-
quarters for his depredations [71] and either in meeting his exactions or in the
considerable rebuilding after the war,[72] Abbot Walter resorted to a wholesale
alienation of every saleable item even to the extent of stripping gold ornamen-
tation from the altars and missals and disposing of sacred vestments, vessels,
and statuary.[73]   Accordingly there would have been little question of being
able to maintain the demesne economic structure, and Abbot Walter became
notorious in Ramsey annals, perhaps unjustly, as an expropriator of abbey
property.   Abbot Walter's alienations of land have been neatly summarized
in the Cartularies, and are transcribed here in Table XV.   Walter's successor
Abbot William (1161-79) probably was responsible for a greater disintegration.
One charter [74] preserves his alienations to relatives: a land in King's Ripton
to his nephew, a carrucate in Cranfield to his brother the seneschal, demesne
lands in Therfield to his niece, and a knight's fee at Walton to his brother.
The two other alienations mentioned in this record were of a different nature:
William sold a virgate at Brancaster to Herbert the reeve for forty marks,
and the monks of Sawtrey were permitted to make a ditch through Ramsey
lands from their abbey to Whittlesey Mere.   The long list of manors under
the title *Occupationes terrarum per villas nostras, secundum juramentum rus-
ticorum* would seem to be an effort at complete listing of the unsatisfactory
land transfers, or 'encroachments' of the traditional manor, during the abbacy
of William.[75]

---

[69] *Carts.*, III, p. 274.
[70] *Ibid.*, p. 277.
[71] J. H. ROUND, *Geoffrey de Mandeville* (London, 1892), Ch. IX, is probably still the
best account in English of this nadir point
in the anarchy from which Ramsey suffered
so much.
[72] *Chronicon*, pp. 333-4: Ea quidem die qua
dominus Galterius post mortem comitis G.
de Magna Villa abbatiam Ramesensem
recuperavit, ejecta prophana tenebrarum
militia, tantum supellectilis ibi non invenit
in qua possent vel unius prandii caules
coquinari. In omnibus teris dominicis
totius abbatiæ unam tantum carucam
reperit et dimidiam, reperit victualium
nihil; debitum urgebat; terræ jacebant
incultæ; multas autem quas raptores
occupaverant adhuc deserere nolebant . . .
Unde factum est quod oportuit præfatum
abbatem XXIII castellas vel amplius
singulis mensibus pro rusticis suis redemp-
tiones seu tenserias præstare, qui tam per
Danielem quam per ipsos malefactores
multum exhausti fuerant et extenuati.
[73] *Carts.*, II, 273-4.
[74] *Carts.*, III, 223-4.
[75] *Ibid.*, pp. 224-9.   The Rolls Series editor
of this volume has been probably misled
by the very summary nature of these
charters in making breaks in the series with
Barton (p. 224), and again with St. Ives and
Hemmingford (p. 228).   Since the manors
on these pages form a continuous series,
they likely all come under the title *Occupationes, etc.*, as examples of encroachments.

TABLE XV

LANDS ALIENATED BY ABBOT WALTER WITHOUT CONSENT OF THE MONASTERY (1133-61) (*Carts.*, II, 270-2)

Therfield..........	1 v(irgate) of d(emesne).
Bradenach........	200 a. from d., 3 v., 80 a. of pasture.
Burwell...........	1 v. of d., 2 v., etc.
Lawshall..........	2½ v., 'land', freed men.
Brancaster........	pasture.
Ringstead.........	20 a. of d.
Holme............	d., *curia, domus, et molendinum*.
Abbots Ripton......	2 v., 10 a. & assarts.
Cranfield..........	1 v. and 30 a. and 3 men of d., 7 a. and 1 man.
Barton...........	40 a. of pasture, ½ hide.
Shillington........	1 v., 1 *cultura*, 1 man.
Bythorn..........	2 arables of d., 1 h., 300 a.
Weston...........	3 v.
Houghton.........	1 h., 7 v., 1 car., 1 arable.
Ellington.........	1 v. and 1 a. and 1 manse in d., 4 v., several manses.
Upwood...........	1 h., 1 v., 1 assarted arable.
Elsworth..........	3 v., 60 a.
Hurst............	1 v., 1 meadow, tithes.
Ramsey...........	4 a. within gates, 4 a. beyond.
Wistow...........	1 v.
Barford...........	manor for £10.
Middelho.........	all to monks of Wardon.
Offord...........	5 h.

Note: This bare listing does not mean that the abbot gave all these lands gratuitously; e.g. the Middelho agreement for 3 pounds of wax per year.

While the short-sighted or emergency spending of an ill-advised baronial overlord soon brought decay to lay or monastic property inheritances, there is no apparent explanation in the Ramsey materials for this decline in administrative control, prolonged over two generations, that permitted alienations by abbots, seneschals, farmers, and tenants down to the most humble villein. A farmer like Simon the Chamberlain was able to extend his private property, or that of others, at the expense of the demesne or of the villein-

age.[76] Parochial churches participated strongly in the new encroachments.[77] There was a wholesale freeing of hides or smaller holdings on
every manor to the perpetual leases for money rents that had been gradually creeping in from the earlier part of the century. Because of the
difficulties in distinguishing the small assart from the encroachment by toft
or croft on demesne and villeinage, this disintegration is most evident where
the larger villein tenant has been able to liquidate his work and service
obligations.[78]

The actual statements from the extents upon the decline of lands *ad opus*
show the following: in Holywell there was a fall from twenty-three virgates
ad opus to fifteen, in Elton from thirty-five to twenty-eight, in Upwood from
twenty-eight to twenty-six and one-half, in Lawshall a decline by six and
one-half virgates, forty acres and one cotland, in Shillington and Pegsdon a
decline by two and one-half virgates, three crofts, in Burwell a decline by
three and one-half virgates and three crofts, Brington by five cotlands, Weston
by one virgate and one croft, Bythorn by one-half virgate and one croft.
In the fenlands the tenements *in landsetagio* bore the obligations for work
and services.[79] The extent of Brancaster, Burnham, and Depedale, notes
one-hundred and fifty-six acres and additional small holdings that *fuerunt in
landsetagio*, while an additional one-hundred and thirty-three acres had been
freed from the demesne in many parcels. At Holme, the whole demesne had
been rented out for a money payment. While the complete disintegration
of the demesne economy at some of the fen manors, and the decline by as
much as thirty per cent of the service-bearing lands in some of the arable
manors, bring clearly to our view the degree of changes at this time, it is
unfortunately impossible to draw the complete picture of the transformation
on Ramsey manors. Thirty virgates were already *ad censum* at Shillington
and Pegsdon in the time of King Henry I; we have already noted that even
Abbot Reginald was interested in the renting of small holdings for money
rents. The term *censum* does not seem to have been employed for the commutation of works owed by cotlands and crofts. But most important, there
could be an extensive annual commutation that has not been recorded in the
extents; and in fact, at Hemmingford Abbots, Hemmingford Grey, Graveley,
Elsworth, Warboys, and Barton, we find the most explicit statements of the

[76] Henry the Archdeacon had built a house
upon the lord's demesne at Stukeley
(*Carts.*, III, p. 275); 'John', the former
Burwell farmer, had taken one virgate out
of villeinage for his own use (*ibid.*, p. 309).
The greatest abuse of the abbot's revenues
seems to have taken place at Outwell
(*Carts.*, III, pp. 296-9), where Walter le
Curteys, parson and *custos* of the village,
appropriated to himself the revenues of the
church and several smallholdings; William
le Curteys, probably brother to the parson
and former farmer of the village, had
appropriated fifteen tenements from the
abbey's property and about thirty 'nights'
of fishing rights in various places, so that

these were sublet and William rather than
the abbey was receiving their revenues.
[77] In Houghton and Wyton there was a seven-
virgate increase by the church, in Ellington,
an increase of one virgate and ten acres,
in Shillington and Pegsdon five virgates, in
Weston one-half hide, in Cranfield one-half
hide.
[78] The study of commutation in the twelfth
century must begin with Professor Postan's
paper, 'The Chronology of Labour Services',
Trans. R. H.S., Fourth Series, XX (1937),
pp. 169-193, which first drew the movements of this century into a more satisfactory chronological perspective.
[79] *Carts.*, III, pp. 268-9.

ad censum arrangement, but slight, if any, complaint of reduction in virgates *ad opus*.[80]

From the early years of Abbot Walter's term of office (1133-61), until the last decade of the century this story of property alienation, purprestures, and losses is cumulative.[81] Needless to say the farming of manors would become stagnant and contribute to this deterioration, so that 'farming' must have become synonymous with decay.[82] A decline by one in the total number of teams on the demesne of four estates, from the nine manors for which there is evidence for both the early and late twelfth century (*supra*, Table IX, Col. IV), is indicative of the retraction in demesne cultivation over the mid-century. Data are usually not available for other livestock changes over the mid-century, though the following declines may be noted:

Manor	Vaccary		Swine	
	T. H. I.	T. H. II	T. H. I	T. H. II
Houghton & Wyton..	11	7	—	—
Elton..............	11	10	100	50
			Sheep	
Brancaster.........	7	5	448	357
Hilgay.............	6	5	—	—
Girton.............	—	—	120	100

While a new body of ecclesiastical regulations primarily concerned with property control set the framework for administrative re-organization,[83] in the economic sphere it was the extraordinary price rise, beginning in the last decade of the twelfth century and continuing well on into the thirteenth that would attract attention to this uneconomic system of fixed rents. The Ramsey materials give insufficient evidence for the tracing of the various stages of this rise,[84] but it appears certain that the price lift was general and

[80] The variation in dates of the extents, and the incomplete condition of several, are, of course, important problems here too.

[81] Cf. KNOWLES, *The Monastic Order in England*, pp. 304-305, for nation-wide trends of the same species.

[82] It may be noted that Jocelin of Brakelond includes the farming of vills among the evidences of decadence (*Chronicle, op. cit.*, p. 1), yet the same farming of Groton and other manors by abbot Samson becomes panegyric material when the manorial production had been stepped up by re-capitalization. In the same fashion, the long-term leases of Ramsey manors over the mid-century — Barford, Middleho, Offord, Walton — were indicted by the alienation lists, but that more adaptable farming of manors which can be seen in the extent organization, receives no criticism as such.

[83] See the following chapter, Section I.

[84] The twelfth-century evidence of the Beveridge Committee on Prices and Wages, whose collections I have been kindly permitted to study in the Institute of Historical Research, should bring out the degree and the range of this price upswing quite clearly. See for example, *Table 1, English Wheat Prices, 1160-1339*, in the Cam. Ec. H., II, p. 166.

considerable.[85]   The value of the plough horse and ox, for instance, has at least doubled by the account roll of 1240's over the extent figures of the late twelfth century.   A list of *redditus* for some year under Abbot Robert the Second (1202-1206), and values for manors farmed in the numerous vacancy rolls under King John tell the story of this price rise in rent amounts that contrast with the *Redditus Annui* column of the mid-twelfth century.   By

TABLE XVI

DOMESDAY PLOUGHS AND PLOUGHLANDS ON RAMSEY ESTATES

Manor	Demesne Ploughs	Villein Ploughs	Ratio	Demesne Plough-lands	Villein Plough-lands
Stukeley	2	6	1:3	2	6
Abbots Ripton	2	12	1:6	2	14
Broughton	4	10	1:2½	?	?
Wistow	2	11	1:5½	3	13
Upwood	2	14	1:7	3	13
Hollywell	2	6	1:3	2	6
Slepe	3	20	1:6⅔	3	21 (or 18 ?)
Houghton	2	10	1:5	2	8
Wyton	2	8	1:4	2	8
Warboys	3	16	1:5⅓	3	17
Sawtrey	2	5	1:2½	?	10
Elton	4	20	1:5	4	20
Hemmingford Abbots	2	8	1:4	?	14
Hemmingford Grey	1	3	1:3	?	4
Bythorn	1	7	1:7	1	3
Brington	1	6	1:6	1	6
Weston	2	7	1:3½	2	11
Gidding	1	7	1:7	1	7
Ellington	2	12	1:6	2	12
Cranfield	2	10	1:5	2	14
Barton	3	9	1:3	3	9
Pegsdon	3	11	1:3⅔	2	12
Shillington	2	12	1:6	2	12
Therfield	3	17	1:5⅔	3½	16½
Elsworth	4	18	1:4½	4	18
Over	2	8½	1:4¼	6	4½?
Burwell	4	12	1:3	3+	13
Girton	2	4	1:2	3	3?

[85] The rapid increase in some revenue totals largely dependent on manorial returns over the second decade of the thirteenth century (e.g. R.A.L. SMITH, *Canterbury Cathedral Priory*, Cambridge, 1943, p. 16, note 1) and the increase in some prices at the same time (e.g. N.S.B. Gras, *Evolution of the English Corn Market*, Cambridge, Mass., 1915, pp. 370 ff. for the maintenance of a different price level after about 1217), suggest an inflationary movement by their general pattern. See Table V, *supra*, for the increase in late twelfth-century manorial values discussed in this paragraph.

the time of King John, the farm of Girton had leaped from twelve to twenty pounds, that of Lawshall from thirty to fifty pounds, in these vacancy rolls. These farms came in a roll showing obvious extortion by the royal administration — it is the only vacancy roll in which the cellarer's revenues were decimated by a £226.20s.3d. *superplusagio* — and a misleading 'increase' may have come from the depletion of manorial stock in these manors in order to satisfy the royal avarice. Nevertheless, a great rise in agrarian revenues was under way, and the level of these manorial rents was to be maintained. Somewhere about this same time came the re-organization in the food and money 'farm' sent to the convent, and this serves as at least a floor for the measurement of the revenues of these manors around 1200: Abbots Ripton has become a full farm worth more than twice its value recorded in the twelfth century *Redditus*; Upwood and Wistow, now 'three-quarter' farms, have increased by forty to fifty per cent in rent value.

For the most part, movements in prices and production have had to be studied in this chapter without direct evidence upon the influence of agrarian productivity and of profits from marketing. The reason is not far to seek. In an era of rising prices the person situated in a position to market agrarian produce would reap the first advantage from the increase; but with the rigidity of the rental structure, from long-term leases of whole manors and static farming, down to customary rents and *censa* from the peasants, the abbey had become isolated from the market. We shall conclude this chapter with some tabular illustrations of how movements in the twelfth century affected the position of the demesne economy and of the villein on Ramsey estates.

Since it is clearly indicated for most of the large arable estates of the Ramsey Domesday how many demesne ploughs were or 'could be', a comparison of these data with the actual number of villein ploughs indicates something of the relative capital wealth of the villeins. As the preceding table shows, the proportion of villein ploughs to those in demesne varied widely; but the demesne ploughs corresponded exactly (if at their complement) with the demesne ploughlands, so that the works required from villeins for the demesne must have varied widely also.[86]

Here, probably, we have a structural explanation for the variety in twelfth-century development. When some villeins could have seven times

[86] Cf. the late Anglo-Saxon 'Rectitudines Singularum Personarum' (*English Historical Documents*, II, p. 814): "The estate-law is fixed on each estate; at some places, as I have said, it is heavier, at some places, lighter, because not all customs about estates are alike." This picture is also confirmed from the thirteenth-century extents where for a number of manors have been given the ploughs necessary for the demesne both in terms of the number of lord's ploughs, and of the villein ploughs, the latter computed as at full time allocation for demesne ploughing (e.g. *Carts.*, I, p. 295: Consuetudo carucarum villæ ad valorem unius carucæ per annum continue æstimantur et amplius):

Manor	Ploughs Necessary for Demesne	
	From the Lord	From the Villeins
Slepe	3	3
Holywell	2	1+
Warboys	4	2
Abbots Ripton	5	2
Broughton	4	2½
Upwood	7	3
Wistow	4	2+

the number of ploughs to those on demesne while others had only twice the
number, it can be readily seen how the former manor could provide freeholds
or virgates *ad censum* without causing great distress to demesne production.
Much the same proportion can be seen above in a comparison of demesne
and derived villein ploughlands.   In column five, the villein ploughlands
have been assumed for the purposes of this general picture, to be represented
by the residue of geldable ploughlands after the subtraction of demesne
ploughlands and those ploughlands clearly taken from the villeinage by
freemen.

This great disparity among the Ramsey manors between the amounts
in villeinage and in demesne may be again seen clearly in the twelfth-century

TABLE XVII

THE DISPOSITION OF VIRGATES FROM TWELFTH-CENTURY EXTENTS [87]

Manor	Total Virgates in the Manor	Virgates *ad opus*	Virgates in Demesne
Brington................	16	12	4
Bythorn...............	16	11+	1
Wistow................	32	27	?
Graveley..............	35	26½	17½?
Upwood...............	40	28	?
Weston...............	40	23+	7
Broughton.............	58½	28	13
Elsworth..............	37 *	17½ & 33 cot.	12?
Knapwell..............	20 *	8	8?
Cranfield..............	40½*	24	?
Ellington..............	45	24	?
Barton................	46 *	32	6
Hemmingford Abbots....	120	78	30
Holywell..............	45 *	15	?
Houghton.............	42	33	?
Wyton................	35	6	?
Shillington & Pegsdon....	80	32½	?
Stukeley..............	28	9	?

[87] The starred items have been completed from the virgate data of manorial hidage summaries in *Carts.*, III, pp. 208-215, and 220-223. The difference between the sum of the villein and demesne virgates against the manorial total is of course due to 'freed' lands.

extents.   But the extents also cut across the process by which lands were
freed from villein services or taken in for money rents so that it is possible
to assess the effects of these twelfth-century developments upon the structure
of the demesne economy (Table XVII, above).   It is at those manors owing
food rents to the convent, expecially Bythorn, Brington, Wistow, Graveley,
Weston, Upwood, that the proportion of virgates *ad opus* to total virgates
in the manor has remained the greatest.   At the other extreme the data
from manors like Wyton, Shillington, and Pegsdon,[88] emphasize how money
rents are shifting the demesne from the centre of manorial life.   It must be
assumed, too, that even the villein had access to a market,[89] and would enjoy
some of the advantages of the property holders in the twelfth-century evolution, for, from the time of earliest extent evidence, a virgate *ad opus* will
be liable to pay from one to two shillings in customary rent.   Indeed, it was
only the *famuli* who were entirely dedicated to works and services for their
holdings.   The general consequences of the twelfth-century rent movements

TABLE XVIII

THE PLACE OF MONEY RENTS IN 12th-CENTURY *VALORS*

Manor	Total *Valor*	*Redditus Assisus* & Tallage	
		Amount	% of Total
Shillington & Pegsdon....	£38. 0s. 0d.	£19. 4s.3d.	50
Barton.................	£22.10s. 1d.	£12. 1s.6d.	55
Cranfield..............	£29.12s. 6d.	£15.13s.9d.	52
Hilgay.................	£13. 8s. 6d.	£ 7. 3s.7d.	53
Elsworth...............	£32. 8s. 4d.	£17. 3s.6d.	53
Brancaster.............	£26.10s.11d.	£12.12s.6d.	46
Ringstead..............	£15.19s. 5d.	£ 6.13s.0d.	40
Walsoken...............	£11.12s. 6d.	£ 4.16s.9d.	36
Burwell................	£21. 8s. 7d.	£ 6. 7s.8d.	29
Wimbotsham............	£ 9. 8s.11d.	£ 2. 1s.5d.	22
Graveley...............	£12. 8s.10d.	£ 2. 4s.8d.	16

[88] The fen manors like Holme, Brancaster,
and Ringstead are most striking in this
context, but their assessment is not
sufficiently clear for such a tabulation.

[89] In the more complete thirteenth-century
extents we are able to see what the villein
was marketing at the time from the tithe
assessment for sales; e.g. *Carts.*, I, p. 320:
Percipit etiam pro pullo unum denarium,
pro vitulo obolum pro agno obolum, pro
capriolo quadrantem; et si vitulus, agnus,
aut capriolus vendantur, decimam partem
denariorum pro eis receptorum percipiet.
In addition, it was the sale of only those
animals essential to maintenance of the
plough team that continued to be strictly
governed by the licence of the lord (see
infra, Ch. VII, Section I, especially footnote 7).

can be brought out more clearly from the *valor* data.   Table XVIII shows the position of money rents (largely payments by the villeins) for some Ramsey manors: the lesser importance of money rents from the manors owing food livery is well confirmed by this evidence from the *valors*.   Peasant livery and service in Graveley was fifty-one percent of the total *valor* for that estate. In other manors the *valor* of these villein services has declined in proportion to the increase of money rent: Burwell (25%), Shillington and Pegsdon (22%), Barton (16%), Cranfield (12%).   This trend shifted the emphasis from demesne production in the manorial organization.   Table XIX (also from the *valors*) indicates the declining importance of the value of the demesne (and the works with it) where extensive money rents prevailed.

In order to appreciate more fully how the villein himself could take an active part in twelfth-century development, it must be recalled that the virgater was not an empty-handed proletarian.   In the Domesday team statistics the Ramsey villeins usually averaged about two tenants per team.[90]

TABLE XIX

THE PLACE OF DEMESNE ARABLE IN 12th-CENTURY *VALORS* [91]

Manor	Total *Valor*	Value (of demesne and *opera*)	
		Amount	% of Total
Graveley.............	£12. 8s.10d.	£ 7.17s. 8d.	63
Burwell..............	£21. 8s. 7d.	£11. 6s. 8d.	52
Elsworth............	£32. 8s. 4d.	£12. 3s. 7d.	37
Barton..............	£22.10s. 1d.	£ 7. 5s. 6d.	32
Shillington & Pegsdon....	£38. 0s. 0d.	£11.16s. 6d.	30
Cranfield............	£29.12s. 6d.	£ 9. 2s. 6d.	30
Ringstead...........	£15.19s. 5d.	£ 4. 5s. 0d.	26
Brancaster....	£26.10s.11d.	£ 6. 7s.10d.	23
Walsoken........... ..	£11.12s. 6d.	£ 2. 9s.10d.	22
Wimbotsham..........	£ 9. 8s.11d.	£ 1.17s. 0d.	21
Hilgay..............	£13. 8s.11d.	£ 2. 0s. 0d.	15

[90] The thirteenth-century extents actually suggest in many instances that each virgater may have had his own plough: e.g. Warboys, *Carts.*, I, p. 310: ..., arabit dimidiam acram, ..., sive propriam et integram habeat carucam, vel junctam cum aliis, pro uno opere. However, it was always possible that the villein plough was in such instances smaller than that of the lord.

[91] It should be noted that these tables are an attempt to picture proportions only.   The precise percentages are impossible since the absolute money income for each year is not known: e.g. the temporary commutation of works and services, or the amount added to the *valor* total to round out the farm price (an amount which may have reflected probable arable profits).

Despite the capital involved, with the large plough teams necessary for arable on Ramsey estates, this proportion does not seem improbable for a virgate holding of thirty to forty acres when the villein had to have extra ploughing resources to fulfil his obligations on the demesne.   The reeves on Ramsey manors were always villeins, and in the thirteenth-century **extent** for Broughton, where the reeve was a virgater, there is found the following provision: And if he be reeve, he may have two of his horses, four oxen, and two cows, pastured with the lord's stock . . .[92]   Or again, 'succession taxes' reveal something of villein property wealth: the widow of Richard Plumb, villein and virgater at Warboys, who died around 1300, was able to pay five marks fine to the lord for her husband's goods, an amount derived from the lord's right to receive automatically one-third of the movable and immovable wealth of Richard.[93]   In addition to his sales in order to meet money rents, the liability of any virgate to be put *ad censum*, as stated for the twelfth-century extents of Elsworth and Warboys — though probably a universal rule on Ramsey estates — must have implied some flexibility in the villein's resources whereby he could apply these works formerly employed on the demesne to discover enough money to pay the *censum* commutation.   An easiest solution to this question is the assumption that the virgater hired at least some proportion of the labour for his works on the demesne, and when his *opus* was put *ad censum*, he merely diverted his former wage commitment to rents.   This is all the more plausible when it is recalled that only the largest land holding units *ad opus* (the virgates) were granted the *censum* alternative.

Yet the twelfth-century peasant did more.   He was able to reduce the virgates *ad opus* through the payment of a money fine.   He was able to apply his resources to assarting or to the carving of new portions out of the fens. The picture of small holding accretions as well as the clipping away of fragments from the demesne and *ad opus* blocks of land is in fact the expected counterpart to a period of rising prices coupled with a system of structural rigidity in rents. The peasant was making a net revenue.   There are, consequently, no references in the twelfth century to those lands 'vacant because no one will rent them', that were to become common in the fourteenth century, even though in the loosening of the twelfth-century demesne structure the *nativus* seems to have been able to gain employment beyond the borders of his home manor.[94] A marginal profit from a holding of twenty or thirty acres of arable land would be a small and a stringent saving at the greatest price increase.   But a peasant's economic perspective is cumulative rather than dramatic; his 'standard of living' increase is the extra few feet added to the holding during his lifetime; so that the great increase in the number of twelfth-century land-

[92] *Carts*, I, p. 338.
[93] *Ibid.*, p. 307, note I; and see further, *infra*, Chapter VIII, Appendix IV, for fines paid by villeins.
[94] *Carts.*, III, p. 246, at the end of the Knapwell extent (Thomas son of Wlvinus, and Herbert son of Harwin); p. 248, at the end of the Graveley extent (Edward, Edmund, Galfridus, Robert); p. 252, at the end of the Elsworth extent (Wimerus, Inglemar son of Radulph); or the four men absent from Warboys, p. 257.   While one *nativus* had settled at Huntingdon and another in Godmanchester, the remaining had only moved to neighbouring villages.

holders in the extents has revealed but periodic 'snapshots' of a process continuing generation after generation to become an expected part of the peasants' life work.   The system of periodic tallages that is outlined in twelfth-century extents, or the succession fines for entry to an inheritance, show likewise how the peasant was expected to accumulate a wealth above the needs of the annual taxes and expenditures.   For the economic development of Ramsey manors in the twelfth century a peasantry, with initiative and with productive capacity, stand out as the most dynamic element.

CHAPTER IV

ADMINISTRATIVE REFORM AND ECONOMIC ORGANIZATION

THE most spectacular period of change from the above-mentioned increases in prices, rents, numbers of landholders, and arable areas continued on to the mid-thirteenth century, and appears to have been largely exhausted around that time. However, by the early thirteenth century there was a new leaven working in the economic life of Ramsey estates that changed the locus and scope of economic decisions. Economic initiative moved upon a different plane, and through administrative channels in a manner divergent from that spirit which typified the twelfth-century structure. There is no extant evidence of policy pronouncements to a new era of 'high farming'; nor does there appear to have been the genius of an Abbot Samson or a Henry of Eastry to grace the Ramsey Abbey directorate. In fact much of the economic policies of Ramsey abbots remained but patchwork rationalizations of their seigneurial position upon the aggressive advance of freeman and peasant over the previous century; and the full sweep of administrative cohesion remained curtailed by the tensions, pulls, and rigidities of the large consumer super-structure. But for the first time in the evidence recorded since the foundation dowry of the abbey, the buyers' market for Ramsey lands was replaced by a fairly consistent long-term trend to property redemption and augmentation; and the farming system at least retired, although it did not disappear altogether, behind a primary emphasis upon the more direct administration of estates.

The starting point of this re-orientation must likely be sought in a Constitution[1] formulated by Archbishop Hubert Walter for Ramsey Abbey which appeared around 1200, a climax to, if not a consequence of, the twelfth-century series of extent investigations, purprestures, and lists of property alienations. It is a misfortune for the administrative history of Ramsey that the key documents for the working out of this central adjustment process relative to the economic exigencies of the period are so few and impersonal; on the other hand, more plebeian sources abound, above all the account rolls, to give a substantial if less comprehensive picture of economic growth from the thirteenth century. Nevertheless, both because the new administrative programme had a decisive impact on economic development, and because some insight into the functioning of the overall framework is necessary for the interpretation of manorial statistics, an effort must be made in this chapter to reconstruct the central structure and guiding spirit of administration before passing on to those elements of more ready economic import.

---

[1] Of the three redactions preserved among Ramsey charters, the most complete version, *Carts.*, II, 204-7, has been used for the quotations of the next few pages.

I

The Constitution of Archbishop Hubert Walter for Ramsey is still another example from an epoch of re-organization in the legal and economic structure of the church effected on international [2] as well as national [3] lines in the late twelfth and early thirteenth centuries. On the other hand, it was a practical reform, directed towards the particular problems of each foundation,[4] rather than a re-formulation of monastic principles. The bulk of the ordinances in the case of the Ramsey Constitution were palpably concerned with removing the specific heritage of mismanagement by Ramsey abbots, in contrast with those contemporary reforms at Canterbury,[5] for instance, which dealt largely with problems of obedientiary control. The personal liberty of the monks was stressed against arbitrary delivery to external courts or excommunication by the abbot. The conventual consent was required for such major decisions as the use of the abbey seal for letters patent, the advancement of the monks to sacred orders, the granting of aids or corrodies, and the appointment of obedientiaries and assistants to the abbot. Any extravagant appointments of supernumerary obedientiaries or servants, beyond the traditional quota, were to be rescinded. The prior was to have full authority in the absence of the abbot.

More novel were the constitutional limitations placed upon the abbot. Apparently for the first time, two monk chaplains were appointed as companions to the abbot, to be his witnesses, helpers, and counsellors in all things; there was to be a keeper of the abbot's seal; and more significantly, two monks and the steward [6] were now to administer all external affairs, only referring to the abbot for the sake of convenience (. . . , *et quæ per eos non poterunt commode expediri, referentur ad audientiam Abbatis, ut per consilium ejus expediantur*). The crux of this administrative control, and the problems receiving most detailed treatment in the Constitution, were revenue matters. Although the steward and two monks had been established as collectors of moneys, an equally important development was the system of treasurers, appearing for the first time in Ramsey documents, and obviously instituted as a means of control over the disposition of the abbot's income. Three times the Constitution emphasizes the absolute control by the treasurers:

---

[2] W., HOLTZMANN, (ed.) *Papsturkunden in England*, II (Berlin, 1936), *passim*.

[3] Dom. David KNOWLES, *The Monastic Order in England*, esp. Ch. XXI.

[4] Dom BERLIÈRE's classical study, 'Innocent III et la Réorganisation des monastères bénédictins', *Revue Bénédictine*, XXXII (1920), brings out well the great variety of problems attacked and solutions provided. See especially pp. 35-42, and 149-153.

[5] R. A. L. SMITH, *Canterbury Cathedral Priory*, Chapter 2.

[6] The appointment of a lay steward is not new, of course, to monastic administration; but the new and broader scope given to his duties is an interesting example of the effort to employ even laymen in the attempt to remedy the complexities of monastic administration. Miss H. M. CAM has pointed out an interesting example of the same development at Bury St. Edmunds. See *Liberties and Communities in Medieval England* (Cambridge, 1944), Ch. 13: 'The King's Government as administered by the Greater Abbots of East Anglia', p. 188, where it is noted that the steward of Bury St. Edmunds was given certain manors to support expenses of the external forum in the early thirteenth century, 'so that the abbot might serve God'.

Omnis vero pecunia ad cameram Abbatis pertinens undecunque proveniens, sive ex mutuo sive ex redditibus, sive ex casibus fortuitis sive aliunde, per præceptum et testimonium dictorum monachorum et Senescalli, tribus Thesaurariis monasterii tradetur, per eos reservanda, qui tres Thesaurarii constituti sunt ad recipiendum et reservandum omnem pecuniam prædictam ad usus necessarios, . . .

Thesaurarii accipient denarios de camera Abbatis, undecunque pervenerint; et consilio Prioris sociorumque ejus expendant in sustentatione domus et quitantiis debitorum; et compotum reddant per quattuor quateria anni.

Nullus firmariorum de camera Abbatis reddat firmam suam nisi Thesaurariis . . .

There seems to have been little if any effort to circumscribe the traditional jurisdiction of the obedientiaries in the same way. There was to be a monk to look after the bread, beer, and wine of the convent, and another to act as porter, but over these the cellarer retained authority *in omnibus*. Nor would there appear to be any novel limitations to the functions of the other four major obedientiaries: chamberlain, almoner, sacristan, and prior of St. Ives. While each obedientiary with his aid must draw up an annual account of the expenses and receipts of his office,[7] the obedientiaries appear to have continued to receive their revenues directly, rather than by a controlled distribution via the treasurers: . . . *ut ipsi Camerarius et Elemosinarius recipiant suos redditus per manus firmariorum terminis statutis, sicut fieri solebat tempore Roberti Abbatis.*

The Constitution of Archbishop Hubert Walter underlines strongly the failure of the early twelfth-century *divisio* to guarantee a security and abundance of conventual needs at Ramsey. The *divisio* would seem to have been fairly successful insofar as its allocation of specific food farms to the convent was concerned, for there are no complaints about a diminution of their farms in the twelfth century; and, as we have seen, the demesne and villeinage supplying these farms from the cellarer's manors remained fairly stable despite the general disintegration. But heavy investments and rental adjustments were inevitable, due to the depredations of a Geoffrey de Mandeville or a King John on all Ramsey manors, or with the reduction in purchasing power of the convent as prices rose from the late twelfth century. Whereas the income of the abbot was adjustable by tallage, new farms, and increments, — in the final analysis, by his powers of lordship — the obedientiaries had remained tied to a fixed rent system. The foundation of this was the conventual farm, with the food rent system of the cellarer which has already received some attention; the charters of the twelfth century also gradually reveal the names and the income structures of other obedientiaries. How these administrators had to depend upon fixed allocations to meet their rising expenses, how they became almost pensioners of the abbot, may be best exemplified by the grants from various spiritualities: Abbot Walter granted twenty shillings

---

[7] Such accounts were not in all probability innovations of the thirteenth century. See   *Chronicle of Jocelin*, p. 123.

from Cranfield church for the repair of books, and five shillings from Shillington church to the almonry.   Later in the century forty shillings were allocated to the almonry from Warboy's church, and by the closing decade of the century the pensions of eight churches were confirmed to the sacristan and infirmarian.   The Prior of the Ramsey cell at St. Ives was the sole obedientiary who appears to have been a beneficiary of the direct property grants in the twelfth century;[8] but later in the century he, too, was coming to depend upon numerous fixed grants from churches at Elsworth, Knapwell, St. Ives (and the chapels of Woodhurst and Waldhurst), Hemmingford, and Abbots Ripton.

Those arranging the division of Ramsey resources between the abbot and convent in the early twelfth century had of course forseen the probability for new needs of the convent, and had made the abbot responsible for deficits in the conventual farms:

> Similiter conventui, et *omnibus supervenientibus*, in pane et cervisia debet (abbas) providere.   Si autem contigerit firmas, in plena solutione antiquæ consuetudinis, sustinere defectum, Abbas, de camera sua, earum, quotienscunque necesse fuerit, debet adhibere *supplementum*.[9]

This meant, in short, that jurisdiction over the collection and disposition of excess revenues was left to the person of the abbot.   The convent would have no immediate discretionary control over a financing of extraordinary expenditures, or a budgeting project attuned to the steady increase in agrarian returns.   On the other hand, it would not appear to have been the intention of the Anglo-Norman *divisiones* that the convent should depend upon a dole from the abbot or anyone else.   During an abbatial vacancy the monks of Abingdon successfully prevented the royal custodian from acquiring a farm of their conventual holdings, that is, granting a fixed revenue to the convent so that he might enjoy excess profits, and exploit the manors.[10]   As has already been noted in Chapter Two, there was a specific division of lands between the abbot and convent, not merely of revenues.   Although we have little direct evidence for Ramsey on this point,[11] it would seem that the early twelfth-century *divisio* of monastic estates left the obedientiary with sufficient seigneurial authority for the administration of his estates and the reception of profits from justice.   But the obedientiary did not become legally independent in the eyes of common law,[12] so it remains doubtful whether he could pursue a

---

[8] And these came at the beginning of the twelfth century where they were associated with the foundation of the St. Ives cell (*Chronicon*, pp. 266 ff.). The prevalence of the farming system in the twelfth century contributed to this rigidity, of course. In 1196, for example, Abbot Robert farmed a marsh of Wimbotsham for twelve years, at four pounds per annum, two for the cellarer, and two for the sacristan (*Carts.*, II, p. 216).

[9] *Carts.*, III, p. 170.

[10] *Chronicon Monasterii de Abingdon*, II, p. 298: " . . . believing that he would be able to obtain the livery of our possessions into his hands, so that, while he would be held to administer our food and clothing requisites, anything that was left furnished revenue (profits)."

[11] See, however, the grants to the sacristan cited in Chapter II, n.60.

[12] *Glanvill*, Book XI, Ch. V: "It should also be observed, that the abbots, and priors of Canons Regular, are received in court,

recalcitrant debtor, or change an unsatisfactory contract in the king's court without the co-operation of the abbot. In any case, since the convent was responsible for the growing domestic needs of the abbey, it was inevitable that their traditional resources should require renewed capitalization and probably the addition of new resources in land. Some adjustments had accrued from the revaluation of food rents, and there was some protection against losses from rising prices by the maintenance of grain rents in kind, but no further revaluation of conventual farms seems to have been made after the late twelfth century. During the buoyant periods of agrarian returns their sole recourse would seem to have been the proscriptive effect of those repeated lists of properties alienated without conventual consent. In the meantime, caught in the web of their feudal status, the abbots of Ramsey were compromising monastic resources by grants for favours, friendship, security, and solvency.

The Constitution attempted to free the convent from the shackles of this system by shifting discretionary control of excess revenues to the treasurers:

> ... qui tres Thesaurarii constituti sunt ad recipiendum et reservandum *omnem pecuniam* prædictam ad usus necessarios, quod ideo institutum est, ut cum redditus conventus ei non sufficient, defectus de redditibus cameræ Abbatis per *Thesaurarium* suppleatur.

This meant, too, that the convent, as repository of revenue control through the medium of the treasurers, was now for the first time in a position to implement, and to benefit from, an effort to increase manorial revenues. In addition, the Constitution left little doubt upon the nature of the issues to be attacked with this authority: that loss of lands to petty baronial sergeancies is again indicted —

> Abbas alienationes rerum immobilium, quas fecit consilio prædictorum, pro viribus suis, studeat revocare; ...

Those injudicious grants that had given hereditary leases of villeinage as well as new lands for money rents, along with the ill-controlled farming of manors that fostered such grants, were specifically attacked:

> Nulla terra detur, neque sartum concedatur, nec terra consuetudinaria libera efficiatur, nisi de communi consilio.
> Nullum manerium, neque de celerario, neque de camera Abbatis, cum vacaverint, ad firmam tradatur, nisi de communi consensu et consilio.
> Prior de Sancto Ivone non habeat sigillum ad terras dandas, vel ecclesiam ad firmam tradendam, ...

In order to appreciate the nature of the problems to be met with in the study of the economic history of these monastic estates, it is important to note here particularly how economic enterprise waited upon adjustments in internal

upon their own authority, without even the letters of their convents. Other priors, whether of canons or monks, even though cellarers, and even though aliens, are by no means to be admitted in court, without the letters of their abbot or grand prior."

discipline. Nothing could testify more fully to the danger of equating too nearly administrative reform with fundamental economic trends in prices, rents, and production, than the lag in the appearance of the new abbey Constitution in relation to late twelfth-century economic movements. Furthermore, it should be a caution against the unity implied by that liberally employed phrase 'economic corporation' that the traditional division of resources indicated by the obedientiary system was never pulled into line with the exigencies of productive development by means of a common capital pool in the hands of the treasurers. In addition, that constant threat which the abbot's independence and 'external' liabilities offered to a healthy economic control was never satisfactorily removed or circumvented. Accordingly a postscript to the Constitution in which it was recorded that the abbot's dignity was to be maintained despite these newly-established constitutional limitations was unnecessary, if not actually misleading. The abbot never became anything like a mere administrative figurehead.[13] Despite the paucity of documents from the abbey treasury, we shall be able to trace fairly fully the economic employment of manorial resources in the thirteenth century through the abbots' charters of allocation. Nor was a more precise division effected between the baronial and conventual departments. The abbot could, in the ordinary course of events, and apparently without fear of protest, impose an unusual demand upon manorial produce, of both demesne and villeinage in all manors, to meet the expenses of fêting the royal court;[14] or heavy taxes were relayed to the villeins to such a degree as scarcely to have avoided diminishing considerably the manorial production capital.[15] In short, the executive consequences of the abbot's legal primacy on one hand, and of his great needs for the forensic administration on the other, never seem to have been fundamentally circumvented. The Constitution of Hubert Walter was primarily directed against incompetence in administration. It was designed, consequently, to set up a system of checks, controls, and accountability. There emerges from this document no new principle for the exploitation of Ramsey estates, or for a re-organization of manorial properties as such. Indeed, the reforms that were initiated from the time of the Constitution came in the name of the abbots of Ramsey, although the ensuing increase in profit-bearing land and the allocation of surplus to the convent appear as such a decisive reversal in policy to the twelfth-century abbatial administration, that they can be clearly attributed to the spirit of the Constitution and the pressure exerted by the abbot's advisers.

[13] A fourteenth century opinion (W. A. Pantin, *Chapters of the English Black Monks*, III, Camden Society, 1937, p. 38) makes it appear unlawful for a Benedictine convent to appropriate such administrative powers from the abbot: Ad istum respondet et dicit quod bona monasterii a tempore fundacionis eiusdem nunquam fuerunt discreta, et quod abbates qui fuerunt pro tempore habuerunt disposicionem, ordinacionem et administrationem, illius manerii sicut ceterorum maneriorum dicti monasterii. ... Item in dicta regula continetur quod omnia sint in disposicione abbatis, non dicit prioris et conventus, quia monstruum esset in uno corpore plura esse capita. Et in constitucionibus Benedictinis, in capitulo *Ne victualia in peccunia administrentur monachis*, est manifeste prohibitum ne monachi recipiant pecuniam etc.

[14] *Add. Ch.* 34672.

[15] Cf. *infra*, Ch. VIII, Section II, where most of the matter discussed in these last two pages is illustrated in greater detail.

The most remarkable contribution by Ramsey abbots to the thirteenth-century revival of that abbey, and certainly a reform more immediate and persistent than the movement towards a direct management of estates, was that made by capital investment in land. Fortunately, enough documents survive to give what appears to be a fairly complete list of these land purchases up until the time of the Black Death. The first stage of this process involved a concerted effort from the time of King John to recover freeholds, in accordance no doubt, with the complaints against twelfth-century alienations. The accompanying fine or payment bears no apparent relation to the value or size of the property acquired, and hence would probably vary with the force of the legal claim:[16] in 1211 two hundred acres were regained in Stukeley for 30 marks, in 1219 the isle of Higney and appurtenances for 20 marks and twelve quarters of wheat, in 1220 eleven virgates were secured in Walsoken by an exchange, and Bodesheye estate came in the same year for 30 marks, in 1221 seven virgates in Bradenach for 17 marks, around 1230 lands in Stukeley and Gidding for 30 marks, and by 1237 the manor of Over was regained from the Peck family after a lengthy lawsuit. Some of these newly-acquired properties were rounded out by further purchases, as the hide gained in Higney for forty shillings, or a hide in Bodesheye for five marks.

It is not easy to see the force of baronial suasion in these property recoveries, especially since recent studies have gradually been bringing to light a more sanguine picture of the freeholder in the thirteenth century.[17] While large religious establishments were apparently earlier in reacting against losses of land, the picture of a running battle was much the same. On Ramsey estates the freeholder was apt, perhaps more often than not, to sustain his claims in a lawsuit from the very beginning of that period of 'manorial reaction'. For instance, the freeholder established his claim for twenty acres at Outwell in 1202, for Walton church in 1224, for two virgates at Burwell in 1228, or for a mill and appurtenances at the same manor in 1259.[18] In some instances, as with the fee of Walton or the estate of Staplewerecroft (near Wimbotsham), the abbey was able to gain a written guarantee to first right of purchase at a 'reasonable' price if the property were ever to be sold.

---

[16] The land transactions listed in the following paragraphs are for the most part from *Carts.*, II, *passim*. See *infra*, Table XX. These data have survived in some cases only because of *Anniversary Rolls*; and in some of these the abbot has specified that these are 'all the acquisitions' made during his period of office. The numerous references in public records (especially the *Patent Rolls*) do not seem to add significantly to the amount or precision of the *Anniversary Rolls*.

[17] F. M. POWICKE, 'Observations on the English Freeholder in the Thirteenth Century', in A. Dopsch (*Festschrift*), *Wirtschaft und Kultur* (Leipzig, 1938). E. g., p. 385: "These cases from the end of John's reign show that, seventy-five

years before the statute Quia Emptores (1290), which put an end to subinfeudation as a consequence of transfer of land, many kinds of difficulty had already to be faced. The statute Quia Emptores was not a blow, an unexpected thunderbolt, directed at feudal relations. It was a natural consequence of the changes in tenure and the increase in the number of free tenements which were characteristic of the 13th century." For another important contribution to this question, see E. MILLER, 'The State and Landed Interests in Thirteenth Century France and England', *Trans. R. H. S.*, Fifth Series, II (1952), 109-129.

[18] See also interesting charters in *Carts.*, II, pp. 279, 280, 286, 288, 312.

Above all, however, the mid-thirteenth-century extents of Ramsey appear in this context as inquisitions on the baronial level which, like the Hundred Rolls of a generation later, found everywhere a history of alienations extending back over two or three generations, and revealed an intricate descent of tenure that often had obscured or lost the service due to the lord. Some alienations were even traced back to the time of Abbot William (1161-79). For instance, five hides had been taken from the demesne in Hemmingford Abbots,[19] and of these, Robert the son of William, the son of Radulph holds two virgates originally given by a certain Robert Clerk, farmer of Hemmingford in the time of William abbot of Ramsey. The inquisition tells us that Robert, while he was the farmer of Hemmingford Abbots, transferred this property 'on his own authority' to his brother Mathew; and Mathew having died without heir, the same Robert transferred the land to his nephew Radulph, the father of William, the father of the present Robert. We are taken back equally far by the story of alienation through a family compact of farmers by the inquisition of Stukeley:[20] one-half of a virgate, which at one time was in demesne is held at this time by Henry the son of Thomas through Henry the archdeacon, formerly farmer, who granted it to Henry the steward, his father, at four shillings a year. At the death of this Henry, his son Thomas succeeded him, and afterwards married the granddaughter of a *Magister Adam* who had succeeded Henry the archdeacon as farmer of Stukeley. Adam himself remitted some of the rent due from this land, so that Thomas, as well as his son Henry in the time of the inquest, paid but two shillings annually. These thirteenth-century extents also provide some information to show that Abbot Robert Trianel (1180-1200), who had come too late for many of the records of alienation in the twelfth century, incurred indictment for the same policy: at Broughton he let one-half virgate of freeland to Richard Parys, 'who then was a villein'.[21] At Crawley, he allowed one-and-one-quarter virgates to be kept out of the hidage;[22] in Barton he gave a croft of the demesne to the parson;[23] and in Weston he also permitted seisin of two cotlands and one rod of meadow beyond hidage.[24]

Many of the instances for which services were not known, or at least clearly ascertainable, probably represent equally ancient alienations. At Wyton the parson held one free hide, 'nor does he do anything (for it), unless that he owes suit to the court at Broughton, but he does not do this'.[25] And the extent continues: 'Moreover, the same man holds free one virgate, which, it is believed, was of the villeinage; and it is not known through whom the church (of the parson) gained entry to that (land); neither (is it known) that he performs any services for that (land), nor that he has been accustomed to'. At Hemmingford Abbots, it is simply stated that while the parish church was accustomed to owe forensic services for three free virgates, *modo non facit*;[26] or at King's Ripton, the two virgates which were accustomed to be

[19] *Carts.*, I, p. 381.
[20] *Ibid.*, I, p. 396.
[21] *Ibid.*, I, p. 339.
[22] *Ibid.*, I, p. 440.

[23] *Ibid.*, I, p. 474.
[24] *Ibid.*, II, p. 36.
[25] *Ibid.*, I, p. 370.
[26] *Ibid.*, I, p. 380.

in *communa villatæ* for tallage and other dues *nulla inde facit.*[27]   At Brancaster, Robert of Brancaster held one marsh containing pasture for six hundred sheep at only forty pence a year; he had gained entry to this pasture before the time of Robert de Brayboc and *nesciunt per quem, vel quo waranto, illam teneat.*[28]

The fact that most, if not all of these tenants were freemen may account for the failure of the abbey to recover twelfth-century alienations. But it does not explain the continuance of alienation from demesne and villeinage in the thirteenth century despite the Constitution of Archbishop Hubert Walter and the ensuing recovery or purchase of many lands ! The frontier economy of the twelfth century continued, of course, and with assarting still active on several Ramsey manors, this would account for such new lands being, for a time at least, let for rents rather than services. At Abbots Ripton, for instance, the inquisitors note: "Jocelin de Roucely holds a certain piece of land, which is called Calurecroft, and it contains four acres which his father assarted with permission of Walter of Stukeley, then steward of Ramsey, (and) for which he does no service to the lord abbot." [29] Or at Cranfield, a 'new assart' is held *extra hydam* in Horley for a money rent, tallage and sheriff's aid only.[30]

Such assart rentals were still only part of a wider picture, however, that of alienation or reduction of services for the sake of increased revenues from money rents. Since the system of leasing manors to a farmer continued to be a policy for many of the Ramsey estates in the thirteenth century, and the farmer was often the immediate recipient of money rents,[31] it is not surprising to find the farmers cancelling services to their own profit. The father of John of Clairvaux had appropriated one virgate from the hidage of Wistow, while he was farmer, and his son still held it in 1252 without services.[32] At Hemmingford Abbots, three crofts had owed monday works in the time that Richard Porter held that manor at farm. Richard's son Nicholas succeeded to him *in ipsa firma usque ad terminum patris sui*, and during that time Nicholas on his own authority changed that service for a payment of twenty-eight pence that he received and still receives himself.[33] In many cases, like that of the croft of Walter at Burwell held for four shillings, *sed*

---

[27] *Ibid.*, I, p. 397.

[28] *Ibid.*, I, p. 413. And the same Robert of Brancaster held one croft from the villeinage, nescitur per quem habuit ingressum. The abbess of Chatteris held some rights in the Ramsey marsh at Crowlode, et nescitur, qualiter habuit ingressum (I, 430). Simon de Hunneye has a small tenement in the same manor; nullum facit opus, sed nesciunt quo waranto, nec a quo tempore (I, 435). At Burwell, it is not known quomodo tenent piscariam (II, 28). The parson of Weston has two rods taken from the villeinage; nesciunt qualiter, nec a quo tempore, eas habuit (II, 36); and in the same manor Winfridus Vitedlon holds one

virgate; nesciunt quod servitium inde facit, nec quomodo habuit ingressum. A delightful precision is given to the report from the inquisitors for Burwell: 'Robertus de Clervaus et Walterus de Barnwelle, et Radulphus de Ovede tenent dimidiam acram de dominio; sed nunquam viderunt illam in dominio, sed audierunt (II, p. 27).

[29] *Ibid.*, I, p. 322.

[30] *Ibid.*, II, p. 13; see also the 'new assarts' of Nicholas, on the same page; of Richard, p. 14; and of Walter and Richard, p. 15.

[31] See for example, *ibid.*, I, pp. 371 and 390.

[32] *Ibid.*, I, p. 355.

[33] *Ibid.*, I, p. 383.

nesciunt quo modo illud tenet sed per firmarios habet,[34] the farmer was likely rewarded by an entry fine.

It is also clear that profit from money rents was the reason for leases of lands and the alienation of services by abbots of Ramsey. Unfortunately, the thirteenth-century extents deal fully with the abbacy of only one thirteenth-century abbot, Hugh Foliot (1216-1231). The extents themselves come early or late in the time of Ranulph (1231-1253); Robert of Reding held office but five years (1202-6), his successor Richard survived but two years (1214-16) under John, so that their names appear only two or three times in the extents. In addition, while evidence on rent of services for profits is quite plentiful for the time of Abbot Hugh, the inquisitions were not always primarily concerned with the economic details of the lease. Some of these leases were no doubt arranged for a substantial fine rather than an increase in the annual rent. Such would be the case with the twenty-four acres held by Roland in Brancaster for four shillings two pence, the same rent as his fellow tenants paid, but Roland owes no works, though the inquisitors only note that 'his father was always *ad opera*, as other *operarii*, up to the time of Hugh the Abbot'.[35] In many cases, moreover, the inquisitors were interested only to record the fact that Abbot Hugh had given a charter to a villein, or allowed some freeman to establish freehold over villein lands, or permitted freeholders to be put 'beyond hidage'. Thus in Chatteris, Robert de Achatour holds one acre with a manse by seven pence a year for all obligations, *et tamen est terra servilis, et habet inde cartam Abbatis Hugonis, ut putant.*[36] In Cranfield, Gervase ad Hokes held one-half virgate at five shillings for all services, which land had been held by a villein Galfridus ad Hille *ad censum*, but Gervase gained seisin through Abbot Hugh.[37] Another smallhold that had been let 'beyond hidage' in the time of Abbot Hugh, had not even paid the money rent due for the twelve years since the present tenant gained entry.[38]

Nevertheless, there are enough detailed cases in the extents to draw the picture of the fundamental forces at work. Brington supplies one of the best examples:

> William Farmer holds three other cotlands, containing fifteen acres, without messuage, and pays to the farmer six shillings annually for them, . . . , and eight pence of an increment, . . . And these cotlands he obtained by the grant of Abbot Hugh. And note that formerly, in the time of Richard Porter these three cotlands were held at two shillings each. And since it seemed to the said Richard that they were paying insufficient service, he took them into the hands of the Abbot, and they were in demesne until the time of Abbot Hugh who transferred them to the above William, . . .[39]

[34] *Ibid.*, II, p. 28, and see also I, pp. 334, 355, 397.
[35] *Ibid.*, I, p. 420.
[36] *Ibid.*, I, p. 430.
[37] *Ibid.*, I, p. 440, and see also at Holywell, I, p. 298, where Cristina de Houghton holds one virgate at four shillings for all services, a virgate which had been freed to Simon Fikebert by Abbot Hugh; or also the villeinage held by heirs of Marshall in Cranfield (I, p. 439), and also that in Chatteris held by Katerina de Coveneye (I, p. 430).
[38] *Ibid.*, I, p. 441; and also II, p. 4 and p. 46.
[39] *Ibid.*, II, pp. 42-3; and also on p. 43: Dabit etiam duas gallinas ad Natale, et duas ad festum Sancti Benedicti, et qua-

In Broughton the abbot bought land from a certain Mathew in order to have the money rent from its tenant;[40] and in the same manor the almoner of Ramsey purchased two virgates from which he received one mark for all services from the five tenants.[41]

The successor to Hugh, Abbot Ranulph (1231-53), almost entirely escaped criticism, coming under censure only twice in the extents for losses of revenues and of rights in abbey lands.[42] While there can be no doubt that lands were recovered from villeins at an earlier period,[43] with Abbot Ranulph we have some very good evidence of the concern for *both* money rents *and* the preservation of non-free tenures. It seems to be no mere coincidence, therefore, that many Ramsey extents, giving such detailed accounts of services and patient records of old alienations, came during the time of Ranulph. In addition, substantial portions have been preserved from the court rolls for Brancaster in 1239[44] and 1240,[45] and for Ringstead in 1240.[46] These rolls show Abbot Ranulph resolutely pursuing both freeman and villein for the alienation of services, even in these East Anglian manors where services had never been heavy. The 1239 roll for Brancaster is concerned with several property transfers touching on two generations of tenants, and is much longer than the extant rolls for 1240 of either Ringstead or Brancaster, so it may well represent one of the first steps in Ranulph's 'reaction' or re-organization. In any case, the court roll of 1239 is sufficiently detailed to throw interesting light on the recovery of services. There are some dozen suits for alienation of villein tenements, as well as the usual entries pertaining to the transfer of property among the tenants themselves.[47] In several instances there was difficulty in establishing the status of the tenants. Gilbert Hardwyn had first to be proven villein before the king's justices in eyre at Norwich, before he so acknowledged himself in the court of Brancaster. Henry the Merchant who, according to the wording of the roll may not have been a resident, acknowledged that he was a villein of the abbot. In two other instances, those of Gilbert Potekyn and Simon Copsi, these tenants had to face a challenge to their freeman status, and, while they acknowledged the villein services due from their tenements, such were to be *salvo corpore suo*. The court, which was presided over by Abbot Ranulph himself, followed the same process in the recovery of all lands, whether these were held by freeman or villein. The villein Gilbert

---

draginta ova ad Pascha. Dicunt tamen, quod ante tempus Ricardi Portarii non dedit virgata nisi tantum duas gallinas ad prædictos terminos.

[40] *Ibid.*, I, p. 333.
[41] *Ibid.*, I, p. 334.
[42] *Ibid.*, I, pp. 439 and 457.
[43] *Ibid.*, I, p. 392: It was recognized in the time of Abbot Richard (1214-16), that two villeins held fifteen acres belonging to the parish church at Stukeley. These were returned to the church and the abbot gave the villeins fifteen acres from the demesne in exchange. We also have a good example of recovery of land at Wistow at this time (*Carts.*, III, p. 315).

[44] *Ibid.*, I, pp. 423-428.
[45] *Ibid.*, I, pp. 428-9.
[46] *Ibid.*, I, pp. 411-412.
[47] Some of these are quite detailed and informative; e.g. *ibid*, I, p. 427: Katerina, quæ fuit uxor Roberti Taylefer, dat domino Abbati dimidiam marcam, ut haberet seysinam de una acra, quam Radulphus Taylefer dedit in maritagio Henrico filio Edwyni cum Margeria filia ejus, et de una acra cum domo constructa super eandem, quam Robertus vir suus emerat de prædicto Henrico viro suo, et habet eam in escambium pro illa acra, quæ data fuit cum ea in maritagio.

Hardwyn, for instance, acknowledged that he had bought twenty acres and one fold of villeinage from Peter son of Hugh a villein of the abbot, through a charter given by Peter. Gilbert Hardwyn resigned the tenement into the hands of the abbot that he might dispose of it like other villeinage, as well as handing over to the abbot all charters relevant to the transaction. In the same fashion, the freeman Gilbert Potekyn delivered these lands into the abbot's hands together with his charters. Gilbert son of Wido resigned in turn his claim to the acre and one-half, also handing over to the abbot the charter he had received with this land in return for seisin of the whole four-and-one-half acres. Gilbert son of Wido, or others, were henceforth to hold these acres directly of the abbot, however, rendering to him ten shillings for services owed.[48] An indemnity of one mark must be paid to Gilbert Potekyn for his claim to the property, probably by Gilbert son of Wido, although this is not altogether clear from the roll.[49]

In general, the tenant who had sold the lord's villeinage was subject to the penalty for the transgression. However, when Gilbert Hardwyn sold two acres of villeinage to another villein Alan, in addition to the six shillings eight pence payable by Gilbert *pro damnis suis*, Alan gave thirteen shillings four pence to the abbot for re-seisin *et pro transgressione sua*. On the other hand, Henry the Merchant was pardoned his fine for selling from the villeinage because of his poverty, but he was able to give one-half mark to the abbot to further a suit for his wife![50] Again in many long-standing cases, as in that of William Marshall who had to deliver to the abbot villeinage purchased by his father, the fine for sale or purchase of villeinage was apparently cancelled, or absorbed in the entry fine. In nearly all cases the present tenant was allowed to regain seisin by the payment of a fine. Throughout all the lawsuits the main concern of the abbot is to regain control of services and customary dues.[51] Although in many instances this recovery of services came to mean that the land was to be held directly of the abbot for services,[52] subletting was not

---

[48] Since there is not here the usual statement, faciendo inde omnes consuetudines serviles et servitia, the services may have been commuted from the four-and-one-half acres.

[49] The *Rolls Series* transcription, *Carts.*, I, p. 425: *Dederunt etiam ex licentia Abbatis, pro custo suo, Gilberto Potekyn, unam marcam*, should probably read, *Dedit etiam*, etc.

[50] *Ibid.*, I, p. 425: Et quia (Henricus Mercator) vendiderat Johanni de Rys dimidiam acram terræ suæ, auctoritate propria, de ipso lancetagio, ideo in misericordia, et perdonatur quia pauper. Johannes autem de Rys, sciens illam dimidiam acram esse lancetagium Abbatis, resignavit cartam in manu Abbatis et terram, et totum jus suum. Et dominus Abbas tradidit eam prædicto Henrico pro servitio debito, ut terra redintegraretur. Idem Henricus dedit dicto Abbati dimidiam marcam, ut haberet considerationem curiæ, si Emma uxor sua

haberet majus jus in medietate duodecim acrarum, quas Simon Copsy injuste detinuit et deforciavit, quas eadem Emma per considerationem curiæ statim dirationavit, et adepta est inde seysinam.

[51] One of the clearest statements of this point is given in the roll of Ringstead, p. 412: Præceptum est, quod tota terra, scilicet quinquaginta acræ et unum messuagium Martini Prioris capiatur in manu Abbatis, quia partem vendiderat, et partem locaverat, quod facere ei non licet, eo quod lancetagium est.

[52] As noted above, the person who had purchased the land, even though illegally, was now usually given the grant by the abbot. For example, Gilbert of Northgate had purchased two acres of villeinage from Simon, and one acre from Peter; he resigned the charters of purchase to the abbot, and was granted seisin again of both properties (p. 427).

forbidden so long as the abbot's 'rights' in the property were preserved.   Thus Gilbert Copsi, *Capellanus*, paid one-half mark to the abbot in order that his son Henry may hold six acres of the villeinage that Gilbert has in Brancaster of the abbot.   And it is permitted when Henry has been pledged to do the services owed from such an amount of land.   Similarly, tenants in villeinage may pursue one another in court over their rights to the tenure of villeinage, as long as the lord's jurisdiction is assured.[53]   Finally, the regaining of customary services did not mean that the abbot needed these for his demesne. From some holdings, at least, they were commuted, for we find Gilbert de Northgate owing *per servitium servile, sicut alii, scilicet pro qualibet acra duos denarios.*[54]

From the mid-century the picture of the abbatial investment in property changes also.   There are fewer lawsuits over recovery and proportionately more outright purchases.   And the number of the small freeholds that are being bought increases rapidly.   There is some evidence that new stringencies in the arable economy (discussed below)[55] may have eased the availability of property from this period.   In any case, the willingness of the abbey to invest money in land must have presented a strong temptation for many a landholder. The large purchases by William de Godmanchester have become notorious examples of this expenditure.   To mention only two transactions, he paid £1,666.13s.4d. for the group of lands comprising Barnwell, Hemington and Crowethorpe manors, a fee in Littlethorpe and the church advowson in Barnwell, and secondly, £500 for the Le Moigne family holdings in Nidding- worth, Holywell, Ramsey, one hide in Woodhurst, one hide in Walton, and one-half hide in Fen Drayton.

The smallhold purchases appear to have been equally expensive, as Abbot William again manifests by his payment of forty marks for a virgate complementary to his new purchase of Barnwell.   Abbot Hugh de Sulgrave (1255-68) who appears to have initiated the policy of heavy investment in land by the purchase of Gravenhurst Manor for 250 marks, purchased some twenty small properties in nine manors.[56]   During his term of office Abbot William acquired small holdings in thirteen manors in addition to the above

---

[53] E.g. Adam de Helinghey in præsentia Ranulphi Abbatis, de licentia ipsius in plena curia, dedit dimidiam marcam Alfgaro et Reginaldo filiis Hamonis Stute pro pace habenda tota vita sua de octo acris et dimidia, et uno mesuagio de lancetagio, quas tenet de domino Abbate in Brancastre, quas ipsi petebant versus eundem Adam coram dicto Abbate in ipsa curia, ut jus suum.   Et idem Adam promisit fideliter domino Abbati se facturum cartam suam, quod nullus heredum suorum aliquid juris exiget in dicta terra post decessum suum, nisi de voluntate Abbatis (p. 427). Another interesting case was given for the following year at Brancaster (p. 428): Editha, relicta Hervei, implacitavit Gilber- tum Potekyn per breve domini Regis de

recto, de viginti quatuor acris de lancetagio Abbatis.   Unde dictus Gilbertus dedit ei centum solidos pro pace habenda.   Et pax illa confirmata fuit per cartam ipsius Edithæ, quam ipse Gilbertus resignavit ipsi Abbati domino suo.   Et ideo ipsa Editha in misericordia de dimidia marca.   Et ipsa Editha invenit plegios, quod nunquam de cetero aliquem implacitabit de homagio Abbatis, nec forisfaciet alicui, . . .

[54] *Ibid.*, I, p. 427; see also Alanus Jumbard, p. 428.   At Ringstead there is an interest- ing example of a villein receiving custody of freehold through his wife (p. 411, Simon).

[55] Chapter VIII, Section I.

[56] *Carts.*, II, 228-30.   An effort has been made to express the value and breadth of these purchases in Tables XX and XXI, *infra.*

TABLE XX

LARGER PROPERTIES RECOVERED AND PURCHASED BY RAMSEY FROM THE BEGINNING OF THE 13th C.

Recoveries

Date	Property	Fine (paid by abbey)
1228-31	Stukeley & Gidding	30 marks
1211	Stukeley (200 a.)	30 marks
1220	Bodesheye	35 marks
1219	Higney, & marsh	20 marks, 40 s., 15 q. wheat, and lease in Walton
1221	Bradenach (7 v.)	17 marks
1220	Walsoken (11 v.)	60 a. exchange
1221	Crawley (1 v., etc.)	30 marks
1218	Over (1 hide)	corrody
1229	Over (1 mess. & 1 v.)	2 marks
1216	Walton	corrody
1237	Over (manor)	0

Purchases

Date	Property	Price
1266-69	Gravenhurst	250 marks
ca. 1275	Barnwell, Hemington, Little-thorpe	£1,666. 13s. 4d.
ca. 1275	Barnwell (1 v.)	40 marks
1267-85	Niddingworth, Holywell, 1 h. in Woodhurst, 1 h. in Walton, etc.	£500.
1317	'manor' of John Hawker in Slepe	500 marks
1307	170 a. arable, 18 a. meadow, 1 mess. in Houghton (for a chantry)	

Note: In particular for the early thirteenth century, there are some two dozen charters involving compromise terms that are impossible to tabulate. These are smaller properties, however, like the one virgate recovered at Gidding for the hereditary lease of another one-half virgate in the same manor.

TABLE XXI

PROPERTIES ADDED TO MAJOR RAMSEY MANORS FROM THE MID-13th CENTURY

Manor	Abbot Ranulph (1231–53)	Abbot Hugh de Sulgrave (1255–68)	Abbot William (1268–85)
Abbots Ripton	assart (£6.)		
Elsworth	2 tenements (60s.)		
Broughton	1 tenement	meadow & one-half dozen small lands	houses & land (40s.)
Slepe	1 tenement (60s.)		
St. Ives	2 mess. & 2 houses (60s.)		
Cranfield	tenement (60s.)	land & woods	
Bythorn	lands (11 marks) *		
Gidding Abbots	land (6 marks) *		
Shillington		3 properties (55s.)	4 v. & mess. (£4.)
Barton		tenement (35s.)	3 lands (16s.8d.)
Therfield		lands (13s.4d)	some dozen lands (60s.)
Graveley		mess., & 80 a. arable (66s.8d)	
Elton		2 tenements (38s.8d)	
Burwell		2 mills, etc. (60s.)	land (£4.12s.4d)
Houghton		tenement (20s.)	land
Hemmingford Abbots		tenement (10s.)	several lands (68s.)
Walsoken		several small lands	2 lands (5s.)
Weston		2s. rent	cotlands (68s.8d.)
Ellington			assart (60s.)
Knapwell			several lands (29s.3d.)
Brancaster			several lands (10s.)
Chatteris			houses & lands (5s.)
Wistow			1 mess. (10s.)

Note : The bracketed figure is, in most instances at least, the value of the annual *redditus* to be paid to the obedientiary holding these lands. Hence they do not represent the purchase price of these properties.

From the early fourteenth century land purchases were more numerous, but of smaller holdings. Most of these purchases were made during a twenty-five year period, and under a mortmain licence for '60 librates', given apparently around 1310. I have been able to find under this licence, purchases amounting to 75 messuages, 539 acres of arable, 1 virgate, 1 carrucate, 38¾ acres, 6 rods of meadow, 11½ acres of woods, 18 tofts, 3 mills, and rents worth 39s.10d. But the location of these properties has not been sufficiently distinguished to allow tabulation according to manors.

* bought by Abbot William Accolt (1253-54).

large investments.[57] The Ramsey Cartularies contain more than a dozen licences for gains in mortmain by Abbot William's successor.[58] Simon Eye (1316-1342) bought smallholds in Abbots Ripton, Weston, Warboys, two messuages and three virgates in Graveley, land worth 100 shillings in Wold-hurst, land worth six marks at Hemmingford Abbots, a stall worth twenty marks at St. Ives, land worth ten marks at Wistow, and land worth twenty marks at St. Ives.[59] A further notion of the purchase value of land to the abbey may be gained from the fact Simon Eye paid five hundred marks for this last-mentioned property of John Hawker in St. Ives which was only returning twenty marks per annum. Robert de Nassyngton's investments (1342-9), somewhat more diversified as they included three stalls at St. Ives and one windmill at Holywell, totalled in all some eleven properties for 354 marks, two shillings and eleven pence.[60]

By these purchases, as well as by the recoveries of land in the first half of the century, the abbots acted as capital investment promoters during the thirteenth-century profit farming. For these lands were almost without exception handed over to the convent, not, as was the case in the twelfth century, in terms of a fixed rent allocation, but as grants in usufruct. In fact, despite the purchase of properties by the abbot, it was now the abbot's treasury (or, as it was more often called, his *camera*) that became more and more the recipient of a fixed pension over this period as increased allocations were made to the conventual portion of the monastic *divisio*. Neither the treasurers appointed by the Constitution of Archbishop Hubert Walter at the beginning of the century, nor a treasury pool of monastic net profits, appear in these arrangements. The officials responsible for consumption expenditure at the abbey remained beholden to the abbot to make up their consistent deficits over the thirteenth century. It was Abbot Richard (1214-16) who assigned the mills of Wistow and Elsworth, and tithes of the latter vill, to 'amend' the cellarer's farms (*ad relevationem firmæ et dimidiæ ad emendationem celerarii*). Abbot Hugh (1216-1231) allocated his tallages from the conventual farms to relieve the insufficiency (*invenimus eam redditu in denariis adeo destitutam, quod ipsa sibi nullatenus potuit sufficere*); and the same abbot gave the island of Higney to the sacristan because he had become destitute (*destituta sit proventibus et redditibus, et tam exilis, quod nullo modo sibi sufficere possit*). The next abbot had to take all the cellarer's manors into his hands because the

---

[57] *Ibid.*, 233-5.
[58] *Ibid.*, 101-127.
[59] *Chronicon.*, App. II, p. 349.
[60] The abbey may have bought out most of the freeholds in its larger Huntingdon manors by 1350. Unfortunately many of the sources give the value rather than the size of these purchases so it would not seem possible to calculate that they included all the lands held by these freemen in the thirteenth-century extents or the Hundred Rolls. However, there is little evidence of property purchase by Ramsey Abbey from freemen after the Black Death, but by the fifteenth and sixteenth centuries the rents from *liberi tenentes* were small items in manorial returns, so these 1250-1350 purchases may have largely wiped out this class of tenants. On the other hand, W. O. AULT (Court Rolls of the Abbey of Ramsey, p. xiii) found that the number of free tenants called to the honour court had not varied noticeably between 1250-1350, so our remarks about the decline of this class must remain tentative.

manorial revenues had 'collapsed'. And these manors remained in the abbots' hands for some thirty years, because, as Abbot William of Godmanchester explained to the visitor, they had to be built up again.[61]

But whether it was the abbot himself, or his counsellors, who directed the economic policies of Ramsey, there was a remarkably consistent effort to place the increasing agrarian revenues of the thirteenth century at the disposal of the obedientiaries. For example, whereas the chamberlain had previously received twenty pounds from Girton for the monks' clothes, he now received from the abbot *quidquid habuimus in Girttone*. The sacristan was to have all appurtenances, services, men, and stock of Higney. Abbot Ranulph purchased lands in Abbots Ripton, Wistow, and Elsworth, in order to pay a fixed revenue to his *camera* 'in recompense' for the loss of Gidding. But any surpluses from these purchased tenements were to be paid into the (cellarer's) farms from these manors. The numerous purchases by Ramsey abbots from the mid-thirteenth century followed the same pattern. Fixed rents were allocated to various obedientiaries, for the most part as anniversary expenditures by the sacristan or almoner, while the residue would go to strengthen the manorial budget.[62] For instance, the purchases of Hugh de Sulgrave in a dozen manors were assigned to the revenues of those manors, but in return each of these manors paid a fixed annual rent to the custodian of the shrine of St. Ives. The more numerous purchases by William de Godmanchester were assigned to their respective manors, while the serjeant or reeve paid an annual tax for these lands to the almoner. The fixed revenue due from these smaller purchases probably approximated their regular rent value, but some of the large investments were handed over almost without fixed commitments, particularly when the cellarer was involved. For the valuable manors of Niddingworth and Holywell, for example, the cellarer had merely to foot the expenses for the services and pittances on the anniversary day of Abbot William de Godmanchester, so that *quicquid autem residuum fuerit de proficuo dicti manerii, completo dicto anniversario modo prædicto, secundum dispositionem et voluntatem dicti conventus nostri, ad augmentationem celerariæ convertatur.* Or for Hemington, the cellarer had only to pay one hundred shillings *per annum* to the abbot, although we know from a charter of the same time that Hemington was being farmed for forty pounds *per annum*.[63] The sacristan

---

[61] The conventual farm manors were probably given back to the cellarer at this time, since large property grants were made to his office (e.g., 1293, *Carts.*, II, p. 240: Hemington). The abbot's immediate intervention continued to be of importance, of course. Around the end of the century Abbot John de Sawtrey (1286-1316) had the unusual experience of facing a 'sit-down' strike in the choir as a protest against the manner in which his debts were pinching the whole community (*Chronicon.*, p. 393). And in 1317 Abbot Simon Eye paid for the convent's corn for one-quarter

of the year because of the poor harvest (*Chronicon.*, p. 349).

[62] See *supra*, Table XXI, where the fixed rents are bracketed.

[63] Despite these economic arrangements, the abbot's baronial position can still be seen in many of these documents. For instance, Abbot William specifies (*Carts.*, II, p. 235), that if the fixed dues were not paid to the obedientiaries from the various smallholds given to the convent's manors, these smallholds were to be taken from the jurisdiction of the manor and farmed to someone who would pay the fixed rent.

was not as fortunate in his custody of Barnwell and Crowethorpe since he had to give sixty pounds a year to the prior and convent.[64]

These grants to the convent and obedientiaries of immediate control over properties with rights to surplus and 'profits', indicate how the administrators of Ramsey were aware of the new economic possibilities of the thirteenth century. It is not surprising to find that in the thirteenth-century manorial inquisitions the *firmarius* has usually disappeared as functional correspondent for demesne organization as well as for contractual payments to the abbey.[65] By the time of the appearance of the first extant cluster of

TABLE XXII

SOME MID-THIRTEENTH-CENTURY CORN SALES

Manor	Year	Amount (bushels)	Value
Wistow............	1247	968 (+ ?)	£49.10s. 2d.
	1250	528	12.13s. 7d.
	1252	552	8.12s.10d.
Upwood............	1247	660	19. 6s. 6d.
	1250	358	5.16s. 4d.
	1252	540	7.16s. 6d.
	1253	316	4.19s.10d.
Broughton..........	1244	280	64s. 2d.
	1250	922	22.12s. 8d.
	1252	370	4.11s.10d.
Warboys............	1250	243	82s. 9d.
	1252	450	6. 5s. 4d.
Abbots Ripton.......	1252	292	4. 8s.11d.
Weston *et al*.........	1252	513	6. 5s.10d.

[64] *Carts.*, II, p. 237: Quicquid autem de proficuo totius manerii, cum suis pertinentiis, ultra prædictas sexaginta libras superfuerit, Sacrista in opere conventualis ecclesiæ Rameseiæ, per visum et consensum conventus expendat.

[65] Where the *firmarius* is mentioned, it is in relation to ancient alienations, or on the abbot's manors; though see the latter part of Section II, this chapter, for notions of a modulated 'farming' by the villeins that should qualify the conception of direct exploitation of estates by the lord, or convent.

account rolls (1243-54) the payment of food rents and cash liveries were being directly credited to the appropriate monastic department rather than through the hands of a 'farmer' as in the twelfth century.   The signs of a considerable surplus in demesne production by the mid-thirteenth century show sufficiently the *raison d'être* of this policy.   Though concerned largely with a period of disruption and loss in farm profits from the Civil War,[66] the conventual manors show, in addition to an oversubscribed livery of corn (*infra*, Ch. VI), a substantial profit from the sale of corn, a profit that was being almost entirely passed on to the treasury.   The profits also varied, of course, with the species of corn sold.   Table XXII above illustrates some sales of this period.

Such surpluses in production were built upon a new demesne production programme.   Miss Neilson has tabulated some figures in illustration of the increased works required per villein holdings,[67] but the increasing fission of tenements, the additions of small parcels owing usually some small work obligation along with a predominantly money rent, and the evidence for increase of hired labour, all suggest that much more labour was employed on the demesne than any satisfactory *opera* calculation would illustrate, even if such were possible.[68]   Taking just the round totals of lands in 'pure villeinage', some idea at least can be gained of a reaction against the late twelfth-century arrangement:

[66] Because of war disturbance the abbey owed £133.6s.8d. to the king for the three years 1248, 1249, 1251 (*Carts.*, II, 390-1) for the fair of St. Ives. The fair was totally prevented in 1248 and 1251 and paid only 25 marks in 1249. The royal farm for these three years should have totalled £150. It seems most logical to conclude that the eventual collapse of the manorial farms was occasioned by the same war. The drastic decline in the manorial stock capital found on these account rolls after the 1240's, as well as the fall in corn profits, points to the early 1250's as the period of collapse of these conventual farms. We may also recall that the inquisitions for the cellarer's manors were made in 1251 and 1252.

Ramsey suffered from the last years of the Barons' War too: "In the year of grace 1266 ... there came lord Nicholas of Segrave to the village of Ramsey with 236 horses and the same number of armed men, and they stayed there for the night. On the morrow the king came up on them with fifty knights, and they depopulated that village by fire, horse, and the sword" (*Cambridge University Library*, Ms. Hh. vi, 11, f. 26).

[67] *Economic Conditions on the Manors of Ramsey Abbey* (Philadelphia, 1898), pp. 50-51, usually an increase of one or two days per week in the harvest season.

[68] Kosminsky found it impossible to count works on Ramsey estates. See his article, 'Services and Money Rents in the Thir-

teenth Century', *Ec. H. R.*, V (1934), 39. Of the thirteen manors in Miss Neilson's table, I have not been able to find an obvious increase in week work for six (Wistow, Broughton, Holywell, Houghton, Stukeley, Girton). In addition I cannot account for her twelfth-century data for Barton and Warboys, and it would appear to be uncertain for Hemmingford and Shillington. This leaves but an evident increase for Upwood and Slepe, and perhaps Brancaster. Miss Neilson's table, showing the heaviest increase in seasonal works through the boon works (*precariæ*), must also be qualified with respect to such works. From the fact that the *precariæ* are mentioned clearly in eight of the twelfth-century extents, and frequently in a very off-handed manner, it must be strongly suspected that reference to them has been merely omitted in many of these summary accounts of villein *opera*. The general reference in the thirteenth-century extents to *lovebones*, that is, extra work apparently given in return for the increased value of food served at the *precariæ*, is a further argument for the much earlier existence of the *precariæ*. Also, if as the term implies, the villein originally came at the request (*preces*) rather than the will of the lord, and was well rewarded, the boon works may have initially attracted the villein and tended to replace some wage labour proper. For further remarks on these works see below, Chapter VIII, Section I.

TABLE XXIII

VIRGATES *AD OPUS* [69]

Year	Wistow	Upwood	Broughton	Warboys	Holywell
ca. 1140	?	28 v.	?	?	23 v.
ca. 1190	27 v.	26½ v.	28 v.	36½ v. 9 c.	15 v.
ca. 1250	30½ v.	27½ v.	30 v.	44½ v. 33½ c.	23 v. 15 c.

Comparisons of ploughs on the demesne are only possible for a few manors, and the poorly enumerated boon and customary ploughworks of the twelfth-century extent make a comparison of demesne ploughs alone of little value. However, some changes can be noted in the following table:

TABLE XXIV

DEMESNE PLOUGHS

Manor	T. H. II	Ca. 1250		
	Demesne ploughs	Demesne ploughs	Customary ploughs	Boon ploughs
Warboys..........	3	4	2	2
Broughton.........	4	4	2½	2 or 3
Upwood...........	4	7	3	—
Wistow...........	3	4	2+	2

With the opening up of new pastures and the increasing interest in pastoral revenues by the abbey's economic administration, the thirteenth-century

[69] Miss Neilson also gives the following increases for virgates *ad opus*; Shillington from 32½ to 47, Ellington from 24 to 27½, Stukeley from 9 to 12½.

demesne stock quota offers another important contrast to the twelfth-century data:

TABLE XXV				
DEMESNE LIVESTOCK				

Manor	Date	Cows	Sheep	Pigs
Warboys...........	12th c.	5	100	20
	13th c.	100 [70]	200	100
Broughton.........	12th c.	4	180	0
	13th c.	20	200	100
Upwood............	12th c.	13	0	79
	13th c.	40	600	26
Wistow............	12th c.	12	120	0
	13th c.	40	300	120

These tables illustrating increases in villein works and demesne livestock show some of the recovery or re-organization that had taken place by the mid-thirteenth century. There is an almost complete gap in the evidence for manorial organization between 1200 and the mid-century so that many important adjustments cannot be investigated. What was the immediate effect of price changes, for example? The plough beasts which had been valued at four shillings each at the close of the twelfth century were valued from

[70] This figure for Warboys seems to approximate the whole cattle total for the manor given in the account rolls. The eastern fen pasture manors of Ramsey seem to have more than doubled their stock after the 12th century if twelfth-century data may be taken from *Valors*. The stock figures of 1303 are from *Add. Ch.* 39715.

STOCK ON SOME OF THE ABBOT'S MANORS *ca.* 1200 (A) AND 1303 (B)

Stock	Brancaster		Wimbotsham		Hilgay		Walsoken		Ringstead	
	A	B	A	B	A	B	A	B	A	B
cows........	7	16	7	11	6	33	15	29	5	13
ewes........	25	88	19	31	11	41	—	—	44	96

nine to thirteen shillings *ca.* 1270;[71] or demesne arable was generally valued at fourpence per acre on the abbot's manors in the twelfth century, but was worth eightpence per acre in the third quarter of the next century.[72]   One obvious reaction to these increases in value of land and production has been seen in those purchases of property, and the revocation of hereditary leases from freemen by the abbots of Ramsey, which set the stage for controlling the new level of profits from these lands.

The conversion,[73] or re-conversion, of villein holdings into demesne, the revocation of 'freed' tenements, or the increase of villein customary services and (or) money rents which would naturally accompany the general rise in agricultural values, would in theory be much more amenable to the lord's will.[74]   It must be admitted, however, that in terms of the various data summarized in the preceding pages, the thirteenth-century re-organization on Ramsey manors was more of a 'reaction' towards the previous high in demesne cultivation than an entirely record-breaking advance.   On the other hand, our sources for this period are piecemeal and we must recognize that large profits were being made from the arable in the 1240's, and that we have no gauge for some possible important factors like the increase of hired labour from the twelfth century.   In contrast, there would seem to be little doubt that the pastoral economic activity was everywhere being pushed to an

[71] *Carts.*, I, p. 53.

[72] *Carts.*, I, p. 55; for value of villein works, see *infra*, Ch. VIII; some notes have already given suggestions on the chronology of these price changes, (*supra*, Ch. III, esp. notes 84 and 85).

[73] The extents only give the example of some Cranfield tenements (*Carts.*, I, 455-456) for this adjustment, and it is not clear whether the one-half virgate, one cotland, and twelve acres here held by the lord from the villeinage were only temporarily in the lord's hands.

[74] The student is liable to miss the vital problems facing abbey administration in the thirteenth century if he does not realize the powerful force of custom at that time. A close acquaintance with the extents and manorial court rolls of Ramsey estates does not leave one surprised with the evidence that purchase of property, rather than arbitrary seigneurial authority, was the most effective means of 'reaction'. While theoretically the lord might have a jurisdiction 'at will' over his villeins, in the practical order custom was upheld as law. We may see a good example of this in the famous lawsuit over services by the villeins of King's Ripton in 1275. The villeins claimed a customary fixed money rent (*Carts.*, III, p. 60) — This was actually about the same amount as the *censum* or the hereditary money rent of the early thirteenth or the twelfth centuries. Rather than simply proving these tenants to be villeins, the abbot presented the extent of this manor in the king's court: Et quod antecessores prædictorum hominum, tempore Regis prædicti, et ante, et post, hujusmodi servitia facere consueverunt prædecessoribus prædicti Abbatis, et non prædictas consuetudines et servitia tantum, quæ prædicti homines proponunt (*Ibid.*, p. 63). And the court of Westminster decides in the same tenor: Et ideo consideratum est, quod prædicti homines, et hii qui de eisdem hominibus exient, prædicta servitia et consuetudines de cætero faciant prædicto Abbati et successoribus suis, Abbatibus de Rameseia, in perpetuum. This acceptance of customary law provided considerable limits to the economic possibilities of the demesne economy in the expansion of the thirteenth century. The value of the villein heriot given for thirteenth-century extents was only the ancient twelfth-century amount of 32 pence at Ringstead, Chatteris, or Brancaster, and, at five shillings for other manors, was still much below the market value for the ox or the horse; the minute definition of villein services had become a limitation to the lord's demands (Ch. VII, Section I, *passim*); and customary law was supported in the courts for the villein as well as the lord (Ch. VIII, Section I). The tallages from many manors granted to the cellarer in the early 13th century (*Carts.*, II, pp. 318-319) were the same in value as these taxes in the twelfth century; and were not to be increased.

entirely new magnitude. A general comparison of money rents between the more complete of the twelfth and thirteenth-century extents, though a vague and unsatisfactory summation, remains the sole means for a comprehensive assessment of these changes. Some of these rents tabulated below suggest that on the one hand, most of those manors in Huntingdon, in particular manors like Warboys, Holywell, or Broughton heavily committed to demesne production for the conventual food farms, showed little change, or even a reduction in the money rents as works and services became a more regular charge for customary tenancy. But on the other manors of the abbey, and particularly those bordering on the 'new fen' areas, additional rents from the increase in numbers of tenants (*supra*, Ch. III, Table X) and the increase in rent values themselves, were simply added to the manorial rent roll:[75]

TABLE XXVI

MANORIAL *REDDITUS*

Manor	12th C.	13th C.
Warboys.....................	£ 4. 0s. 5d.	£ 4.14s. 3d.
Houghton & Wyton..........	6. 2s. 9d.	4.15s. 1d.
Holywell....................	4. 0s.11d.	3. 8s. 9d.
Broughton..................	3.15s. 5d.	2.15s. 4d.
Burwell....................	6. 7s. 8d.	15.13s. 8d.
Brancaster.................	12.12s. 6d.	23. 0s. 0d.
Ringstead & Holme.........	6.13s. 0d.	8. 6s. 6d.
Cranfield..................	8.18s. 4d.	12.16s. 1d.
Shillington................	19. 4s. 3d.	29.10s. 2d.

It is difficult to assess what the abbots contributed to these developments by their personal direction. The huge expenses[76] of defending, recovering, and maintaining the extensive fen properties of the abbey were probably borne by the abbot's exchequer. But Abbot Robert's purchase (1342-3) of seventy-two head of cattle at the cost of £20.8s. to restore the 'vaccary' of Henny Hill[77] is the sole example of direct investment to restore manorial capital, although the restoration of the *maneria collapsa* after the mid-thirteenth century may have involved a heavier personal investment by the abbot in

---

[75] From all the increases by the thirteenth century, the taxation *valors* of Ramsey manors for 1272 (*infra*, Ch. VIII, Section II, Table LV) were over twice the figure for the earlier *valors* (above, Ch. III, Section II), though it is impossible to compare concretely the two methods of evaluation. The increase in money rents *from* the late thirteenth century, however, can be traced in detail, (see *infra*, Ch. VIII, Table LIII, and Appendix II).

[76] See *infra*, Ch. V, esp. Section V.

[77] Ch. VIII, Appendix V.

stock in place of a full scale revival of corn production.[78]   The lack of evidence for such investment is not surprising since the abbot seems to have left most[79] of his manors in the hands of 'farmers' or 'custodians' in the thirteenth century and these contractors would be responsible for the maintenance of stock in the ordinary course of events.   The main features of such rentals do not seem to have changed much since the twelfth century.[80]   Perhaps the farming of manors appealed to the abbot's desire for independence, for, as there remains no hint that the abbot had his own administrative organization for the more direct control of manorial production, his use of regular monastic machinery would be tantamount to a treasury check of his revenues.   Such at least would seem to be the case in the following example.   Whereas the Ramsey Constitution had specified that all of the abbot's 'farms' were to be handled by a three-man administration along with the treasurers, the farming of manors appears to imply an exemption from the regular administrative controls in a charter of Abbot Hugh de Sulgrave (*ca.* 1260):

> Uni autem fratrum nostrorum, quem de communi consilio elegerimus, et uni clericorum nostrorum, concessimus custodiam omnium maneriorum ad cameram nostram pertinentium, *præter illa, quæ de assensu capituli nostri tradidimus ad firmam*, ut ipsi de prædictis maneriis, et omnibus sibi pertinentibus, habeant dispositionem in omnibus, per consilium nostrum, ad commodum et profectum ecclesiæ nostræ, et ad acquietantiam omnium debitorum nostrorum.[81]

II

As was the case with other Benedictine abbeys,[82] the new interest in the profits of land at Ramsey invigorated and developed a whole system of administrative direction and control during the thirteenth century.   A large part of this administration functioned on a simple, though minutely organized, plane of accounting.   Upon one hand there were 'standards' of account — the catalogues or calendars.   These gave the number of seigneurial dues expected from the manors,[83] especially the sheriff's aid and small food farm items —

---

[78] See further, Chapters VI and VIII.

[79] There were only the large manors of Shillington, Houghton, Barton, Cranfield, and Girton not at farm in 1201, of some twenty manors belonging to the abbot. While such figures must be used with caution, the *redditus* from non-farmed manors in the 1254 vacancy account (£32.10s.9d.) seems to be about the same as that in 1201 (£32.2s.0d.) which suggests that only a few manors were being directly exploited.   The farmer is as obviously the contractor in the mid-thirteenth-century extents for Houghton, Hemmingford, and Stukeley, as was the case in the twelfth century.   See further, footnote 80 of this chapter.

[80] See Appendix D, and compare with Chapter III, Section II.   When a term of years was given, the farm contract seemed to be for about seven years in the thirteenth century;

e.g. lease of Wimbotsham, Dunham Market, the Hundred and one-half of Clacklose in 1262, or agreements concerning Hemmingford or Ellington, esp. *Carts.*, II, 244 ff.   It is doubtful, however, whether a farm conception should exclude the general 'custody' functions of the villeins (see Section II, this chapter).

[81] *Carts.*, II, 231; the abbot's revenues that entered the treasury were usually handled by a receiver.   For the receiver's revenue, see *infra*, Table XXVII.   The few extant treasury rolls suggest a decline in the receiver's importance at least from the 13th century (*ca.*1300 — £504.10s.2d; 1318 — £121.4s.7d.; 1425 — £86.13s.6d.).

[82] E. g. H. W. SAUNDERS, *An Introduction to the Rolls of Norwich Cathedral Priory* (Norwich, 1930); R. A. L. SMITH, *Canterbury Cathedral Priory*.

[83] E.g. *Add. Ch.* 34758.

usually fowl, pork, mutton and corn to the value of about 10 shillings — that went regularly to the abbot. Another roll catalogued the conventual farm dues, with full details upon the days for payment of money rents as well as of the food items.[84] When the sale of works became a regular business a calendar of the works expected from each manor and their commutable value was also compiled.[85] This more static chain of catalogues and calendars was complemented on the other hand by various direct seasonal inquisitions. There is one fragment of a thirteenth-century *progressus* of Ramsey manors — March 17, Upwood; March 18, Wistow and Warboys; March 28, Slepe and Holywell, etc. — from which a report was made upon crop returns together with all the detailed allocation of corn for various manorial obligations.[86]

Against these *standards* of account would be measured those *actual* movements of goods and money, checked initially by the receipts or tallies of the reeves and other officials, and then preserved for the central account by such documents as the *solutiones firmarum* of 1272.[87] Despite the efforts to increase manorial productivity, or, from the close of the thirteenth century at least, to augment the revenues from money rents, this checking off of receipts within a framework of fixed standards remained the basic principle of accounting. Although it is difficult to make a comprehensive estimation from the few dozen *disjecta membra* that survive of the central administration, the main 'view of account' at Ramsey seemed to centre in the *status obedientiarum* and *status maneriorum*[88] rolls in which two groups of officials were directly concerned — the obedientiaries and the reeves. These rolls were presented to the Treasury as synoptic accounts of only three items — income, expense, balance. As such they would simply demonstrate whether or not the monastic administration and the manorial management were working on a solvent basis: how much was received by the obedientiary or reeve? had it been sufficient for allocations?

There survives none of those documents from the central office of Ramsey, if such ever existed, that have served as guides to policy or at least to an elaboration of the accounting procedure for some abbeys.[89] In turn, the obedientiary accounts, which are especially numerous from the late fourteenth century, present a disappointingly barren calculus of fixed rents. For, even from the late thirteenth century, stability in obedientiary accounts is beginning to reflect an insulation from direct economic trends, as may be seen in the following table:[90]

---

[84] E.g. *Add. Ch.* 39707.
[85] *Add. Ch.* 34341.
[86] *Add. Ch.* 34713.
[87] *Add. Ch.* 34710, 34711.
[88] E.g. *Add. Ch.* 34912, 39671, 39672, 39736.
[89] E.g. SAUNDERS, *op. cit.*, Chapters II-IV. Much more to be deplored, for purposes of this study, is the lack of notes outlining new programmes of centralized direction, such as have been found for Canterbury or Winchester.
[90] The accounts are from *Add. Ch.* 34652 and 34722. This stability in revenues is, of

course, a consequence of the major dependence upon rents and farms. While most of the obedientiaries received direct allocations of land, as has been noted above, it would appear that only the cellarer and chamberlain took an immediate responsibility in the administration of any manor. In the late thirteenth century the cellarer incorporated in his account the direct receipts from arable profits and the expenses for demesne maintenance for the manors of Over and Welles, though he received money rents from several other manors and the

TABLE XXVII

REVENUES FROM TREASURY ACCOUNT ROLLS

Obedientiary	*ca.* 1300	*ca.* 1318
Cellarer.................	£555. 13s.	£528. 10s. 8d.
Chamberlain..............	128. 2s.	131. 9s. 1d.
Sacristan.................	87. 8s. 1d.	94. 17s. 1d.
Infirmarian...............	12. 13s.	12. 3s. 8d.
Almoner..................	75. 7s. 8d.	80. 22s. 8d.
Receiver.................	504. 10s. 2d.	120. 24s. 7d.
Master of Works...........	37. 9s.	31. 8s. 4d.
Pittancer................	15. 1s.	14. 5s. 4d.
Custodian of the Chapel.....	12. 0s. 11d.	15. 14s. 8d.
Custodian of the Shrine......	32. 6s. 3d.	21. 18s. 7d.
Refectorian...............	produce	produce

But of one type of Ramsey administrative documents large numbers have survived. This is the manorial account roll, and as it reveals, albeit *post factum*, the story of most adjustments in manorial economic organization, and of the movements of produce as well as the simply administrative account balance, some further elaboration of its position is necessary.

Few mediæval institutions have elicited more attention and interpretation than the account roll. As the main structure of the Ramsey manorial accounts varied little from those studied in numerous manorial descriptions,[91] only some points of perspective that may be helpful in relation to the extensive use of account roll materials in the forthcoming chapters will be noted here. On the Ramsey estates the account roll was the major report of the manorial economy. As such it fully reflected the complexity which followed upon that conjunction in the same records, on one side, of returns from manorial small holdings held freely or simply at money rent and, on the other, of the centralized abbatial dispositions involving food rents and baronial jurisdiction. But below both these sets of entries there lay the basic complicated pattern determined by the demesne organization itself. Accordingly, the account roll told at once more and less than the story of demesne production. Such

---

large farms from the home manors (*Add. Ch.* 34710, 1278). The chamberlain had direct arable profits from Lawshall, and Girton, and stock and money rent payments from Slepe and Walton (*Add. Ch.* 34638, 1285).

[91] J. S. DREW, 'Manorial Accounts of St.

Swithin's Priory, Winchester, 1248-1400', *E. H. R.* LXII (1947), 20-41, and D. OSCHINSKY, 'Mediæval Treatises on Estate Accounting', *Ec. H. R.*, XVII (1947), 52-61 have been found useful, along with the relevant sections of those estate histories referred to throughout this study.

normal manorial returns as customary rents, entry fines, and hallmote profits were entered in the revenue column of the Ramsey accounts, though they bore no direct relation to demesne profits.   In the evolution of the manorial economy these incidents will be seen to provide useful guides to the shifting organization, obligations, and prosperity of the peasantry.

At the same time, the *compotus* remained an incomplete account of economic decisions touching the entire manorial life.   Supramanorial decisions only appeared in the account roll as consequences of long run changes in policy, such as the decision to reduce food rent liveries in the late fourteenth century. However, simple external interference in current affairs was rare over the period of main concern here.   From the late thirteenth century there appears to have been no investment in manorial capital of the large arable estates by the central authorities, beyond sheep flocks; at the same time impositions of extra livery were rare, and then usually scrupulously concerned with avoiding dilapidation of demesne capital.   In addition, the intermanorial movement of stock inscribed on the account rolls was both insignificant and infrequent, and then carefully subtracted from the regular transactions.   As a result of all this, those annual administrative judgments that had to choose between extra investment in demesne capital and cash livery, or between full livery of the corn quota and diminished amounts available for seed, may be largely seen as they eventuated on the manorial level, whether they were decided originally by the monastery, by the steward, or solely by the reeve.   There are formative forces behind any large administrative complex.   Thus, even in the highly developed modern business corporation the account balance may fail to touch exactly the full exigencies of the profit picture: a 'declaration' of returns to shareholders moves within a set of discretionary arguments for ploughing back profits and for the promotional value of large share dividends — arguments which are not easily reducible to audit columns.   But within these parameters the business management moves with its own independence and initiative.   In analogous fashion, though subsidiary to the larger arguments of the monastic economy, and although not all manorial surplus moved in the money terms by which the balance was 'struck', too much must not be abstracted from the positive discretionary elements reflected in the manorial account roll.

The most obvious contribution of the account roll to economic history appears in the inventory of demesne stock and production.   The following statistical chapters are largely derived from this source, and are designed to bring out variations in capital, and movements of surplus over long periods. Considered as an annual survey, the account roll was, indeed, not far removed from the manorial 'farm' contracts, with their complex of extents and stock quotas.   The revenue column indicated, with varying degrees of detail, the regular customary and time rents due, and the exemptions or failures in their payment.   Particularly as the sale of works increased, the account roll itemized to the last subdivision of a unit the amounts of various seasonal works due.   From the earliest extant rolls, the description of initial stock of animals and corn, and of their increases and disposition to various uses, was very complete for the Ramsey accounts. But these documents were much more than surveys. The account roll was a *real* account, positing much responsibility on the manorial level, and revealing consequently much of the dynamics of adjustment to economic conditions. For an appreciation of this responsibility it must be recalled that the villeins were administrators who could and did act in concert to rent a large demesne, to administer the intricate decisions of 'champion' husbandry, to govern the active functioning of the hallmote. For example, a subsequent chapter will show that arable profits were maintained longer and with more consistency over generations of fluctuating returns in Ellington and Hemmingford manors, that were rented to the *villata* from the thirteenth century, than in other manors devoted to corn production under more direct monastic control. The same groups of villeins earned the indictment of the abbot for their efficiency in extracting profits through manorial courts.[92]

The farming of the demesne by the corporate body of customary villeins (*villata*) was of course known as early as Domesday, particularly for the manors of the Canons of St. Paul's Cathedral. When the larger body of the villeins were concerned in any case with every detail of work[93] on the demesne it would seem that an outright lease to them of the demesne might be a practical mode of eliciting responsibility. It was apparently unusual, however, for farms to be granted on such long terms as those given by the Canons of St. Paul;[94] the corporate functioning of the vill was so real, and their customary obligations to the demesne so clearly determined, that a formal contract would have been in most cases superfluous. In attempting, no doubt, to put a stop to the disintegration of the villeinage, the twelfth-century extents of Ramsey bring out quite clearly the group responsibility of the *villata*, or as it is called in the Barton extent, the *communitas villæ*. Even for an East Anglian manor like Higney, there is the service obligation on *all* tenants:

> Hæc est consuetudo ipsius villæ, scilicet Helingeie. Quod omnes homines totius villæ, cujuscunque tenuræ sint aut homagii, si firmarius voluerit, ter arabunt in hieme. Et ter in Quadragesima. Et habebit cibum suum, sicut statutum est, in curia. Et in Augusto, aut flagellabunt, aut metent, una die, ad cibum firmarii.[95]

[92] Court Rolls of Ellington, P.R.O. *Sc.* 2, *Port.* 179, 16, m. 2d, transcribed incorrectly as Elton in G. C. HOMANS, *English Villagers in the Thirteenth Century*, (Cambridge, Mass., 1942), p. 331. A large number of the sources for this study by Homans, which gives an interesting social and legal review of the virility of the 13th-century village unit, were taken from Ramsey manors. Note also how the farm agreement of Hemmingford manor made in 1279 for seven years with the men of Hemmingford (*Carts.*, II, 244-5) is more concerned with the abbot's judicial profits (*infra*,

Ch. VIII) than with a fear of incompetence in demesne management. The villeins were not to be subject even to the annual view of the bailiff: Quieti autem erunt de serviente in autumno singulis annis, præterquam in ultimo autumno, in quo habebunt servientem, per cujus visum, secundum consuetudinem abbatiæ, fiet implementum.
[93] See below, Chapter VII, Section I, for a discussion of the villein obligations in preparation and delivery of food farms and of works in general.
[94] See *supra*, Chapter III, Section II.
[95] *Carts.*, III, p. 289.

Commutations preserve the same corporate terms. At Graveley, for instance, *tota villata dat per annum octo denarios ad allec*; or the villagers receive wages in the same group fashion, as at Elsworth: *Dominus Abbas debet villatæ, postquam falcaverunt pratum, duodecim denarios.* The *villata* of Hemmingford, who held a certain meadow called Alvo for thirty shillings, illustrate, in turn, how the villagers could work together for their own advantage as well as at the behest of the lord.

The Ramsey administration did not neglect this villein expertise when the manors were being 'directly administered'[96] for profit. The village authorities, the reeves, were usually elected by the customary tenants (the election is often mentioned in fourteenth and fifteenth-century rolls), and this group commitment would serve as an initial guarantee for that co-operative effort so essential to the success of the open-field system. The fact that Ramsey reeves were always recipients of lands rather than wages would be another useful factor in this policy. Again, this office seemed to continue for long periods in the hands of one family, both in the extents where 'reeve' is almost a surname, and in thirteenth and fourteenth-century account rolls. The lord for his part could, of course, confirm or revoke the election of a reeve, but in the actual appointment a responsibility not far removed in nature from a custody was allowed, since, villein though he be, the demesne and stock were sometimes at least handed over to the reeve through the indenture contract.[97] He was, therefore, under obligation to maintain the stock, the conditions of cultivation, and of livery,[98] subject to directives from superior authority. Such directives did not spurn the reeve's valuable knowledge and experience; and the abbot frequently made the reeve even the personal executor of his allotments.[99]

[96] This phrase is employed here in its now traditional sense as a contrast to 'farming', though the central administration does not seem to distinguish farmed and non-farmed manors (see Constitution) — probably because of the 'food farm' payments from the home manors. As mentioned below, it would seem more proper to designate the reeve's administration as a type of 'custody' emanating from the self-administration of the traditional services and the payments of *feorm* to the lord and further determined by the contractual actions of the *villata* which were independent from the obligatory tradition (e.g. the farming of the whole or portions of the demesne). Some students of manorial history have called attention to the latter farming by the *villata*. See references by Marjory HOLLINGS, *The Red Book of Worcester*, IV, p. iv; and 'Communitas Villæ' by Joan WAKE, *E.H.R.* (1922), 406-413; or on *villata* administration, C. S. ORWIN, 'The Open Fields', *Ec. H.R.* (1937-8), pp. 133 ff.

[97] See example from Elton in App. E. This range of responsibility of the reeve over the maintenance of corn and stock capital was

very real. Even on those manors devoted to supplying the conventual farm the cellarer had to purchase from the reeve any foods he found necessary beyond his rent allocations for that year, even though the latter were below the farm quota.

[98] The organization at Ramsey would seem to be much the same as that of St. Peter's, Gloucester, where there is given the following description of the reeve's obligations with regard to the livery (*Cartularium Monasterii*, III, p. 108): Et præpositus qui malum misit brasium, in pœnam sui delicti bonum brasium emptum a braciatore de bonis suis propriis aquietabit. Et provideat etiam subcelerarius in quantum potest quod conventus jugiter cervisiam habeat defæcatam.

[99] *Cart.*, II, p. 229 (Abbot Hugh de Sulgrave, 1255-68): Ita tamen, quod propter assignationem omnium supradictorum, servientes vel præpositi subscriptorum maneriorum solvant, singulis annis, custodi feretri Sancti Ivonis, qui pro tempore fuerit, subscriptum redditum ad duos anni terminos, . . .

This position of the reeve comes out most clearly in his judicial functions. In the thirteenth and fourteenth-century court rolls of Ramsey manors it is common to find that the reeve and his chief assistant, the beadle, are to distrain for this or that offence, or they are distrained themselves for failing to distrain others, or they go pledge.   At the manor court of Broughton in 1301, for example, it is noted that the reeve and beadle did not distrain John King to show his charter for the one acre that he had bought from Richard Edward.   So John King is to be distrained to 'correct' his charter at the next court; and it is noted that he is a tenant of the lord and does 'fidelity'.[100]   In fact, it is clear from the records of Ramsey estates that this power of distraint is a logical consequence of the reeve's judicial responsibilities.   The reeve collected the heriots, fines for marriage, entry fines to lands, and fines for leave of absence from the manor; it was in the reeve's account roll, rather than in the manorial court rolls of the thirteenth and fourteenth centuries, that such seigneurial incidents were enrolled.[101]   While the hallmote prosecuted for torts and delicts at its frequent meetings, the standing authority, with judicial as well as administrative functions, remained the reeve.

This responsibility[102] of the reeve is again impressively remarked in the system of arrears.   The office carried a personal obligation — usually seen in such a form as Richard Onty owes the abbey so much because of a deficit in the balance, or occasionally the abbey owes the reeve so much for over-drawing.   Whether variations in marketing conditions and in villein incomes accounted for some of these debts, or for his ordinary turnover of business some 'cash on hand' would be a praticable policy, the fact remains that the reeve was personally responsible for the debt.   The apparent hazard in making a virgater or half-virgater responsible for the whole manor can only be explained away when one realizes how much reliance was placed upon the economic efficiency of the reeve and the co-operative machinery of manorial adminis-tration.   To make this responsibility real the reeve must have much freedom of action: the proceeds of customary rents and various sales of produce on the manor were employed by the reeve for his expenses.   No doubt the purchase of stock and expenditure on manorial production and upkeep allowed a similar

---

[100] *Ad. Ch.* 39913.
[101] For some abbeys, like St. Peter's, Glou-cester, it was clearly stipulated that all land transfers were only allowed through the hallmote — though it is not clear that they were to be enrolled (*Cartularium Monasterii*, III, 217): Item quod non permittatur consuetudinariis aliquas ex-cambias facere terrarum, pratorum, sive quorumcumque tenementorum sine licentia, et tunc coram halimoto.   The reeve still had wide jurisdiction on the manors of this abbey (*ibid.*, p. 219): Item, quod quilibet præpositus habeat potestatem concedendi cuicumque nativæ ut possit se maritare tam extra terram domini quam infra, acceptis tamen salvis plegiis pro ea de fine faciendo ad proximam curiam cum si forte præsentiam ballivi expectasset in

partibus remotioribus agentis casu interve-niente forte nunquam gauderet promotione maritali.
The reeve's jurisdiction was apparently the same for Ramsey estates (*Carts.*, II, p. 245): Nullus etiam custumarius finem faciat pro filiabus suis alleviandis, vel maritandis, absque nostra præsentia, sed coram nobis fiant gersumæ earum, præsentibus præ-positis, vel aliquibus de firmariis, qui dictam pecuniam habeant et colligant, versus firmam suam.
[102] H. S. BENNETT, *Life on the English Manor* (Cambridge, 1948), has some useful corrective remarks to make on the mislead-ing generalizations of Fleta and Walter de Henley concerning the duties of the reeve.   See especially pp. 166-168.

range of discretion. The reeve handled the profits of the manorial courts, sometimes allocating those profits to his expense account, although he usually handed on these amounts, and the larger livery from manorial sales and commutations, to the treasury in 'round sums'.[103] Finally, the steward presided at the manorial court and perhaps audited the account, but it was in the reeve's name that the account was drawn up and 'viewed' in the treasury roll.[104]

The reeve's account roll was the natural expression of a manorial system with its roots in the mutual obligations and advantages of champion husbandry. In the happier days before the fourteenth century, his accounting regimen illustrated reciprocal profits from this co-operative interdependence, for instance, with the large regular or piecework employment of villeins on the demesne, and the profitable renting of bits of arable and pasture to the villeins. When artificial controls began to be introduced to stabilize the profits of demesne production the villeinage reserves shrivelled. But even with the twilight of champion husbandry the reeve was already being forced to disappear from manorial administration; the period of his greatest responsibility had coincided with the era of greatest communal activity by the *villata*.

This chapter began with a study of the new Constitution for Ramsey Abbey which, however, was found to manifest more concern with improvements in the control of revenues than dissatisfaction with the traditional economic organization as such. The latter point was probably best borne out by the prevalence of the problem of loss of services and revenues until towards the mid-century, and the persistence to an important degree of the system of farming manors right through the century. But on the the whole the administrative emphasis pointed towards a more immediate control of increasing agrarian revenues. This was seen in the recovery or purchase of properties, the maintenance of more land directly in the hands of obedientiaries, and the indirect evidence for large increases in manorial capital and profits.

[103] Some good examples of the reeve's use of various types of revenue, seigneurial or market, and of his passing on debts to other villeins, may be seen in the payments of the heavy taxation in the late thirteenth century (Ch. VIII, Section II). While a distinction among *sources* of revenue can be useful for various purposes, those efforts to make an accounting distinction between revenues of demesne farming and seigneurial returns (see A. E. LEVETT, 'the Economic Organization of the Manor', *Ec. H. R.*, I, 1927, p. 69; or F. M. PAGE, *Wellingborough Manorial Accounts*, Northants. Record Society, 1936, pp. x-xii) are putting artificial limits to the actual revenue and profit disposition on the manor which can be seen in the commitments of the reeve.

[104] There is no direct evidence from Ramsey on the method of auditing the manorial accounts. Indirect evidence (especially the manner in which the reeves were accounted in the treasury) would suggest that the reeve appeared in person to render his account, like the obedientiaries, at the abbey; perhaps like the custom cited in Pantin, *Chapters of the English Black Monks*, III, p. 41 (no. 13): . . . nam ballivi et prepositi maneriorum coram deputatis et senioribus conventus ac uni perito maneriorum seculari annuatim compotum reddunt, quibus compotis redditis, celerarius vel administrans in compoto suo de receptis omnibus et singulis ad plenum respondet ac se onerat; . . .

However, it became evident that little could be seen of the concrete realities of the manorial economy by this level of inquiry. For example, even though farming persisted, the system was rendered flexible through the use of short term leases, or quasi-custodies by villeins. Furthermore, even in an era of rising prices the conventual farms could not be maintained, and we shall see in Chapter Eight that purchase of property was not always a sign of prosperity or even solvency at the abbey. Through the data of the following chapters we shall be able to penetrate to the local movements on Ramsey estates and approach more closely to the real terms of their economic development.

CHAPTER V

MANORIAL STATISTICS — I: LIVESTOCK

T HERE were thirteen manors in Huntingdonshire, all but four in one solid block of land, that had become intimately connected with livery to Ramsey, and were to remain most consistently under the direct administration of the abbey. These manors formed also an independent block in those details of inter-manorial supply and production that have been mentioned in various charters. Finally, it is for these manors that the most extensive account roll series have been preserved, covering, with considerable variations in continuity, a period of more than two hundred years. These Ramsey 'home' manors provide, accordingly, a unique opportunity for statistical studies of agricultural organization and production despite the grave *lacunæ* in the records of the central department.

The account roll *exitus grangiarum* was divided neatly into corn and livestock quotations, and the following two chapters have kept to the logic of this division. For convenience of space only those elements of the *exitus* which played a major rôle in manorial profits have been tabulated. This has meant neglecting the production of cheese and poultry-raising among other important manorial occupations.[1] The accompanying remarks are intended to be largely technical and descriptive, as aids to the presentation and interpretation of tables. The significance and analysis of trends will be dealt with in later chapters of this study.

An attempt has been made, where possible, in the following tabulations, to isolate the natural rhythm of manorial productivity. That is, beyond those infrequent excess impositions by the overlord,[2] or the occurrence of inter-manorial and supra-manorial subsidies in stock and seed, the attention is directed in these columns to the gradual build-up or decline of stocks and production over long and short periods. Finally, to facilitate the interpretation of gross figures by the more vital aspects of manorial life, some functional indices have been provided for ploughteams, vaccaries, and so on.

I

HORSES AND PLOUGH TEAMS

The manorial account roll summation of livestock opens with a detailed list of the working animals, the horse and the ox. In those earliest extant rolls,

---

[1] Considerable studies have been made of the typical details of milk, cheese, and poultry production in Nellie NEILSON, *Economic Conditions on the Manors of Ramsey Abbey* (Wistow), and especially by S. C. RADCLIFF, *Elton Manorial Records, 1279-1351* (Cambridge, 1946), Introduction.

[2] The impositions upon Upwood, during a

dated around the mid-thirteenth century, all horses were classified as the common stots, except for Broughton manor which boasted some carthorses. This manor, which often served as an entrepôt for liveries to the abbey from other estates, and was active as the seat of the hundred court and a residence of the abbot, may have had particular needs for the specialized animal. But by the late 13th century the carthorse was to be found listed in every manor. Sometime in the second quarter of the 14th century, the affrey replaced the stot, although there is nothing to indicate that this is more than a change in terminology.

Right after the horses come a large number of animals classed as oxen. The account roll stock data bear no references to plough teams as such, but it seems safe to conclude that at least the stot and the ox were thus employed. The low-bred stot was valued at the same level as the ox, whereas the specialized carthorse was worth considerably more, so the former two animals alone are here calculated as beasts for the plough. Although they include a quota for the plough teams expected from the demesne, the mid-thirteenth-century inquisitions fail to give the size of the team. For this figure, therefore, the evidence from twelfth-century extents has been used, or for manors such as Slepe and Abbots Ripton, where no 12th-century evidence is available, the mean average of eight is used. The proportionate numbers of horses to oxen in the teams seem to have undergone little change over the previous century,[3] though there is no longer any evidence to assume that the full team of oxen alone was being employed.

Some possible limitations of these tabulations might be observed. No doubt colts and steers were being set aside and trained for use on the plough sometime in the following year, but as these were not yet classified as stot or ox in the roll they have not been taken into the team picture of the present tables. In addition the farm manager's programme is necessarily pragmatic:[4] prospective sales or purchases of stock would turn upon seasonal needs, there would be, perhaps, variations in the size of the team according to stubble or pasture ploughing, there might even be the employment of the carthorse or cow on the field to take full advantage of a dry interval in a wet season or the slack carting season at the time for spring ploughing. The more powerful and ironshod carthorse would surpass the efficiency of the stot or ox, so that some reduction in the size of the team would become possible. With his greater speed, the horse, and perhaps above all the carthorse, would be more

---

year when a visit of the king's children created an extra demand, show that the tax by the abbot's kitchen was not a heavy burden on the major livestock. This livery was, of course, exclusive of the cellarer's farms. It is summarized from *Add. Ch.* 34672 (1348-1349?): 6 wethers, 1 ewe, 3 lambs, 4 sk', 18 goats, 8 porkers, 2 heifers, 14 geese, 16 hens, 54 chickens, 259 pigeons, 266 eggs.

[3] See Appendix C, *infra*.

[4] There would also be variations in the demesne ploughing stock if the villeinage was undercapitalized, since several extents permit the villein to convert his plough-works to something else if he has no plough or plough beasts (e.g. *Carts.*, I, 415, 419, 487). Miss Neilson's words should be recalled in this context: "The total amount of work was distributed according to the number of ploughs, demesne and in villeinage, of the manor, not according to the number of villeins." (*op. cit.*, p. 31.)

suitable to the lighter cultivation implements, especially the harrow.[5] But in the final analysis the heavy carting and ploughing season that followed Michaelmas, makes the inventory a 'working picture' of manorial teams.[6] Indeed, a more detailed study of stock movements shows no tendency towards depletion in total numbers of horse and ox over the winter season, with a correlative increase in the spring.   So the following tables contribute towards the total picture of the numbers of animals to be fed on the manor over the winter, as well as providing an inventory of the work animals employed.

[5] The Crowland manors illustrated another variation in the ploughteam combinations: "There were some ploughteams on the manors, and, contrary to the usual practice, the stronger animals were put to the cart for a few years and returned to the plough-team when past their prime." (Mildred WRETTS-SMITH, 'Organization of Farming at Croyland Abbey, 1257-1321', *Journal of Economic and Business Review*, IV, 1931-2, 190).   Even as late as the 19th century, six or eight horses were being used for summer fallow ploughing over much of Hunts. (R. PARKINSON, *General View of the Agriculture of Huntingdonshire*, London, 1811, p. 102).

[6] In so far as fluctuations in seasonal numbers of stock can be traced in the Ramsey manorial accounts it may be suggested that there was no great reduction at the 'Martinmas slaughter'; cf. also W. G. HOSKINS, *Essays in Leicestershire History*, (Liverpool, 1950), p. 174.   But, in any case, the account rolls were drawn up before this season, and as remarked above (Chapter IV), such rolls provided a sort of workable 'stock and corn' bond for the incoming reeve.

TABLE XXVIII

PLOUGH TEAMS AND HORSES

S. indicates the stot, O. the ox, H. the horse, and T. the team. The bracketed figure before the number of ploughteams represents the actual number of animals by which the account stock failed to reach this round number; the bracketed figure after the team number gives the amount by which account stock exceeded this number.

For all manorial statistics, unless otherwise stated, the date is that from the first year of the account roll. In Ramsey documents, C generally indicates a long hundred until the fifteenth century.

13th-century data for Broughton probably include King's Ripton.

Year	Wistow						Upwood						Broughton						Year
	S.	O.	H.	−	T.	+	S.	O.	H.	−	T.	+	S.	O.	H.	−	T.	+	
1244	—	—	—	—	—	—	—	—	—	—	—	—	10	25	3	(3)	4	—	1244
1247	12	17	0	(3)	4	—	14	24	0	—	5	(3)	8	21	6	(1)	3	—	1247
1250	13	20	0	—	4	(1)	13	18	0	—	4	(3)	9	29	6	(2)	4	—	1250
1252	12	16	6	(4)	4	—	14	21	0	—	5	—	—	—	—	—	—	—	1252
1297	6	12	6	—	3	(1)	—	—	—	—	—	—	—	—	—	—	—	—	1297
1307	6	25	6	(1)	4	—	—	—	—	—	—	—	—	—	—	—	—	—	1307
1314	—	—	—	—	—	—	6	22	7	—	4	—	6	16	6	—	2	(2)	1314
1316	7	35	7	—	5	(2)	—	—	—	—	—	—	—	—	—	—	—	—	1316
1318	—	—	—	—	—	—	9	?	6	(3)	—	—	—	—	—	—	—	—	1318
1319	7	—	6	—	—	—	6?	12	6	—	3	—	10	?	5	—	—	—	1319
1324	8	4	6	(4)	2	—	—	—	—	—	—	—	7	12	6	(1)	2	—	1324
1326	—	—	—	—	—	—	—	—	—	—	—	—	—	—	—	—	—	—	1326
1335	5	21	6	—	3	(2)	6	13	8	(2)	3	—	—	—	—	—	—	—	1335
1340?	4?	15	6	—	2	(3)	—	—	—	—	—	—	—	—	—	—	—	—	1340?
1342	—	—	—	—	—	—	—	—	—	—	—	—	6?	13	5	(1)	2	—	1342
1343	—	—	—	—	—	—	6	24	6	—	4	(2)	—	—	—	—	—	—	1343

TABLE XXVIII (*Cont'd.*)
PLOUGH TEAMS AND HORSES (*Cont'd.*)

Year	Broughton S.	O.	H.	T. −	T. +	Upwood S.	O.	H.	T. −	T. +	Wistow S.	O.	H.	T. −	T. +	Year
1351	—	—	—	—	—	—	—	—	—	—	6	26	7	(2)	4	1351
1357	—	—	—	—	—	6	23	6	—	4 (1)	4	11	5	(1)	2	1357
1368	—	—	—	—	—	6	18	6	—	4	—	—	—	—	—	1368
1371	—	—	—	—	—	—	—	—	(4)	—	—	15	6	—	2 (3)	1371
1378	6	19	4	(5)	3	—	—	—	—	—	—	—	—	—	—	1378
1379	4	16	4	—	2	—	—	—	—	—	4	15	6	—	2	1379
1380	—	—	—	—	—	—	—	—	—	(4)	—	—	—	—	—	1380
1384	—	—	—	—	(3)	8	13	7	—	3	—	—	—	—	—	1384
1385	6	17	5	—	2	4	14	5	—	2	—	—	—	—	—	1385
1386	—	—	—	—	—	3	18	5	—	3	4	24	5	(4)	4	1386
1388	—	—	—	—	2	—	—	—	—	—	5	24	6	(3)	4 (3)	1388
1389	5	14	3	(1)	—	—	—	—	—	—	4	15	6	—	2 (4)	1389
1392	—	—	—	—	—	3	10	5	(1)	2	4	16	6	—	2	1392
1393	—	—	—	—	—	—	—	—	—	—	—	—	—	—	—	1393
1394	—	—	—	—	—	—	—	—	—	(1)	—	—	—	—	—	1394
1406	—	—	—	—	—	4	18	6	(1)	3	—	—	—	(3)	—	1406
1408	—	—	—	—	—	5	15	7	(2)	3	4	9	5	—	—	1408
1412	—	—	—	—	—	6	20	12	—	4	7	12	5	—	2	1412
1419	—	—	—	—	—	3	16	9	(2)	3	—	0	3	—	2	1419
1420	—	—	—	—	—	—	—	—	—	—	—	0	1	—	2 (3)	1420
1422	—	—	—	—	—	—	—	—	—	—	7	—	—	—	—	1422
1445	—	—	—	—	—	—	—	—	—	—	1	—	—	—	—	1445
1456	—	—	—	—	—	—	—	—	—	—	—	—	—	—	—	1456
1466	—	—	—	—	—	—	—	—	—	—	4	9	6	(3)	2	1466

TABLE XXVIII (*Cont'd.*)

PLOUGH TEAMS AND HORSES (*Cont'd.*)

Year	Slepe S.	Slepe O.	Slepe H.	Slepe –	Slepe T.+	Abbots Ripton S.	Abbots Ripton O.	Abbots Ripton H.	Abbots Ripton –	Abbots Ripton T.+	Holywell S.	Holywell O.	Holywell H.	Holywell –	Holywell T.+	Weston S.	Weston O.	Weston H.	Weston –	Weston T.+
1297	6	18	4	—	3 (1)	11	30	8	—	5 (1)	5	12	8	—	2 (1)	9	15	6	—	3
1307	6	19	4	—	3 (3)	—	—	—	—	—	—	—	—	—	—	—	—	—	—	—
1309	—	—	—	(4)	3 (3)	—	—	—	—	—	—	—	—	—	—	—	—	—	(3)	3 (4)
1311	6	21	4	—	3 (4)	—	—	—	—	—	—	—	—	—	—	8	20	6	—	—
1313	6	26	4	—	3	11	21	6	(1)	4	—	—	—	—	—	—	—	—	—	—
1314	5	15	5	—	3	8	23	6	—	4	5	13	8	—	2 (2)	8	13	6	—	3
1324	3	19	5	—	3	—	—	—	—	—	—	—	—	—	—	—	—	—	—	3
1342	4	24	4	—	—	—	—	—	—	—	5	21	9	—	3 (2)	—	—	—	—	—
1351	—	—	—	—	—	—	—	—	—	—	8	19	6	—	3 (3)	—	—	—	—	—
1352	—	—	—	—	—	7	22	6	(1)	4	—	14	11	(1)	2	—	—	—	—	—
1356	—	—	—	(2)	—	—	—	—	—	—	—	—	—	—	—	6	13	5	(3)	2
1362?	—	—	—	—	—	—	—	—	—	—	—	—	—	—	—	—	—	—	—	—
1364	—	—	—	—	2	7	21	5	(3)	4	—	—	—	—	—	—	—	—	—	—
1366	4	9	5	—	—	—	—	—	—	—	—	—	—	—	—	—	—	—	—	—
1369	—	—	—	—	—	4	18	4	(1)	3	2	8	6	(3)	1 (2)	—	—	—	—	—
1371	—	—	—	(2)	3	—	—	—	—	—	—	—	—	—	—	—	—	—	—	—
1375	—	—	—	—	—	—	—	—	—	—	—	—	—	—	—	—	—	—	—	—
1381	3	23	5	—	—	6	4	13	(4)	2	—	13	10	—	2	—	—	—	—	—
1383	—	—	—	—	—	—	—	—	—	—	—	—	—	—	—	—	—	—	—	—
1385	—	—	—	—	2	—	—	—	—	—	—	—	—	—	—	—	—	—	—	—
1387	4	10	4	—	—	5	12	5	—	2 (3)	—	—	—	—	—	—	—	—	—	—
1388	—	—	—	—	—	5	13	6	—	2 (2)	—	—	—	—	—	—	—	—	—	—
1390	5	11	4	—	2	—	—	—	—	—	5	7	6	—	2	—	—	—	—	—
1394	5	9	5	—	2	4	13	5	—	2 (1)	6	8	7	—	2	—	—	—	—	—
1395	—	—	—	—	—	6	21	5	—	3 (3)	6	10	5	(4)	2	—	—	—	—	—
1396	—	—	—	—	—	—	—	—	—	—	6	11	5	(2)	2	—	—	—	—	—
1399	—	—	—	—	—	—	—	—	—	—	5	—	1	—	1 (1)	—	—	—	—	—
1401	—	—	—	—	—	—	—	—	—	—	—	—	—	—	—	—	—	—	—	—
1402	—	—	—	—	—	—	—	—	—	—	—	—	—	—	—	—	—	—	—	—
1404	—	—	—	—	—	—	—	—	—	—	—	—	—	—	—	—	—	—	—	—
1405	—	—	—	—	—	—	—	—	—	—	—	—	—	—	—	—	—	—	—	—
1416	4	4	4	—	1	—	—	—	—	—	—	—	—	—	—	—	—	—	—	—
1417	5	14	5	—	2 (3)	—	—	—	—	—	—	—	—	—	—	—	—	—	—	—

TABLE XXVIII (Cont'd.)

PLOUGH TEAMS AND HORSES (Cont'd.)

The bracketed figure before the number of ploughteams represents the actual number of animals by which the account stock failed to reach this round figure; the bracketed figure after the team number is the amount by which account stock exceeded this number.

S. indicates the stot, O. the ox, H. the horse, and T. the team.

Year	Houghton					
	S.	O.	H.	−	T.	+
1307	14	28	6		5	(2)
1319	16	3	6		2	(3)
1326	10	16	6		3	(2)
1336	7	21	5		3	(4)
1365	6	13	6		2	(3)
1369	6	14	5	(4)	3	
1371	6	14	5	(4)	3	
1372	6	13	6		2	(3)
1380	5	12	5		2	(1)
1383	4	9	5	(3)	2	
1387	4	12	5		2	
1388	5	16	6	(3)	3	
1389	4	15	5		2	(3)
1392	5	10	6	(1)	2	
1393	5	10	6	(1)	2	
1395	4	10	5	(2)	2	
1403	6	6	6	(4)	2	
1404	4	4	6		1	
1405	4	6	5		1	(2)
1406	4	6	5		1	(2)
1407	4	6	5		1	(2)
1410	4	6	5		1	(2)
1419	4	5	6		1	(1)
1445	0	0	12			
1449	0	0	12			
1450	0	0	12			
1451	0	0	12			
1453	0	0	12			
1454	0	0	12			
1460	0	0	4			

TABLE XXVIII (*Cont'd.*)

PLOUGH TEAMS AND HORSES (*Cont'd.*)

For all manorial statistics, unless otherwise stated, the date is that from the first year of the account roll. In Ramsey documents *C* generally indicates a long hundred until the fifteenth century.

Year	Warboys			Year	Elton		
	S.	O.	H.		S.	O.	H.
1250	11	18	0	1286	10	18	2
1255	10	14	0	1297	8	19	3
1307	4	21	6	1311	8	25	4
1318	6	6	6	1313	9	31	4
1324	7	18	7	1324	11	21	4
1335	4	22	6	1345	8	24	4
1336	6	21	6	1349	8	16	4
1342	6	21	6	1350	8	19	4
1344	4	15	6	1360	9	17	4
1346	4	15	6	1380	6	13	4
1348	4	23	6	1383	4	15	5
1353	5	21	7	1387	5	10	4
1354	4	20	7	1392	4	14	4
1359	4	32	6	1422	4	12	5
1360	4	25	6	1443	4	12	5
1362	4	34	6	1448	0	4	2
1363	4	30	6	1451	0	4	2
1366	3	21	5	1452	0	4	2
1371	1	15	2	1461	0	0	2
1373	3	14	5				
1374	4	13	6				
1375	4	16	6				
1377	4	16	5				
1378	3	15	6				
1379	4	15	6				
1393	4	12	6				
1404	3	10	6				
1413	4	14	6				

II

CATTLE

All age and sex groups of cattle were tabulated in the annual account. But the use of younger stock for food or work appears to have been rare, so there is no real objective to be gained in tabulating separately the cumbersome data upon *juvenci, juvencula, boviculi, bovicula*, etc.   In order to have some notion of the size of herds for the winter feeding problem, however, all the cattle, from the oxen and cows to the youngest calf, are included in one total figure.   These total stock tables also show the devastation from disease, and the very great gradualness with which stock were often rebuilt, when almost entirely dependent upon natural reproduction.   Evidence of a disease among cattle comes out strikingly in the rolls for 1319: in Broughton there were only six remaining while a total of 48 was given as dead of the disease; 56 died in Houghton; in Upwood, where only four cattle had died of natural causes in 1316, there were 45 *mortua* in 1319 leaving only two cows.   The effect of this catastrophe on ox teams can be seen in Table XXVIII.   Only after twenty years did the stock totals approximate again those in the first decade of the 14th century.

As only a carcass or two, probably sometimes supplied from stock that had died from natural causes, were necessary for annual meat supplies, the most important function of cattle after supplying the ox teams, was the vaccary.   The maintenance of ox teams by purchase was not infrequent; and surprisingly enough upon first consideration for a region where rich marsh grasses abounded, the vaccary never became an important commercial enterprise on the Ramsey estates.   The milk was used mostly for making cheese; there is no evidence of the use of milk from sheep or goats for this purpose.   Even though most of the livery of this item to the cellarer had been commuted by 1250, few cheeses remained for sale after the manorial uses had been supplied.

The herd of cows rarely numbered over two dozen.   With this herd there was always one bull on each manor, and it is impossible to estimate the fertility of these herds; only on one roll does the remark appear that 'nearly all the cows were sterile this year'.

With the break-up of the old food rent system after the Black Death, the vaccary ceased as a cheese producing unit, and the cows were left to 'run in the marsh with their calves'.   This serves indeed as a vital clue to the conservative development of the vaccary: the abundant marsh grasses were at some considerable distances from the manor for convenient pasture for milch cows, and winter hay does not seem to have been of an abundance to ensure a very great surplus after the feeding of horses and oxen.   The fens were to develop largely as sheep pasture in the Ramsey economy.

Table XXIX

CATTLE

v.—vaccary; s.—total herd.

Year	Wistow v.	Wistow s.	Broughton v.	Broughton s.	Upwood v.	Upwood s.	Slepe v.	Slepe s.	A. Ripton v.	A. Ripton s.	Holywell v.	Holywell s.	Year
1244	—	—	12	47	11	46	—	—	—	—	—	—	1244
1247	21	70	—	—	8	36	—	—	—	—	—	—	1247
1250	—	52	—	73	7	39	—	—	—	—	—	—	1250
1252	15	51	—	111	—	—	—	—	—	—	—	—	1252
1297	—	69	—	—	—	—	—	—	—	—	—	—	1297
1307	—	87	—	—	—	—	16	60	29	91	—	—	1307
1309	—	—	—	—	—	—	20	60	—	—	—	—	1309
1313	—	—	—	—	—	—	21	76	—	—	—	—	1313
1314	—	—	—	24	15	51	19	70	—	—	—	—	1314
1316	—	93	—	—	2	10	—	—	—	—	—	—	1316
1319	—	15	—	6	5	26	9	36	11	43	4	21	1319
1324	19	54	—	—	—	—	—	—	—	—	—	—	1324
1335	—	—	—	—	—	—	—	—	—	—	—	—	1335
1336	21	74	—	36	7	35	—	—	13	34	—	—	1336
1340?	20	78	—	—	19	67	—	—	—	—	—	—	1340?
1342	—	—	14	44	—	—	26	64	—	—	—	—	1342
1351	—	—	—	—	4	72	22	78	—	—	—	—	1351
1352	—	—	—	—	—	—	—	—	—	—	—	—	1352
1356	—	—	—	—	—	—	—	—	—	—	26	109	1356
1357	—	—	—	—	—	—	—	—	5	30	—	—	1357
1364	16	52	—	—	—	—	10	47	—	—	18	59	1364
1366	—	—	—	—	—	—	—	—	—	—	—	—	1366
1368	—	—	—	—	—	—	—	—	8	50	—	—	1368
1369	—	—	—	—	—	—	—	—	—	—	—	—	1369
1371	—	—	—	—	5	32	—	—	—	—	7	28	1371

Year	1	2	3	4	5	6	7	8	9	10	11	12
1375			38	7								
1378									47	8		
1379											54	12
1380									46	11		
1381	46	8	40	12	83	20						
1383												
1384			44	11			82	21				
1385			44	11			75	18				
1386			41	12	80	27	103	20	61	12		
1387												
1388					86	33					73	20
1389			52	10			81	24	31	1	60	17
1390			55	10	110	32						
1392											51	13
1393											52	12
1394												
1395												
1396												
1399	67	22									48	11
1401	64	23										
1402	65	19					37	12				
1403							33	8				
1404	75	21										
1405	71	25										
1406							42	6				
1408	38	17										
1409	38	17			94	34						
1412												
1417											29	5
1419											25	4
1422											?	3
1445												
1449												
1450									3	2		
1456									3	2	8	4
1466											28	6

TABLE XXIX (*Cont'd.*)

CATTLE (*Cont'd.*)

Elton

Year	v.	s.	Year	v.	s.
1286	15	21	1380	16	60
1297	29	79	1383	19	52
1311	20	85	1387	11	54
1313	23	95	1392	21	57
1324	17	61	1422	11	28
1345	22	70	1443	11	28
1349	22	86	1448	1	8
1350	27	69	1451	1	8
1360	18	64	1452	1	8
			1461	1	3

Warboys

Year	v.	s.	Year	v.	s.	Year	v.	s.
1250	7	40	1353	24	82	1377	11	46
1255	?	57	1354	21	90	1378	14	49
1307	19	70	1359	15	101	1379	12	43
1318	17?	?	1360	20	95	1393	10	41
1324	16	65	1362	35	123	1404	11	46
1335	17	57	1363	28	92	1413	8	38
1336	17	73	1366	15	55			
1342	22	72	1371	14	47			
1344	11	60?	1373	12	56			
1347	26	85	1374	9	55			
1348	30	96	1375	10	49			

Houghton

Year	v.	s.	Year	v.	s.	Year	v.	s.
1307	8	69	1392	12	42	1453	0	3
1319	4	9	1393	12	47	1454	0	3
1324	8	56	1395	11	37	1460	3	4
1336	14	56	1403	10	33			
1338	8	70	1404	6	24			
1365	9	44	1405	6	22			
1369	6	41	1406	5	20			
1371	10	41	1407	6	22			
1372	12	46	1410	4	17			
1380	12	46	1417	8	23			
1383	14	46	1445	0	3			
1387	11	61	1449	0	3			
1388	16	73	1450	0	3			
1389	16	75	1451	0	3			

III

HOGS

With the extensive forests supplying plenty of pannage the hog had been an important animal on Ramsey estates from earliest times. Bacon was a product employed extensively for local manorial needs as well as in livery of food rents. This livery of bacon, as was the case with cheese, had been for the most part commuted by the 13th century. Along with the cellarer's bacon supply the abbot's kitchen received three or four flitches a year from most manors, and upon extraordinary occasions, as for instance in 1297, this demand might be raised to twenty or thirty animals.

Besides all the supplying of these food requisites, there was a regular sale of fifteen or twenty hogs from each manor which gave an important boost to the money income. Since the hog was such a basic item of sale and internal consumption the fluctuations in gross numbers of animals remaining at Michaelmas that have been tabulated below reflect much more than vicissitudes in natural reproduction. There were occasionaly such 'natural' vicissitudes, as in Broughton during 1342 when forty-five animals died of disease. But the evidence of much disease mortality is very rare. As purchase for re-stocking was unusual, the renewal of herds of swine must have depended largely upon the one boar and three sows which appeared regularly as the Michaelmas quota on these large manors.

TABLE XXX

HOGS

s. — total

Year	Wistow	Brough-ton	Upwood	Slepe	A. Ripton	Holywell	Elton
	s.	s.	s.	s.	s.	s.	s.
1244	—	69	—	—	—	—	—
1247	63	—	49	—	—	—	—
1250	53	60	—	—	—	—	—
1252	12	65	—	—	—	—	—
1286	—	—	—	—	—	—	73
1297	66	—	—	—	—	—	70
1307	122	—	—	87	81	—	—
1309	—	—	—	70+	—	—	—
1311	—	—	—	—	—	—	110
1313	—	—	—	85	—	—	123

Table XXX (*Cont'd.*)

HOGS (*Cont'd.*)

Year	Wistow	Brough-ton	Upwood	Slepe	A. Ripton	Holywell	Elton
	s.	s.	s.	s.	s.	s.	s.
1314	—	59	—	—	—	—	—
1316	—	—	82	—	—	—	—
1319	—	74	82	—	—	—	—
1324	87	—	103	74	96	12	130
1326	—	40	—	—	—	—	—
1335	60	—	—	—	—	—	—
1340 ?	97	—	75	—	—	—	—
1342	—	66	117	—	123	—	—
1345	—	—	—	—	—	—	104
1349	—	—	—	—	—	—	113
1350	—	—	—	—	—	—	68
1351	103	—	—	106	—	—	67
1352	—	—	—	129	—	—	—
1356	—	—	—	—	—	207	—
1357	—	—	97	—	—	—	—
1360	—	—	—	—	—	—	103
1364	—	—	—	—	74	73	—
1366	—	—	—	78	—	—	—
1368	66	—	—	—	—	—	—
1369	—	—	—	—	72	—	—
1371	—	—	32	—	—	34	—
1375	—	—	—	—	87	—	—
1378	—	64	—	—	—	—	—
1379	79	—	—	—	—	—	—
1380	—	68	—	—	—	—	114
1381	—	—	—	43	—	—	—
1383	—	—	—	—	—	73	87
1384	—	—	94	—	70	—	—
1385	—	—	88	—	—	—	—
1386	—	102	80	—	—	—	—
1387	—	—	—	67	—	—	68
1388	70	—	—	—	99	—	—
1389	102	—	—	—	—	—	—
1390	—	—	—	69	90	—	—
1392	—	73	64	—	—	—	69
1393	89	—	—	—	—	—	—
1394	75	—	—	69	—	—	—
1395	—	—	—	—	75	—	—

TABLE XXX (*Cont'd.*)

HOGS (*Cont'd.*)

Year	Wistow	Brough-ton	Upwood	Slepe	A. Ripton	Holywell	Elton
	s.	s.	s.	s.	s.	s.	s.
1396	—	—	—	—	77	—	—
1399	—	—	—	—	—	77	—
1401	—	—	—	—	—	73	—
1402	—	—	—	—	—	67	—
1404	—	—	—	—	—	79	—
1405	—	—	—	—	—	85	—
1406	—	—	72	—	—	—	—
1408	—	—	59	—	—	—	—
1409	—	—	—	—	—	29	—
1412	—	—	87	—	—	21	—
1417	—	—	—	62	—	—	—
1419	31	—	—	—	—	—	—
1420	—	—	57	—	—	—	—
1422	11	—	—	—	—	—	14
1443	—	—	—	—	—	—	14
1445	14	—	—	—	—	—	—
1448	—	—	—	—	—	—	7
1449	—	23	—	—	—	—	—
1450	—	23	—	—	—	—	—
1451	—	—	—	—	—	—	4
1452	—	10	—	—	—	—	7
1461	—	—	—	—	—	—	7
1466	27	—	—	—	—	—	—

Warboys

Year	s.	Year	s.	Year	s.
1250	68	1347	113	1373	93
1255	77	1353	114	1374	80
1307	105	1354	110	1375	55
1318	110	1359	102	1377	67
1324	33	1360	92	1378	72
1335	57	1362	105	1379	56
1336	50	1363	91	1393	55
1342	68	1366	77	1404	85
1344	97	1371	61	1413	42

TABLE XXX (Cont'd.)

HOGS (Cont'd.)

Houghton					
Year	s.	Year	s.	Year	s.
1307	71	1389	87	1445	24
1324	93	1392	71	1449	25
1336	98	1393	77	1450	25
1365	69	1395	57	1451	25
1369	90	1403	38	1453	25
1371	66	1404	21	1454	25
1372	87	1405	30	1460	8
1380	72	1406	30		
1383	73	1407	30		
1387	81	1410	38		
1388	91	1417	18		

IV

SHEEP

As sheep farming was pre-eminently a market project directly responsible to the abbey department which handled the collection and sale of wool, the manorial account roll gave a much more fleeting picture of the overall management of flocks than is obtainable for other species of livestock. Throughout the latter half of the 13th and during at least the first half of the 14th centuries, the reeve was concerned mainly with some six or eight carcasses used for manorial sustenance and livery, and the carcasses, hides and skins of dead animals which were sold from the manor. As far as the valuable wool was concerned, the reeve merely sent the fleeces, unweighed and unvalued, to Ramsey.

The documents do not reveal when this centralized marketing of wool was first organized. The account series may open upon a transition stage in the mid-thirteenth century. For the fen manors (Chatteris, Hilgay, etc.) and some clayland manors (Therfield, Broughton, Warboys) show at that time a sale of wool taking place through the hands of the reeve on the manor itself. But for most of the Huntingdon manors (Wistow, Upwood, Abbots Ripton, Houghton?) no sheep flocks are mentioned at all, or these are practically negligible (9 at Upwood in 1252, 28 at Abbots Ripton in 1252). The maintenance of considerable flocks on some of these manors would not seem to have turned directly upon the recovery of vast stretches of marsh by the abbey at this date (cf. *infra*, Section V), for Wistow and Upwood commoned in the fens with Warboys, and 'could' support considerable flocks according to the extents of *ca.* 1250 (*supra*, Table XXV, in Chapter IV). It would be unusual to find that disease or civil war had decimated some manors while those immediately contiguous were unaffected, so it remains to conjecture that a central department handled both the stocking and marketing accounts of the sheep in some areas at this time.

In any case there is no doubt about the disposition of sheep flocks towards the close of the thirteenth century. When the sole surviving account of the central department at the abbey is taken as supporting evidence to the rolls (*infra*, Table XXXII), it is clear that the sheep farming on Ramsey remained disposed towards the manorial grouping rather than becoming concentrated in one large specialized sheep run as had been sometimes a feature of Benedictine management.[7] The reason for this seems fairly obvious. Nearly every Ramsey manor participated in fen rights and included substantial meadows within its boundaries, so the winter foldage accessible on manorial flats and fallow and sometimes the hay which was preserved to feed other livestock, were the determining factors in this decentralization, while commoning in the large summer marsh and fen pastures would provide the practical advantages of centralization over drier seasons. Indeed, the precarious nature of fen pasture would argue strongly in favour of a manorial dependence; and the manors seem to have maintained their own shepherds to guide the flocks far up into the drying meres. At the same time, Table XXXII makes clear that sheep raising was less important for the non-fen manors, in particular the Bedford manors of Cranfield, Barton, Pegsdon and Shillington.

The account roll data remain, therefore, of vital importance to the history of sheep farming on Ramsey, and tables have been constructed to show the size of flocks remaining at Michaelmas, as well as the number of fleeces sent annually to the abbey. Only occasionally were a few fleeces kept on the manor for local usages. The peak period for flocks was in the spring when, with more pasture drying up, ewes were purchased for their wool and lambs, and young lambs were arriving; but the Michaelmas totals usually bear a fairly close approximation to the numbers of fleeces. The manorial data are equally important for a picture of the natural reproduction rate among the manorial flocks, and the number of new lambs reported have been tabulated for some manors as illustrations of natural increase.

The decline in size of flocks was nearly always due to natural causes rather than sale or consumption, so the frequent downtrends in the size of flocks

---

[7] See F. M. PAGE, 'Bidentes Hoylandie', *Economic History*, I, pp. 603 ff., although this concentration was more common to Cistercian sheep runs. The sheep flocks often grew as an appendage to the old demesne core of the Black Monk manors. See R. A. L. SMITH, *Canterbury Cathedral Priory*, Ch. X, and E. M. HALCROW, 'Administration and Agrarian Policy of the Manors of Durham Cathedral Priory' (B. Litt. thesis, Oxford), Ch. 5. Crowland manors in or along the fens had little upland; the sheep of this monastery were concentrated at Welland.

serve as a guide to the incidence of disease, as well as to the capital problem of maintaining this valuable investment. As the sheep appears to have suffered more than any other animal from disease in mediæval times, it would be valuable to have some criterion of the mortality rate. In the Ramsey account sales it is easily observable that the major fluctuations in the number of pelts move in a very proximate order of magnitude to the numbers of those listed as 'dead from disease', when the latter are specified. In Holywell, for example, there were 342 hides in 1364 and 280 'dead', 105 hides in 1371 and 111 dead, 164 hides in 1409 and 128 dead, whereas the normal number of hides was 20 or 30. These proportions of mortalities from disease to hides might well be higher, since afflicted sheep would be killed off to save the flesh. But as hides were a more regular market item than carcasses, and were thus listed more consistently in either or both the sales column and the inventory than figures of those dead through disease, the tables of hides have been added for some manors as an index to the impact of natural deaths in manorial sheep stocking. It may be noted that 'murrain' decimated the lamb more than the sheep of any other age category, although a considerable number of ewes always seemed to die at the lamb-bearing season. At Houghton manor in 1393, for example, there were 53 lambs alone dead of disease, only six remaining as the seasonal *exitus*.

Largely because of the endemic 'murrain', rapid and substantial increases in the size of flocks had to be made by purchases. This varied in turn with the investment policy of the abbey. There seems to have been a considerable drop in the size of flocks on the Ramsey manors towards 1320, but with only light investment the flocks were slowly built up again towards the mid-century. With a new policy after the Black Death, however, the flocks were built up to record numbers by purchase over a few years. An epidemic took heavy toll of these flocks around 1370, but on most manors they were quickly replaced by purchase. From the third quarter of the 14th century all of the sale and purchase of sheep seems to have taken place through the manorial account, so that a more complete study of the maintenance problem can then be made. Through numerous payments for driving sheep from market it appears that Wisbech was a common source for Ramsey purchases.

TABLE XXXI

SHEEP

Year	Flock	Fleeces	Hides	Lambs	Sold	Bought
Holywell						
1307	421	210	9	40	—	—
1356	540	404	31	224	—	55
1364	264	353	342	—	—	21
1371	119	111	105	2	60	—
1383	431	375	23	81	—	172
1399	500	496	45	32	90	91
1401	491	485	23	32	47	40
1402	493	490	24	61	66	71
1404	527	541	11	45	59	65
1405	528	551	104	20	44	57
1409	0	143	164	—	—	107
Abbots Ripton						
1252	28	—	—	6	—	—
1307	271	202	53	27	—	29
1324	144	128	29	43	22	20
1342	210	174	22	—	16	20
1364	411	582	20	76	—	—
1369	500	?	—	—	—	—
1371 ?	291	284	121	—	—	—
1375	321	?	—	58	—	—
1385	306	211	33	101	—	55
1388	435	364	43	80	—	—
1390	384	370	50	66	—	3
1395	573	483	45	107	—	40
1396	871	613	74	207	—	55
Slepe						
1313	—	508	82	—	—	—
1324	149	110	16	—	—	—
1351	180	397	151	—	—	—
1352	405	322	—	—	—	—
1366	—	290	—	—	—	—
1381	—	250	—	—	—	—
1387	333	288	30	—	—	—
1390	287	—	—	—	—	—
1394	260	256	—	—	—	—
1417	504 ?	515	—	—	—	—

TABLE XXXI (*Cont'd.*)

SHEEP (*Cont'd.*)

Year	Flock	Fleeces	Hides	Lambs	Sold	Bought
			Houghton			
1307	375	291	68	—	—	—
1319	209 ?	176	—	28	—	—
1324	147	—	51	49	6	16
1336	232	—	—	45	—	27
1338	355	299	67	52	—	—
1365	491	—	—	80	—	40
1369	388	319	40	63	17	—
1371	174	128	215	21	7	—
1372	197	149	17	53	1	4
1380	576	—	—	130	3	2
1383	361	340	94	81	—	—
1387	554	—	—	109	—	4
1388	536	—	—	121	—	17
1389	554	—	—	95	—	—
1392	347	322	65	66	—	—
1393	288	303	60	33	43	—
1395	422	463	129	6	161	10
1403	280	—	—	—	—	—
1404	89	—	—	12	—	—
1405	352	360	—	20	—	—
1406	331	360	176	40	100	15
1410	119	—	—	—	—	—
1417	416	45	36	134	—	—
1445	120	—	—	—	—	—
1449	120	—	—	—	—	—
1450	120	—	—	—	—	—
1451	120	—	—	—	—	—
1453	120	—	—	—	—	—
1454	120	—	—	—	—	—
1460 ff.	0	—	—	—	—	—

TABLE XXXI (*Cont'd.*)

SHEEP (*Cont'd.*)

Year	Flock	Fleeces	Dead
		Wistow	
1307	215	100	—
1318	192	144	—
1336	246	?	136
1340?	219	160	164
1351	190	164	18
1352	231	188	—
1368	286	249	—
1379	418	?	—
1388	221	?	—
1389	306	?	—
1393	389	324	—
1394	468	400	—
1419	353	259	—
1422	0	0	—

Year	Flock	Fleeces
	Upwood	
1252	9	0
1325	192	?
1357	344	323
1371	74	?
1385	265	264
1386	279	249
1392	249	225
1406	414	348
1408	299	255
1414	448	?
1420	60	0

TABLE XXXI (*Cont'd.*)

SHEEP (*Cont'd.*)

Year	Flocks	Fleeces	Ewes	*Exitus* (Lambs)
		Elton		
1286	153	118	49	38
1297	182	103	73	54
1311	623	492	218	175
1313	620	521	219	161
1324	249	206	88	44
1345	365	356	60	130
1349	246	?	113	70
1350	300	237	94	75
1360	448	514	160	64
1380	243	?	54	52
1383	268	328	121	66
1387	453	?	134	121
1392	420	?	156	124
1422	220	?	121	?
1442	220	?	121	?
1447	140	—	—	—
1451	140	—	—	—
1453	140	—	—	—
1461	140	—	—	—

Year	Flock	Fleeces	Bought	Sold
		Broughton		
1244	181	118	13	33
1250	215	120?	?	?
1252	71	?	3	2
1314	231	218	13	23
1319	134	?	?	?
1325	82?	?	16	12
1342	214?	247	8	15
1378	257	?	27	11
1380	175	210	34	44
1386	332	?	0	0
1392	262	233	0	0

TABLE XXXI Cont'd.)

SHEEP (Cont'd.)

Year	Flock	Fleeces
Warboys		
1252	223	?
1307	162	?
1318	206	165
1324	195	145
1335	301	?
1336	328	255
1342	149 ?	156
1344	255	215
1347	241	180
1348	243	203
1353	290	186
1354	423	271
1359	705	621
1360	918	748
1362	1,005	894
1363	267	228
1366	393	332
1371	187	138
1373	348	?
1374	339	313
1375	163	?
1377	241	259
1378	514	397
1379	579	459
1393	638	538
1404	675	582
1413	441	290

TABLE XXXII

GROSS WOOL LIVERY TO THE ABBEY (1361) *

* From *Add. Ch.* 39720.

Manor	Fleeces	Weight		
Therfield.............	513	1½ Woolpacks,	6	stones
Bigging..............	532	2 ”	9	”
Abbots Ripton.........	1,132	4½ ”		
Elsworth.............	562	2½ ”	4	”
Graveley.............	304	1 ”	10	”
Knapwell............	274	1½ ”		
Slepe...............	617	2½ ”	5	”
Upwood.............	464	1½ ”	6	”
Warboys.............	749	3 ”	4	”
Holywell.............	643	2½ ”	12	”
Houghton............	541	2 ”	5	”
Wistow.....	494	1½ ”	12	”
Broughton............	763	3½ ”	3	”
Weston..............	574	2 ”	7	”
Bythorn.............	199	1 ”		
Shillington...........	275	1 ”	3	”
Pegsdon.............	131	½ ”	1	”
Barton..............	180	½ ”	6	”
Elton...............	433	1½ ”	6	”
Burwell.............	274	1 ”	5	”
Cranfield............	232	(?	?	)

V

PASTURE LANDS

In Domesday the marsh appurtenant to Holywell (one league by one league) and Warboys (one league by one-half league) manors had alone received mention, though even these were not evaluated. There is no evidence that such lands entered into the economy of the manors at all. The fen area generally was only accounted in terms of its fishery value to the abbey itself in 1086. It is difficult to place a precise date upon the beginning of a large scale movement by Ramsey Abbey to exploit the fens for pasture. Many of the twelfth-century lawsuits of the abbey involving these properties were concerned with fisheries rather than fen pastures. For example, the Cistercian monks at Sawtrey were forced by a legal decision of 1192 to block up trenches detrimental to Ramsey fisheries between Whittlesey Mere and Uggmere.

But the foundation of commoning rights in the fens was very ancient,[8] and inquests were being made into the bounds of Ramsey and Thorney rights in Whittlesey during the twelfth century.[9] Such subsidiary manors as Little Raveley and Niddingworth, which became more noticeably associated with Wistow and Holywell respectively over the twelfth century, included considerable fen properties. Probably all the manors were gradually bringing more lowlands into use under the initiative of farmers and tenants. A comparative tabulation of the cartloads of hay livery due to the cellarer in the late eleventh century, set off against the livery requisites given in a document of the early thirteenth century, may supply one criterion of this evolution, as well as incidentally illustrating the early importance of fen hay for winter feeding.

TABLE XXXIII

FEN LIVERY DUE THE ABBEY (CARTLOADS)

Manor	ca. 1095	ca. 1200	
	Fen	Fen	Forage
Houghton	5	15	5
Slepe & Holywell	10	15	8
Warboys	5	10	5
Wistow	5	15	5
Upwood	5	15	5
Abbots Ripton	5	15	5
Elton	5	15	—
Ellington	5	—	—
Total	45	100	33

The fen frontier was well in the limelight of the thirteenth-century profit farming re-organization by the abbey. Such new acquisitions as the isle of Higney and Bodesheye were almost entirely investments in the fens. But the dozen Huntingdon manors themselves needed extensive pastures in order to carry some hundred head of stock and three to four hundred sheep as an

---

[8] N. NEILSON, *A Terrier of Fleet, Lincolnshire* (Oxford, 1920), Introduction, 'Intercommoning in Fenland', p. xxxviii.

[9] *Red Book of Thorney*, Cambridge University Library Ms, fols. 166 ff., and 173 ff.

average on each. The actual system of intercommoning in the fens has already been well reviewed by Miss Neilson,[10] so it will not be further discussed here. Those notorious lawsuits undertaken between Ramsey and her neighbours to stake out now more precisely the former unknown wilds of the fen show something of the vastness of these marsh pasturelands: in 1281 there were 3,800 acres of marshland in dispute against Ely and Thorney, and in 1342 a settlement was reached involving 1,000 acres of marsh at Walton.

Such lawsuits, which became especially important from the second quarter of the thirteenth century, mark a new economic phase in the fenland rather than a simple descent into litigation. Like the farmers of the Lincolnshire fens in the sixteenth century,[11] the thirteenth-century plaintiffs began to force the defendants to give up common rights,[12] to restrict common rights,[13] or, as was the case with Ramsey's suit of 1281, to claim a *quid pro quo* in the neighbours' fens by the writ *quo iure*, as the need for more pasture was being felt.

The rise of concentrated sheep farming in the south-western fens[14] is an intriguing question. In Lincolnshire[15] the fens were associated with dairy farming, while sheep were restricted to the salt marshes along the coast. The water grasses of the more southerly fens were traditionally noted for cattle herds in manorial charters,[16] and in the ancient regulations of intercommoning in the fens rents were usually mentioned solely in terms of cattle.[17] The heavier concentration of sheep flocks in the south-western fens from the thirteenth century by Ramsey and her neighbours[18] must be looked upon as a new phenomenon — a phenomenon probably due to large scale organized drainage of the fen marshes.[19]

[10] NEILSON, 'Intercommoning in Fenland', especially Chapter II, and Map following p. 214.

[11] Joan THIRSK, 'Lincolnshire Farming Regions', an unpublished chapter of a forthcoming book which the author has kindly placed at my disposal.

[12] NEILSON, 'Intercommoning in Fenland', p. xxxiv.

[13] *Ibid.*, p. xxiv. And from the Ramsey *Carts*: e.g. the Weremeremore — Episcopus et abbas concesserunt . . . totus prædictus mariscus dividatur in duas medietates equales (I, p. 201); the concord between Ramsey and William Bardolf in 1281 *de separatione marisci* of Staplewere (II, p. 322): the settlement sometime after 1237 — nec dictus Abbas de Thorneye, nec ejusdem loci conventus, vel aliquis, nomine eorum, in prædicto marisco de Wardeboys, aliquam communam pasturæ, cum averiis vel animalibus suis, habere possint, . . . (II, p. 325); and concerning the marsh of Falche — vel super fossato facto inter ipsum mariscum et mariscum domini Abbatis de Thorneye (II, p. 327); of Ramsey Mere, 1224 — quæ pars est versus Rameseiam remaneat ipsi Abbati de Rameseia sine communa aliqua . . . et versus Faresheved, remaneat ipsi Abbati de

Thorneye . . . sine communa aliqua . . (II, pp. 364 ff.).

[14] No sheep flocks were given for the Hurstingstone Hundred manors in Domesday and in the twelfth-century extents sheep data are given for only half of these manors, never in greater numbers than 180. Contrast the tables of this chapter for the late thirteenth century.

[15] THIRSK, 'Lincolnshire Farming Regions'.

[16] Dairy cattle were especially important at the Ely manor of Doddington; there was a concentration of cattle at Crowland. See WRETTS-SMITH, *op. cit.*; and cattle kept at least their earlier proportionate importance to sheep in the Ramsey manors of the east fens over the thirteenth century (Chapter IV, note 34).

[17] NEILSON, 'Intercommoning in Fenland', xix, xxx, li.

[18] See F. M. PAGE, 'Bidentes Hoylandiæ'.

[19] E. H. CARRIER, *The Pastoral Heritage of Britain* (London, 1936), p. 35: "As a rule cattle rather than sheep are associated with a marsh pasture, as sheep suffer from footrot when on a damp lair. The Romney Marsh sheep, however, have apparently acquired immunity from this disease, . . possibly on account of efficient draining of the ground between the ditches, . . ."

The important question of fen drainage in mediæval times is badly in need of a thorough investigation. It has been too long taken for granted that mediæval fen drainage was a primitive, individualistic enterprise.[20] Two points may be suggested here from Ramsey documents. First, mediæval men were well capable of extensive drainage projects: the men of Holland drained a large area for arable at an 'early period' (12th c. ?);[21] and the Nene River was dammed near Outwell in 1301 in order to drain new lands for the manor of the Bishop of Lichfield and Coventry at Coldham (Cambs.).[22] Secondly, the opening up of the south-west fens to large scale sheep pasturing in the thirteenth century corresponds with the decisive drop in the water level of this area effecting the drying up of the old West Water (branching from the Ouse at Earith to flow into the Welney river). The extensive regional knowledge of fen hydrology, and the co-operation manifested in the lawsuit against the dam at Coldham manor, suggest very strongly that the blocking of the old more sluggish fall towards Wisbech in order to turn the flow to the Wash through Kings Lynn was not a freak development from a local ditch at Littleport, but a large scale co-operative enterprise by west fen interests.[23]

Unfortunately the most positive evidence only appears with investigations by the sewage commissioners, and in lawsuits from the late thirteenth century. The tracing of the earlier constructive development of fen pastures must turn upon an elaborate and interrelated study of the charters of the region.[24] As one side of intercommoning, the co-operative drainage of the fens was an equally real tradition.

At least from the time of Domesday, each manor had a sizeable meadow field too, which was probably used for the ploughteams and vaccary. As

---

[20] See L. E. HARRIS, *Vermuyden and the Fens* (London, 1953), Ch. I, where the 'primitive and elementary' mediæval drainage works are mentioned. Unfortunately Professor Darby (see especially Cambs., V. C. H., II) has paid little attention to this need for fresh study of mediæval drainage history.

[21] NEILSON, 'Intercommoning in Fenland', p. xxxiv.

[22] *Carts.*, III, pp. 121-2: ..., quod cursus cujusdam aquæ, quæ vocatur Nene, ..., ratione desiccandi manerium suum de Coldham (in Elm), quod situatum est in terra maresca in comitatu Cantebrigiæ, obstruere fecit prædictum cursum apud Utwelle in Comitatu Nortffolciæ, de terra et sabulone, quod nullus est ibidem transitus navium seu navicularum versus portum de Lenne, sicut antiquitus consuevit ... A further plea mentions whether the dam could be constructed alio modo quam per obstructionem cujusdam aquæ vocatæ Weldam.

[23] The effects of the dam at Coldham were traced and evaluated by the plaintiffs from five counties (Norfolk — losses of £200 *per annum*; Cambridge — £200; Huntingdon — £10 to the king's lands and 600 marks to others; Lincoln — 1,000 marks;

Northampton — 50 marks). The judgment was against the lord of Coldham, and the expenses of removing the dam were disposed throughout the men affected in the four counties (see the account in *Carts.*, I, 74-77). The whole account of this lawsuit (*Carts.*, III, 121-157), serves as an interesting illustration of how the men of the time estimated to precise numbers of feet the effect of this dam on fen drainage twenty to thirty miles away. See selections from this inquest in Appendix F.

[24] The Ramsey Ms (B. M., Harl. 5071) provides useful data on drainage for use with the *Red Book of Thorney*, and the Ely Mss (Cotton, Claud.). The function of drainage for some manors of northern Huntingdonshire was summarized in a lawsuit of 1342 (*Carts.*, I, p. 175 ff.): Querelam diversorum hominum comitatus Huntedoniæ accepimus, continentem, quod diversæ ladæ et trencheæ in villis de Waltone, Sautre, et Conyngtone in eodem comitatu, tam pro salvatione partium illarum et terrarum, pratorum, et pasturarum hominum inibi morantium contra aquas dulces ibidem, descendentes, quam pro navibus et batellis quorumcunque hominum blada, turbas, et alias res ad diversa loca, etc.

the following table indicates, some of these meadows were expanded over the next couple of hundred years.

Manor	1086	*ca.* 1390
Table XXXIV		
DEMESNE MEADOWS ON SOME RAMSEY MANORS		
Broughton.............	10 a.	29 a., 3 r., 11.5 p(oles)
Slepe..................	60 a.	67 a., 13 p.
Abbots Ripton...........	16 a.	30 a., 1 r., 35 p.
Upwood................	6 a.	53 a., 18 p.
Warboys...............	3 a.	31.5 a., 30 p.
Wistow................	24 a.	26.5 a.

Despite the basic custom of intercommoning for the stock of villeins as well as freemen, there might be considerable variety in the economic employment of pasture lands, and from this various restrictions tended to arise. At Holywell, for example, there were eight meadows that could be mown, and one of these, Breyhurst, was to be mown for two years and in the third year left as pasture with the fallow (*et tertio anno jacebit ad pasturam cum warrectis*). After the grass had been cut anyone having horses could let them run among the hay cocks, although the animals were to be fenced in if they harmed these, and the cocks to be fixed up again.   Once the fen grass was removed, however, all from St. Ives, Niddingworth, and Holywell, could turn any animals into the flats.   On most of the Huntingdon manors of Ramsey the freemen and villeins enjoyed this privilege once the hay had been removed. In contrast, the meadows at Broughton were much more restricted: after removal of the fen hay only four animals of four ploughmen could be pastured with the lord's beasts; and if the lord sowed any part of the meadow that portion was to be enclosed.

The managers of the estates of Ramsey Abbey knew well how to exploit the lush grasses of the fen marsh.   At Holywell two marshes were to be cut twice a year in the proper season.   Many of the lower lying meadows could also be cut twice a year.   At Upwood, for instance, two of the ten meadow lots could be cut twice a year, but only in a wet year!   This dependence of the fen economy upon a sufficiency of moisture for the marshy grasses can easily be overlooked in light of the later emphasis upon drainage.   At Chatteris it was noted that the meadow of Hunneye was worth practically nothing because it had dried up; and since it had affected the rents, there was likely to have been a long run problem of water level, rather than merely an accidental dry season, behind this entry.

The rights to pasture in the woodland were equally varied, although there was usually a general permission for all to common in the woods except for one section set aside to pasture the lord's animals only. At Abbots Ripton, for example, there were two woods: and in Westwood everyone had pasture for herbage, but in the other wood, Hauland, there were no common rights. At Upwood certain freemen could pasture in the lord's separate wood.[25] On the other hand, there seems to have been in practically no instance the right to feed pigs freely on the forest mast. The following table shows the pannage dues from villeins in several manors:

TABLE XXXV

PANNAGE RATES FROM THIRTEENTH-CENTURY EXTENTS

Manor	1 year old	½ year	Young pig	Sow & young
St. Ives	2d.	½d.	0	1d.
Holywell	1d.	½d.	0	0
Warboys	2d.	1d.	½d. (¼ year old)	0
Abbots Ripton	2d.	1½d.	1d. or ½ d.	0
Broughton	2d.	1d.	½d. (¼ yr.)	0
Upwood	2d.	1½d.	1d. (¼ yr.)	0
Wistow	2d.	1½d.	1d. (¼ yr.)	0
Shillington	pannage as they ought, if mast.			

It is interesting to find that the pannage is arranged as a source of revenue for the lord, rather than as a tax upon excessive demand for a limited amount of mast. At Shillington, the villein was obliged to use pannage from the lord's forest when there was any, and not from elsewhere. He was to pay what he ought, or to pay nothing if there was no pannage. At Upwood and Wistow a 'suitable price' was to be arranged if pannage was scarce. But on the Huntingdon manors pannage dues had almost become an annual tax on the villein's hogs. On these manors he had to pay the pannage in the following fashion: at St. Ives 'whether he fed his pigs at home or not, and whether mast was plentiful or not', at Holywell 'whether mast or not', at Warboys, Broughton, Abbots Ripton, Upwood, and Wistow, 'as long as there is a supply of mast, whether he keeps his pigs at home or not'.

[25] Broughton (*Carts.*, I, p. 332) provides one of the most detailed examples for the use of manorial woods: Ad dictum autem manerium pertinet unus boscus, qui dicitur boscus de Broughtone; pars cujus bosci vestitur tamen quota pertinet ad parvam Ravele, ut dicitur; in quo bosco omnes de Broughtone et Ravele minori, tam liberi quam villani, communicant cum averiis suis, praeterquam cum capris et porcis in tempore defensionis; et extra dictum boscum versus Ryptone remanet quaedam viridis placia domino ad pasturam separalem. In quo bosco nullus de viridi vel sicco capere potest sine licentia.

CHAPTER VI

MANORIAL STATISTICS — II: CORN

DESPITE the fluctuations in corn returns and the advent of large-scale pastoral farming, the cultivation of corn in the arable uplands remained the foundation of the abbey manorial system. As a consequence, considerable efforts have been made in the following tabulations, often at the risk of tedious gross summations, to present substitutes for the serious lack of yield and acreage figures in the thirteenth and early fourteenth-century rolls. On the other hand, few eccentricities appear in the account roll system of enumeration. The bushel in which the yield was calculated is translated into rings or quarters on every document. The ring — a measure comprising four bushels — was only translated to the more peculiar livery measurements in the *exitus* balance[1] when corn was sent to the monastery.

I

SEED AND YIELD

The first *responsio* or yield ratio to seed was entered on the account rolls only in 1324. Nevertheless, the amounts sown[2] are entered from the earliest account rolls, and although the harvest from this seed is rarely computable

---

[1] A document from among the Ramsey charters (*Carts.*, III, pp. 158-9) illustrates this livery system of measurement: Memorandum, quod octodecim communes ringæ faciunt unam magnam quarteriam; excepto Boreuuelle, quod facit viginti communes ringas, unam magnam quarteriam.

Et quattuor communes ringæ, duo busselli, faciunt mittam gruti.

Et quinque communes ringæ brasei et præbendæ faciunt mittam.

Nota, quod mitta gruti debet mensurari sic: Videlicet, cum fuerit cumulata et imprimata per impressionem pugni usque ad cubitum semel per quatuor partes mittæ de residuo gruti per impiessionem, debet fieri circulus per exteriorem costeram mittæ, ad altitudinem palmæ, videlicet, ad summitatem pollicis, et denuo debet cumulari usque ad summum, quantum vas potest sustinere.

Et hoc facto, continet mitta gruti quattuor communes ringas, duos bussellos.

Mitta brasei eodem modo debet mensurari, excepto quod ultima cumulatio non debet fieri, nisi ad altitudinem pollicis, ut prius.

Et sic continent quinque communes ringæ mittam.

Mitta avenæ omnino sicut braseum debet mensurari.

Nota, quod septem disci cumulati de wouk' faciunt parvam mensuram rasam.

Quæ mensura, sexies impleta et iasata, facit unam mensuiam cumulatam.

Quæ mensura, sic mensurata, continet unam communem ringam de Huntingdonia. Since even the 'rased' measures are reduced to the ring there are no complications in these measurements. In any case the following tables have been calculated from the common bushel measure which never seems to have been a 'rased' measure when employed in the *exitus* totals.

[2] There is no evidence from the extents that the villeins used some of their own seed in sowing the demesnes of those manors for which statistical data are given in this chapter. The villein obligation of sowing with his own seed *ad hybernagium* is found only for some of the abbot's manors: Hemmingford (*Carts.*, I, 384; III, 276), Shillington (*Carts.*, I, 461), Stukeley (*Carts.*, I, 397), Ellington (*Carts.*, II, 24), Barton (*Carts.*, I, 475), King's Ripton (*Carts.*, I, 399); although this obligation was owed on the conventual manors as late as the

owing to the lack of rolls for consecutive years, over long periods the variations in amounts sown are so slight that major variations in productivity are traceable. This is also possible because the *exitus* data are fairly specific in their indication of the sources of the grain quantities therein enumerated, with the result that the gross output of various crops may be summated. Although the *exitus* specifies the demesne corn harvest in distinction from those various amounts left in the granary from the previous year, or derived from purchase, multure,[3] and intermanorial transfer, there were until the 14th century occasional sums of a dozen rings or so whose origin has not been specified. On the assumption that these sums derived from cultivation of some additional property for that year, they have been included in the gross yield. Such factors emphasize that the gross output figures are rough calculations only, but in any case, these variations from the certain harvest totals represent a very small percentage.

Table XXXVI has been constructed from each manor therefore, to illustrate, for the designated years, the gross returns from each type of grain harvested that year, and the amounts sown for the next year. As the gross figures offer at least a different visual picture of yield trends from the *responsio*, they have been carried on into the 14th century, to overlap considerably with these yield data. Although the variations in seed per acre among grains must not be forgotten, it has been thought useful to add some totals of all corn sown and harvested. In an economy where grains so often replaced each other and were inter-mixed in various uses gross production must have been an important factor.

It will be obvious from the following data on corn sown and harvested that a radical change had taken place on the Huntingdon manors of Ramsey

---

early thirteenth-century extents of Brington (*Carts.*, II, 44) and Elton (*Carts.*, I, 487). This villein obligation to sow some of the wheat on the lord's demesne would seem to have been commuted on other manors to the one bushel of *benesede* owed to the lord by the virgater (e.g. St. Ives, *Carts.*, I, p. 287).

[3] The multure payments were only received, of course, when the mills were not farmed. The only customary corn payments received in any amount were the fodder corn payments in oats (usually about 30 rings per manor). The tithe-corn, which can be an important consideration, especially in manorial statistics of corn yield (see R. LENNARD, 'Statistics of Corn Yields in Mediæval England. Some Critical Comments', *Economic History*, III, pp. 173-192), has been excluded from the following tabulations. The tithe-corn had been commuted for land on some Ramsey manors (e.g. Ringstead, Barton), and on others the harvest of a few acres was allocated for tithe payments in the same fashion as thirteenth-century food payments to abbey servants (*infra*, Ch. VII). These tithe payments were properly deducted by the reeve *after* his estimation of harvest returns. The tithe acreage was a fixed quota, and usually combined with a tax *pro schepa*. An entry for the Stukeley extent (I, p. 394) shows that this *schepa* (or *scepa*) was also a measure of wheat sown by the villein on the lord's demesne: Et ad seminandum illam dimidiam acram, dabit de frumento proprio octavam partem unius quarterii, scilicet unam scepam. With the tithe, this was commuted for one or two acres in the accounts from which statistics have been derived below. The tithe acres as given in the extents have been collected below, Table XLIV. There is no clear evidence in accounts for *Acrae Inbladatæ* (as payments to servants *at* the abbey), so these payments may have been commuted by the late 13th century. In any case for the purposes of this study, and even in themselves, such dues were a very small percentage of total corn production on Ramsey estates (see the example worked out for Wistow by R. LENNARD, 'Statistics of Corn Yields, Additional Critical Questions', *Economic History*, III, p. 339).

between 1250 and the early fourteenth century. There appear to have been two phases in this change: first, a total decline of corn sown on the demesne (Upwood, Abbots Ripton, Warboys, Wistow, Weston?)[4] between 1250 and 1300; and secondly, there was an increase in the total amount of corn sown on some manorial demesnes (Upwood, Warboys, Abbots Ripton, Wistow, Elton, Bythorn) over the generation after 1300. The latter increase came with a change in proportions of corn sown on all manors through the more extensive employment of legumes and barley. This was to become the standard crop rotation system on Ramsey manors from this time, and is illustrated in detail in the last section of this chapter.

Because of the paucity of evidence for Ramsey manors over the latter half of the thirteenth century, it is difficult to trace the first stage with any great chronological precision. Some indirect evidence will be adduced in Chapter VIII, to suggest that a depression in agrarian returns from Huntingdon manors was felt from the 1260's until the close of the century. This depression turned largely upon corn production, and the following tables show that the large amount of oats sown — about fifty per cent of all corn at Upwood, Wistow, and Abbots Ripton, ca. 1250 — had gradually dwindled to insignificance, or had disappeared altogether by the fourteenth century. The thirteenth-century decline in sowing of oats did not coincide with the considerable increase[5] in legumes and barley sown — since the latter increase only becomes important from late in the first quarter of the fourteenth century, and in most cases (e.g. Abbots Ripton, Wistow, Warboys) only moves in an inverse ratio to the decline in oats from that time. It is necessary to look beyond a simple change in the system of crop rotation for causes of the earlier change.

Some decrease in oat acreage may have occurred on marginal lands. The renting around 1250 of many small arable plots at Upwood for twopence an acre,[6] for example, may have meant that marginal lands were under production in the open fields. Since there were only occasional bits of coarse

---

[4] For two sets of grouped manors — Broughton and King's Ripton, Weston and Bythorn — it has not been possible to establish whether demesne lands sown on each manor were accounted in the mid-thirteenth-century grange rolls. As a consequence, these manors have usually to be omitted from the discussions of the next few pages.

[5] There was some increase in beans and peas sown on all manors ca.1300 in comparison with the mid-thirteenth century; but only at Warboys did this increase replace anything like the decline in amounts of oats sown over the half century. There is no evidence from the rolls that dredge was anything more than a new term for the corn mixture (wheat, barley, peas — though dragetum was usually a mixture of barley and oats in 14th-century accounts of Ramsey) classification employed ca.1250.

The amount of mixed corn had increased somewhat from the mid-thirteenth century, except at Broughton and Warboys where there was a considerable decline. But the increased sowing of this mixture over the hundred years (1250-1350) was never appreciable. The mediæval rye (that is, siligo; see Sir William ASHLEY, Bread of Our Forefathers, Oxford, 1928) has only been found employed on the Huntingdon manors of Elton and Holywell, and never gained a great importance or continuity in the cropping of these manors.

[6] Carts., III, 348-9. Of course the rent of small plots varied considerably. The occasional butts and forelands are awkward 'extra' plots, and expected to be cheaper. But generally it might be accepted that extra 'acre' holdings on Huntingdon manors were rented at a penny per rod in the mid-thirteenth-century extents.

gravel on Ramsey manors the geological structure gives slight *prima facie* reasons for marginal lands.[7]   Nor is there any evidence from thirteenth or fourteenth-century documents that unproductive 'outfields' were rested for long periods.   But the notion of marginal lands is relative.   On the heavy clay lands of Huntingdon the arable will be reduced to a medium pasture. ground today if there is not sufficient cultivation, drainage, and manuring.[8] Again, however, there are a number of factors which militate against this suggestion of an outfield in Huntingdon — a field less liable to the economic care and preparation given to the 'inland' at this time.   Some manors of similar terrain[9] did not so perceptibly change their sowing of oats in the second half of the thirteenth century; and the great variety in the rate of evolution of the rotation system of all manors contiguous or not, from 1300, suggests that the dramatic decline in oats sown on these one-half dozen manors after 1250, was too uniform for a natural causation.

The early date of the decline in conventual farms seems to give the most important clue for this transformation coming earlier on the Huntingdon manors facing the fen than in other Ramsey lands, or non-Ramsey lands in the district.   The abbot had taken these manors into his hands at this time,[10] and the sheep flocks were rapidly increased sometime over this same period (Ch. V), so some of the most available, if not less productive, demesne arable was probably turned into pasture.   The manors showing a large decline in cropping during the thirteenth century were clustered along the fen, and with little meadow available here, even fairly productive arable lands may have been necessary for winter pasture.

[7] The Norfolk brecklands were a proximate regional example of marginal land cultivation. See J. SALTMARSH and H. C. DARBY, 'Infield-Outfield System on a Norfolk Manor', *Economic History*, III, pp. 30-44.
[8] F. W. FRYER, *The Land Utilization Survey of Britain, Huntingdonshire*, p. 417.
[9] See Warboys and Broughton. The sample table of seeding at Graveley given *infra*, illustrates, by the large proportion of dredge employed, how variations occurred on clay lands within a few miles of the Huntingdon manors.   Professor Darby (V.C.H. Cambs., II, p. 61) has given an interesting table of variations on types of seed with soil differences along the south-west fen border (14th century): Graveley on the extreme west was on clay; Kennett in the east, on a light gravelly soil; Dry Drayton, Oakington, and Cottenham, forming a continuous strip running from chalk to the clay; Great Shelford, on chalk and clay; and Soham, on the edge of the fenland:

PERCENTAGES OF TOTAL AREAS SOWN

Manor	Wheat	Barley	Rye	Dredge	Maslin	Oats	Peas
Cottenham	16	7	18	—	25	25	9
Dry Drayton	40	8	3	—	6	30	13
Oakington	25	—	—	37	8	8	22
Kennett	11	29	20	—	—	33	7
Shelford	25	33	—	15	22	3	2
Soham	17	22	3	13	13	9	23
Graveley	30	38	—	—	—	7	25
Total	23.4	19.6	6.3	9.3	10.6	16.2	14.3

[10] See *supra*, Ch. IV, Section I.

Nevertheless, while the advent of commercial sheep farming may have been the occasion,[11] or the most apparent turning point, in the history of corn production, it does not explain the inertia and long run trend in the arable economy from the thirteenth century.[12]

[11] As a supporting corollary to the previous paragraph it may be noted that arable cultivation was intensified on some manors along the fens *ca.* 1310 (see Ch. VIII), whereas the sheep flocks were left in fewer numbers than for previous decades (see Ch. V). Nevertheless, this suggestion concerning the origin of the change in arable cropping remains very much an hypothesis. Some nearby manors (Dry Drayton, Oakington) of Crowland Abbey, for which the seed data have been tabulated below, illustrate that the oat was a very high proportion of total seed in 1267 (the approximate time of the abbot's holding of these home manors at Ramsey). But for the Crowland manors, too, there has been a drastic decline in amounts sown by the late thirteenth century. The evolution in crop rotations was thus at work at least from the last quarter of the thirteenth century in this region. But the decline in oats (and barley) was largely replaced by dredge (barley and oat mixture) at Oakington; while a few miles away into the midlands from the Huntingdon manors, another Crowland manor (Wellingborough) continued to give a heavy emphasis to oats until well into the 14th century.

[12] See Ch. VIII, Section I. I am under obligation to Professor Postan and members of the Seminar on mediæval agrarian problems at the Institute of Historical Research for reviewing some of the above points by discussion.

In the following table (XXXVI), the dots indicate that data are available for these entries, but have been omitted, since such material is presented more clearly by the following table of yield ratios (Table XXXVII).

TABLE XXXVI

SEED AND YIELD (Quarters and Bushels)

W. = Wheat; B. = Barley; O. = Oats; R. = Rye; B. & P. = Beans and Peas; M. = Mixed; D. = Dredge.

Upwood

Year	Seed						Year	Yield					
	W.	B.	O.	B.&P.	M.	Total		W.	B.	O.	B. & P.	M.	Total
1247	79	15	139	4	13	250	1247	264	98	308	6	85	761
1250	56	11	123	3	10	203	1250	158	78	365	21	30	652
1252	40	8	125	4	15	192	1252	198	84	237	21	116	656
1299 ?	35	21	47	12	16	131	1299 ?	212	85	76	38	58	469
1302 ?	35	14	74	14	21	158	1302 ?	125	48	88	50 ?	48	359
1306	36	19	47	13	21	136	1306	155	118	147	55	85	560
1312 ?	28	20	35 ?	?	19	?	1312 ?	175	131	67 ?	?	47	?
1319	34	17	49	20	17	137	1319	170	114	51	58	58	451
1324	45	27	36	21	17	146	1324	125	100	55	68	55	403
1326 ?	37	20	36	21	17	131	1326 ?	112	120	75	62	56	425
1343	29	20	28	28	17	122	1343	192	108	36	72	31 ?	439
1384 ?	9	36	0	23	0	68	1384 ?	.	.	.	.	.	.
1385	13	27	0	20	0	60	1385	57	344	0	64	0	465
1386	15	31	0	20	0	66	1386	57	178	0	53	0	288
1392	15	33	0	27	0	75	1392	58	223	0	64	0	345

Wistow

Year													
1408	13	33	0	26	0	72	1408	·	·	·	·	·	·
1412	5	54	.0	27	0	86	1412	·	·	·	·	·	·
1420	11	45	0	26	0	82	1420	·	·	·	·	·	·
1247	38.4	16	99	0	0	153.4	1247	263.2	125	267.6	0	0	656
1250	36.4	14.4	86.4	3.6	6.5	147.7	1250	158	104	301	28	57	648
1252	37.4	19	84	4.4	7.6	152.6	1252	220	133	264	17	0	634
1297	30	11	62.4	10.4	15.4	129.4	1297	196	50	93	37	49	415
1298	34.4	—	—	—	—	—	1298	—	—	—	—	—	—
1307	32	19.4	28.4	10.4	19.4	110	1307	181	140	101	59	85	566
1311	41.4	32.4	39	17	27	157	1311	211	91	68	47	72	489
1315	31.4	16	—	—	—	—	1315	—	—	—	—	—	—
1318	41	15.4	54.4	18.4	15.4	145	1318	137	66	90	61	52	406
1335	32	27	23	29	16	127	1335	106	108	23	135	105	477
1346	37	18	7	34	13	109	1346	91	121	8	147	84	451
1351	—	18	18	35	21	—	1351	—	127	7	54	65	253?
1352	39	18	7	34	13	109	1352	—	—	—	—	—	—
1368	37	—	5	31	0	—	1368	—	227.4	—	104.2	0	332?
1379	17	31	3	39	0	90	1379						
1388	19	46	4	37	0	106	1388						
1389	19	44	4	36	0	103	1389						
1393	16	49	4	33	0	102	1393						
1394	18	40	4	25	0	87	1394						
1403	19	50	4	31	0	104	1403						
1419	7	—	0	30	0	—	1419						
1422	—	—	0	17	0	—	1422						
1423	5	60	0	30	0	95	1423						

TABLE XXXVI (*Cont'd.*)

SEED AND YIELD (Quarters) (*Cont'd.*)

Warboys

Seed

Year	W.	B.	O.	B. & P.	M.	Total
1250	47.2	12.2	58	3.1	44	164.5
1254	42.2	18.4	56.3	3	27.2	147.3
1307	42.6	19.2	38.6	20	19.4	140.2
1316	46.3					
1318	42.7	23.7	41.3	20.5	21.1	149.7
1324	41.2	8.3	35.5	24.5	12.6	122.5
1328	41.7	32.1			12.1	
1335	34.1	29	47	16.1	0	126.2
1341	38.2	20.3	30	29.3	10	128
1342	38.7	16.2	26.5	27.7	10.5	120.2
1343	34.5	29.5	29	23.5	0	116.7
1344	29.6	26	21	25.5	0	102.3
1346	34.5	26.7	16.5	34.6	0	112.7
1347	31.3	33.3	15.5	28.6	7.1	109.1
1348	30	33	12.5	32.3	6	115.1
1353	?	28.3	22.2	23.2	0	
1356	36.6	35.5	12.2	28.6	9.3	113.3
1359	32.4	21	11.3	43.1	10.4	117.3
1360	32	28.6	11.4	32	?	114.6
1363	28.2	?	?	24.1		
1366	22.2	34.7	11.2	30.1	0	98.4
1371	26	31.2	3.6	28.1	0	89.1
1373	23.7	44.6	3.5	32.2	0	104.4
1375	?	29.2	0	24.3	0	
1377	17.2	30.5	0	25.1	0	73
1378	20.2	27.1	0	26.3	0	73.6
1379	13.5	25.4	0	13	0	52.1
1393	13.7	40.1	0	41.1	0	95.1
1404	25	55.1	0	27.2	0	107.3
1413	16	43	0	33.4	0	92.4

Yield

Year	W.	B.	O.	B. & P.	M.	Total
1250	182.6	131.5	133.4	36	155.6	639.5
1254	277	128.1	171.3	28.6	176.2	781.4
1307	177.2	143.1	59.6	56	80.7	517
1316	126.7					
1318	284.5	164.7	68.4	70.7	74.6	663.5
1324	125.1	162.5	37.6	75.2	51.1	451.7
1328	79.2	64.7			44.4	
1335	86.5	130.4	65	48	0	330.1
1341						
1342	194.7	162.5	87.4	75.2	55.5	575.7
1343						
1344						
1346						
1347						
1348						
1353						
1356						
1359						
1360						
1363						
1366						
1371						
1373						
1375						
1377						
1378						
1379						
1393						
1404						
1413						

Elton

Seed

Year	W.	B.	O.	B. & P.	D.	R.	Total
1286	43.3	57.7	46.5	7.7	0	0	155.6
1297	47.6	60	56.6	11.1	7.6	3.2	186.5
1311	43.6	70	44.1	12.1	0	7.6	177.6
1313	42.4	88.6	45.5	15.2	0	2.2	194.3
1324	37.4	70.4	62.7	18.6	0	6.1	196
1345	?	79.4	?	23.4	0	0	—
1349	43.4	100.1	19	7.4	0	0	170
1350	35	85.1	13.4	7.5	0	0	141.2
1380	27.1	70.2	5.4	31.6	0	0	134.5
1383	?	73.7	7	33	0	0	—
1387	23.7	55	9.3	29	0	0	117.2
1392	22.6	70.2	7.3	30.2	0	0	130.5

Yield

Year	W.	B.	O.	B. & P.	D.	R.	Total
1286	132	259	109	31.4	38.4	0	570
1297	243	245	112	32	7.4	20.4	660
1311	186	446	92	42	0	14	780.4
1313	179.4	462.4	81	76.4	0	32	831.4
1324	162.4	452	143.4	72.4	0	0	830.4
1345	?	373	72.4	45.4	0	0	—
1349	86	179	34	7.4	0	0	306.4
1350	85	167	36.4	8	0	0	296.4
1380	.	.	.	.	.	.	.
1383	.	.	.	.	.	.	.
1387	.	.	.	.	.	.	.
1392	.	.	.	.	.	.	.

Broughton and Ripton Regis

Seed

Year	W.	B.	O.	B. & P.	M.	Total
1244	48	21	6	6	73	154
1250	49	20	11?	8	50 D.	138
1252	60	31	0?	14	72	177
1310	—	35?	—	—	61	—
1311	39	52	9	20	34	154
1318*	58	34	0?	25	72	189
1325*	28	11	0?	15	58	112
1341*	30	30	0?	—	34	—
1342*	37	23	0?	21	26	115
1344*	33	—	—	—	—	—
1346*	35	—	6	—	—	—
1378*	23	23	5	20	0	72
1380*	19	47	5	19	0	90
1386*	19	39	2	29	0	92
1392*	17	45	—	21	0	85

Yield

Year	W.	B.	O.	B. & P.	M.	Total
1244	202	148	12	53	234	649
1250	408	139	33?	?	109 D.	689
1252	318	235	0	91	469	1,113
1310	127	83	21?	23?	56	525
1311	173	158	?	73	121	404
1318*	110	109	0	41	144	—
1325*	76	—	0	55	99	(419)
1341*	—	—	0	—	—	—
1342*	159	202	0	58	140	302
1344*	—	—	0	—	—	311
1346*	138	145	17	67	0	424
1378*	73	193	18	51	0	459
1380*	49	210	19	78	0	
1386*	117	242	9	80	0	
1392*	128					

* Broughton manor only.

TABLE XXXVI (*Cont'd.*)

SEED AND YIELD (*Cont'd.*)

			Seed			
Year	W.	B.	O.	B. & P.	M.	Total

Abbots Ripton

Year	W.	B.	O.	B. & P.	M.	Total
1252	49	23	113	13	0	198
1307	38	30	56	16	0	140
1324	42	30	55	25	15	167
1342	44	48	48	48	0	188
1364	?	54	12	20	0	?
1375	20	32	20	34	0	106
1385	22	48	21	38	0	129
1388	22	62	21	?	0	?
1390	21	49	21	22	0	113
1395	16	41	21	?	0	?
1396	16	40	21	33	0	110

		Seed			
Year	W.	B.	D.	B. & P.	Total

Weston

Year	W.	B.	D.	B. & P.	Total
1252	57	0 ?	138	29	224
1297	39	22	52	22	135
1311	52	31	61	29	173
1324	43	38	63	33	177
1368	21	42	0	39	102

Bythorn

Year	W.	B.	D.	B. & P.	Total
1252	22	0	42	5	69
1297	19	13	22	12	66
1314	20	13	—	—	—
1324	22	25	26	15	88

TABLE XXXVI (Cont'd.)

SEED AND YIELD (Cont'd.)

			Seed			
Year	W.	B.	D.	B. & P.	O.	Total

			Slepe			
1307	31.5	22.4	25	10.1	39.2	128.4
1309	40	58.2	0	9	27.4	134.6
1313	30.5	25.3	0	13	45	114
1314	46?	42.4	—	—	—	—
1324	27.3	26.6	30.2	27.7	22.3	134.5
1345	41.1	—	0?	19	—	—
1351	24	43.1	0	25.5	5.6?	98.4
1366	21.5	62.5	0	34.2	4	122.4
1387	17	45.4	0	35.2	3	100.6
1394	—	—	0	29	3	—

			Seed				
Year	W.	B.	D.	B. & P.	O.	R.	Total

				Holywell			
1307	30.1	26.1	6	6.2	28.1	8.1	104.6
1324	20.1	42.1	0	14.7	16.5	10.5	104.3
1364	16.2	66	—	18.1	7	—	—
1371	20.4	39	0	16.4	2	0	78
1383	19	39.3	0	25.4	2.4	0	86.3
1399	20.1	40.3	0	30.5	2	0	93.1
1401	21.1	36.2	0	23.2	2	0.2	82.7
1402	17.4	35.2	0	20.2	2	0.4	75.4
1404	16.4	38.3	0	25	2	0.4	82.3
1405	18	34.4	0	21	2	0.4	76
1409	8.2	21.1	0	28.6	2	0.4	60.5
1410	7.6	21.1	0	6.5	0	0	35.4
1412	7.6	21.1	0	6.5	3	0	38.4

TABLE XXXVI (Cont'd.)

SEED AND YIELD (Cont'd.)

Year	W.	B.	D.	B. & P.	O.	Total
			Seed			

Houghton

Year	W.	B.	D.	B. & P.	O.	Total
1308	—	38.4	82.4	—	—	.
1316	50.5	0	125.3*	15.5	9.2	.
1319	—	0	128.3	30.3	—	.
1320	47.4	0	0?	—	—	.
1324	50.3	0	125.3	23.5	0	.
1334	46.5	0	106.1	28.2	0	.
1338	6?	44.1	63.5	24.1	0	.
1364	29.4	—	—	26	2.5	.
1372	27.2	73.5	0	24.5	3.1	.
1379	31.5	56.6	0	26.2	2	.
1383	—	87.6	0	22	0	.
1387	—	84.2	0	20.6	0	.
1388	35.4	59.4	0	24.2	1.4	.
1389	23.7	63.3	0	47.6	1	.
1393	—	74	0	19	0	.
1394	20.1	63	0	21	0	.
1396	28.1	60.5	0	30.6	0	.

* Barley was entirely mixed with dredge for the next few years.

Graveley (Cambridgeshire) *

Year	W.	B.	D.	B. & P.	O.	Total
1307	27.2	24.3	47.5	13.7	0	.
1314	30.6	0	68.4	13.5	0	.
1319	5.2	0	69.3	15.7	0	.
1324	24.2	0	72.1	10.3	0	.
1347	21.2	0	57	14.1	0	.
1358	42.2	0	0	15.4	0	.
1384	(46a.)	(58a.)	0	(40½a.)	(15a.)	.
1393	(52a.)	(65a.)	0	(37a.)	(8a.)	.

* These data are taken from V.C.H. Cambs., II, p. 61. It is there noted that Burwell (Cambs.) had 128 a. in wheat, 130 a. barley, 10 a. in oats, and 9 a. in peas in 1348.

TABLE XXXVI (*Cont'd.*)

SEED AND YIELD (*Cont'd.*)

SOME CROWLAND ABBEY MANORS

	Seed						
Year	W.	B.	B. & P.	O.	D.	R.	Total
Dry Drayton (Cambs.)							
1258	38	19	5	71.6	0	2	135.6
1267	41.4	13	7.4	91.1	0	0	153.1
1314	32	12	16	48	10.4	3	121.4
1322	20.3	0	17.3	37.4	4.5	11.4	91.3
Oakington (Cambs.)							
1258	14.5	10.4	3.2	19.5	0	5.4	53.4
1267	16.1	9	4.5	31.4	0	5.4	66.6
1292	18	12.4	5.5	2	7	4	49.1
1314	10	9	14.1	14.3	18.3	4	69.7
1322	12.7	0	13.7	7.4	34.1	0	68.3
1361	9.4	0	12.2	3.6	40.4	0	66

Table XXXVI (*Cont'd.*)
SEED AND YIELD (*Cont'd.*)

SOME CROWLAND ABBEY MANORS

Year	Seed							Total
	W.	R.	B.	Bolemon	D.	O.	B. & P.	
				Wellingborough				
1258	20.4	21.1	37	0	0	72.4	6	157.1
1267	29	23	40	2	0	60	5	159
1276	12.1	0	10.5	0	0	29.5	0	52.3?
1280	40.5	0	25.5	0	0	107	0	173.2
1281	33.1	0	29.4	0	0	96	0	158.5
1282	43.4	0	36	1	0	96	0	176.4
1283	25.4	13	30.4	0	0	100.4	0	169.4
1285	16.2	23.2	29	2	0	103.2	0	173.6
1289	40	0	42	0	0	101.4	3	186.4
1290	23.4	12	46.2	16	0	75.5	0	173.3
1291	16.7	17	33.2	0	0	65	0	132.1
1292	26.2	14.1	28	5	0	112	0	185.3
1296	24.4	9.4	27	4	20.4	69	0	154.4
1297	15	19	18	0	0	69	0	121
1298	24	8	19	3.5	0	74	0	128.5
1299	20.5	14.4	22.5	4.1	20	48.1	0	130
1302	24.4	14.4	18.3	3	27.4	51.1	0	139
1304	28.1	14	26.4	0	0	87.4	0	156.1
1305	26.1	7.1	30	4	44	51.1	1	163.3
1307	32.3	11.1	33.1	0	43	75.4	5.4	200.5
1308	26.4	13.4	31.3	0	26.1	65	4	166.4
1310	29	22	36	0	22	79	0	188
1312	29	13.4	42	0	33	68	0	185.4
1314	21	17	46.4	4	20.1	90.4	0	199.1

II

YIELD RATIOS

The *responsio* was always written as the number of times the seed had been increased, with an addition or subtraction of the rings and bushels that varied from this ratio.   In addition to their late appearance, two other factors disappoint in the construction of tables giving yield rates from this source.   The note on yield percentage was often crowded into the margin of the roll in a very small hand, and the *exitus* portions of the roll being the first to suffer mutilation, the extractable information on yields is still much less frequent than the regular computable information on corn.   Secondly, there are given only very occasionally figures for amounts of corn sown the previous year that might be used in fractioning the awkward quantities to be added or subtracted from ratio figures.   The gross seed figures do follow a fairly regular order of magnitude, however, and as the amounts of grain to be added to or subtracted from the ratio are very seldom as much as eight or ten per cent, these variations are designated by the plus (+) or minus (−) sign only. Where a considerable variation does occur, the proximate decimal number has been interpolated.   Finally, except for Warboys, tables of yield have been brought together under the same species of corn rather than in manorial blocks.

TABLE XXXVII

YIELD RATIOS

WHEAT YIELD

Year	Wistow	Broughton	Upwood	Houghton	Holywell	Abbots Ripton	Slepe	Weston
1324	.	.	3½+	3½ −	1½+	2½	.	2
1336	.	.	.	4	.	.	.	.
1342	.	3½+	.	.	.	3½+	.	.
1343	7½+	.	4 +	.	.	.	.	.
1351	5 +	.	.	.	.	.	5 —	.
1352	.	.	.	.	.	.	5 —	.
1366	.	.	.	4 +	.	.	.	.
1372	.	3 —	.	.	.	.	.	.
1378	.	.	.	.	.	.	.	.
1379	8½+	.	.	.	.	.	.	.
1383	.	.	.	.	5 +	3 —	.	.
1385	.	.	.	.	.	.	.	.
1386	.	6 —	.	.	.	.	3½+	.
1387	.	.	.	4 +	.	.	.	.
1388	5 —	.	.	4½ −	.	4 —	.	.
1389	.	.	.	3½ −	.	4		.	.
1390	.	.	.	.	.	.	.	.
1392	.	5½+	.	3½+	.	.	.	.
1393	4		.	.	3½+	.	.	.	.
1394	7 +	.	.	3 +	.	5 +	5 —	.
1396	.	.	.	.	.	.	.	.
1401	.	.	.	.	3½	.	.	.
1402	6½+	.	.	.	3	.	.	.
1403	.	.	.	.	4 —	.	.	.
1404	.	.	.	.	3½ −	.	.	.
1405	.	.	.	.	1½ −	.	.	.
1409	.	.	.	.	.	.	.	.

TABLE XXXVII (Cont'd.)
YIELD RATIOS (Cont'd.)

BEANS AND PEAS YIELD

Year	Elton	Slepe	Abbots Ripton	Holywell	Houghton	Broughton	Upwood	Wistow	Year
1324	4 –	3 +	5 –	3½+	1½		4 –		1324
1336					3 +				1336
1342			1½+					1½+	1342
1343							3 +	1 +	1343
1349	1 –								1349
1350	1 +			3 +					1350
1351		1 –	1 –						1351
1364									1364
1366	1 +								1366
1372									1372
1378					1½+	3 +		1½ –	1378
1379					3 –				1379
1380						3 +			1380
1383					1½+				1383
1385									1385
1386		1½+	1 –			4 +			1386
1387					3½–				1387
1388					3			3 +	1388
1389			1 +		3 +			3½–	1389
1392						3 –		1	1392
1393									1393
1394					4				1394
1395									1395
1396									1396
1399				4					1399
1401		1 +	1½ –	1 +					1401
1402			1	1½				1 +	1402
1403				1½+					1403
1404				3					1404
1405				1½					1405
1409									1409

Table XXXVII (*Cont'd.*)

YIELD RATIOS (*Cont'd.*)

BARLEY YIELD

Year	Elton	Slepe	Abbots Ripton	Holywell	Houghton	Upwood	Broughton	Wistow
1324	6 +		6¾	5½		4½		
1342			6			4 + —	2	
1343								+
1349								
1350	3 —	1½						5
1351	2 —	4½ —	5⅓	4½	5 +			
1364				5 +	5 —			+
1366					3½ +		4½ +	
1372							3 +	9 —
1378								
1379								
1383							4½ +	
1385		4 —	1 —		1½ +			6½ —
1386					3½ +			
1387					4 +			
1388								
1389			6 —				6 +	
1390								
1392								4½ —
1393		4 —	3 +		5½ —			4½ +
1394			5 —		4 +			
1395					4 +			
1396								
1401				3½ +				
1402				3 —				3½ —
1403				3½				
1404				6				
1405				1				
1409								

TABLE XXXVII (Cont'd.)

YIELD RATIOS (Cont'd.)

OAT YIELD

Year	Elton	Slepe	Abbots Ripton	Holywell	Broughton	Upwood	Wistow	Warboys	Year
1324	2 -	1 +	1 +	1 -	.	1 +	.	1 -	1324
1342	.	.	2	.	.	1½-	.	6½+	1342
1343	1 -	.	.	.	.	.	.	.	1343
1344	.	.	.	.	.	.	.	.	1344
1352	.	.	.	3 +	1 +	.	+	.	1352
1364	.	.	1 -	.	3½+	.	1	.	1364
1378	.	.	.	.	.	.	.	.	1378
1379	.	.	1 -	.	.	.	.	.	1379
1383	.	.	.	.	1 +	.	.	.	1383
1386	.	.	.	.	.	.	.	.	1386
1389	.	.	.	.	.	.	1	.	1389

DREDGE YIELD

Year	Slepe	Holywell	Houghton	Upwood	Wistow	Warboys	Year
1324	3½+	6 -	2 -	1 +	.	5 +	1324
1336	.	.	1 -	.	.	.	1336
1342	.	.	.	3 -	.	5½+	1342
1343	.	.	.	.	.	.	1343
1352	.	.	.	.	3½+	.	1352

TABLE XXXVII (*Cont'd.*)

YIELD RATIOS (*Cont'd.*)

WARBOYS YIELDS

Year	Wheat	Barley	Oats	B. & P.	D.
1344	6½ +	9 +	1+	4½+	.
1347	5 +	8½ +	1−	6 +	.
1348	5½ −	7½ −	1+	5 −	.
1353	?	6 −	1−	1½−	.
1356	7 −	9½ +	1+	4 −	.
1359	7 +	11½ +	1−	5 +	4 +
1360	5½ +	11 +	1−	?	11 −
1363	3 +	5½ +	.	1 +	.
1366	?	?	1−	4 −	.
1371	?	6 −	?	3½−	.
1373	?	?	.	4 −	.
1375	?	7½ +	.	1½−	.
1377	7 −	9½ −	.	4 −	.
1378	11 +	10 +	.	1½+	.
1379	5½ −	9½ +	.	1 +	.
1393	5 +	5 +	.	1	.
1404	4½ +	6½ +	.	3	.
1413	3½ +	4 −	.	1	.

III

LIVERY

All the conventual manors were obliged to send yearly quotas of grain to the cellarer for the sustenance of the monks and their servants. The several documents which relate to this quota after the twelfth century do not show any change in total quantities or types of grain. But, *de facto*, alterations seemed to be made according to the exigencies of demesne production. First, great variations occurred in the annual volume of livery from the manors, and these were not covered by supplementary cash payments, such as was done for cheese and bacon, nor were deficits compounded from year to year. Deficits in livery to manorial *famuli* were debited to the manor, but not so the conventual livery. There was considerable administrative co-operation among the manors: Holywell always sent the manorial livery through Slepe, or Bythorn and Brington through Weston, and manors outside Huntingdon owing corn often deposited this at Slepe or some other intermediary station. But this was a system of transport rationalization, and the extra-manorial corn was carefully accounted, both on passing in and out of the local grange. Most of the smaller intermanorial movements of corn, which seem to have practically disappeared by the fourteenth century, were related to administrative needs (especially of the Broughton court). The fact that fluctuations in the volume of livery from all the manors tended to move together, is a further consideration against the existence of some method of spreading the burden of deficits in poor harvest years. There were huge storage granaries, of course, which would tide the convent over bad harvest periods, at least for a year or two. At the death of Abbot Simon Eye (1342) there was left in (his?) granary three hundred quarters of wheat and one thousand quarters of malt.

Secondly, the content of the livery varied with the changing nature of demesne production. The large amounts of oats that had traditionally been sent to the abbey stables from Huntingdon manors for use as fodder, were reduced to a pittance by the fourteenth century.[13] From the fourteenth century the various types of grain began to be classified a second time in the roll, according to their use as malt, meal (*grutum*), or people's bread (*wouk'*). Barley seems to have been the main variable in the first two confections, being largely used for malt in one year or for meal the next. But in most cases, until well into the fourteenth century, barley tended to be used for the making of meal, while malt was produced from dredge. From *ca.* 1350 barley became the single source of malt. The allocations for workers' bread had been entirely of wheat in the twelfth, and at least earlier thirteenth, centuries. It is common to find equal proportions of wheat, barley, and peas in the early fourteenth century. But *wouk* of fifty per cent wheat and fifty per cent peas was adopted everywhere from the first quarter of this century, until the people's bread disappears in the fifteenth century. Beans and peas were sent in only small amounts as livery to the abbey; they usually served as a more all-purpose corn for feeding of stock, supplementing servants' wages, etc.

[3] Apparently oats was still needed at the abbey; see *Add. Ch.* 34714, wherein 385 quarters of oats were mentioned as used, largely from Walsoken, in 1419-20. Since much of the precarious fen arable was only useful for the sowing of oats (see Edward MILLER, *The Abbey and Bishopric of Ely*, p. 79) the newly-opened fen lands in the thirteenth century may have provided enough oats for the abbey needs, and thus would be an additional circumstance in that large reduction of oat production on Huntingdon demesnes. This relation of demand to corn production is a very complicated question, however: e.g. the villeins of Graveley (largely a clayland manor) rendered five quarters of oats to one of wheat for their customary livery in the twelfth century.

TABLE XXXVIII

CORN LIVERIES TO THE CELLARER

* 1284 values for all manors are from the receiver's roll, *Add. Ch.* 34711.

Warboys (Quota 3202 b.)

Year	Livery
1250	2808
1255	2870
1284 *	1200
1307	2332
1318	3524
1324	2419
1331	1404 ?
1342	2828
1344	2998
1347	1908
1348	2851
1353	1252
1356	1449
1359	1950
1360	2441
1362	2052 ?
1363	1870
1366	2887
1371	1728
1373	1412
1375	2136
1377	2532
1378	2112 ?
1379	2063
1393	2098
1404	1538
1413	3699

Abbots Ripton (Quota 3202 b.)

Year	Livery
1284	2785
1307	3642
1324	2720
1342	2903
1375	755 ?
1385	592
1388	808
1390	1320
1395	926
1396	1032

Slepe and Holywell (Quota 3202 b.)

Year	Livery
1284	1541
1307	1778
1309	1575 ?
1313	3428 ?
1314	1448
1324	1528
1351	310
1360	1096
1366	1297
1387	976

TABLE XXXVIII (*Cont'd.*)

CORN LIVERIES TO THE CELLARER (*Cont'd.*)

Upwood (Quota 2502 b.)		Wistow (Quota 2502 b.)	
Year	Livery	Year	Livery
1247	2476	1247	1800 ?
1250	2870	1250	2216
1252	2608	1252	2450
1284	2307	1297	2286
1297 ?	1788	1307	2872
1306	1586	1311	1743
1319	1799	1318	1724
1324	1438	1335	1433
1325 ?	1634	1340 ?	2114
1343	2168	1352	1212
1385	1919	1388	1862
1386	1384	1389	1412
1392	1030	1393	1270
1406	696	1394	1344
1408	324	1403	883 ?
1412	920	1423	1887
		1466	888

Houghton	
Year	Livery
1324	1564
1336	3170
1338	2510

TABLE XXXIX

NON-CORN LIVERY : ELTON

The farm quota is given in parentheses under each item.

Year	Cash (£4)	Cheese (10 pond' or £4)		Bacon (10 pond' or £5)	Hens (138)	Geese (14)	Sucklings (20 or 66s.8d.)	Lambs (16 or 4s.10d.)	Sheep (4 or 6s.8d.)	Year
1286	4	2 &	64s.	0	£5	138	14	0	66s.8d.	0	4s.10d.	0	6s.8d.	1286
1297	4	6 &	32s.	0	£5	138	14	0	"	0	"	0	"	1297
1307	4	8 &	16s.	0	£5	138	14	0	"	0	"	0	"	1307
1311	4	6 &	32s.	0	£5	138	14	0	"	0	"	0	"	1311
1313	4	6 &	32s.	0	£5	138	14	0	"	0	"	0	"	1313
1324	4	3 &	56s.	0	£5	138	14	0	"	0	"	0	"	1324
1345	4	6 &	32s.	0	£5	138	14	0	"	0	"	0	"	1345

Year	Fresh Cheese (24 or 12s.)	Butter (16 or 16s.4d.)	For Eels (6s.8d.)	Eggs (2760)	Beef (½ carcass or 2s.)	Honey (8 boll')	Year
1286	0 12s.	0 16s.4d.	6s.8d.	4d. +2660	2s.	0	1286
1297	0 "	0 "	"	2760	2s.	0	1297
1307	0 "	0 "	"	2760	2s.	0	1307
1311	0 "	0 "	"	2760	2s.	0	1311
1313	0 "	0 "	"	2760	2s.	0	1313
1324	0 "	0 "	"	2760	2s.	0	1324
1345	0 "	0 "	"	2760	2s.	0	1345

TABLE XXXIX (Cont'd.)

NON-CORN LIVERY : WARBOYS

Year	Cash (£4)	Cheese (10 or £4)	Bacon (10 or £5)	Hens (138)	Geese (14)	Sucklings (20 or 66s.8d.)	Lambs (16 or 4s.10d.)	Sheep (4 or 6s.8d.)	Year
1250	4	3½ + 60s.6d.	1½ + £5.2s.	?	14	0 66s.8d.	0 4s.10d.	0 6s.8d.	1250
1255	4	2½ + 60s.	6 + 42s.6d.	138	14	? 60s.	0 "	0 "	1255
1303	4	½ + 76s.	0 + £5	138	14	0 66s.8d.	0 "	0 "	1303
1306	4	2 + 64s.	0 + £5	138	14	0 "	0 "	0 "	1306
1316	4	2 + 64s.	0 + £5	138	14	0 "	0 "	0 "	1316
1318	4	2½ + 60s.	0 + £5	138	14	0 "	0 "	0 "	1318
1324	4	1 + 72s.	0 + £5	138	14	0 "	0 "	0 "	1324
1325	4	0 + £4	0 + £5	138	14	0 "	0 "	0 "	1325
1330	4	1 + 72s.	0 + £5	138	14	0 "	0 "	0 "	1330
1336	4	0 + £4	0 + £5	138	14	0 "	0 "	0 "	1336
1342	4	0 + £4	0	138	14	0	0	0	1342

Year	Fresh Cheese (19 or 12s.)	Butter (16 or 16s.4d.)	Eels (6s.8d.)	Beef (½ carcass or 2s.)	Honey (8 boll')	Eggs (2880)	Year
1250	0 12s.	0 16s.4d.	6s.8d.	0 2s.	0 7s.2d.	960 + 4s.8d.	1250
1255	0 12s.	0 "	"	0 "	2½ + 4s.1d.	960 + 5s.6d.	1255
1303	0 12s.	0 "	"	0 "	?	1080 + 5s.6d.	1303
1306	0 12s.	0 "	"	0 "	0 8s.	?	1306
1316	0 12s.	0 "	"	0 "	0 8s.	2760	1316
1318	0 12s.	0 "	"	0 "	0 8s.	2760	1318
1324	0 12s.	0 "	"	0 "	0 8s.	2760	1324
1325	0 12s.	0 "	"	0 "	0 8s.	2760	1325
1330	0 12s.	0 "	"	0 "	0 8s.	2760	1330
1336	0 12s.	0 "	"	0 "	0 8s.	2760	1336
1342	0	0		0	0	2760	1342

IV

CROPPING AND DEMESNE AREAS

While many of the conclusions upon the evolution of the rotation system over the late thirteenth century must remain largely hypothetical, the pattern of the fourteenth-century development is fairly clear. The farming of portions of the demesne began to become a regular alternative to cultivation.[14] At most of the manors not so greatly affected by the thirteenth-century revolution in cropping (especially Warboys and Elton), the sowing of oats gradually declined, but continued in large amounts until well into the second quarter of the century. By the mid-century, however, the sowing of oats had practically disappeared from Huntingdon manors.

The decline in oat cultivation from the mid-century was replaced by a marked increase in the seeding by barley and legumes.[15] From the second half of the century, it is also possible to see that this rotation system now turned upon an intensive[16] sowing of the high yielding barley. Like many administrative regulations for mediæval agrarian estates, the regulation *quota* of sowing was wonderfully standard and rigid, but in practice this quota became quite flexible. The rolls first gave a standard regulation in practically invariable ratios which are exemplified in the accompanying tables for Wistow and Broughton. But this regulation amount was varied in the actual sowing especially with respect to the high yielding barley which might be doubled in seed intensity. The table for Houghton has been compiled from a more complete series of acreage figures and amounts sown to illustrate this latter point.

---

[14] See *infra*, Chapter VIII.

[15] This concentration upon the cultivation of barley, with legumes usually a close second crop, and wheat a less important third, was to become fairly common in the east midlands from the late middle ages (W. G. HOSKINS, *Essays in Leicestershire History*, pp. 160-167; Joan THIRSK, *Fenland Farming in the Sixteenth Century*, Table III, p. 37 and R. H. HILTON, *The Economic Development of some Leicestershire Estates in the Fourteenth and Fifteenth Centuries*, Oxford, 1947, pp. 63-66, 133, 136, App. III). The cultivation of wheat remained fairly stable at Ramsey manors after the mid-fourteenth century, being governed by the fixed bread requirements of the abbey and the *famuli*. Since wheaten bread tended to be something of a luxury food, its production for home consumption varied with the wealth of the farmer in some areas (see Joan THIRSK, *Lincolnshire Farming*

Regions). While malt barley was the the important corn for market production (THIRSK, *ibid.*) in some areas, there is no evidence that any of the barley sent to the Ramsey bakery was marketed from the abbey. The heavy purchases by the master of the bakehouse in 1422 (see *infra*, Chapter X, Table LXVIII), presumably for domestic uses, show a demand that would easily dispose of the total malt barley livery over the late fourteenth century.

[16] It should be noted that this emphasis upon the high yielding barley from *ca.*1350 permitted a livery total often not far from the level of the early 14th century despite the decline in total amounts of corn sown and the farming of large portions of the demesne (Chapter IX, App. III), and see the more complete series for Warboys (this chapter, Tables XXXVI, XXXVII, XXXVIII).

TABLE XL

SEED PER ACRE QUOTAS (bushels)

Year	Wheat	Barley	B. & P.	Oats
Wistow				
1379	3	5	—	5
1389	3	5	3½	4
1393	3	5	3½	4
1394	3	5	3½	4
1398	3	5	3½	4
1403	3	5	3½	4
Broughton				
1380	2½	5	2½	5
1386	2½	5	3	4
1392	2½	5	3	4

TABLE XLI

ACTUAL BUSHELS PER ACRE SOWN

Year	Wheat	Barley	B. & P.	Oats
Houghton				
1379	3	4	3½	–
1383	–	6	3½	–
1387	–	6	3¼	–
1388	3	5	4	4
1389	2½	6¼	4¾	4
1393	3	6	4½	–
1394	3½	7	3½	–
1396	3	9	5	–
1407	–	–	4	–
1418	2¾	4	4½	4

The names of arable fields and their areas are only given in Ramsey accounts from the third quarter of the fourteenth century. Furlongs were being sown in smaller parcels by this date, and only rarely can a nominal coincidence be found with the *culturæ* listed in the thirteenth-century extents. Finally, it is difficult to throw light upon the rotation cycles because of the infrequency with which an annual sequence of account rolls occur, and the varied divisions of even small fields from year to year. The following example from Holywell appears to be typical of the system on other Huntingdon demesnes.[17]

---

[17] This rotation would seem to be much like that retained in the numerous open fields of Hunts. in the 18th century, that is: first fallow, second wheat or barley, third legumes, fourth barley or wheat (G. MAXWELL, *General View of the Agriculture of Huntingdonshire*, London, 1793). The actual disposition of these crops in the fields would be a much more elastic matter. In addition to the fact that legumes were being sown instead of oats, the late fourteenth and early fifteenth-century cropping on Ramsey demesnes manifest an obvious emphasis upon legumes as intermediate to a second sowing of wheat or barley (see Table XLII, 1401 and 1402) in contrast to the eighteenth-century report by the Board of Agriculture for this region. These eighteenth-century data have been summarized thus (D. W. FRYER, *The Land Utilization Survey of Britain*, p. 445): "The Common Fields were divided into three parts, one part was annually fallowed, half being undunged and sown with barley in the following spring. The part producing wheat was then broken up and sown with oats and the part that produced barley was generally sown with peas or beans, the land reverting to fallow in the third year."

TABLE XLII

SOWING IN HOLYWELL FIELDS

Field	1400	1401	1402	1404	1405
Bradeway	barley (24a.1r.)	peas (24a.1r.)	wheat (23a.1r.)	barley (24a.1r.)	peas (24a.1r.)
Northrup	,, (15½a.)	,, (15½a.)	barley (15½a.)	,, (15½a.)	,, (15½a.)
Crowholdale	,, (14a.1r.)	,, (2a.)	,, (9a.1r.)	,, (9a.1r.)	,, (9a.1r.)
Hogfurlong	peas (34a.1r.)	wheat (30a.) barley (4a.1r.)	fallow	peas (28a.1r.) wheat (11a.)	wheat (23a.)
Sevonacre	,, (13½a.)	wheat (13½a.)	fallow	peas (13½a.)	wheat (13½a.)
Whaddon	,, (11a.1r.)	,, (6a.3r.) oats (4a.)	,,	,, (11a.1r.)	,, (11a.1r.)
Thynenacre	?	barley (21½a.)	peas (21½a.)	fallow	barley (21½a.)
Schepingfurlong	?	,, (6a.1r.)	,, (6a.1r.)	,,	wheat (6a.1r.)
Eastlong	?	peas (5a.)	barley (5a.)	barley (5a.)	peas (5a.)
Subcroft	?	barley (4a.)	fallow	oats (4a.)	oats (4a.)
Prestade	?	fallow	barley (11a.3r.)	wheat (11a.3r.)	fallow
Wodebroke	?	barley (2a.1r.)	peas (2a.1r.)	fallow	barley (2a.1r.)
Bafedele	?	,, (6a.1r.)	,, (6a.1r.)	,,	,, (6a.1r.)
Mareway	?	fallow (7a.1r.)	wheat (7a.1r.)	wheat (7a.1r.) ,, (1½a.)	fallow
Redholmacre	?	fallow (10½a.)	,, (10½a.)	,, (10½a.)	,,
Brerecroft	?	,, (4a.)	oats (4a.)	fallow	,,

Table XLIII

DEMESNE ACRES SOWN

Year	W.	B.	B. & P.	O.	Total
Broughton					
1380	60a. 2r. 24p.	77a. 19½p.	59a.1r.27½p.	7a.3r.8p.	204a.3r.39p.
1386	77a.19½p.	66½a.33½p.	57a.3r.36p.	9a.	210½a.1r.9p.
1392	65½a.37½p.	74a.14½p.	59a.1r.7½p.	4a.	202½a.2r.19½p.
Wistow					
1379	46a.	50a.	83½a.1r.5p.	5a.	184½a.1r.5p.
1388	47a.22½p.	63a.3r.14½p.	79a.3r.10p.	10a.1r.8p.	201a.15p.
1389	45a.32½p.	60a.3r.3p.	78½a.13p.	7a.½r.13p.	191a.3r.1½p.
1393	47a.1½r.16p.	69a.1r.13p.	56a.1r.12p.	8a.	181a.½r.1p.
1394	59a.1½r.4p.	67a.1r.15½p.	69a.3r.14p.	8a.	204a.1½r.33½p.
1403	55a.	63a.1r.	67a.	6a.	191a.1r.
Slepe					
1387	73½a.23p.	55a.2r.3p.	57a.1r.12p.	6a.	192a.1r.38p.
1390	45a.3r.8p.	74½a.13p.	60a.3r.37p.	6a.	187a.1r.18p.
1394	—	67a.1r.3p.	62a.23p.	6a.	—
1417	57a.13p.	74½a.13p.	60a.3½r.17p.	6a.	198½a.23p.

Houghton

Year					
1379	71a.	104a.	58a.	0	233a.
1383	69½a.21p.	119½a.1r.20p.	49a.13½p.	0	238a.2r.14½p.
1387	61½a.13p.	115a.1r.3p.	52a.3r.35p.	0	229½a.1r.11p.
1388	92½a.10p.	93a.18½p.	43a.3½r.½p.	3a.	231½a.3½r.29p.
1389	80a.3r.29p.	78½a.26p.	57½a.27p.	2a.	219a.1r.20p.
1393	58½a.38½p.	96a.3r.9p.	33a.3r.9½p.	0	188½a.3r.17p.
1394	44a.34½p.	70a.29p.	49a.35p.	0	163a.2r.18½p.
1396	74a.3½r.11p.	51a.39p.	47a.3½r.½p.	0	174a.10½p.
1399	66a.	69a.	45a.1r.	0	180a.1r.

Upwood

Year					
1385	48a.3r.4p.	57½a.3p.	60½a.28½p.	0	166a.3r.35½p.
1386	49a.3r.19p.	57½a.9p.	66a.3r.5p.	0	173½a.2r.33p.
1392	42a.24½p.	52a.36½p.	68a.3r.16p.	2a.	165a.½r.17p.
1406	34a.1r.	65a.	82a.	2a.	183a.1r.
1408	34a.1r.	54a.	65a.1r.	2a.	155a.2r.
1412	14a.	94a.3r.	72a.1r.	1a.	182a.
1420	31a.1r.	78½a.	66a.	0	175½a.1r.

Warboys

Year					
1379	69a.23p.	51a.32p.	45a.	(2)	167a.1r.15p.
1393	43a.33p.	59a.1r.10p.	74½a.4p.	(2)	179a.7p.
1404	67a.1r.	76a.	62a.	(2)	207a.1r.
1413	62a.	70a.1r.	76½a.	(2)	210a.3r.

The revolutionary nature of the late thirteenth and fourteenth-century changes in cropping of the demesne may be seen by contrasting the above tables with the tables of tithe acres. The tithe acres, as taken from the extents which, it will be recalled, were around 1250 or earlier, probably represent the earlier cropping proportions since these commuted tithe arrangements seem not to have been changed again. As such, they show the great importance of oat crops at this period:[18] in nine of the thirteen manors oats was at least as heavily represented by the tithe acre as was wheat, only from seven manors did barley pay tithe acres and in two cases it was equal, in one case of a greater acreage, than oats. In short, the distribution of tithe acres among various crops roughly corresponds to that concentration upon wheat and oat yield found in the account rolls of the mid-thirteenth century (above, Table XXXVI, this chapter).

TABLE XLIV

TITHE ACRES [19]

Manor	Wheat	Oats	Barley	Rye
St. Ives................	4a.	4a.	0	0
Holywell..............	2a.	2a.	1a.	1a.
Warboys..............	3a.	4a.	1a.	0
Abbots Ripton..........	2a.	2a.	0	0
Broughton.............	3a.	2a.	1a.	0
Upwood..............	2a.	1a.	1a.	0
Wistow...............	2a.	1a.	1a.	0
Houghton.............	6a.	2a.	4a.	0
Brancaster............	½a.	3a.	2a.	3a.
Cranfield.............	4a.	4a.	0	0
Weston...............	1a.	1a.	0	0
Brington.............	1a.	1a.	0	0
Bythorn..............	1a.	1a.	0	0

[18] The fact that the villeins paid corn rents only in wheat (*benesede; scepa*) and oats (foddercorn) from the twelfth century, may be a further indication that these had been the predominate manorial crops. The twelfth-century documents show *famuli* 'wage acres' in wheat and oats only (*Carts.*, III, pp. 164, 239). Since the composition of meal and malt varied, it is not possible to draw any conclusions from the earlier food farm arrangements.

[19] For many of these it is mentioned not only that the wheat must be from the manorial demesne but also oats, a fact that would explain the sowing of oats after fallow (e.g. *supra*, Table XLII). It should also be noted that this tithe acreage, rather than any system of rotation, accounts for the continued sowing of a small acreage of oats in the fourteenth century (*supra*, Table XLIII).

CHAPTER VII

MANORIAL STATISTICS — III: WORK, WAGES, AND PRICES

I

WORK

THE basic pattern of the work due from the villein is fairly clear. It was determined by the nature of the demesne production, and hence involved routine weekly work throughout the year, as well as a concentration at certain periods for seasonal needs. Within these two general divisions there were, of course, further subdivisions, that is some obligations more regularly necessary and others more immediately urgent. The most regular obligation was that of the weekly ploughing. The autumn sowing of wheat, the preparation over winter for the spring sowing of barley and oats, and the summer fallowing presented a fairly consistent demand for plough services throughout the year. In addition, ploughing with the large eight or ten stock team must have been the slowest portion of arable cultivation, and consequently, it could be less satisfactorily corrected by boon works. Equally important was the fact that ploughing depended upon almost the entire manorial capital in plough animals, so that a recruitment of all the ploughs at short notice for work on the demesne must have been difficult. The first problem was met by the obligation of one day's ploughing every week for all those having ploughs. In practically all the twelfth-century extents,[1] the virgater owed work with his plough on the lord's demesne one day per week, usually Friday, from Michaelmas to the following August,[2] except for the holydays at Christmas, Easter, and Pentecost. In the more detailed thirteenth-century extents the weekly obligations were the same, although it was specified that the villein had a week exemption from ploughing at Easter and Pentecost, and on most manors an exemption during thirteen or fifteen days at Christmas. During the heavy harvest work season of August and September the weekly plough service was not required.

For these plough services it was the plough and team, not the person of the villein, that were most important. Hence, the extents emphasized the utilization of the full villein ploughing potential: 'he ploughs, whether he has his own plough or not, as he ploughs his own land'; 'he ploughs with as many animals as he has in the plough'; 'he ploughs, one day per week with his own

---

[1] At Shillington, Pegsdon, and Elsworth, this obligation was measured as one-half acre per week, rather than one day's ploughing.

[2] There were some variations from this general pattern, particularly in the Cambridgeshire manors where the fens were so important. At Elsworth there was no ploughing after Pentecost; at Girton, none in January. On the other hand, ploughing was required every week throughout the year at Higney.

plough if he has one, and proportionately more if joined with others'.[3] This second problem, that is, the assurance of availability of plough capital, was further enforced by a consistent refusal to commute ploughing services. Often, even when land was being widely freed in the twelfth century, along with the suit to the hundred court there was added 'he ploughs'.[4] The more detailed regulations for commutation given in various extents, also allow us to see the emphasis upon this maintenance of plough services: "If he is not at works, he gives two shillings a year, and ploughs every Friday, and will be quitted from all other works except boon works, and will give three pence halfpenny towards the twenty shillings."[5] Important *famuli* like the reeve, beadle, forester, and *akermanni*, might be exempt from other works for their lands, but not from the ploughing services.[6] A villein may be sick in bed for a year and hence be excused from services, but not from his ploughing obligations; even if he dies, his relict was usually excused from all obligation from the tenement for thirty days, but not from the ploughing; for, as the inquisitors of one manor emphasize, 'the ploughing must always be done'.[7]

For other works required over fairly long periods during the year more flexibility was possible, so that the extents employed a general formula such

---

[3] E. g., arabit unam sellionem, cum quot capitibus habet in caruca (I, p. 289); sive propriam et integram habeat carucam vel junctam cum aliis, pro uno opere (I, p. 310); Ad omnes etiam precarias carucarum veniet cum caruca sua, sive habeat carucam suam integram vel junctam cum alio; et eodem modo singulis septimanis anni arabit super terram domini uno die, sicut super propriam (I, p. 336); Et præterea, arabit uno die cum quot capitibus habet in caruca, ita quod quælibet caruca arabit unam sellionem, sicut jacet, et hoc nisi festum impediat (I, p. 398); Et in qualibet hebdomada, arabit die Veneris, scilicet, si habeat carucam, unam sellionem, si non, quotquot fuerint associati ad unam carucam arabunt unam sellionem, sicut jacet in campis (I, p. 493). I, p. 310: ... ad omnes precarias carucarum venit cum caruca sua sicut jungitur; et non possunt plures in hyeme jungi quam tres, in æstate quattuor, et cum tres simul jungantur vel quatuor, veniant omnes ad prandium, sicut junguntur, et nullus eorum alibi quam ad carucam sine licentia eodem die operabitur, vel ad aliud intendet. And for Ellington, see *Carts.*, II, p. 23.

[4] E. g. *Carts.*, III, p. 278 (Houghton): Thurkillus de Wittona tenuit antiquitus duas virgatas, pro quinque solidis. Et sequebatur comitatum et hundredum, et arabat omni die Veneris. Et modo tenet Reinaldus eandem terram pro eodem servitio.
Wlfricus tenuit tunc duas virgatas pro quinque solidis, et sequebatur comitatum et hundredum, et arabat. Quas modo tenent Thomas et Ricardus, pro eodem servitio. See also III, p. 258, and 263-4. In some

instances the weekly ploughing obligations of freeholds had apparently been commuted to a certain acreage. See III, pp. 242, 272, 276, 282, 258.

[5] *Carts.*, III, p. 243; and see also pp. 254, 256; and for the thirteenth century, I, p. 478: Si virgata sua ponatur ad censum, dabit pro ea per annum quatuor solidos ad tres terminos æqualiter, ut supra. Arabit qualibet septimana, ut virgatarius, ad opera, et herciabit quicquid arat. Or see p. 488.

[6] E.g. *Carts.*, I, p. 346.

[7] At Lawshall the virgater was free from work during the week after Easter, and the week after Pentecost, 'except for the ploughing which begins from the fifth *feria* of the week' (III, p. 282). It is interesting to note also that the only real limitations put upon the villein sale of stock were for the preservation of manorial ploughs. Ordinarily, the entry is very short and to the point, like this example from Holywell (I, p. 298): Nec potest vendere boviculum, nec pullum masculum, ex quo ponitur in opere, sine licentia domini. But the entry for Wistow (I, p. 358) points out that the lord has the first right to purchase for this purpose: Non potest suum equum, pullum masculum, vel bovem vendere, quousque quæsierit a ballivo, utrum ad opus domini eos emere voluerit. And for Warboys (I, p. 312), the extent indicates that this regulation applies only to those animals actually ready for the plough: Non potest equum, bovem, vel pullum suum de proprio nutrimento, vendere sine licentia; sed pullum, et boviculum biennem, infra biennium bene potest; pro licentia habenda vendendi nihil dat.

as 'he works two or three days a week'.   The work to be done on these days
was at the discretion of the reeve or farmer and varied with the seasons
and with the demesne economy peculiar to different regions.   Only with the
more complete thirteenth century extents were such works first described in
detail for the Ramsey estates.   Over the winter the villein might be employed
during this one or two days a week at cleaning or extending ditches, at repairing
fences and hedges, or at threshing in the manorial grange.   When the cultivation and sowing of the spring crop was completed there was still the hoeing
and reworking of the fallow.   On most of the Ramsey manors the mowing,
gathering, and carrying of fen grass and meadow hay was a major annual
work.   At some manors, like Hemmingford, an additional day per week was
required to help with the mowing of the fen; at Elsworth, an extra day per
week and an extra labourer each day were required from Pentecost until
August 'to clean the fields and gather the fen grass'.   In regions where the fen
mowing was not important extra days had not to be added, or if they were,
they did not last until August.   In the twelfth-century extent of Houghton,
for example, it is only mentioned that 'at the time for mowing the fen, he will
mow one day when he is able'.

At the opposite extreme from the weekly ploughday came the immediate
tasks for which everything else had to be set aside, sometimes even the weekly
ploughing.   Students of manorial extents have been perhaps too impressed
by the tedious enumeration of works in the thirteenth-century extents.   At
Ramsey the twelfth-century extents actually may have left the virgater subject
to heavier obligations at the busy season owing to the unspecified nature and
period of many works.   Thus in the twelfth century at Graveley the virgater
had to supply the harvest labour of four days a week as long as the harvest
lasted, at Holywell he had to work all week while the mowing of the fen lasted,
or at Ellington he had to work all week except Saturday while the harvest
lasted.[8]   For other manorial obligations, too, the lord found it impossible to
commit labour to any particular time of year and sometimes even to any
particular day of the week.   This was particularly true for the preparation and
delivery of the conventual food farm in the twelfth century: at Graveley, whenever the winnower (*vannator*) came the virgater was to thresh on Monday and
on Tuesday, Wednesday and Saturday carry to the mill and thence to Ramsey;[9] at Elton when the winnower came all were to go to the manor house every
day to prepare the corn until the food farm was ready.[10]   These general commitments left the villeins liable to very heavy obligations, for, in the thirteenth,
and early fourteenth centuries, though there was yet but little commutation
of *opera*, much labour had to be hired for the threshing at Ramsey manors.

The thirteenth-century extents were, of course, constructed for the same
pattern of economic needs.   Hence in addition to the regular ploughing

---

[8] The obligation also held *quamdiu messis durat* at Hemmingford Grey, Elsworth, Brington, Hemmingford Abbots.

[9] *Carts.*, III, p. 247; or see Elsworth, III, p. 250.

[10] *Carts.*, III, p. 259; Brington, III, p. 311; or Knapwell, III, p. 301: Quacumque die vannarius de Ramesia venerit, omnes simul, qui habent virgatas, et qui habent cotlandias, venient ad curiam; et verberabunt bladum, quantum vannarius rogaverit; et deducent Ramesiæ.

obligations, the villein at Holywell will perform the extra day's work 'as long as the harvest lasts', or at Houghton he will work the four days a week until Michaelmas 'if it should be necessary'. The thirteenth-century extents were particularly like those of the earlier century in maintaining the right of the lord to many villeins' carrying services at will. But repeated comparative readings of the twelfth and thirteenth-century extents for Ramsey manors not only emphasize the vast amount of detail added to the later documents, but reveal as basic to such detail a regulative principle at work between lord and villein that limited the obligations of the latter by defining them as work units. It is probable that this principle was effective before the thirteenth century if only for the purpose of more efficient organization of villein obligations and for their commutation, although the twelfth-century extents cite less than a dozen examples of its employment.[11] With the thirteenth-century documents, however, there was an effort to define precisely the amount of various services that made up one 'work' on every manor. At St. Ives, for example, 'if he ought to work at piece work, he will thresh twenty-four sheaves of wheat or rye, and thirty sheaves of barley, beans, or oats, for one work; he gathers in the woods and will carry one bundle of poles to the manor house, or one bundle of branches, . . . ; he will construct enclosure in the field facing the woods for one-and-one-half rods, in the fields of Waddon or Wodebroc for two rods, in other fields adjacent to the town of St. Ives for one-and-one-half rods, . . . On the level land he will dig a ditch of one rod sixteen feet in length, of five feet in width at the top and two feet at the bottom, and in depth a good two *spadegrafes* . . . He will spread the manure for one furrow . . .'[12]

In many instances a further precision was obtained by specifying the 'man-hours', that is the length of the day to be spent for 'one work day'. At Abbots Ripton, for example, after indicating the amount of wood to be collected, the extent continues: 'for whatever other kind of work is prescribed to him, he will work from morning until the hour at which the ploughs are unhitched, until Hokeday; and from Hokeday until after harvest he works for the whole day . . . He will harrow for the whole day in winter, and during Lent until after none (*post nonam*), . . . If he ought to cut wood, he will cut until none; and if the lord wishes to feed him he will work until evening (*ad vesperam*)'. Or at Wistow, 'he will harrow during the winter and Lent from morning almost (*fere*) until evening, and this is allocated to him for the work of one day . . . He hoes however throughout the whole day. But he mows (only) until none, whenever he ought to mow. And when piling the fen, he works for the whole day.' At Stukeley, 'if he ought to enclose, to ditch, to thatch, or to build walls, or to do any other work, except in the woods, he will work from the rising of the sun until its setting. If he is to work in the woods,

---

[11] At Hemmingford Abbots some of the work to repair the mill could be counted as regular *opera*, as also with two days' mowing at Warboys; the virgater was free from regular work while carrying for the lord at Lawshall and Burwell, and while sowing one-half acre of the demesne at Ellington; at Upwood his ploughing of one-half acre counted for one day's work, as did his malting at Brington.

[12] *Carts.*, II, 288 ff.

cutting trees, or any other type of work, he will work until none, without food, or for the whole day if given his food.'[13]

This definition of villein obligations was applied to even the most urgent seasons and obligations of the year, and consequently tended to leave less and less discretion to the reeve, farmer, or 'will of the lord'. At St. Ives the load for one carrying work of one virgater was one ring of wheat, or six bushels of barley or oats.   Two virgaters from the same manor were to take one weight of bacon or cheese to Ramsey, and for each weight of cheese or bacon will be given bread and ale at Ramsey.   At Broughton the virgater will carry one cartload of grain, when ordered, and it does not take the place of works; but after this first load, every two cartloads take the place of one work.   Or at Upwood every virgater and his companion must carry four cartloads of fen hay from Northwood meadow to the manor, but carrying from other meadows is to be considered as works.   At Houghton, for harvesting the wine, each virgater had to give one man at the expense of the virgater when the *custos* of the vines wanted him, but his work was to be accounted by the farmer as the work for one day.   It was particularly important for the lord to have full disposition over carrying services at market times, or to transport the food farms.   Most of the thirteenth-century extents repeated the common prescription of the twelfth century that the virgater will carry 'whenever and wherever the lord wills'.   But there was usually some qualification in the thirteenth century: at Houghton, the extent continues 'if however he wishes to have carrying services on Monday, or Tuesday, or Wednesday, these take the place of the work for that day'.[14]   It is, of course, obvious that many of these carrying services, as with the work cited in the previous paragraph, would take much less than the full day to accomplish.   For all manors the number of carrying services beyond the shire was limited, and the villein was being rewarded by some payment if the distance was great.

While the detailed definition of *opera* must have been useful for management of the demesne and for the commutation of *opera* to money rents, there nevertheless emerges with these thirteenth-century extents strong evidence

---

[13] While the definition of a work unit for threshing, ditching, etc. could have been derived for administrative reasons alone, the limitation of the agrarian day for such employment as was not easily organized as piece work — leaving the harrowing or mowing when almost complete, for example — must have imposed administrative complexities for the reeve. It is not surprising to find that arrangements were commonly made whereby the villein could be rewarded for completing the day. As is suggested in the following pages, it was in this evolution from the villein dependence upon the ill-defined will of the lord, to a custom whereby the villein was rewarded for extra services, that the transition from predial services to money rent can be most clearly depicted.

[14] At Shillington it is noted (*Carts.*, I, 462):

Et quotiencunque curtum averagium fecerit, si forte sit per diem operabilem, allocabitur pro uno opere similiter. Summagium autem, tam longi averagii quam curti, cujuslibet generis bladi, erit dimidium quarterium de manerio ... Summagium carnium est unus porcus, duo carcos multonum, quarterium bovis. Crawley (I, 449): Averabit in dorso usque Rameseiam, vel alibi, ad remotius, ubi possit per unum diem ire, et per alium diem redire,et portabit duas aucas, vel tres capones, vel quinque gallinas, vel duodecim pullos, vel centum ova. Girton (I, 494): Si averabit, ducet apud Cantabrigiam vel Ellesworthe, vel Over, dimidium quarterium frumenti, vel alterius bladi, ad placitum domini, et allocabitur ei unum opus. Si portat de Cantebrigia cibum, vel potum, vel aliud nuntium faciat allocabitur ei unum opus.

that the villein of this period was not a person 'without the law', a serf at the beck and call of the lord's whim or necessity, but a tenant owing services to the lord as a real obligation for land, such services being limited in turn according to the mutual contractual obligations of the lord and tenant. Although this conception runs through the whole enumeration of villein services, it may be recognized perhaps most clearly in the lord's obligation to pay for services exacted, beyond the villein's due.

The lord was willing to pay the villein for extra services for all the more urgent demesne requirements, especially carrying, mowing, and harvesting, although ploughing might be encouraged by certain rewards too;[15] and at Brancaster, the lord had to feed the villeins during all employment on the demesne, even the regular weekly obligations throughout the year. The carrying services were usually rewarded according to the length of the day. These rewards, like the wages of the *famuli* at the time, might be either in food or in money. From Barton the virgater was to make three carrying trips to London, or to Ramsey, at the farthest, each trip being accounted as the work due for one day of that week. For going to London he will have one penny for one load; for going to Ramsey he will have his dinner, and fodder for his horse. Whenever he makes a carrying trip to sell corn, he will have one penny for the full load. At Shillington, the virgater was to make twelve long carrying trips between the feast of St. Michael and the following August, that is to London, St. Albans, or Cambridge; and for each trip, he will have the customary payment of four pence, and at Ramsey he will have bread, ale, *companagium*, and fodder and hay for his horse. By the late twelfth-century extents it had been pointed out that the whole vill received eight pence for cutting the meadow at Knapwell, and twelve pence at Elsworth, but the thirteenth-century extents reveal that in addition to this general payment an individual reward was being given to the villein for his mowing services. This daily reward was usually as much hay as the mower could carry on his scythe. At Warboys, for example, the villeins shared sixpence among themselves for mowing the meadow, together with the bundle of hay each per day; at Holywell the villeins received a *scythacre* reward of six acres of meadow, and at St. Ives one acre of meadow, together with the individual bundles, for mowing the demesne meadow.[16]

It was in the arrangement of boon works, of course, that the mutual contractual obligations of lord and villein were most clearly described. The boon work, as much as the various piece works, or the weekly ploughing, met an essential demand for villein labour, although the demand for boons was

---

[15] E.g., *Carts.*, I, p. 371: Item ad tramesiam uno die, cum Abbas habeat carucas villanorum, tunc arabit dimidiam acram, et habebit tres quadrantes, sicut villani.

[16] The meeting of service and wage may be well seen in this entry from the extent of Shillington (I, p. 462): Tempore vero falcationis, per totum diem falcabit in prato de Bradephen, et non allocabitur pro opere. Sed ipse, et omnes in eodem falcantes, habebunt de bursa Abbatis duodecim denarios de consuetudine; et in sero habebit quantum herbæ poterit in hasta falcis suæ portare, quæ si frangatur, perdat herbam. Alias vero falcabit usque ad nonam pro uno opere, et si usque ad vesperam pro opere, et habebit tunc herbam sicut prius. Falcabit etiam ipse, et omnes alii de villata, pratum, quod dicitur Wytemers, et non allocabitur eis, quia habent unam acram prati in loco assignato, pro qua fenum adunabunt, et carriabunt.

much more elastic. The thirteenth-century manorial extent was organized to provide several hundred men for 'extra' boon days, if necessary, while at the same time it was allowed that no, or few, boon works might be necessary in a particular year.[17] It was probably from this vague elasticity, not from the lack of real obligation in this service, that the term boon finds its origin. Despite the overtone of benefaction in the word boon itself, there is no indication that the obligation had been any the less real for the villein than the obligations behind such words as *donum* or *elemosina*, by which a sale to a feudal superior might be expressed. But the thirteenth-century arrangements differed in the precisions that were made for this contract, particularly with regard to food payments. The villein usually had to commit all his manual resources when called to do boon work for the lord. This was most frequently described as 'all the villein's workers, except his wife', for, as the extent of Ellington explains, the wife, or someone else, must look after the villein's home.[18] About one-half dozen of the extents further specify that if the villein has four men he can stay at home himself (Holywell), or merely direct them at work (Warboys, and other manors).

In return for the harvest boon works, the lord or farmer had been obliged from the earliest extents to pay the labourers the full cost of their daily maintenance (*corredium, cum cibo, ad cibum domini*, etc.).[19] Immediately after the passage citing the obligation of the villein and his labourers to appear for boon work, there are long paragraphs in the thirteenth-century extents specifying the lord's obligations to the villeins for these works. The villeins were to have a real feast of bread, meat, *potagium*, cheese and ale. If the boon works extended over several days, one of the days was usually to be a 'fish' day, for which the labourers received eels rather than meat. When the boon works lasted several days the food payments, and the boon obligations themselves, gradually tapered off until only the usual week work was owed. But the striking feature of these arrangements is the extra obligation that the villein was expected to have incurred by his food consumption at the full boon. By the third day he was expected to supply the same labour for the same amount of food, but without ale. Above all, he often had to supply a man for one day's work just in payment for the food of the first boon day.[20]

---

[17] E.g. *Carts.*, I, p. 367: Præterea, si firmarius facere voluerit tres precarias in autumno, ... For reasons of simplicity we shall be concerned only with the harvest boons, and the obligations of the larger villein tenements, in the following paragraphs. The same remarks apply to the general pattern of other boon works, and to the boon obligations of lesser men.

[18] At Broughton, where it is mentioned that either the villein or his wife must accompany the workmen, there is also a clause to the effect that if the villein is ill his wife may stay at home to care for him while the labourers work (*Carts.*, I, p. 336-7).

[19] *Carts.*, III, p. 312: Et ter facit precarias firmarii, et comedit cum eo totidem vicibus.

[20] E.g., in recompensatione prandii precariæ precedentis, sine cibo at St. Ives; Et inveniet unum hominem in crastinum, ad reddendum cibum diei præcedentis at Holywell. This obligation was apparently called *hungerbedrype* at some manors, e.g. *Carts.*, I, p. 477. It should be noted that this was not the same obligation as that of supplying again the regular week work day that had been overlapped by the boon. At some manors, such as Barton, the boon work cancelled the regular work; but at several manors this work was simply transferred. The extent of Ellington (*Carts.*, II, p. 24), signifies quite clearly the two obligations — an extra day for food, and another as the regular week work day.

Since the cost of feeding the labourers so evidently tended to outweigh the worth of labour rendered, it is not surprising to find attempts to standardize and control their consumption. While *potagium* and ale were to be given 'in sufficiency', in many instances it was noted that one 'measure' of cheese was to be given, one firkin of meat between two labourers, or six eels for each. In all cases, the amount of bread to be given the labourers was carefully specified. This was most frequently to be one loaf for each workman, or in some instances two men were to receive three loaves. There was a concern for both the composition and the market value of the loaf. At Holywell the loaf was to be of wheat and rye, but mostly of wheat; at Houghton it was to be of wheat, but 'as it has fallen from the sheaves'.[21] The loaves at Broughton or Upwood were to be worth three farthings each, if purchased. This evaluation of bread was not apparently undermining the feast as the price of corn rose, for there was still a basic concern for consumption necessities. At Broughton, for instance, every two labourers received two loaves so that *quorum alter panis eis ambobus sufficiat.*[22] The lord was gaining recompense for adverse price changes in another way. As an early student of Ramsey documents has suggested,[23] the food supply of the villeins had evidently become a fixed quota, and with the rising prices for farm produce against the levelling off of wages, the villein was receiving in food value more than his labour was worth. In order to rectify this, most manors had established that in addition to the boon day without drink, an entirely unpaid-for gift of labour, or 'loveboon', could be solicited. This was usually the labour of one man for a day without his food; or at some manors it was the mowing of one furrow (*sellion*) of corn, without food.[24]

The data from boon works in some account rolls will allow us to see the large amount of labour available on the Ramsey manor.[25] But it is also important to recognize in the dependence upon villein tenants for this supply of labour the important intermediate position of the villein in the employment of manorial labour. Three or four pairs of hands had to be supplied by each virgater at the boon works, and for his many weekly and seasonal works on the demesne throughout the year he was to 'supply' of 'find' one or two men. If the villein could supply such labour from his own family, he could save much in the way of wage expenditure, and through the maintenance obligations and increment payments of the lord significant additions could be made to the family sustenance. The possibility of family subsistence generation after

---

[21] At Brington, (*Carts.*, II, p. 45), the labourers' loaves were to be simply of wheat.

[22] And for Holywell, *Carts.*, I, p. 300: et duo homines habebunt tres panes, ita quod quantitas panis unius duobus ad prandium sufficiat; ... For lawsuits instituted by villeins because of insufficiency of food owed them at the boon, see *infra*, Ch. VIII. Scattered remarks attest to the increasing preference of the lord for money wages over payments in kind or food wages proper. For example, at Ringstead (I, p. 411), all who worked in the autumn were now to

receive from the purse of the abbot 12d. for the sheaves they were accustomed to receive. Or at Cranfield (II, p. 18), the villagers have six pence for drink when they cut the lord's meadow.

[23] Nellie NEILSON, *Economic Conditions on the Manors of Ramsey Abbey*, pp. 45-46.

[24] Some loveboons might also be required for food given at other than harvest boons, e.g. for carrying loveboons (*Carts.*, I, p. 286).

[25] See *infra*, Chapter IX, Appendix IV.

generation upon a fixed plot of land, becomes more understandable with this flexibility of employment. The children of the villein could be employed by their father as well as among the wage labourers of the desmene. Again we may better appreciate, too, that the prosperous villeins would be sufficiently acquainted with these problems of labour employment on the manor to be able to rent large portions, or even all, of the demesne. Further opportunity to control more land and labour lay open to the enterprising villein through service as an important *famulus*, such as reeve or beadle.

II

WAGES

Whether or not the villein was ever responsible for all the work on the demesne, the closely defined obligations of the villein during the intensive agrarian production of the thirteenth century meant that both regular and temporary hired labour would also be necessary in considerable quantitites for the demesne. The account rolls reveal that workers were necessary in large numbers on the arable manors of Ramsey. Indeed, these wage labour groups were not incomparable with the numbers found in regions with a negligible villeinage tradition.[26] For example, in Broughton during 1252 an annual wage was paid in cash and food to fifteen *famuli*, and another fifteen men were hired from the Ascension to the Feast of St. Michael, in addition to the piece rate payments that went to winnowers, threshers, and artisans. On each of the Huntingdon manors at least, full annual wages were paid to eight or ten men, in addition to the part-time and piece-rate employments, until the end of the fourteenth century.

These men supplemented rather than replaced the traditional *famuli* and officials who were paid by a grant of land which they held exempt from the ordinary villein service and customary rents.[27] The reeve, beadle, and several ploughmen were always to be found as tenants on these conditions. For an example from Broughton again, the account rolls list the following tenement exemptions from the heaviest customary rents and services:

1244	reeve, beadle,	4	ploughmen,	woodward, carpenter.
1250	” ”	3	”	woodward, smith.

[26] E.g. R. A. L. Smith, *Canterbury Cathedral Priory*, pp. 124 ff.

[27] The thirteenth-century extents give a more elaborate description — but not one substantially different from the twelfth-century data (*supra*, Ch. II) — of payments in *acræ inbladatæ* to servants at the abbey. The most detailed fourteenth-century rolls only mention the *acræ inbladatæ* of the parson and *pro schep*, so presumably the other *acræ* had been compounded for wages (the reeves and beadles always received land, the woodward a money and corn wage, in account rolls). This paragraph on *acræ inbladatæ* from the Upwood 13th-century extents (*Carts.*, I, p. 351) is typical: "The following receive sown acres at Upwood: to the chamberlain one acre of wheat in the field next to that chosen for seed; to the parson two acres of wheat next to that of the chamberlain, and one acre of barley after dunging, and one acre of oats; the reeve, beadle, and woodward receive three one-half acres of wheat, and three (one-half) acres of oats in the field next to the parson; to the launderer of the church two acres of oats; to the carpenter, mason, and carter of Ramsey in the same fields

1252	reeve, beadle, 4 ploughmen,			woodward, smith, carpenter.
1307	”	”	4	”	smith, 4 virgates *ad censum*.
1311	”	”	3	”	4 virgates *ad censum*.
1312	”	”	3	”	4 virgates *ad censum*.
1314	”	”	4	”	3 virgates *ad censum*, woodward.
1319	”	”	4	”	4 virgates *ad censum*, woodward.
1326	”	”	4	”	4½ virgates *ad censum*.
1342	”	”	4	”	
1344	”	”	4	”	

There must have been some strong arguments from the point of view of managerial efficiency for the use of wage labour against the simple development of the minute equation of demesne needs and villeinage *opera*.[28] The customary rigidities facing the legal enforcement of *opera* in relation to new or increasing complexity of the agricultural arts, were undoubtedly important. But that increased interest of the abbey in the exploitation of land at a period of apparent ease in the labour market, to judge by the pre-Black Death history of wages, would be a more positive factor in the growth or maintenance of the wage labour group.   Despite fluctuations in such real values as corn prices, money wages of labour on Ramsey manors remained practically fixed over the hundred years before the Black Death.   In some cases there had been a slight rise in this portion of the wage by 1300; but on the other hand, payments in corn, which represented over seventy-five per cent of the *famuli* wages, generally fell from about one ring per month to a ring for six weeks, so that total annual wages would have fallen somewhat in the hundred years after 1250.[29]

There were some variations in money wages among manors until the mid-fourteenth century, though these were seldom by as much as a shilling. Within each manor the ploughmen, carters, shepherds, swineherds, cowherds,

---

three acres of wheat, and three acres of oats. And note that the reeve eats in the manor house in the autumn, and he eats with the winnower when he comes to make the 'quarters' (for livery), but at no other time.''

[28] An example from the 13th-century Ringstead extent (*Carts.*, I, 408) shows the close relation between *opera* and wages (in cash or food) in the manorial economy: Si dominus voluerit, custodiet (a tenant on twenty-six acres) faldam suam, vel sequetur carucam suam, et tunc quietus erit de prædictis operibus, et si custodierit faldam, habebit pro stipendiis suis duos solidos, et unam acram siliginis, et unam rodam hordei, de meliori siligine unum panem, et unum allec, vel caseum. Habebit etiam tertium agnum meliorem de falda, et melius vellus de velleribus domini. Et habebit faldam super terram propriam per quindecim dies ante Natale, et per quindecim dies Natalis, et per quindecim dies post Natale . . .
Et præterea, qualibet die Mercurii, habebunt singuli ad vesperam duos panes, et caseum, vel duo allecia.

Si custodierit carucam inveniet unum hominem sicut prius, et habebit cibum sicut prius, et tantum unam acram siliginis, et unam acram hordei, et octo panes, ad metendum illas, et companagium sicut prius.
There is no way of determining whether the ploughmen who held lands exempt from works on every manor (as in the example from Broughton above), were always the same men as those ploughmen receiving money wages on every manor (see Tables *infra*, this chapter).

[29] The rise in price of corn probably accounts for that reduction in broad payments of *acræ inbladatæ* by the late 13th and early 14th centuries (*supra*, n. 27).   The arrangements at Gloucester show clearly the attention given to this increased value of wages in kind: (*Cartularium*, III, p. 218) Item quod nullum bladum trituratum alicui solvatur per remunerationem alicujus servitii, sed si necesse illud exposcerit, vendatur bladum et solvantur denarii pro mercede.

and dairymen usually received the same wage. The *seminator* who was found on all manors in the thirteenth century but seems to have disappeared by the fourteenth, was a different type of employee. His sowing performance was checked by a tally; he was perhaps a freeman like William Le Boys (Weston, 1307, 1313), or Simon Le Waleys (Slepe, *ca.* 1300), and his part-time wage was greater than the current annual money wage of the *famuli*. Another employee receiving a higher wage was the woodward: both his money wages and wages in corn were consistently greater than those of the above-listed *famuli* group. From the mid-fourteenth century, the woodward usually had a half-mark added to his wage 'for his robe', perhaps owing to the increasing importance of his work,[30] or he may by then have usually been a freeman.[31] Part-time workers grouped with the *famuli* usually included servants of the bailiff and assistant shepherds for the fens during the summer months. The thirteenth-century rolls occasionally mention a *mercator* hired for a few weeks; two fishermen were being hired at Weston in the late fourteenth century; there was a keeper of goats at Abbots Ripton until *ca.* 1375; and most of the manors paid for an accountant before the mid-fourteenth century. By the late fourteenth century a 'cook' — probably the malt maker — had appeared on all manors.

In addition to his regular annual wages, the labourer received a 'gift' of usually one halfpenny at Christmas and one farthing at Easter. This sum has not been included in the table of money wages given below. With the short supply of labour after the Black Death this gift was often increased, especially until the stabilization of the money wage at 6s. around 1360. The simple table of *famuli* 'stipends' also fails to show the increased earnings of this labour group from meals taken at the expense of the manor house, which seem to become more frequent when men were being employed for extra seasonal works, owing to the shortage of customaries after the mid-fourteenth century. Towards the close of the fourteenth century the money wage was often supplemented by a 'reward' bonus of one-half mark (e.g. Houghton in Tables, *infra*). The account roll mentions occasionally (e.g. the carter and one ploughman at Warboys who received 8s. each extra in 1393 because they were freemen) that this was due to his being a freeman. But this reason was not always appended to the 'reward' item, and the reward sometimes varied. Accordingly, this bonus may be taken as an evidence of increased shortage of labour perhaps resulting from the freeing of more men, or from the large numbers working outside the manor *ca.* 1400.[32] The wages of seasonal workers often provide another example of wage elasticity in response to short supply at this time. For example, a ploughman who was taken on at Slepe from February 15th to Michaelmas in 1417 received (in addition to the usual corn rents) the same total money wage as the ploughmen hired for the full year.

---

[30] See Chapter X, n. 26.
[31] See further *infra*, this chapter.

[32] See further, Chapter X, for these points.

TABLE XLV

MONEY WAGES OF *FAMULI*

S. = sower; B. = shepherd; P. = pigman; E. = accountant; Cart. = carter; W. = woodward; D. = dairyman; Bed. = beadle; Caruc. = ploughman; V. = cowherd; M. = *mercator*.

When more than one, the number of workers is put in brackets. The wages are in shillings, pence, and are annual unless otherwise indicate1.

Broughton

Year	S.	Cart.	Caruc.	B.	W.	V.	P.	D.	M.	E.
1311	—	—	2.8 (4)	2.8	4	2.8	2.8	—	3	—
1312	4s.	3.2	2.8 (4)	2.8	4	2.8	2.8	2.8	—	—
1314	4	3.8	3 (4)	3	4	—	3 (2)	3	3	5
1326	4	3.6	3 (4)	3	4	—	3	—	—	5

								Bed.	Cook	Servant
1344	—	—	3.6 (3)	3.6	4	3.6	3.6	4	—	—
1346	—	—	3.6 (3)	3.6	4	3.6	3.6	4	—	—
1378	—	6	6	6	10.6	—	6	6	6	6
1380	—	6	6	6	10.8	—	6	—	6	6
1386	—	6	6	6	—	—	6	6	6	6
1392	—	6	6	6	10	—	6	—	6	6

Houghton

Year	Cart.	Caruc.	B.	W.	V.	P.	D.
1316	3.6	3.6 (4)	3.6	4	3.6	2.8	3.6
1324	3.6	3.6 (4)	3.6	—	3.6	2.8	3.6
1336	3.6	3.6 (4)	3.6 (2)	—	2.6	2.6	—

Year							Cook
1338	3.6 (2)	3.6 (4)	3.6 (2)	—	—	—	—
1364	6	6 (3)	6 (2)	—	6	6	6
1369	6	6 (4)	6	—	6 (2)	6	—
1371	6	6 (3)	6	4	—	6	5
1372	6	6 (4)	6	—	—	6	—
1383	6	6 (4)	6	—	—	6	6
1394	13.4	6 (3)	6	—	—	6	—
1396	10	10 (3)	13.4	—	—	8	6
1399	13.4	10 (4)	13.4	—	—	8	13.4
1407	6 (2)	6 (2), 6.8 (1)	6	—	—	—	13.4 5
1418 *	20	13.4 (2)	8	—	—	—	—

* for 48 weeks, except the shepherd, who was paid for 6 months.

Slepe

Year	S.	W.	E.	Cart.	Caruc.	V.	B.	P.	D.	Cook	M.	Pr.
1307	20	10.8	6	3.6 (2)	3.6 (3)	3.6	3.6 (2)	3.6	3.6	—	—	—
1314	20	10.8	6	3.6 (2)	3.6 (2)	3.6	3.6 (2)	3.6	3.6	3.6	—	—
1324	—	10.8	4	3.6 (2)	3.6 (3)	—	3.6	3.6	3.6	—	2	4
	Ball.											
1342 ?	22	—	—	3.6 (2)	3.6 (3)	3.6	3.6 (2)	3.6	—	3.6	3.6	—
1351	—	—	—	6 (2)	6 (2)	4	6	6	—	6	5.4 *	—
1366	—	—	—	6 (2)	6 (2)	6	6	6	—	6	—	—
1387	—	—	—	6	6 (4)	6	6	6	—	6	—	—
1390	—	—	—	6	6 (4)	6	6	8	—	—	—	—
1417	—	—	—	6	6 (4)	6	6	6	—	10	—	—

Ball. — bailiff Pr. — prepositus

* servant.

TABLE XLV (*Cont'd.*)

MONEY WAGES OF *FAMULI* (*Cont'd.*)

Cap. — custodian of goats.

Abbots Ripton

Year	Cart.	Caruc.	B.	P.	V.	Cap.	Cook	W.
1252	3.8	3.8		3.8	3.8	—	—	—
1307	4.4 3.8	3.8 (5)	3	3	3	—	—	—
1313	4.4 3.8	3.8 (5)	3	(2) 3	3	3	—	—
1324	4.4	3.8 (4)	3	(2) 3	3	3	—	—
1342	4.4	3.8 (4)	3	3	3	—	—	3.4
1364	6	6 (2)	6	(2) 6	6	6	6	6
1375	6	6 (4)	6	6	—	6	6	10.8
1385	6	6 (2)	6	6	—	—	6	10.8
1388	6	6 (2)	6	8	—	—	6	
1395	10	8 (2)	10	10	—	—	8	10.8
1396	10	10 (2)	10.6		—	—	10	11.2

Holywell

Year	Cart.	Caruc.	B.	P.	V.	Cook	W.
1307	3.6	3.6 (2)	—	3.6	—	—	—
1324	3.6	3.6 (3)	—	3.6	—	—	—
1354	3.6 (2)	3.6 (2)	—	3.6 (2)	3.6	—	4
1356	5 (2)	5 (2)	—	5 (2)	5	—	4
1364	6	6 (2)	—	3 (2)	6	—	4
1371	6	6 (2)	—	6	6	—	4
1383	6	6	6	6	6	6	4
1399	6	6 (2)	6	6	6	—	3.4
1401	6	6 (2)	6	6	6	—	3.4
1402	6	6 (3)	6	6	6	—	3.4
1404	6	6 (3)	6	6	6	—	3.4

Upwood

Year	Cart.	Caruc.	B.	P.	V.	Cook	W.
1252 *	—	2.10 (5)	3	2.10	2.10	—	2.10
1312	3	3 (3)	3	2	3	—	—
1371	—	6 (5)	6	6	6	6	10

* The mid-13th-century wage at Wistow (*ca.* 2.11) and Warboys (*ca.* 2.10) showed about the same increase as Upwood over the next one-half century; but generally the mid-13th-century data are difficult to abstract since they were given in broad seasonal terms rather than in years.

III

WAGES IN KIND

Both the composition and the quantity of the corn livery to the *famuli* varied somewhat, from the time of the first available evidence until the early fifteenth century.   Around 1250 the *famuli* livery was made up of fairly equal proportions of wheat and barley.   By 1300, peas, with smaller amounts of dredge and other grains, were being introduced to these wages in kind. At the Weston group of manors in 1297, for example, the *famuli* received corn from an allocation of 81r. 2b. wheat, 14r. 2b. tolcorn,[33] 18r. 2b. barley, and 49r. 3b. beans and peas.   Slepe and Holywell employed considerable amounts of rye for such purposes around 1300.   After the mid-fourteenth century the *famuli* livery was always composed of equal proportions of wheat and peas on the Huntingdon manors.

Around 1250 the wages in kind were usually at a bushel per week or a ring for five weeks (Broughton, Wistow, Upwood, Warboys).[34]   After 1300 the *famuli* received regularly a ring for six weeks — except for the sower and woodward who continued to receive a bushel per week.[35]   This arrangement continued on down through the century until the disappearance of the system in the fifteenth century — the only modification being the change of the woodward's livery from the bushel per week to one quarter per ten weeks.

Since peas were usually worth about a shilling per quarter less than barley, this change in composition of livery represents some fall in wages, from the value of the corn as well as the amount.   Thus, while his money wages may have gone up by a few pence between 1250 and 1350 (cf. Upwood), the carter, ploughman, etc., whose livery was reduced from a ring per five weeks to a ring per six weeks, would be receiving about one quarter of corn less per year, that is three or four shillings worth — in addition to a five to ten per cent reduction in the quality (value) of his corn wages.   It is not at all certain, however, that this fall in real wages reflected the actual money values of the *famuli* wages.   The price of corn sales to various workers on the manor failed to vary much over the hundred years (this chapter, section IV), but corn prices were rising throughout the country.[36]   If the *famuli* were receiving marketable corn which had appreciated with the general price rise, their total wages in money terms may have varied little in the hundred years after 1250, despite the relative decline.   The tables in this section show something of the composition, and of the importance in bulk terms, that these wages in kind manifested on Ramsey manors.

---

[33] This appears to be multure from the manorial mill on Ramsey estates.

[34] Although it is interesting to note that at Abbots Ripton, which had higher money wages at this date, the livery was one ring for six weeks.

[35] The sower was usually employed for only the short sowing season.   For example, at Holywell in 1324 he received one bushel per week for six weeks.

[36] E.g. J. E. Thorold ROGERS, *The History of Agriculture and Prices* (London, 1866), I, Ch. XIII.

Village labour acquired considerable earnings from piece-rates for threshing and winnowing, since, especially before 1349, a large proportion of this work was let out to wage labour. The winnower was most frequently paid a penny for eight rings of corn. Threshing rates varied more with the value of the corn — a frequent ratio in the early fourteenth century was a penny per ring for wheat, a halfpenny farthing per ring for barley and halfpenny per ring for oats. These threshing rates were doubled by the late fourteenth century. Other employment was afforded to the village tradesmen in varying work for the repair of mills, manorial buildings, etc.

While some index of village welfare in the twelfth and early thirteenth centuries can be obtained from the increase in numbers of small holdings hewed out by purpresture and assart, the thirteenth and fourteenth-century study of such economic conditions among the villagers must turn upon *employment* of village labour on the demesne. For Ramsey materials at least, there are no twelfth-century data of a sufficiently comparable nature to enable the measurement of increase in villagers' wage receipts when demesne cultivation was re-organized in the thirteenth century. The large number of two to four acre holdings in the mid-thirteenth-century extents indicate that the small plot and wages were still the basic components of many villagers' existence at that period. But the life of the non-land holding villager and even the small-holder, is only obliquely touched upon in account and court rolls, which are the only sources for later periods.

In order to acquire some impression of this importance of the demesne economy to the villager, and to help in the understanding of the insistence upon *opera* over the late Middle Ages, it is useful to have some notion of the dependence of demesne cultivation upon labour. Elton manor had been unable to regain many tenements to the *ad opus* after the Black Death. By 1383-4 the total wage bill (autumn expenses, money wages, threshing and winnowing, plough boons, custody of the mill, harrowing and mowing, to the bailiff, to 'forensic' errands exclusive of 57½ quarters of corn to the *famuli*) came to a money total of £32.5s.10d. And this in a year when the *total* receipts of the reeve were £62.9s.2d!

TABLE XLVI

FAMULI WAGES IN KIND

Year	Amount and Kind	Total
	Weston and Brington	
1297	81 r(ings) 3b. W. + 14r. 2b. tolcorn + 18r. 2b. B(arley) + 49r. 3b. B. & P.	164r.2b.
1311	?	126r.
1324	?	134r.
1368	73r.2b.3p. W. + 41r.2b.3p. P(eas) + 12r. mixed	127r.6p.
	Abbots Ripton	
1307	(W. + B. + P.)	95r.
1324	32r. 2b. W. + 10r. B. + 54r.½b. P.	96r.2½b.
1342	50r. 3b. W. + 45r. P.	95r.3b.
1364	42r.2b. W. + 42r. P.	84r.2b.
1375	42r. 2b. W. + 42r.2b. P.	85r.
1385	30r. 2½b. W. + 30r.2½b. P.	61r.1b.
1388	30r. 2½b. W. + 30r.2½b. P.	61r.1b.
1395	30r. 2½b. W. + 30r.2½b. P.	61r.1b.
1396	35r. 3½p. W. + 35r. 3½p. P.	70r.7p.
	King's Ripton	
1297	14r. W. + 32r. B. + 7r. P.	53r.
1307	25r. W. + 23r. 1b. P.	48r.1b.
	Slepe	
1307	(W. + rye + B. + P.)	93r.2b.
1309	47r. W. + 18r. rye + 23r. 2b. P. + 24r. B.	112r.2b.
1313	50r. W. + 5r. 3b. rye + 7r. B. + 26r. P. + 17r. 3b. tolcorn	106r.2b.
1314	53r.1b. W. + 4r.2b. B. + 44r. P.	101r.3b.
1324	31r.½b. W. + 15r.1b. B. + 20r.3b. P. + 9r. dredge + 24r. tolcorn.	100r.½b.
1345	47r.2b. 2p. W. + 47r.2b. 2p. P. + 1r. dredge	96r.1b.
1351	45r. W. + 45r. B.	90r.
1366	37r. 2½b. W. + 37r.2½b. P.	75r.1b.
1381	40r. 1b. W. + 40r.1b. P.	80r.2b.
1387	35r.1b.3p. W. + 35r.1b. 3p. P.	70r.2b.6p.
1394	49r.3b.4p. W. + 49r.3b.4p. P.	99r.2b.8p.

TABLE XLVI (Cont'd.)

FAMULI WAGES IN KIND (Cont'd.)

Year	Amount and Kind	Total
	Bythorn	
1297	21r.1b. W. + 15r. 3b. B..............................	37r.
1324	16r. W. + 6r.2b. Beans + 1r.2b. B. + 20r. tolcorn..............	44r.
	Broughton	
1244	48r.1b. W. + 79r. B...............................	127r.1b.
1311	22r.3b. W. + 19r.3b. P. + 49r. W. + 49r. P.....................	140r.2b.
1312	74r.3½b. W. + 68r.3½b. gross *blad'* *.....................	143r.3b.
1314	(W. + dredge + P.)..............................	138r.
1319	62r.½b. W. + 4r.3b. B. + 47r.1½b. P.....................	114r.1b
1342	41r.1b.3p. W. + 41r.2b. P........................	82r.3b.3p.
1346	42r. W. + (?)...............................	?
1378	?....................................	78r.1½b.
1380	?....................................	72r.
1386	34r.2b.3p. W. + 34r.2b. 3p. P.......................	69r.6p.
1392	?....................................	70r.3b.

* This is defined in several rolls as 'produce of the mill'.

Year	Amount and Kind	Total
	Holywell	
1307	15r. W. + 8r. rye + 2r. B. + 18r.2b. P......................	43r.2b.
1324	17r. W. + 5r.2b. B. + 8r.2b. P. + 23r. tolcorn................	54r.
1356	38r.1b. W. + 8r. rye + 2r.3b. P. + 28r. mixed..................	77r.
1364	40r.1b. W. + 11r.3b. rye + 2b. P. + 28r. *exitus* of mill..........	80r.2b.
1371	30r.1b. W. + 30r.1b. P..........................	60r.2b.
1383	31r.2b. W. + 31r.2b. P..........................	63r.
1399	35r.1b. W. + 35r. 1b. P...........................	70r.2b.
1401	36r.1½b. W. + 36r.1½b. P.........................	72r.3b.
1402	36r.1½b. W. + 36r.1½b. P.........................	72r.3b.
1404	36r.1½b. W. + 36r.1½b. P.........................	72r.3b.
1405	36r.1½b. W. + 36r.1½b. P.........................	72r.3b.
1409	21r.1b. W. + 21r.1b. P...........................	42r.2b.

IV

PRICES

The compilation of price statistics from the manorial accounts is complicated by the variable effect of those 'internal factors' which have a bearing on stock and corn transactions, that is, the age and sex divisions among animals, or the season and purpose of the stock and corn sale or purchase. Nevertheless, since the great bulk of the transactions come year after year under certain regular categories, a simple tabulation gives a fairly complete picture of manorial prices. To be specific: the hog was self propagating and very rarely were there purchases of this animal. Towards the late fourteenth century, purchases of brood sows or very young porkers occur for the first time on some manors, for example, at Houghton, four porkers were bought for two shillings in 1379, six porkers at sevenpence halfpenny each with five hogs at three shillings each in 1393, and one brood sow for three shillings, fourpence in 1396. On the other hand, considerable numbers of hogs had always been sold, occasionally at prices varying greatly throughout the year. In the following tables only these sales prices have been used, and they are weighted to include annual variations.

For the horses and cattle an equally simple price picture may be drawn. Until the late fourteenth century the sale price of horses and cattle was usually much below the purchase value of these animals, and, although this is only indicated for extremely low valuations, it may be assumed that such stock were the *senile* and *debile*. As a consequence, the following tables give the purchase prices only for horses and cattle. These, too, are weighted prices, and as the exceptional sales of colts or calves have been omitted, they represent the prices of the full grown animal only.[37]

Although the purchase and sale of sheep was very occasional and in small numbers before the late fourteenth century, it has been possible to tabulate some prices for the earlier period. Since both the sale and purchase of various classifications appear more often after 1350 the sheep prices have been collected in a separate table in order to handle the heavier concentration of data. These prices, too, are weighted.

Except for wheat, which was often obtained in some rather small quantities for seed, the only very frequent corn purchases were made for beans and peas. These were seldom more than the few quarters to make up the livery quota of this grain to the cellarer. The mid-thirteenth-century sales of corn had been made as far afield as London. But from the late thirteenth century it is only for a few instances, and most of these come in the late fourteenth century,

[37] Miss WRETTS-SMITH has noted ('Organization of Farming at Croyland Abbey', p. 191) that cattle were seldom sold or purchased in the intermediate stage of yearling bullock, or steer.
The extraordinary lack of variety in the numbers of horses (see Ch. V, Table XXVIII, *supra*), whether the stot or carthorse, is largely due to the policy of purchasing the necessary animals rather than depending mainly upon reproduction.

that there were sales 'in the market' — presumably that of St. Ives. The purchases likely took place on the manor itself or on some adjacent manor; the sales from the late thirteenth century were nearly all made to the part-time workers. Although the prices varied very little at these sales throughout one year, perhaps because most of the sales took place around the threshing time in the winter, the following tables are weighted. The fact that the prices of corn sold to labourers, expecially for wheat, were usually much below the figures given by Rogers and others, and varied less over the long run, suggests that the quality may have been inferior. Perhaps the large part of sales to village labourers involved low grade leavings.

TABLE XLVII

PRICES (shillings and pence)

Houghton

B. — *bought*; S. — *sold*.

Year	Wheat		Barley S.	Oats B.	Beans & Peas		Meal B.	Mixed S.	Hogs	Ox & Stot	Horse (cart)	Year
	S.	B.			S.	B.						
1319	.	.	.	.	.	2.6	.	.	3.11	13.3*	.	1319
1324	4.6	.	2.8	.	2.3	.	.	.	4.1	14.9	.	1324
1328	.	.	3.6	3	3.2	.	.	.	.	9.3	.	1328
1334	4	.	.	.	2.2	4.4	4	.	2.6	.	.	1334
1336	.	.	4	.	.	2.4	.	.	2.11	.	.	1336
1338	4.6	.	.	.	.	.	Malt S.	.	3.7	11.6	.	1338
1364	.	.	.	.	.	.	.	.	4.1	13.7	.	1364
1369	.	6.8	.	.	.	.	6	9	.	.	27.1	1369
1371	.	10.3	.	.	.	5.4	.	.	.	9.6	39.10	1371
1372	2.4	.	.	.	.	.	4.3	3.7	5.4	.	40.1	1372
1379	.	.	.	2.4	.	.	.	.	2.6	.	.	1379
1383	3.4	6.8 (s)	.	.	.	2.4	3.8	.	.	10	24	1383
1387	.	.	.	.	.	3.4	.	.	.	12	.	1387
1388	.	.	.	.	.	1.6	.	.	.	13.4	.	1388
1389	.	.	.	.	.	1.8	.	.	.	.	24.2	1389
1393	.	6	.	2	.	1.8	3.4	.	.	.	.	1393
1394	.	4.2	.	.	.	2	.	.	.	.	30	1394
1396	3.4	3.6	.	.	.	2.6	.	.	.	11.6	23.7	1396
1407	.	.	.	.	.	.	3	.	.	12.9	26.4	1407

(s) corn purchased for seed; all corn prices are per quarter.

* Cows were bought this year for 9s. ob.

TABLE XLVII (Cont'd.)

PRICES (shillings and pence) — (Cont'd.)

Broughton

Year	Wheat S.	Wheat B.	Barley S.	Dredge S.	Beans & Peas S.	Beans & Peas B.	Meal B.	Malt B.	Hogs	Ox & Stot	Horse
1244	5.8	.	.	.	1.10	.	.	.	5.1	.	.
1250	.	.	.	.	1.11	.	2.4	2.4	.	9.3	.
1252	5	.	4	2.6	2.4	.	.	.	.	9.2	.
1307	.	.	3.8	3	2.8	.	.	.	3.7	.	20
1311	.	.	.	.	.	3	Oats B.	.	3.5	.	.
1312	4	.	3.4	4.4	2	.	.	.	3.3	15	.
1314	6.4	.	.	3	4	.	.	.	4.3	12.3	19
1319	4	.	2.8	2	2.8	.	.	5	3.3	11	20
1326	4.6	5.4 (s)	.	.	4.4	.	.	.	2.1	.	.
1342	.	.	.	.	.	.	2.2	.	2.2	9.6	20.7
1344	.	.	.	.	.	2.8(s)	1.6	.	2.1	.	.
1346	.	.	.	.	.	.	.	.	.	.	.
1378	.	.	.	.	.	3.1	2.4	2.10	.	11.4	.
1380	.	.	.	.	.	.	.	4	.	.	.
1386	.	.	.	.	.	.	.	.	.	13.3	21
1392	.	.	.	.	.	2 (s)	.	.	.	.	.

TABLE XLVII (Cont'd.)

PRICES (shillings and pence) — (Cont'd.)

Holywell

Year	Wheat		Rye		Dredge S.	Peas B. & P.		Horse B.	Hogs S.	Beans B.	Oats B.	Barley B.	Year
	S.	B.	S.	B.		S.	B.						
1307	4.10	.	3.8	.	3.4	.	.	.	.	.	.	.	1307
1324	5.4	.	4.	.	Malt S.	3.	.	24.11	1.11	2.6	2.8	.	1324
1347	.	3.4	4.	.	.	.	.	.	.	.	.	2.8	1347
1356	.	.	5.	.	6.	.	.	.	.	.	.	.	1356
1364	.	15.4	.	.	.	.	6 (s)	.	3.4	.	.	.	1364
1371	.	5.3	.	.	.	.	.	43.4	4.8	.	.	.	1371
1383	.	5.4	.	4	4.	.	.	17.4	.	.	.	.	1383
1399	.	6 (s)	.	4.8	.	.	.	.	.	.	1.10	.	1399
1401	.	10 (s)	.	6.8 (s)	.	.	.	23.2	.	.	2.2	.	1401
1402	.	.	.	.	.	.	2.8 (s)	.	.	.	2.	.	1402
1404	.	.	.	.	.	.	.	8.3 (approx.)	.	.	1.8	.	1404
1405	7.4	6.8	.	.	.	.	3.4	.	.	.	1.4	.	1405
1409	.	.	.	.	.	.	.	.	.	.	1.6	.	1409

TABLE XLVII (Cont'd.)

PRICES (shillings and pence) — (Cont'd.)

Slepe

Year	Wheat		Barley		Peas		Hogs S.	B. & P. B.	Oats B.	Horse B.	Stot B.	Meal B.	Malt S.	Year
	S.	B.	S.	B.	S.	B.								
1307	4.8	.	4.	.	2.8	.	3.6	1.11	1.3	25.	10.1	.	.	1307
1313	4.10	.	3.2	.	2.6	.	3.4	1.7	2.4	.	.	.	.	1313
1324	.	.	.	.	3.3	.	.	.	.	16.	12.	.	.	1324
1345	.	3.	.	.	.	.	2.7	.	1.3	.	.	1.11	.	1345
1347	.	.	.	.	.	.	2.2	.	1.11	.	.	.	.	1347
1351	.	.	.	.	.	.	2.1	2.10	1.11	24.	.	.	.	1351
1366	.	.	.	.	.	.	4.3	.	2.8	26.8	.	.	.	1366
1381	.	.	.	3.	.	3.4	.	.	2.	33.4	13.	.	3.	1381
1387	.	.	.	.	.	.	.	.	.	.	.	.	.	1387
1390	.	5.	.	4.	.	.	4.2	.	2.	.	.	.	4.6	1390
1417	.	4.8	.	.	.	2.4	.	.	2.	25.6	13.4	.	.	1417

Table XLVII (*Cont'd.*)

PRICES (shillings and pence) — (*Cont'd.*)

Sheep

Note: These statistics of sheep prices are from account rolls of Warboys, Houghton, Holywell, and Broughton.

Year	Wethers		Lambs		Ewes	
	B.	S.	B.	S.	B.	S.
1244	.	1s.4d.	.	.	.	.
1252	.8	.	.	.	.8	.
1255	.11	.	.	.	.	.
1307	1.9	.	.	.	.	.10
1310	.	.	.	.	.	1.6
1314	.	.8	1.3	.	.	.
1316	.	.	1.8	.	.	.
1318	.	3.7	.	.	.	.
1319	.	1.11	.	.	.	.
1324	.	1.10	1.6	.	.	.
1325	.	2.2	1.11	.	.	.
1326	1.10	2.4	.	.	.	.
1328	1.4	.	1.1	.	.	.
1330	1.7	1.4	.	.6	.	.
1334	1.8	.10	.8	.	.	.
1335	.	.9	.	.	.	.
1336	.	.7	.	.	.	.
1342	.	.9	.	.	.	.
1344	.	1.	.	.	.	1.
1347	.	.7½	.	.	.	.7½
1351	.	1.3	.	.	.	.6
1353	.	.	1.2	.	.	.
1356	2.3	.	.	.	.	.7
1364	2.	1.6	.	.	.	1.1
1371	2.2	.9	.	.	.	.
1372	2.4	1.3	.	.	.	1.
1378	.	1.	.	.	.	.
1379	.	1.6	1.2	.	.	.11
1380	2.	.11	.	.	.	.
1383	2.	.	.5	.	1.6	.
1387	.	1.1	.	.	.	.11
1393	1.11	.	.	.	.	.
1394	.	.8	.	.	.	.
1396	1.6	.8	.	.	1.6	.7
1399	1.10	.8	.	.	.	.
1401	2.	1.2	.	.	.	.
1402	2.	1.2	.	.	.	.
1404	2.2	1.6	.	.	.	1.3
1405	2.	1.8	.	.	1.11	.
1407	2.1	1.4	.	.	.	.
1408	.	2.	.	.	.	.
1409	2.4	.	.	.	.	.

CHAPTER VIII

RETRENCHMENT IN ARABLE PRODUCTION AND ORGANIZED STABILITY IN MANORIAL REVENUES

I

THERE is little hope of isolating from the Ramsey account rolls 'normal' conditions of full agrarian prosperity over any great length of time, if such ever existed. When the regular series of rolls commences towards the end of the 13th century, the buoyant era in agrarian profits that had brought administrative re-organization on the Huntingdon manors was over, and the novel feature of these accounts is the cut-back from that bustling life of full employment on the demesne for market production, which had been realized at the mid-century. That all was not happy with manorial revenues was first disclosed early in the third quarter of the century with continued failures in the food farms,[1] which were largely a matter of corn livery by this time. It seemed to be accepted that the decline in production was chronic, for henceforth the gap in conventual revenues from farm deficits was filled by the abbot's purchase of lands in response to complaints by the convent,[2] rather than by increased capital expenditure on home demesnes; and there was still an underpayment in the livery, usually of about twenty per cent by the standard of earlier liveries and prevailing quotas, from at least the last two decades of the century.[3] At the same time there was a significant disappear-

TABLE XLVIII

CORN SALES ON ELTON MANOR
(to nearest quarter)

Year	Quarters	Year	Quarters
1287	16	1313	23
1297	6	1324	15
1307	11	1345	0
1311	12	1350	5

[1] See *supra*, Chapter IV, Section I, especially n.61 and text.
[2] *Supra*, Chapter IV, Section I, and *infra*, Chapter VIII, Section II.
[3] Corn livery to the abbey, 1284, *Add. Ch.*

34711; and many manors post 1300, especially Slepe, Holywell, Wistow, Upwood (see Table XXXVIII, Section III, Chapter VI).

ance of corn sales as important market items on the home manors. Henceforth only a few quarters were sold to villagers working on the demesne; the above table for Elton is typical of conditions on the home manors.[4]

The manorial mills also, which had been turning over valuable quantities of 'multure' to the lord at the mid-century, had all been let out for a money farm by the last decade.

Corn prices did not seem to have a basic position among the causes of this trend. In the first place, in view of the small sales of corn, prices were of minor importance in the actual accounting balance of the reeve. Moreover, in the prices that have been tabulated in Chapter VII, as well as from the general statistical evidence for the country as a whole over this period,[5] there was, if anything, a gradual rise rather than a chronic fall in prices — a trend in itself perhaps not unconnected with decline in production relative to a steady rise in population.[6] Furthermore, an elastic effect of prices upon corn production would not be easily established for the Middle Ages in England. For example, the revival for some years of the early 14th century brought a fairly long trend to increased production despite some considerable drops in prices. Or again, the cellarer was able to gain large profits from the sale of corn in those manors allocated to supplement his revenues, such as Lawshall, at the very period of lower returns in Huntingdon.

[4] Compare Table XXII in Chapter IV for corn sales at the mid-thirteenth century. An account roll for the abbot's chamberlain (1267, *Cotton Charter* XIII, 25) indicates something of profits from corn sent on to the abbey after settlement of expenses and livery. This document may be the more indicative when it is recalled that the conventual manors were in the abbot's hands at this time. Except for Abbots Ripton (and it is not clear whether the large sum bracketed after that manor below was actually from sales on that manor), there would seem to have been no net profits from sale of corn on many home manors at this date. It will be recalled that Broughton manor also handled the corn from King's Ripton, and that neither manor was burdened with livery for the convent. As the following table illustrates, the profits from sales outside Huntingdon were still important, even from Burwell, Elsworth, and Therfield which also sent large corn liveries to the cellarer:

PROFITS FROM SALE OF CORN IN 1267

Manor	£ s. d.	Manor	£ s. d.
Cranfield	7 . 13 . 3 .	Hilgay	8 . 5 . 0
Shillington	27 . 13 . 8 .	Elsworth	13 . 6 . 0 .
Barton	16 . 0 . 0 .	Therfield	36 . 10 . 4 .
Ringstead	5 . 12 . 5 .	Slepe	3 . 13 . 4 .
Broughton	20 . 8 . 10 .	Abbots Ripton	3 . 6 . 8 .
Burwell	10 . 0 . 0 .		(+ 31 . 16 . 8 . ?)
		Bythorn	11 . 10 .

[5] J. E. Thorold ROGERS, *The History of Agriculture and Prices*, I and II, passim.
[6] On general population, see J. C. RUSSELL, *British Medieval Population* (Albuquerque, N. Mexico, 1948); and for Ramsey, *supra*, Chapter II, Table X. There was likely an increase in numbers of landholders on the fen manors until the fourteenth century (a tax roll of 1315, Oxford, Bodleian, Rawlinson 333, 62 ff., lists 20 to 30 per cent more tenants than were numbered in the thirteenth-century extents for Ringstead and Welles). The sale of corn to villagers of the manor may have only appeared from the late thirteenth century, according to the evidence of Huntingdon account rolls.

TABLE XLIX

RETURNS FROM CORN SALES IN LAWSHALL

Year	Return	Year	Return
1273	£32.13s.2d.	1351	£4.14s.5d.
1279	£48.15s.8d.	1357	£9.8s.0d.
1335	£24.3s.0d.	1367	£16.13s.1d.
1347	£22.16s.2d.	1370	£12.6s.10d.
1348	£7.4s.0d.		

It is also singularly elusive and on the whole unrewarding, to make the fall in corn production over the latter half of the 13th century a simple *sequitur* of decline in yields.   Certainly, marginal lands were being cultivated in many parts of the country, and perhaps at Ramsey;[7] very little new assart lands were to be brought under the plough and two generations of intensive cultivation may have exhausted the primal heart of the soil.   But yield ratios are not by themselves convincing proof of this.   The ratios of returns to wheat and oats sown, the main crops around 1250, seem to have been frequently as high as 5 and 3 respectively, and the barley returns were in some cases exceptional. Over the longer period for data available towards the end of the century, there were years of somewhat lower yields, but they were not exceptional variations from the 1250 scene, and the whole pattern of corn returns for this later period fails to present any consistent evidence for a fall in the rates of yield since the mid-century.

Upon closer examination the inadequacy of this evidence from yield ratios is not surprising.   Yield ratios are themselves functions of important variables. One of these is the efficiency of cultivation; another, and almost a corollary of the first, is the intensity of seeding.   Upon the first point, it may be recalled from Chapter VI that a revolution in the old crop rotation system was well under way by the end of the thirteenth century.   A fall in productivity may already have been felt, therefore, and steps were being taken to redeem the situation; or, following Walter de Henley's advice,[8] it was simply a matter of reduction in costs.   Whether the two course crop also involved a primitive exploitation by repeated seedings of oats, the Ramsey documents do not

[7] Ch. VI, Tables XXXVI and XXXVII, and the accompaning observations.   There would seem to be no economic reason from the part of market demand for a decline in oat production. See Lawshall, Girton, or the manors of Clare in Suffolk (G. A. HOLMES, The English Nobility in the Reign of Edward III, Ph. D. dissertation, Cambridge, 1952), where oats continued to be an important item of production and sale in the fourteenth century.

[8] E. LAMOND (ed.), *Walter of Henley's Husbandry* (London, 1890).

reveal, but in any case, the fact that fifty per cent of the arable sown was in an oat crop rarely giving a return of 3 to 1, and in the fourteenth century seldom returning more than seed, would be a sufficient argument in itself for some rotation change that would introduce more of the high yielding barley.

But the introduction of the more efficient system of rotation only appears *after* a long period of deficits in demesne returns! One reason for this paradox may be fairly obvious — if something like the fourteenth-century 'standard' of seed per acre were employed,[9] there was on most of the demesnes, which averaged from two to three hundred acres of arable sown annually, only some dozen acres sown each year until the fourteenth century with the restoring legume.[10]   In short, the three course system was not conceived in the 13th century on Ramsey estates as a panacea to the problem of productivity maintenance.   And even later, over hard times and good times in the fourteenth century, it was found necessary to increase the sowing of beans and peas until they became the second crop, surpassing in acreage sown the much more valuable wheat, and only exceeded by the high yielding barley.   Throughout all this evolution, legumes were important additions to the diet of livestock, but there was no apparent correlation between the outstanding increases of stock in the 13th century, and the more extensive cultivation of beans and peas.   In fact the new grains may have brought a decline in the quality of bread: a few quarters of beans and peas had always been included in liveries to the abbey, but with the changes in harvest over the fourteenth century, beans and peas began to supply 30 to 50 per cent of the *famuli* wages in kind that were at an earlier period made up solely of wheat and barley.   It would appear to be the crop rotation system, geared to the production of barley,[11] which encouraged the large sowing of legumes.

Throughout the interplay of these many elements, there is no explicit evidence that the rate of corn yield set by itself the initial stage of the thirteenth-century recession, or was in turn the catalyst of early fourteenth-century prosperity.   There may have been more predominant forces over cyclical turns, such as climatic perturbations and stringencies in those capital commitments necessary to more intensive cultivation and seeding.   And it has been suggested in Chapter VI, that conversion to pasture may have been a first step in the fall of arable returns.   But in any case, amidst the various complicated threads of manorial production, the argument for diminishing returns continually asserts itself, whether in the long run retrenchment over the late 13th century, or during the secular stagnation in demesne cultivation over the 14th century.

The retrenchment accompanying deficits in total production was accompanied simply by a restrictive trend in cultivation.   It may be recalled from

[9] See Chapter VI, Section IV.
[10] The legumes might only be said to have reached their full-fledged part in the rotation system (Ch. VI, Section IV) upon most of the Huntingdon manors from the mid-fourteenth century.   Previous to that, and especially before the fourteenth century,

their presence usually accorded with small dietary demands of the food farms.
[11] This may have been much like the increase in intensity of sowing on Canterbury manors at the beginning of the fourteenth century (R. A. L. SMITH, *Canterbury Cathedral Priory*, p. 133).

TABLE L

TENEMENTS *AD CENSUM* IN THE LATE THIRTEENTH AND EARLY FOURTEENTH CENTURIES

Year	Wistow	Upwood	Broughton	Warboys	Houghton	Abb. Rip.	Weston	Holywell	Slepe	Year
ca. 1250	0	0	0	0	?	0	?	0?	0?	*ca.* 1250
1297	4½v.2c.	1v.	—	—	—	—	2c.	—	—	1297
1303	—	1v.1c.	—	6v.8½c.	—	—	—	—	—	1303
1306	5v.	4v.	4v.	6v.8c.	—	—	—	—	—	1306
1307	—	—	—	—	—	8v.	—	8v.	16v.	1307
1311	5¾v.1c.	—	—	—	—	0	2c.	—	—	1311
1312	—	2v.3c.	4½v.	—	—	0	—	—	—	1312
1313	—	2v.5c.	—	—	—	0	—	—	—	1313
1314	—	—	—	—	—	0	—	—	16v.	1314
1315	—	—	—	—	—	½v.	—	—	—	1315
1316	6v.1½c.	—	—	—	—	—	—	—	—	1316
1318	—	—	—	1¼v.7c.	—	—	—	—	—	1318
1319	—	1v.5c.	4v.	—	15v.10cr.	—	—	—	17v.	1319
1324	5¼v.6½c.	4½v.2c.	—	2¼v.7c.	22v.1c.10cr.	3v.	2c.	8v.	18½v.2c.	1324
1325	—	—	4½v.	(?) 3c.	—	—	—	—	—	1325
1328	—	—	—	—	24v.½c.10cr.	—	—	—	—	1328
1329	—	—	—	½v.4c.	—	—	—	—	—	1329
1334	—	—	—	—	25v.½c.10½cr.	—	—	—	—	1334
1335	5½v.3c.	—	—	½v.4c.	—	—	—	—	—	1335
1336	—	—	—	½v.4c.	20v.8cr.	—	—	—	—	1336
1338	—	—	—	—	27v.22c.12cr.	—	—	—	—	1338
1342	—	—	2v.	—	—	¾v.	—	—	—	1342
1343	—	4v.5c.	—	2c.	—	—	—	5v.6c.	—	1343
1344	—	—	2v.	—	—	—	—	—	—	1344
1345	—	—	—	—	—	—	—	—	16v.	1345
1346	4v.4c.	—	2v.	—	—	—	—	—	—	1346
1347	—	2½v.3c.	1¾v.	—	—	—	—	—	19½v.	1347

the chapter on corn statistics that drastic reductions in seeding by the low yielding oats were reflected directly in the total decline in the volume of corn sown by as much as twenty-five per cent. Whether or not there was a conversion of some demesne lands to pasture with this trend, it is clear that labour was employed less on the land, as the reeve helped make ends meet by the rental of larger villein holdings and the sale of villein works.

Sometime over the second half of the thirteenth century, all the conventual 'home manors' adopted a regular policy of commuting for an annual sum the principal customary rents and services owed from some tenements, thereby, in accounting terminology, putting some of the tenements *ad censum*. This renewal of the twelfth-century policy contrasted with that of the mid-thirteenth century, when there had been infrequent, if any virgate or cotland holdings *ad censum*.[12] The preceding table is concerned, unfortunately, in large part with the early fourteenth century when some recovery in demesne cultivation had set in. The number of lands *ad censum* may have been much more extensive a generation earlier.

Some further constriction of demesne cultivation may be noted in the sale of villein works which now became a regular item of manorial revenue. Works were not sold with any frequency or in a detailed fashion around 1250;[13] but from a charter of 1293,[14] a systematic project for the sale of villein *opera* comes to light and there were heavy sales at certain seasons on Ramsey manors. From the fact that *opera* were not sold with equal consistency throughout the year, it may be assumed that this was a complementary rather than alternative policy to the placing of lands *ad censum*. That is, until well into the fourteenth century, on none of the manors investigated would there appear to have been sufficient excess works throughout *every season*[15] for a number of years, that would permit the commutation of all works demanded from one of the larger tenements (in short, additional *ad censum* in place of the *vend' op'*), even if the numbers of excess works were always predictable. The sale of *opera* was simply a meticulous pricing of work obligations owed to the lord as determined by seasonal needs, decisions to spend less on cultivation, and of course, efforts to bolster dwindling agrarian revenues.

---

[12] The *ad censum* arrangement was mentioned of course in the 13th-century extents. From the extent evidence the *ad censum* appears to be emphasized in those manors obviously farmed at the time, i.e. Houghton, and the Weston group. In addition to the manors in the above table, the mid-thirteenth-century accounts show no tenements *ad censum* at Therfield, Ringstead, Brancaster, Hilgay, and Walsoken. It should be mentioned that the money 'farms' paid by the villeins for former freeholds (like the *terra Clairvaux* at Wistow), or any of the traditional *redditus*, are quite distinct from the *ad censum* payments when they are mentioned in the Ramsey manorial accounts.

[13] There is mention of some sort of commu-

tation of works (usually 'relaxed', instead of the 'sold' designation of later rolls) in only 9 of the 20 mid-13th-century accounts. Four of these payments were for carrying services; and only at Weston did these exceed 10s. At Therfield 4s.6d. was paid for autumn works; the reeve commuted a few works at Warboys in 1250, and Broughton regularly commuted the *op.' bras'* for about 10s.

[14] *Add. Ch.* 34341.

[15] The work seems to have been sold at only one season, or at least so it may be deduced from the one rate, in the late 13th and early 14th century. After the first quarter of the 14th century the sale of works became scattered over the whole year, as the following tables indicate.

TABLE LI

WORKS SOLD [16]

Upwood Manor

Year	@ ob.	@ 3f.	@ 1d.ob.	@ 1d.	Total Sales
ca. 1250	0	0	0	0	0
1297	580	0	0	0	£1.4s.2d.
1303	322	418	387	0	£4.9s.0d.
1306	754	459	449	0	£5.16s.2d.
1312	429	947	297	0	£5.14s.2d.
1313	600	421	149½	0	£3.10s.0d.
1319	0	0	824 *	0	£1.4s.4d.
1324	912½	341	21	333	£4.9s.8d.
1343	696	155	39	71	£2.5s.4d.
1347	172	407	0	0	£1.12s.7d.
1357	480	136	106	60	£2.5s.1d.
1371	360	287	141	167	£3.5s.1d.
1385	172	189	127	55	£1.19s.7d.
1386	166¾	71¾	146½	50	£1.18s.3d.
1392	170	152	106¾	58¾	£1.16s.0d.
1398	496	69½	184	126¾	£2.12s.9d.
1406	175	165	48½	31	—
1409	257	118	28	80	£1.8s.3d.
1412	272	77	21	0	£1.3s.2d.

* All works were sold together in 1319 @ f.; in these tables ob. = halfpenny; f. = farthing.

The cash renting of villein holdings and the sale of services meant that more of the burden of maintaining stable agrarian revenues was being thrown upon the peasant. This preference for rents must be considered as part of the same plan which had brought heavy investment in the purchase of rent-paying freeholds from the second half of the thirteenth century. In addition, much of the upward pressure on customary obligations, whether in the total number of works or in the commutation value of works and services, must be merely a rental adjustment to that doubling of manorial values which had come with price changes from the twelfth century.[17] However, by

---

[16] See Appendix I to this chapter for further tabulations of works sold.

[17] See *supra*, Ch. IV, Section I, for investments in freeholds and for some evidence of the degree of changes in prices and in total manorial values.

reducing the natural flexibility of the *opera* system, and that at a period of poor agrarian returns — to judge by the Huntingdon demesnes — the increase of works, coupled with a minute exploitation of the commutation system, brought many difficulties.

It has been noted in a previous chapter[18] that the customary money rents and dues in kind had remained practically constant from the twelfth century, and that the increase in rents from customary lands, until the mid-13th century at least, took place through recoveries or efforts to achieve additions to the obligatory services. Since many of these services were not evaluated, it is usually impossible to gain a detailed monetary picture of the total advance in terms of money rents. For example, the virgate in Cranfield was usually paying five or six shillings for all works and services in the twelfth century;[19] in the mid-thirteenth century a virgate *ad censum* in Cranfield paid five shillings, but also had to give boon ploughing, to plough one acre each season, to harrow one day each season, to perform some carrying services, to appear at both boon works, and to pay sixpence of the customary rents.[20]

On some manors, moreover, the increase in rents can be seen reflected in the *ad censum* rates by the mid-thirteenth-century extents. In Elton there were seven virgates *ad censum* in the late twelfth century, six of these at six shillings, no week works, and very few seasonal works, and one at five shillings with a few seasonal works. By the mid-thirteenth century the virgate *ad censum* would pay eight shillings and considerable works: "And the virgater *ad censum* ploughs and harrows, one day each week, like the *operarius*, and he does boon works in the autumn, and gives hens, etc."[21] Or in Burwell, where the twelfth-century rents had been much the same as those at Elton, the thirteenth-century extent shows the virgater giving eight shillings for his work, seventeen pence of the customary money dues (that is, all but sixpence), and all the ploughing of a land *ad opus*.[22]

While the charters of the late thirteenth century do not give much detail on the amount of work still performed by a *censuarius*, the *censum* itself by this period was from twelve shillings sixpence to sixteen shillings on Huntingdon manors.[23] The following calculation suggests that this rent for a bulk

---

[18] See Ch. IV, note 74.

[19] This was, in fact, the most common rent for the larger (i.e. 30 acres) virgate in Huntingdon and adjacent clayland manors in the 12th century. As has been suggested (Ch. VII, Sect. 1), some boon works were probably formally expected with the *ad censum* arrangement in the 12th century, even though not mentioned in the summary extents. However, in the lapse of services at that time, and from the injudicious grants *ad censum*, it may be expected that *de facto* only the *censum* was collected in many instances. While the term *censum* may refer to simple money rents of any kind in twelfth-century documents, the sense of the word that was to become common in the thirteenth and fourteenth centuries (as commuted works and services)

is usually quite distinguishable in the twelfth-century extents.

[20] *Carts.*, I, 445.

[21] *Carts.*, I, 488-9 (Elton).

[22] *Carts.*, II, 29. From the very complete *valor* of Whiston (1271) it can be easily calculated that the virgate *ad censum* for 8s. still owes work valued at 6s.6d. (*Carts.*, I, 55-6).

[23] That is, the rent value of villein holding as expressed in commutation terms had increased $2\frac{1}{2}$ to 3 times since the twelfth century (*supra*, note 19). There is no means of measuring the increase, if such, in the rents paid for the numerous freeholds purchased by Ramsey abbots from the mid-13th century, and presumably rented to villeins, since payments of this nature are seldom distinguishable from the omnibus

commutation may have included a special tax which raised the villein's payment above that due for piecemeal *opera* commutation.

As the *ad censum* rates and the value of *opera* remained fixed over long periods, a summation can be made to illustrate that the worth of a virgater's services for even the busiest year, when added to the customary rents commuted by the *ad censum* arrangement, comes to a figure below the *censum* itself.   In Broughton, for example, over 1314-1315 the virgater had to supply 114 works worth a halfpenny each, 15 at a penny, 29 at twopence, 15 again in the autumn at a penny and three or four days of extra works.   The total value of these comes to near 12s.6d.   The *ad censum* agreement also exempted the tenant from the main customary rents called *heusire* and maltsilver, which came to less than 1s.6d. for a virgate.   So even with a liberal calculation, the commuted obligations from one virgate of Broughton *ad opera* in 1314 comes to less than fourteen shillings, while the *censum* was actually 14s.8d.[24]   Although any peasant might desire the free disposition of his own labour acquired by this block commutation, especially if he were wealthy or childless, neither the ease of hiring labour[25] nor the general economic conditions of the late 13th century, could have favoured this *ad censum* agreement in the eyes of the villein.[26]

There were likely to be similar problems in the system of *opera* sales. The manorial extents definitely allowed for a certain flexibility in the work quota, such as the two or three boon works at ploughing according to needs.[27]

---

redditus item in the manorial accounts. On Ely estates, however, a later survey gives more comparable data on money rents, and some of this information pertains to several manors held by this abbey in Huntingdon.   Money rents seem to have been increased in the early 13th century (Edward MILLER, *The Abbey and Bishopric of Ely*, esp. p. 107, n. 4) when works were being increased (*ibid.*, p. 101); and many money rents had quadrupled or tripled between 1250 and the early 14th century (*ibid.*, pp. 110-111).

[24] Since the account rolls do not declare that 'all works are commuted' (this phrase was first used in the rolls after 1350 with the *arentata*; see Ch. IX, Section I) it must be assumed that some works were still performed along with this heavy money rent payment by the *censuarius*. From the *valors* of Whiston and Doddington in 1271, and the *arentata* (Ch. IX, App. I), the total value of 30 acre virgates was around 20s.

[25] It is important to recall that the *largest* holdings (virgates or semi-virgates) were usually *ad censum*, that is, the more wealthy villeins who could pay the money rent involved.   As a corollary, these more wealthy tenants who would be more liable to be affected by the advantageous labour supply (cf. references to large tenants' *operarii* — often as many as four being called to boon works —, 13th-century extents, *passim*) would have their wage bill

displaced by a money rent from the *ad censum*.   Finally, there seems to have been very little concentration of customary lands at this period (*infra*, Ch. X), that is, small opportunity for the *censuarius* to turn the 'extra labour' (from commutation) to further employment on the land. Consequently a fall in demand for village wage labour by the customary tenants might be expected to accompany increases in the *ad censum* in the late 13th century (see Ch. VII for evidence of a fall in *famuli* wages between 1250 and the early 14th century).

[26] A chance summary of the offending remarks from a suit for libel in the manorial court of Elton (1278; see MAITLAND, *Select Pleas in Manorial Courts*, I, p. 95) brings out clearly the villein attitude towards the *ad censum* in the late thirteenth century: "... charging him (the reeve) ... of taking gifts from the richer tenants as a consideration for not turning them into tenants at money rents, and with obliging the poorer tenants to become payers of money rents."

[27] One means of increasing works was to take advantage of this flexibility; e.g. the 13th-century extents of Weston (*Carts.*, II, p. 38): Dicunt etiam, quod si festa evenerint diebus Lunæ et Mercurii, unum illorum debet eis allocari, et aliud Abbati. Et si unicum evenerit festum aliquo dictorum dierum, illud eis allocabitur; tamen a tempore Ricardi Portarii dicunt quod

As has already been discussed in some detail in Chapter VII, both the terminology and the contractual spirit of boon work arrangements suggest further that a spirit of mutual obligation underlay the relations between villein and lord at periods of extra labour need in more affluent times. The lack of *opera* sales at the mid-century may bear out this traditional flexibility, for even at a time of relatively 'full employment' of demesne arable, climatic conditions, variations in harvest bulk, and irregularities of crop rotation must have caused some elasticity in the volume of work required.

The commutable value of the individual 'work' does not seem to have been advanced over the latter half of the thirteenth century. The villein at Broughton was paying at halfpenny, penny, and twopence, for release from various works in the account rolls from the end of the thirteenth century. The 1252 extent for Broughton gives the same values, (and, incidentally, indicates how the *ad censum* and *vendita opera* were both based upon the evaluation of individual weeks): "Moreover, the lord is able to put all of his (i.e. the villein's) work *ad censum*, if he wishes; which works are valued in winter and summer at a penny per day, and in the autumn at twopence, except piecework which is valued at a halfpenny for any day."[28] However, we have not been able to establish that there was anything like a doubling or tripling in the amount of customary work due after the twelfth century.[29] It would appear, therefore, that the great increase in *censum* by the thirteenth century was largely due to the increased evaluation of the individual work. This suggestion should not indeed be surprising, since, unlike the amount of customary work due, both the decision to commute and the commutable value of works were entirely at the will of the lord or of his officials in the extent regulations of all periods. The slight extant evidence of commutation values from an earlier period suggests the pattern of this increase. From Elsworth were due 1590 *opera* at a halfpenny (from Michaelmas to Gules of August) and 582 *opera* at a penny (Gules of August to Michaelmas) in the *valor* we have attributed to the late twelfth or early thirteenth century. However, by 1293 the *opera* receipts were being divided into four groups on all Ramsey manors, and while the majority of the work required over the long winter period was still being valued at a halfpenny, the works in the summer (from June, or Trinity, to Gules of August) were usually worth halfpenny farthing each, from August to the Nativity of the Blessed Virgin were worth three halfpenny, and thence to Michaelmas were sold at a penny.[30]

---

nullum fuit eis allocatum, et ideo in dispositione Abbatis. Another such example comes in the court rolls of Wistow (AULT, *Court Rolls of Ramsey*, etc., p. 210) where the customaries complain that they were at one time not obliged to perform their plough services the week after the Nativity of the Blessed Virgin. From the late 13th century the villeins as well as the abbots were more watchful lest custom should 'run against them'. This is well exemplified in the court roll of Elton (1300). See S. C. RADCLIFF, *Elton Manorial*

Records, p. 93, where the villeins claimed, and were upheld in court, that they were not bound to load the lord's carts, but only did it out of 'special affection' if they were asked by the reeve.

[28] *Carts.*, I, p. 337. Or for Wistow, *Carts.*, I, p. 359: Licebat etiam domino, pro voluntate sua, ad censum opera sua ponere; quæ quidem opera, cum dominus voluerit, sunt æstimanda.

[29] *Supra*, Ch. IV, Section I.

[30] It has not been possible to establish that these increases in value were related to

There is little distinction between works and payment for works in disputes over customary burdens of the thirteenth century, but it may be taken for granted that the sale of works at various seasons throughout the year would impose the same stringencies that have already been noted for the *ad censum*. That is, the detailed pricing of these works removed something of the control of his most adaptable source of wealth from the villein — his hours of work — both by the more careful itemization and the price demanded for commutation at a period of agrarian depression.

Opposition by villeins to the burden of these conditions flared up on Ramsey manors, as in many other parts of the country,[31] around the beginning of the last quarter of the thirteenth century. The famous legal dispute[32] between the abbot of Ramsey and the villeins of King's Ripton was initiated in 1275; on other Ramsey manors, where that appeal to the ancient liberties used at King's Ripton could not be made, the peasants apparently resorted to 'incidents'[33] and appeals to customary rights, when prevailing economic conditions magnified the burden of their services.

Although the previous pages have emphasized the commutation of services as an important element of demesne management,[34] and not least of all because this system provided a more manageable calculus of villein obligations, the complete *corpus* of the villein and demesne inter-relationship must be born in mind for a study of the villeins' opposition. In addition, it would seem most useful to regard villein *opera* as a form of rent — even as a contractual rent[35] — for the analysis of economic causation. From this viewpoint the

---

such real elements as the length of the 'work day', or the additions to the number of men required for certain boon periods by the 13th century.

[31] E.g. Steventon (1288), see Marjorie MORGAN, *The English Lands of the Abbey of Bec* (Oxford, 1946), p. 106; Staughton (1276), see R. H. HILTON, *The Economic Development of Some Leicestershire Estates in the Fourteenth and Fifteenth Centuries*, p. 72; the first wholesale evasion of works on some manors of St. Albans (1282), see A. E. LEVETT, *Studies in Manorial History*, (Oxford, 1938), pp. 179 ff.

[32] See MAITLAND, *Select Pleas in Manorial Courts*, I, pp. 99-106; and *Carts.*, III, pp. 59-64.

[33] Concerted opposition or neglect of *opera* by customary workers first appears *ca.* 1279. See W. O. AULT, *Court Rolls of the Abbey of Ramsey*, etc., pp. 183, 184, 186, 201 for Wistow, Upwood, and Broughton; and S. C. RADCLIFF, *Elton Manorial Records*, p. 2. The opposition to *opera* becomes almost chronic thereafter on some manors, e.g. *Elton Manorial Records*, p. 117 (1306), pp. 154-5 (1308), p. 193 (1312), p. 249 (1320), p. 256 and 259-260 (1322), pp. 298-9 and 301 (1331).

[34] The previous remarks have merely attempted to isolate the predominant function of commutation from a long-run viewpoint.

An administrative tool which was as flexible and multifaceted as commutation might be manifested in various permutations according to the size of the villein tenement, the number of *opera* due, the number of *opera* in relation to money rents, accessory wages paid to the villein, etc. For example, commutation was an obvious alternative when the virgater had no beast for his plough, (Edward MILLER, *The Abbey and Bishopric of Ely*, pp. 147-8), or if the villein was too weak to work on the demesne (A. E. LEVETT, *The Black Death on the Estates of the See of Winchester*, Oxford, 1916, p. 217, *addendum* no. 3); and profits from commutation brought a corresponding emphasis and need for *all* the non-commuted works (see complaints of this given for *The Estates of Crowland Abbey*, F. M. PAGE, p. 113).

[35] This is but another aspect of the *villata* concept so wanting in investigation (see above, Ch. IV). A few indentures between villein and lord are still extant (e.g. M. MORGAN, *The English Lands of the Abbey of Bec*, p. 108; and A. E. LEVETT, *Studies in Manorial History*, p. 192). On Ramsey estates a manorial *Register*, which does not appear to be extant, was frequently the last court of appeal in the disputes between customary tenants and the abbot, which appear on the court rolls.

revolts against services appear to be a reaction against the burden of rents at a time of depressed agrarian returns. In support of this, it may be pointed out that there is no tendency to the increase of labour services on Ramsey manors after 1250, above all where these can be counted in account rolls from the late 13th to the 15th century. And the court verdicts at this time, and over the following generations, give a further substantiation of this fact: As already noted in Chapter IV, the decision was handed down that the extent of Kings' Ripton had traditionally allowed the same services that were now being demanded by the lord and disputed by the villeins.[36] Finally, it was the largest villein tenancies which owed the most works. And when the court rolls inscribe opposition to works, it was not on the part of the poverty-stricken fringe, although poverty was taken into consideration in manorial lawsuits,[37] but it was an opposition by the main body of customary tenants. The conclusion appears strongly that the villein was often finding his traditional obligations too heavy by the late thirteenth century, probably owing to the decline in the profit margin for arable, and the milching of his free cash by special taxes, and large entry fines.[38] Furthermore, it is not surprising that decline or fluctuations in demesne arable profits should be reflected in their

---

The contractual nature of *opera* often appears in relation to villein rights in the manorial common, as well as with respect to his holding proper. For instance, extra boon works which certain villeins had failed to pay at Elsworth in 1290 (cited in G. C. HOMANS, *English Villagers in the Thirteenth Century*, p. 260) were apparently due for common of pasture.

The laboured emphasis on *opera* as rent throughout these pages has been thought necessary because of the concentrated study still necessary on this question, although more useful work is being done in recent decades. See e.g., E. A. KOSMINSKY, 'Services and Money Rents in the Thirteenth Century', *Ec. H. R.*, (1934-5), 24-45; Edward MILLER, *The Abbey and Bishopric of Ely*, especially, pp.101 ff.

While services due for rent, and wages received for services, might be closely bound up in one contract, expecially with regard to manorial officials (see *supra* Ch. VII, Section I, for an example from Ramsey extents; or E. MILLER *op. cit.*, p. 92), the two elements have not always been clearly distinguished. E.g. A. E. LEVETT, *The Black Death on the Estates of the See of Winchester*, seems to identify money payments to villeins who were rendering works (p. 34); but she fails to make clear distinction between the works and their value on one hand from the small payments to the villein in the nature of a wage on the other: "The *Arrura de prece*, on the contrary, was actually performed, and the bishop paid ½d. per acre for it, though it is carefully noted that it is really worth 6d. or 8d." (p. 63).

As already noted in Chapter VII, it is

often easier to trace the effect on villein economic conditions through these pay-. ments he received — usually in the form of meals or of loaves of bread at boon time on Ramsey manors — rather than by the performance of works. With the price of farm produce increasing vis-à-vis the relative stability of wages the economic trend moved to the disadvantage of the lord. An interesting case in point arose at Broughton in 1279 (W. O. AULT, *Court Rolls of the Abbey of Ramsey*, etc., p. 201) when all the workers left the great harvest boon because the loaves of bread given them were smaller than usual. The verdict was against the villeins, not because the loaves were smaller, but because the *Ramsey Register only required a loaf worth three farthings* for every two men. (The extraordinary number of fines for bad brewing which appear on the court rolls of all Ramsey manors in the late thirteenth century, was possibly another issue along the same basic pattern, i.e. with the price of ale fixed by the Assize, the brewers were being tempted to lower the grain content of their mixture because of higher grain prices.)

[36] And see the legal decisions in the cases cited *supra*, n. 31; Marjorie MORGAN, *op. cit.*, p. 109; R. H. HILTON, *op. cit.*, p. 75; G. C. HOMANS, *English Villagers of the Thirteenth Century*, the case of Hales, pp. 276-284.

[37] Many fines were being pardoned because of poverty *ca.* 1280, e.g. W. O. AULT, *Court Rolls of the Abbey of Ramsey*, etc., pp. 183, ff.

[38] These factors are illustrated below, Section II, this chapter.

closely integrated counterpart, the villein economy.   Especially will this be expected when, as will be discussed below, the system of *opera* sales was being used to cushion the fall in demesne revenues.

It is difficult to chart the effects of late thirteenth-century conditions on the non-land holding villagers.   The number of *famuli* declined, and the part-time employed in particular were fewer.   The decline was not so noticeable among annual wage earners, except in a ploughman less on some manors. As already mentioned, the use of less villein services on the demesne would be thrown back on the villeinage, probably effecting a decline in the hiring of wage labourers among villeins themselves.   In many ways overall retrenchment in demesne cultivation could not fail to depress the body of landless who depended upon boon works and odd jobs as a boost to their annual wage.[39]   But measurements of conditions among the peasantry are difficult, for labour was cheap and it may have been more economical for the reeves to sell *opera* and to hire wage labour in its place.[40]   In addition, the abbots were showing considerable concern for paupers in wills entailed during the second half of the 13th century,[41] so that the hiring of more wage labour would be an obvious welfare policy[42] for the villages.   In any case, while the total wage bill might fall considerably after the mid-13th century, to take threshing and winnowing as illustrations, there was sometimes a considerable preference for wage labour over villein services from the late 13th century, often at variance with the cycle of corn production, as in Upwood, 1324 (see Table LIII below).

[39] The large number of paupers (*supra* n. 37) who were unable to pay the fine of a few pence may have been from a village 'proletariat'.   But it is easy to illustrate that the margin for a smallholder could be very precarious too. See N. S. B. GRAS, *The Social and Economic History of an English Village* (Cambridge, Mass., 1930), pp. 71-4, where the author estimates that the surplus of the ¼ yardling might drop from 15s.11d. in a good year to 6s.9½d. in a bad year.

[40] The full-time labourers' wage would, to take a sample (e.g. Houghton *ca*.1300 — 4 quarters of corn @3s. plus 3s.6d.), be much the same amount as the virgaters' commuted works (i.e. the *ad censum* of 16s. for Houghton *ca*.1300).   But the *censuarius* still likely helped at boon works etc., and the *famulus* was available every day of the week, and more at the disposition of the reeve than the *ad opus* obligation.

[41] *Carts.*, II, *passim*.   The bequest of Abbot William is one of the most specific (p. 235): ... quicunque futuris temporibus fuerit sacerdos, per priorem et conventum electus, percipiat singulis annis, per manum Elemosinarii, quinque marcas ad duos terminos. Et unusquisque pauperum prædictorum percipiat cotidie unum panem et dimidium, ad quantitatem panis militis, de puro frumento, sicut cadit gerba, sine mixtura alterius bladi.   Dimidiam lagenam cervisiæ, potagium, et dimidium ferculum ad pran-

dium.   Die carnis dimidium ferculum carnis.   Et die piscium tria allecia, aut dimidium ferculum alterius piscis.   Et ad cœnam unum allec, aut unam portionem casei.   Unam tunicam singulis annis ad festum Omnium Sanctorum, aut tres ulnas panni lanei.   Et unum par sotularium, aut quatuor denarios.

[42] It is not unusual to find wage labour considered in welfare terms in the thirteenth-century extents; e.g. for Ramsey, *Carts.*, I, 473-474 (Pegsdon): "No one in the vill does, nor ever was so accustomed, nor is he under any obligation, to hold his land by following the lord's plough.   Nevertheless, if any strong virgater, or any other man of the abbot, should wish to drive or to hold the lord's ploughs on account of poverty, he shall receive the same wage as any non-villein (outsider) so employed, and shall defend his own land by livery or works."   At Halton, Bucks., it is specifically mentioned that gleaning was to be a means of support only to those who were physically incapable of earning wages by regular farm work (cited, G. C. HOMANS, *English Villagers in the Thirteenth Century*, p. 102).   Miss F. M. PAGE has made some very useful studies of this subject. See her article 'The Customary Poor Law of Three Cambridgeshire Manors', *Cambridge Historical Journal*, III, no. 2; and *The Estates of Crowland Abbey*, pp. 108-112.

Table LII

WAGE EXPENSES FOR THRESHING AND WINNOWING

Upwood		Warboys	
Year	Amount	Year	Amount
1250	19s.3d.	1252	31s.1d.
1252	34s.7d.	1306	17s.7d.ob.
1303	25s.1d.	1316	8s.11d.ob.
1306	12.11d.ob.	1318	13s.4d.
1312	10s.8d.	1324	10s.8d.
1319	9s.3d.	1325	8s.9d.ob.
1324	21s.6d.	1335	6s.5d.
1343	9s.9d.	1336	(10s.)
1357	9s.9d.	1342	10s.7d.ob.

The total aggregate of land rents had increased considerably from the mid-thirteenth century, owing to the addition of 'farms' from the freehold purchases of the abbot, as well as from the increases in the *censa*. Since customary rents varied only with the putting of lands *ad censum*, and the farmed parcels from the demesne did not appear until the fourteenth century, a simple total of all money rents from manorial accounts shows the consequences of the above-mentioned (farm + *censum*) rentier policies:

Table LIII

MANORIAL RENT ROLL : UPWOOD[43]

Note: The ob. is the half penny, g. the farthing.

Year	Amount	Year	Amount
1247	104s.1d.	1319	168s.8d.
1250	136s.9d.g.	1324	204s.7d.ob.g.
1252	130s.7d.	1344	220s.4d.ob.
1296	155s.2d.g.	1347	271s.9d.ob.g.
1306	180s.1d.ob.g.	1357	253s.6d.g.
1312	182s.1d.ob.		
1313	178s.1d.ob.g.		

[43] See Appendix II, this Chapter, for further examples.

But these new revenues from rents were not net profits. They became absorbed immediately, for the most part, by the costs of demesne management, in the same fashion as the petty corn or stock sales on the manor and the sale of 'works'. Some of the *redditus assisus* continued to be passed on to the abbot in cash, in 1303 as in 1252 at King's Ripton, for example; or in those manors such as Slepe, where the abbot had bought out many small holdings, cash rents in considerable amounts were allocated to his chamberlain for anniversary expenditures. But the *censa*, and, apparently, many of the rents from small holdings bequeathed to the convent, can be seen to have remained in the hands of the reeve. This means that the grant of small holdings to the manors with the abbots' purchases were actually being used to subsidize a faltering demesne economy; and the *ad censum* policy was deliberately forced on the reeve by the necessity of balancing his account.

Through these means it became possible for the cash liveries, especially the important farms of the cellarer, to become fairly stable over the first half of the fourteenth century. Those amounts which went to the abbot's chamberlain, on the other hand, still depended to a considerable degree upon the fortunes of the harvest and the stock surplus of the year, in those manors where the demesne was not farmed. The following example from Upwood is typical; the cash livery from some other manors may be seen in Appendix III, *infra*.

TABLE LIV

CASH LIVERY FROM THE MANOR: UPWOOD[44]

Year	To the Cellarer	To the Abbot
1247	£11.3s.4d.	£14.12s.11d.
1250	£10.14s.3d.	£ 2.14s.4d.
1252	£ 9.0s.3d.	£ 1.0s.9d.
1297	£ 5.18s.2d.	£ 3.13s.10d.
1303	£16.6s.5d.	£ 3.14s.6d.
1306	£13.17s.9d.	£ 3.19s.3d.
1312	£13.6s.9d.	£11.10s.11d.
1313	£13.14s.9d.	£ 2.16s.0d.
1319	£13.5s.4d.	£ 2.6s.0d.
1324	£13.13s.4d.	£ 6.6s.2d.
1343	£14.1s.4d.	£12.16s.4d.
1347	£14.1s.4d.	£12.3s.6d.

[44] See Appendix III, this Chapter, for further examples.

II

This tightening of demesne production and the development of restrictive policies pervading the whole manorial structure cannot be studied apart from financial conditions in the entire monastic administration: the manors provided the main source of abbey revenues, for example; and in return, capital investment from above in stock and lands often remained exigent for the rapid recovery of manorial prosperity. There was an involved relationship here, which would defy any simple unilinear description of economic fluctuations, as long as the abbey was directly interested in the profits of manorial production. A further hindrance to a complete and unified analysis of when and where new formative influences entered the system, lies in the paucity of rolls from the central administration. Nevertheless, an important point of departure may certainly be found in new drains upon the abbot's exchequer.

From the second half of the 13th century heavy vacancy charges began to be levied on Ramsey abbots when they took up their new offices. The charge had only been 300 marks in 1267, but John de Sawtrey paid 2,000 marks in 1285, and Simon Eye paid 660 in 1316.[45] Papal and royal taxation was a far greater burden. Part of this was due to the intransigent assessment and regularity of the tax. For example, the papal tenth levied for six years from 1275, as based on a *valor* system rather than profits, was static rather than adjustable to seasons and prices. In addition, it must have involved considerable double taxation, since the obedientiaries' revenues (and properties) were assessed separately from those of the abbot, while at the same time, as will be seen below, the abbot could assess all manors in the view of frankpledge in order to pay off his debts and taxes.

TABLE LV

The true Value of all the Income Pertaining to the Church of Ramsey, in the Eighth Year of Abbot William, as Conceded to the Lord Pope for Six Years.

Shillington 100 marks, tenth £6.13s.4d.	Walsoken 15 marks, tenth 20s.
Barton 60 marks, tenth £4.	Chatteris 30 marks, tenth 40s.
Cranfield 80 marks, tenth £5.6s.8d.	London 8½ marks, tenth 10s.
Hemmingford 60 marks, tenth £4.	Sawtrey 3 marks, tenth 4s.
Broughton 50 marks, tenth £3.6s.8d.	Barnwell 6½ marks, tenth 10s.
Ellington 60½ marks, tenth £3.14s.	Abbot's increment 40 marks, tenth £3.
Brancaster 50 marks, tenth £3.6s.8d.	3s.4d.
Ringstead 50 marks, tenth £3.6s.8d.	Total 669½ marks; Total of Abbot's
Higney 41 marks, tenth £3.4s.8d.	tenths £44.12s.8d.
Wimbotsham 20 marks, tenth 26s.8d.	Total in pounds £446.6s.8d.

---

[45] By the 14th century the vacancy fine was set at 2,000 marks for the year, with proportionately less to be paid for shorter periods, 'and the king also receives fees, escheats, advowsons, etc.' (*Carts.*, III, pp. 17 ff.). John of Sawtrey was only able to pay off 1,000 marks during the first year after his becoming abbot (1286); he managed another 40 marks in 1287, 200 in 1288, 50 in 1289. Thus he still owed some 700 marks five years after his accession (*Carts.*, III, pp. 13-15).

TABLE LV (*Cont'd.*)

The true Value of all the Income Pertaining to the Church of Ramsey, in the Eighth Year of Abbot William, as Conceded to the Lord Pope for Six Years.

Elton 100 marks, £6.13s.4d.	Granges 30 marks, tenths 40s.
Weston 100 marks, tenth £6.13s.4d.	In pounds (total) £104.6s.10d.; Total
Ripton 100 marks, tenth £6.13s.4d.	156 marks 7s.10d.
Warboys 100 marks, tenth £6.13s.4d.	Total tenths £10.8s.9d.
Upwood and Wistow 140 marks, tenth	Lawshall and Girton 128 marks, tenths
£10.	£9.4s.
Houghton 100 marks, tenth £6.13s.4d.	Total in pounds £92.
Slepe 100 marks, tenth £6.13s.4d.	Almoner £53.11s. Tenths 106s.1d.
Holywell 50 marks, tenth £3.7s.8d.	Sacristan £59.13s.4d. Tenths 119s.4d.
Elsworth and Knapwell 100 marks, tenth	Pittancer £26. Tenth 52s.
£6.13s.4d.	*Custos* of the Shrine £17. Tenth 34s.q.
Graveley 50 marks, tenth £3.6s.8d.	Infirmarian £12. Tenth 24s.
Burwell 100 marks, tenth £6.13s.4d.	*Custos* of the Chapel £10. Tenth 20s.q.
Therfield 75 marks, tenth £5.	Master of Works £32. Tenth 44s.
Total 1,125 marks,	Gidding £24. Tenth 48s.
Total tenths £75.; true income 574	Total from the obedientiaries and Gid-
marks 9s.2d., of which the tenth	ding £41.14d.
is £38.6s.2d.	Total from all the farms both of the
Total in pounds £750 (?). In pounds	abbot and obedientiaries – 300 marks
£383.2s.11d. (?)	for all tenths.
Total tenths pertaining to the abbot	Total of all income 2,425 marks 10s.
with increase £157.18s.11d.	Total of all tenths of the abbot £157.
Over 76½ marks, tenth 102s. in pounds	18s.10d.
£51.	And in deficit 74 marks 9s.2d.
Redd. Assis. of Ramsey 9 marks, tenth 12s.	Total tax of all the house of Ramsey,
Fisheries at Ramsey 10 marks, 3s.6d.;	3,000 marks, which is in pounds
tenth 13s.8d.	2,000. Whence total tenths 300
Welles 27 marks, tenths 36s.	marks, i.e. 200 pounds.[46]
Pensions 3 marks, 11s. Tenths 5s.1d.	

Another important element about these taxes was their size and peremptory imposition. Abbot John de Sawtrey writes off in panic to a friend:

Quum nos, amice, sicut hactenus bene nostis, ex exactione ponderosa mille librarum domino Papæ pro Principe nostro subito solvendarum simus importabiliter onerati, ac nos per amicorum aliorum subsidium inde solverimus nonagentas et quinquaginta marcas, debeamusque alias quingentas et quinquaginta die Paschæ nunc instante solvere de prædictis mille libris, sub pœna amissionis illarum nonagentarum et quinquaginta marcarum, et sub pœna essendi in primo statu quem continet obligatio principalis si deficiamus in futura solutione; . . .[47]

---

[46] Another paragraph dealing with the actual payments through the dioceses of Lincoln and Norwich is appended to this Ms, P.R.O. *Rentals and Surveys*, Roll 314. It is not clear how some of the above 'totals' are derived, nor are the simple summaries always correct.

[47] *Chronicon*, pp. 399-400. This, and the following references, are from later documents printed as appendices to the 12th-century chronicle.

Or again he sends a hasty note to his clerk:

> . . . vos rogamus quatinus apud Brancestre et Ringstede et alia loca nostra singula de partibus Norfolchiæ personaliter accedere velitis, et de bladis et aliis mobilibus disponere et custodes eorundem informare quomodo melius et consultius levare possint ad opus nostrum XX marcas ad minus ad solvendum pro decima nos in partibus illis contingente . . . Et quia similiter summam magnam pecuniæ solvere tenemur eodem die Oxoniæ, . . .[48]

The important point for economic history is the similar fashion and spirit with which heavy monetary demands were translated to the conventual revenues and the manors. A chronicler notes that 'the king extorted one-half of the abbey's provenance by taxation' during the time of John de Sawtrey.[49] Around 1300 the abbot's debts were so heavy that they jeopardized monastic discipline.[50] Abbot Simon Eye had to face the consequences of pestilence and storms.[51] Abbot Richard entered office (1348) with a debt burden of 2,500 marks, although some must have carried over from his predecessor.[52]

The freemen and villeins fared equally ill. They were taxed by the view of frankpledge for huge sums which were usually as much as 25 to 30 per cent of the gross revenues received by the reeves on the convent's manors; and on the abbot's own manors the percentage was often much higher. The rolls in which some of these payments were inscribed have survived from the central department, and are tabulated below both to show their contrast with the 'normal' view charges, where possible, and their significance within the gross income structure of the manors. On five manors the collection at the view of frankpledge was insufficient to meet the tax exaction, so that the regular manorial revenues had to be called upon. In order to balance his accounts in the face of this problem, the reeve was allocated such seigneurial revenues as sheriff's aid and wood sales, to take an example from Barton in 1289; or sometimes the reeve passed on the debt — such as the seventy-three shillings owed to *famuli* in Cranfield by 1289, or thirty-two shillings twopence owed to wage earners of Barton after the same year. The ordinary solvency of the manor was attacked, therefore, and the extensive deficits for which the reeve was held to account often contained many *heusire* payments and other items from regular customary rents. More frequently, however, it was the view of frankpledge charges themselves that had extended the resources of both freemen and villein. Even after the normal taxation of 1290 in Wistow, for example, the freeholds of the Le Moignes, Clairvaux, and others still owed twelve shillings, twopence halfpenny from taxes of former years; the peasants in turn owed more than thirteen shillings: six shillings four pence by the dairyman and maid, eighteen pence by the swineherd, and the debts of five lesser men totalled five shillings eleven pence.

---

[48] *Chronicon*, p. 387.

[49] And on top of all these taxes John of Sawtrey was sued for debt by the Bishop of Coventry and Lichfield *ca.*1300 (*Carts.*, III, pp. 20-21).

[50] *Chronicon*, p. 393.

[51] See Appendix G, *infra*, for the abbot's description of some of the factors which debilitated his excheqeur.

[52] *Chronicon*, p. 342.

Table LVI
STATUS MANERIORUM[53]

Manor	Year	Total Receipts	Total Allocations	View Receipts	View Allocations	Total Debts
Warboys	1288–9	£47.8s.4d.	£43.12s.3d.	£9.17s.5d.	£11.6s.8d.	49s.4d.
	1289–90	£38.12s.5d.	£36.0s.3d.	18s.9d.	2s.11d.	£4.9s.9d.
Broughton	1288–9	£85.5s.3d.	£81.8s.10d.	£15.16s.–d.	£15.16s.11d.	£5.8s.–d.
	1289–90	£47.17s.3d.	( )	£ 5.–s.–d.	£ 2.17s.6d.	£3.8s.–d.
King's Ripton	1288–9	—	—	£23.7s.5d.	£21.18s.6d.	—
	1289–90	—	—	8s.8d.	—	—
Graveley	1288–9	£42.12s.–d.	£37.5s.–d.	£17.9s.10d.	£13.11s.3d.	£5.12s.–d.
Cranfield	1288–9	£70.3s.–d.	£75.19s.2d.	£33.4s.7d.	£28.9s.2d.	£4.3s.9d.
	1289–90	£65.13s.3d.	£65.1s.9d.	—	—	16s.4d.
Barton	1288–9	£88.10s.5d.	£81.9s.7d.	£20.6s.4d.	£24.15s.8d.	£5.18s.3d.
	1289–90	£59.13s.7d.	£56.–s.15d.	—	—	£2.2s.11d.
Shillington & Pegsdon	1288–9	£170.11s.11d.	£147.11s.5d.	£42.3s.3d.	£39.17s.2d.	£23.6s.–d.
	1289–90	£90.2s.5d.	£82.8s.7d.	—	—	—

53 *Add. Charters* 34912, 39671, 39672, 39736. The total receipts include the 'view'; half pennies and farthings have been omitted. These *visum* totals are incomplete for Slepe and Holywell, and probably for Cranfield (1289–90) also.

Table LVI (*Cont'd.*)

STATUS MANERIORUM (Cont'd.)

Year	Manor	Total Debts	View Allocations	View Receipts	Total Allocations	Total Receipts	Year
1288–9	Therfield	£2.6s.3d.	£14.4s.8d.	£19.13s.6d.	£62.3s.10d.	£60.5s.4d.	1288–9
1289–90		8s.8d.	9s.–d.	—	£50.19s.1d.	£50.10s.1d.	1289–90
1288–9	Burwell	1s.7d.	£19.14s.8d.	£23.2s.3d.	£85.1s.10d.	£85.2s.6d.	1288–9
1288–9	Elsworth	£5.2s.7d.	£26.15s.8d.	£27.17s.6d.	£97.17s.5d.	£103.–s.1d.	1288–9
1288–9	Knapwell	—	£3.12s.5d.	£4.3s.10d.	£10.10s.10d.	£11.15s.8d.	1288–9
1288–9	Chatteris	£3.5s.6d.	£18.13s.3d.	£19.–s.6d.	£96.13s.11d.	£89.9s.6d.	1288–9
1288–9	Elton	10s.8d.	£24.19s.3d.	£19.–s.13d.	£80.19s.11d.	£81.7s.7d.	1288–9
1289–90		£1.4s.6d.	—	—	£63.6s.–d.	—	1289–90
1288–9	Weston	£5.4s.	£21.2s.1d.	£21.12s.–d.	£69.2s.9d.	£74.6s.9d.	1288–9
1289–90		£3.14s.8d.	—	—	£55.–s.11d.	£56.6s.10d.	1289–90
1288–9	Bythorn	£3.17s.8d.	£2.3s.4d.	£5.5s.9d.	£11.14s.–d.	£15.1s.9d.	1288–9
1289–90		£2.4s.10d.			£10.15s.–d.	£13.8s.–d.	1289–90
1288–9	Abbot's Ripton	£9.18s.9d.	£21.5s.6d.	£26.9s.1d.	£83.14s.5d.	£93.13s.3d.	1288–9
1288–9	Slepe	—	£15.8s.7d.	£13.11s.–d.	£96.15s.–d.	£95.2s.5d.	1288–9
1288–9	Holywell	£11.16s.1d.	£6.12s.6d.	£6.19s.10d.	£50.12s.11d.	£51.19s.10d.	1288–9
1288–9	Houghton	£12.15s.10d.	£19.6s.1d.	£25.12s.9d.	£78.?7s.7d.	£91.–s.17d.	1288–9

Like their twelfth-century predecessors, the abbots of Ramsey over these years seemed to be 'strongest in debt'. Their baronial authority made it possible to transgress routine administrative limits, and to reach down to the last peasant in these matters of taxation. As a consequence, the convent seemed to become more peculiarly beholden to 'handouts' from the abbot's exchequer; and the peasant economy was transformed by a system of overhead charges paralleling the liquid demands on a higher level.

Upon the first point, the convent reacted against dilapidation of its resources, so that most of the property purchases by the abbot, from the late 13th century, came rather as a consequence than a contradiction of the tightening in monastic revenues. Thus it may be noted that it was as a result of episcopal visitation concerning the decline of conventual farms that Abbot William de Godmanchester 'purchased Barnwell, Hemington, Niggingworth and increased other abbey lands by £25 per year'. These purchases for monastic usage were not dependent upon the affluence in Abbot William's treasury, and he only gradually paid for the new estates by mortgaging his own resources:

> Adquisivit etiam terram apud Lawishalle ad augmentationem tunicarum et coopertoriorum et habituum conventus. Contulit pro Bernewelle et Hemington MMD marcas, et a tempore quo emit manerium de Bernewelle usque ad terminum vitæ Domini Berengarii, contulit eidem C marcas quolibet anno quoad vixerit, qui XI annis postea vixit et eas recepit. Et manerium de Chatteris habuit dictus miles cum omnibus proficuis in dictæ venditionis conventione ad terminum vitæ, quodque redemit CCCC marcis.[54]

The next abbot (John de Sawtrey, 1286-1316) was liquidating £50 of a £240 debt owed to Sir William de Bereford early in his reign; and by 1300 he was forced to establish a sinking fund by which his heavy debts could be wiped out:

> ... concedimus pro nobis et successoribus nostris quod proventus, scilicet quadraginta libræ, de duobus maneriis nostris ad cameram nostram specialiter spectantibus, videlicet Hemmingford et Elyngtone, per manus præpositorum maneriorum eorundem ad Thesauriam conventus per manus receptorum ejusdem conventus singulis annis plenarie pérveniant, donec tota summa pecuniæ ad quam per sigilla nostra toto tempore nostro sumus obligati in solidum de dictis maneriis fuerit soluta et penes conventum recepta ac deposita ... Concedimus etiam quod pecunia de hominibus nostris ad dicti debiti subsidium levata vel levanda per manus receptorum dictorum recipietur, et in thesauria usque in eventum solutionis faciendæ deponetur. Volumus etiam et bona fide promittimus quod ad dictum debitum solvendum quam cito facultas se obtulerit, de aliis bonis monasterii ad cameram nostram spectantibus curam apponemus diligentem ...[55]

The peasant economy, in the meantime, had attracted considerable advances in entry fines,[56] in addition to the general effects following upon

[54] *Chronicon*, App. II, p. 348, note 3.
[55] *Chronicon*, p. 394.

[56] For these reasons, of course, from the late thirteenth century, Ramsey abbots were

restrictions in demesne production and the frequent taxes. The functioning of Ramsey manorial courts is camouflaged, unhappily, with regard to these seigneurial incidents. Although the abundant court rolls give ample details upon village affairs in distraint and enforcement of customary laws, the land conveyances themselves were enrolled on the reeve's account. And here the fines and *gersumæ* came in a finely clipped list mixed in with heriots and merchets. As a result, there was all too often an insufficient definition of that specific element in the fine which might explain unusual varieties in the tax, that is, whether the tenement was partible or impartible, by lineal or collateral descent, and whether there was a *post obitum* or an *inter vivos* succession agreement. But the general pattern is clear enough over the long run. When the son was entering to the family estate the whole 'land' or virgate was fined usually for sums of a mark or twenty shillings, and the quarter and half virgates proportionately, around 1250; after 1300, the villein was often paying over three pounds when succeeding to his father's virgate. Warboys manor will serve as an illustration:

TABLE LVII

LAND ENTRY FINES ON WARBOYS MANOR[57]

Holding	1250	1253	1303	1306	1318	1324	1325	1329
¼ *terra*	4s.; 5s.(2)	—	10s.	—	—	45s.	—	—
½ v.	8s.; 6s.8d.	6s.8d.	—	40s. (3)	—	30s.	40s.	—
1 *terra*	10s.	10s.	—	—	—	—	—	—
1 v.	—	20s.	66s.8d.	66s.8d.	(40s.)	—	20s.	40s.
1 cr.	—	—	—	13s.4d.	—	(4s.); 2s.; 3s.4d.	—	—
cottage	—	—	—	12s.	—	—	—	—
cot.	—	—	—	4s.	—	—	—	—
messuage	—	—	—	3s.4d.	—	—	—	—

very careful to keep control over customary inheritances when the manor had been farmed (e.g. Ellington, Hemmingford Grey), and even when a manor like Hemington had been given to the convent.

[57] For further examples, see Appendix IV. It was the 13th-century custom at Warboys to allow entry into both the property and the stock of the deceased for 5 marks (66s.8d.) when he had died without issue (*Carts.*, I, p. 307, n. 1). In the early 14th century, however, the 5 marks fine appears to have been a usual charge when the son succeeded to his father's entire estate (e.g. Upwood, Broughton, Warboys — *Add. Ch.* 39693, an extract of manorial *gersumæ* in 1309-10). When other than the son entered to the property the fine was frequently 40s. for the one-half virgate; but at times this type of fine varied greatly — perhaps in accordance with the stock of the land or the wealth of the recipient. In some parts of the country this increase in entry fines brought legal action by the tenants; see John F. NICHOLS, 'An Early Fourteenth Century Petition from the Tenants of Bocking to their Manorial Lord', *Ec. H. R.*, II (1929), 300-7.

The first decade of the 14th century brought an agricultural revival to the Huntingdon manors. Lands *ad censum* were decreased in the manors of Upwood, Broughton, Warboys, Houghton, and Abbots Ripton.[58] There was considerable decline in the sale of works on some manors, such as Broughton and Wistow, but on other manors (e.g. Warboys, Upwood) there was little variation in these sales.[59] Newly purchased holdings such as the lands from the Le Moigne family, Roger de Norton, and the Clairvaux in Houghton were sown by the reeve; some assart accretions appeared in Abbots Ripton and King's Ripton among the cultivated arable. Mills were withdrawn from farm, or if left, as at Wistow, Warboys, Broughton, Abbots Ripton, and Holywell, the farm was increased by about ten per cent.[60] The result of this new agrarian prosperity was an oversubscription of livery on some manors, — such as Warboys, Abbots Ripton, Slepe and Holywell — where the cellarer was receiving one hundred per cent more in liveries than thirty years earlier. Greater quantities of corn were sown, too, at this time; and a more complete conversion to the three course system ensued.[61]

But there was not a whole-hearted return to the earlier system of demesne cultivation. No decreases came in the amounts of land *ad censum* for Wistow, Slepe, Weston, or Holywell, for instance. Even more surprising was the farming of considerable portions of the demesne on some manors. Abbots Ripton let out a field worth £5 *per annum* to sixteen villeins; Upwood continued to rent for a slight premium increment a field that the vill seems to have held for some fifty years. At the same time the villeins were purchasing more pannage and herbage from the reeve. Probably the wealthier villeins were alone able to take advantage of these new opportunities, for the *redditus* totals and the entry fines show little evidence of effective demand by lesser men.[62]

To distinguish warp from woof among these interwoven threads of early fourteenth-century economic conditions is a difficult matter. On one hand the level of regular expenses expected from the abbot seems to have risen tremendously over the previous century. In addition to the tax burdens, visits to Parliament had become costly affairs,[63] royal vacations at Ramsey threw unreasonable demands on the larder, and corrodies were a constant anxiety.[64] But even with this heavier expense overhead, the abbot's net

---

[58] See *supra*, Table L.

[59] See *supra* Table LI, and App. I, *infra*.

[60] See Appendix VII, Chapter IX, *infra*.

[61] See Ch. VI for tables of corn statistics. This period probably witnessed a new high in the total money revenues from Ramsey estates, even over the level of the mid-13th century, due partly to the increased rents, entry fines, etc., as well as better crops. But the livery remained a very large percentage of total revenues, and variations in corn prices cause difficulties in estimation of the change in total *real* revenues.

[62] The *redditus* item is too general to be more decisive on this point. But the general suggestion from Huntingdon accounts and

court rolls at this time concurs with that tendency on the neighbouring Crowland estates to the decrease in the number of small holdings while the larger holdings were being increased (F. M. PAGE, *The Estates of Crowland Abbey*, pp. 83 and 89 for Cottenham and Oakington).

[63] A thirteen-day trip to London by the abbot and his entourage cost £28.9s.11d. in 1332 (*Add. Ch.* 34517); altogether, travelling to London in that year, and returns, cost more than £150.

[64] These points come out in the very valuable set of letters of Abbots John of Sawtrey and Simon Eye (1285-1332), printed in *Chronicon*, Appendix, pp. 368-417. See

income was sufficient at some periods of higher revenue returns to invest monies in abbey buildings, drainage and re-stocking of manors, and real estate purchase. One administrative weakness, which became prominent, lay in the lack of long-run financial policies. The various biographical notes and summaries over the 1250-1350 period mention only one example of deliberately accumulated savings in the abbot's exchequer, — a building fund established by Simon Eye. Consequently the abbots were left more at the mercy of short-run financial crises. Some examples have already shown how the enforced liquidation of debts further curtailed the flexibility of the abbot's income, by mortgaging lands or leasing demesnes. This system continued. In 1330 for example, immediate cash needs forced the abbot to lease his wealthiest manors, Shillington and Pegsdon, which previous to this time had been directly exploited, probably for over one hundred and fifty years. The pattern of the abbots' burdens and expenditures in the decade before the Black Death continued to parallel that of the late 13th century. In 1338, because of the financial burden of royal visits, Ramsey was given the right to retain chattels of felons.[65] But, as Appendix V to this chapter illustrates,[66] the expenditure in taxes, lawsuits, and corrodies had continued to outweigh by far the investment in real estate and demesne capital.

The singular dependence upon the abbot's exchequer for capital, from the late thirteenth century, had a blighting influence on the traditional conventual interest in direct production.[67] Funds from the abbot were employed to purchase property, to liquidate debts, and generally, to re-organize revenues. But they were not invested in demesne capital. The convent, in turn, was inactive, submissive to reductions in corn livery and cash farms, and content to fill in revenue gaps by rents from the abbots' gifts of property. The interest in arable profits was still manifested by the corn sales from those manors outside Huntingdon in the late thirteenth century, notably Lawshall, Girton, and the estates purchased by Abbot William in Northampton. But from 1300 it was obvious that even the cellarer was content to absorb profits as they came. They came for only two decades in the early fourteenth-century revival, and then a decline set in, both at the distant as well as the 'home' manors. Despite the considerable profits after 1300, no capital seems to have been available, or at least none was voted, to shore up the manorial revenues after the next fluctuation. With the decimation of cattle herds in 1319, for example, the reeve was left gradually to rebuild by his own available resources over the next fifteen to twenty years. During this same period, the cycle of increased putting *ad censum* and selling of *opera* was renewed.[68]

A slight increase in agrarian profits over the 1340's brought another reshuffle, and tenements were withdrawn from the *ad censum* for more intensive cultivation of the demesne at Wistow, Broughton, Slepe, and Upwood. But the attraction which agrarian production held for the convent was now

---

infra, Appendix H, for a letter of 1331 concerning the burden of corrodies.
[65] *Chronicon*, pp. 259 ff.

[66] Appendix V: An Abbot's Expense Account.
[67] See Ch. IV, *supra*.
[68] See Tables L and LI, *supra*.

restricted to even fewer manors, and to still less demesne land on these, than in the first decade of the century.   Probably the objectives of re-organization on the above manors were circumscribed by livery needs, for quotas were not oversubscribed as they had been around 1315.   The direct control of demesne production was gradually handed over to groups of 'customaries' — likely the leading landholders of the village.   Farming of large fields to these men was proceeding rapidly, especially at Broughton, Slepe and Upwood, when the plague struck.

The feature most fundamental to the period under review in this chapter was the long run stagnation in corn production at the Huntingdonshire estates of Ramsey, broken by only the two short periods of prosperity of the early years of the fourteenth century and of the early 1340's.   This adverse movement in production was to a considerable extent counterbalanced since the abbey could take advantage of higher corn prices to draw more revenues from rents in the form of commutation of services, higher entry fines, and the renting of purchased tenements.   No doubt the long periods of insolvency at the abbey over the late thirteenth century and from the 1320's favoured this emphasis upon stable money rents rather than a policy of increased investment for production, but it is noteworthy that when money was available for investment the augmentation of money rents remained of paramount importance and there was only a half-hearted renewal of interest in the profits of arable after 1300 and 1340.

APPENDIX I

WORKS SOLD

Broughton

Year	@ ob.	@ 1d.	@ 2d.	@ 1d.	Total Sales
1306	1,484	0	0	0	£3.2s.0d.
1311	528	0	0	0	£1.2s.0d.
1314	868	0	301	0	£4.4s.8d.
1319	871	34	143	0	£3.2s.6d.
1325	969	0	298	0	£4.10s.0d.
1342	618	58	45	163	£3.1s.7d.
1344	176	0	27	185	£1.7s.3d.
1346	571	116	0	25	£1.15s.7d.
1378	486¼	34¾	482¾	1½	£1.16s.0d.
1380	929	122½	137	36	£1.14s.8d.
1386	465¾	163¾	159	6	£3.0s.1d.
1392	285½	56½	49	83½	£1.17s.7d.

Wistow

Year	@ ob.	@ ob.g.	@ 1d.ob.	@ 1d.	Total Sales
ca. 1250	0	0	0	0	0
1297	260	0	0	0	10s.10d.
1307	908	0	462	0	£4.19s.9d.
1311	182	75	339½	0	£2.14s.8d.
1316	168	104	0	0	13s.6d.
1324	329	0	51	147	£1.13s.7d.
1336	0	0	262½	0	£1.10s.3d.
1347	147	92	90½	138½	£1.14s.8d.
1351	0	137	185	102	£2.0s.3d.
1352	91	115	92½	64	£2.17s.11d.
1368	80	104	260	9	£2.13s.3d.
1379	67	39¼	59¼	26	14s.7d.
1388	110½	52½	132¾	3	£1.4s.7d.
1389	160¾	120¾	167	26½	£2.0s.5d.
1393	144	90½	174	16½	£1.14s.9d.
1394	172½	80½	203	23	£1.19s.3d.
1403	324	148	20	0	£1.5s.7d.

Appendix I (*Cont'd.*)

WORKS SOLD (*Cont'd.*)

Warboys

Year	@ ob.	@ 1d.	@ 1d. ob.	@ 1d.	Total Sales
1303	1,008	0	272	0	£3.9s.0d.
1306	1,488	920	215	0	£7.15s.8d.
1318	1,822	917	377	101	£10.(?) 10d.
1325	1,804½	728½	372	0	£9.2s.4d.
1326	192½	914½	405	0	£10.6s.6d.
1329	2,034	919½	222	53	£9.13s.6d.
1335?	1,523	0	0	0	£3.13s.5d.
1336	387	1,231	0	373	£9.1s.10d.
1342	2,442½	1,083½	370	284½	£13.2s.0d.
1344	1,321	1,292½	1,054	252	£12.4s.8d.
1347	1,665	980	243	80	£10.8s.1d.
1348	1,572	257	0	170	£4.19s.8d.
1351	1,471	460	0	298	£9.10s.2d.
1353	1,465	1,154	207	47	£10.6s.2d.
1354	1,276	688	192	510	£7.12s.10d.
1359	1,291	506	340	230	£7.17s.0d.

Houghton

Year	@ ob.	@ 1d.	@ 2d.	@ 1d.	Total Sales
1319	1,243	196	72	732	£7.1s.11d.
1324	1,626	307	361	371	£9.3s.10d.
1336	?	933	0	456	£6.(?)2d.
1369	200	112	158	287	£3.9s.8d.
1371	398	86	68	58	£1.19s.11d.
1372	159	20	97	254	£2.5s.7d.
1379	0?	79	99	111	£2.12s.4d.
1383	91	123	14	188	£1.11s.3d.
1387	130	99	55	134	£1.13s.0d.
1388	23	165	2	50	£0.19s.3d.
1389	34	54	108	206	£2.0s.1d.
1393	25	123	44	119	£1.15s.4d.
1394	98	233	151	146	£3.0s.2d.
1396	36	290	33	153	£1.13s.4d.

APPENDIX I (*Cont'd.*)

WORKS SOLD (*Cont'd.*)

Slepe

Year	@ ob.	@ 1d.	@ 2d.	@ 1d.	Total Sales
1307	1,862	0	0	0	£3.17s.7d.
1313	1,412	702	160	254	£8.11s.4d.
1319	1,312	756	165	0	£6.11s.5d.
1324	451	198	0	189	£7.16s.9d.
1345	1,320	?	388½	0	£12.19s.4d.
1351	1,276	497	332	0	£6.2s.3d.
1366	78	66½	50½	0	£0.13s.0d.
1387	448	351½	161	36	£3.7s.4d.
1390	577	36	66½	37	£1.18s.10d.
1417	0	287	261	0	£3.17s.6d.

Holywell

Year	@ ob.	@ 1d.	@ 2d.	@ 1d.	Total Sales
1307	1,076	0	0	0	£2.4s.10d.
1324	240	94½	29	41½	£1.6s.2d.
1347	158	5	0	130	£0.17s.5d.
1364	29½	0	0	0	£0.1s.3d.
1371	161	72	8	177	£2.0s.1d.
1383	472	147	162	164	£3.12s.7d.
1399	659	151½	246	139½	£3.18s.7d.
1401	741	233	171	55½	£4.3s.5d.
1402	723½	188½	202	136½	£4.10s.11d.
1404	839	257	240	124	£5.6s.6d.
1405	937	234	238	0	£4.18s.2d.
1409	471	0	0	0	£0.18s.9d.

Abbots Ripton

Year	@ ob.	@ 1d.	@ 2d.	@ 1d.	Total Sales
1307	348	580	0	0	£3.3s.3d.
1314	744	699	0	0	£5.4s.9d.
1324	386	728	0	133	£4.17s.6d.
1342	1,090	715	98	125	£7.18s.7d.
1364	28	409	98	0	£3.9s.8d.

APPENDIX II

MANORIAL MONEY RENT ROLLS

Broughton		Abbots Ripton	
Year	Amount	Year	Amount
1244	112s. 10d.	1252	54s. 9d.
1250	123s. 4d.	1307	380s. 6d.
1252	112s. 7d.	1315	268s. 8d.
1307	197s. 3d.	1324	344s. 1d.
1312	209s. 3d.	1342	308s. 0d.
1314	195s. 3d.		
1319	206s. 11d.		
1326	221s. 7d.		
1342	169s. 10d.		
1344	157s. 6d.		
1346	223s. 1d.		

Wistow		Warboys	
1247	87s. 1d.	1250	67s. 5d.
1250	114s. 7d.	1255	75s. 2d.
1252	99s. 10d.	1303	246s. 0d.
1297	186s. 7d.	1306	264s. 4d.
1307	340s. 4d.	1318	221s. 8d.
1311	227s. 0d.	1324	227s. 2d.
1324	301s. 8d.	1325	191s. 2d.
1335	275s. 2d.	1330	212s. 9d.
1346	331s. 4d.	1335	194s. 7d.
1350	158s. 7d.	1342	246s. 11d.
1351	290s. 5d. ?	1344	438s. 2d.
		1346	467s. 2d.
		1347	467s. 2d.
		1348	464s. 2d.

Holywell	
Year	Amount
1307	283s. 8d. (mill farm included)
1324	220s. 0d. (mill farm not included)
1347	307s. 11d. (mill farm included)

Note: A considerable percentage of the increase from the late thirteenth century has been due to the farming of mills (for these, see Appendix VII, Chapter IX). The entries for Holywell indicate the importance of the mill farm to the total.

Appendix III
CASH LIVERIES FROM THE MANORS

Year	To the Cellarer	To the Abbot
	Warboys	
1250	£25.2s.7d.	£1.15s.4d.
1255	£15.1s.10d.	£0.14s.11d.
1303	£18.16s.8d.	£4.0s.10d.
1306	£18.15s.8d.	£4.3s.6d.
1316	£17.19s.2d.	?
1318	£17.15s.2d.	£5.10s.2d.
1324	£18.7s.2d.	£2.6s.7d.
1325	£18.15s.2d.	£9.0s.0d.
1330	£19.3s.2d.	£11.5s.7d.
1336	£18.15s.0d.	£4.12s.3d.
1342	£17.19s.2d.	?
1344	£19.6s.2d.	£22.17s.5d.
1346	£18.3s.2d.	£20.13s.2d.
1347	£17.15s.2d.	£16.7s.0d.
1353	£13.12s.0d.	£11.12s.3d.
1354	£18.15s.2d.	£4.11s.9d.
1359	£17.0s.0d.	£7.6s.0d.
1360	£16.10s.0d.	£4.10s.0d.
1362	£12.2s.4d.	£6.3s.4d.
1363	£13.0s.0d.	£12.12s.3d.
1366	£16.10s.0d.	£8.6s.8d.
	Houghton	
1319	£14.15s.2d.	0?
1324	£18.17s.2d.	£7.10s.3d.
1328	£17.10s.10d.	£5.18s.0d.
1334	£18.17s.3d.	£9.1s.10d.
1336	£19.13s.2d.	£12.6s.11d.
1338	£18.9s.0d.	£5.3s.3d.
1364	£16.1s.0d.	£4.4s.0d.
1369	0	£26.8s.8d.
1371	0	£26.0s.0d.
	Abbots Ripton	
1252	£12.12s.3d.	£0.7s.1d.
1307	£20.17s.2d.	£16.5s.2d.
1315	£16.15s.2d.	£3.7s.11d.?
1324	£17.19s.2d.	£9.5s.9d.
1342	?	£11.12s.0d.
1364	£4.9s.0d.	£12.4s.6d.

Appendix III (*Cont'd.*)

CASH LIVERIES FROM THE MANORS (*Cont'd.*)

Year	To the Cellarer	To the Abbot
Wistow		
1247	£14.2s.11d.	£19.17s.8d.
1250	£14.2s.1d.	£2.4s.6d.
1252	£9.14s.5d.	£1.3s.7d.
1297	?	£3.2s.9d.
1307	£14.1s.6d.	£7.7s.9d.
1311	£14.4s.4d	£7.4s.0d.?
1316	£14.5s.2d.	£14.1s.10d.
1324	£11.2s.4d.	£7.14s.2d.
1335	£14.1s.8d.	£11.10s.10d.
1346	£13.17s.10d.	£14.0s.6d.
1351	£10.4s.4d.	£3.0s.0d.
1352	£8.8s.11d.	£7.5s.8d.
1368	£3.3s.8d.	£16.14s.9d.
Weston & Bythorn		
1252	£17.7s.7d.	£4.16s.7d.
1297	£20.3s.9d.	£10.9s.9d.
1311	£18.12s.1d.	£15.14s.11d.
1324	£17.19s.2d.	£14.12s.10d.
1368	£3.18s.6d.	£14.10s.0d.
1394	0	£52.14s.10d.
Slepe		
1307	£29.8s.0d.	£8.6s.2d.
1313	£28.14s.0d.	£9.10s.1d.
1319	£26.0s.0d.	£7.16s.0d.
1324	£27.14s.7d.	£15.0s.0d.
1347	£18.17s.2d.	£26.15s.6d.
1351	£19.3s.2d.	£31.13s.6d.
1366	£18.0s 0d.	?
1381	0	£24.11s.11d.
1386	0	£53.0s.9d.
1387	0	£33.5s.0d.
1389	0	£59.13s.1d.

Note: Since some minor payments to the abbots in the arrear column, and some smaller liveries in kind, were not always calculable, these totals may in some instances be about a pound off the complete figure. But the ratio has not been affected thereby to any significant degree.

APPENDIX IV
ENTRY FINES

Wistow

Holdings	1252	1297	1298	1307	1311	1316	1324
1 v.	20s. (15s.)	—	—	—	—	(10s.) 40s. (3) 26s.8d.	40s. 13s.4d.
½ v.	10s.	20s.	—	—	—		
ter.	—	26s.8d.	13s.4d.	10s.	—	2s.	—
cot.	—	—	—	6s.8d.	5s.		—
¼ ter.	—	—	—	—	13s.4d.	—	—

Upwood

Holdings	1250	1297	1303	1304	1312	1319
1 v.	20s. (3); (26s.8d.)	(10s.)	—	19s.4d.	—	53s.4d.
½ v.	13s.4d. (2)	—	33s.4d.	—	—	—
cot.	(6s.)	—	—	—	5s.	—
cottage	—	—	—	—	6s.8d.	—
ter.	—	—	—	—	—	10s.

Broughton

Holdings	1312	1314	1319	1326
1 v.	66s.8d.	40s. (2)	—	—
½ v.	40s.; 26s.8d.	20s.	13s.4d.	10s.
¼ ter.	6s.8d.	—	—	2s.
¾ ter.	—	—	—	16s.
cr.	—	—	—	2s.

Houghton

Holdings	1319	1324	1334	1336	1338
1 v.	—	20s.; (6s.8d.)	40s.; 20s.	—	—
½ v.	20s.	—	—	—	—
cot.	2s.	10s.	—	6s.8d. (2)	—
½ cr.	6d.	—	—	—	5s. (2)
1 cr.	—	2s. (3)	—	—	—
cottage	—	—	—	6d.	—

APPENDIX IV (*Cont'd.*)

ENTRY FINES (*Cont'd.*)

Holywell, Weston, Abbots Ripton, Bythorn, Ellington

Holdings	1297	1307	1311	1314	1324
1v.	—	40s.	—	—	40s.; 53s.4d. (2)
½ v.	18s.; 20s.; 26s.8d.	—	26s.8d.; 20s.	9s.; 16s.8d.; 20s.	20s.; 13s.4d. (3)
cr.	—	6s.8d.	—	—	—
cottage	2s.	—	—	—	5s.; 1s.
cot.	—	13s.4d.	—	—	10s. (2)

APPENDIX V

AN ABBOT'S EXPENSE ACCOUNT FOR THE ABBEY

Money delivered outside his wardrobe and expenses paid which are not computed among common expenses.

To the king at the vacancy of the church.................	£4
To the king for 19 sacks of wool.........................	£96
To the king for 10 sacks of wool.........................	£50
To the king for five complete tenths in five years..........	£653.13s.1d.
To the king for one-half of a tenth in one year............	£50.6s.7d.
Diverse expenses at the coming of the queen..............	£98.17s.10d.
To the queen at the vacancy of the church...............	£40
To the children and relatives of the queen................	£50.12s.10d.
Gift to the king.......................................	£66.13s.4d.
TOTAL	£1,110.3s.8d.

Buildings for the vaccary at Henny Hill..................	£11.19s.6d.
New ditches at the same place...........................	£24.9s.10d.
72 head of cattle for the same place......................	£20.8s.
Ditches made and willows planted at Walsoken and Chatteris.	£12.9s.5d.
Ditches and houses at Ramsey and environs...............	£13.15s.
New houses (Broughton, Bigging, St. Ives, London)........	£414.19s.6d.
TOTAL	£498.1s.3d.

Tenements bought at Ramsey............................	£49.2s.11d.
Lands and tenements at Walton..........................	£16
A tenement in Weston..................................	£5
A stall at St. Ives.....................................	£28.13s.4d.
A stall at St. Ives.....................................	£16
A stall at St. Ives.....................................	£26.13s.4d.
One-half tenement at Holywell..........................	£33.6s.8d.
Mill bought at Holywell................................	£16
Lands and tenements at Chatteris.......................	£16.13s.4d.
Property at Huntingdon.................................	£12
To the wife of William Hotoft for her dowry in Weston......	£16.13s.4d.
TOTAL	£236.2s.11d.

In forensic expenses, namely in pleas against Hervett Bonum about a corrody......................................	£143.15s.11d.
Pleas against Thorney and Ely...........................	£308.10s.8d.
Various amounts through servants at the abbey beyond wardrobe expenses......................................	£96.10s.2d.
TOTAL	£548.16s.9d.

Note: This account is taken from *Add. Ch.* 34332, probably of Abbot Robert (1342-49). The totals are mine, since the charter totals do not seem to tally correctly; most of the entries have been synopsized.

CHAPTER IX

ADJUSTMENTS AFTER THE BLACK DEATH AND THE ORGANIZATION OF A NEW LEVEL OF DEMESNE PRODUCTION

I

THE shock of the Black Death on Ramsey manors was countered immediately by a programme of tactical adjustment to avoid the underemployment of land with a view to stabilizing revenues as much as possible. That by now familiar pattern of the *ad censum* resolved both these problems to a degree, by loosening the *opera* in order to encourage cultivation by the villein of his own land, which production, in turn, served to guarantee much of the traditional *censa* rents from the villeinage. Broughton, Wistow, Upwood, Slepe, Holywell, and Abbots Ripton were able to allocate several additional holdings in this fashion. A further type of money rent was introduced under the novel title of *arentata* (or *arrentata*), no doubt to encourage artisans, wage labour, and other former landless, to come forward and take up a holding.[1] This species of rent probably offered a peculiar attraction to the peasant, since it appears to have commuted all,[2] or nearly all, of the customary works and services. The rent level of the *arentata* was consequently higher, but the greater freedom from villein services brought a substitution of this alternative on several manors where the *censum* could not be adopted.[3] Broughton, Wistow, Upwood, Abbots Ripton and Holywell, were each able to allocate a few lands in this fashion; Houghton manor, where the number of tenements *ad censum* declined drastically, had nearly fifty per cent of the villeinage in *arentata* after a few years; on the other hand, Slepe and Weston did not employ this rent immediately after 1349. Finally, the effect of diminished labour services no longer available for the demesne due to such rentals, was offset by a farming of many parcels of the demesne in both large

[1] See Tables, Ch. X, Section I, for examples of the paradoxical increase in total numbers of landholders within a generation after the Great Pestilence.

[2] Although the account rolls only mention occasionally that 'all works are commuted' for *arentata*, this condition must usually be assumed, since there is no mention of work obligations in relation to these *arentata* in the detailed descriptive account and court rolls of the late 14th and early 15th centuries. There is no evidence that the 'term' (i.e., *ad voluntatem*, life, etc.) of *arentata* differed at first from the tenancy *ad censum* or the *ad opus*, but it would undoubtedly involve some insurance against conversion to *opera*. As the table in the following footnote illustrates, the *arentata* tended to depend upon whatever individual contract could be obtained, whereas the *censa* rents continued fairly successfully as fixed rents for holdings of certain sizes.

[3] The many conditions governing the entry to lands (especially allowances for dilapidation, for the end of the 14th century; see Ch. X), and the variations in size of tenancies and rents, make it difficult to tabulate satisfactorily the rents for this period. The following evidence from Houghton may be taken as typical, although there was usually a smaller fall in the *censum* after 1348 on those manors with few *arentata* leases. In any case, variations in the size of the *censum*, either before or after the Black Death, cannot be taken as direct evidence of the rise or fall in money

and small amounts, though, as will be seen below, it is questionable how immediately or widely this policy could be adopted.

On the whole, the bulk of tenemental vacancies seem to have been rapidly taken up by these methods.[4]   At Wistow manor, for instance, there were four virgates left on the lord's hands by 1351, but this condition was wiped out by 1352; Slepe manor had eight virgates *in manu domini* in 1351, but by the next extant account roll (1366) there were none; other manors, such as Upwood, had fairly successfully wiped out the vacant tenements by a decade after the plague.   The extent and rapidity of these replacements offer a tempting gauge for the measurement of mortality rates among Ramsey tenants.   To take as an example that predominant type of pre-plague holding, the tenement *ad opus*, Upwood manor shows a decline in such virgates from 22 in 1347 to 15 in 1357, in cotlands from 15 to 10; or in Houghton the virgates *ad opus* in 1336 were 36½ and by 1364 had become 24, the cotlands at these dates were 17 and 8.   While these figures would point to a death toll of something like one-third of the population there is a considerable variation from manor to manor, and the lack of concentrated evidence for the 1348-60 period[5] excludes the possi-

---

rents since the account rolls do not reveal precisely the degree of *opera* commuted at each level of *censa*.   Some further illustra-

tions of the *ad censa* and *arentata* values have been given in Appendix I to this chapter.

LATE 14th-CENTURY MONEY RENTS AT HOUGHTON

Year	Ad Censum	Ad Arentatum
1338	27v. @ 16s.; 12 cot. @ 8s.4d.	0
1364	7½v. @ 12s.; 2 cot. @ 6s.	1v. @ 15s.; 12½v. @ 14s.; 1v. @ 13s.; 1v. @ 12s.; 3v. @ 10s.; 5 cot. @ 6s.; 5 cot. @ 7s.
1371	8v. @ 12s.	2v. @ 16s.; 1v. @ 15s.; 14v. @ 14s. (?)
1396	1v. @ 12s.	1v. @ 15s.; (18)v. @ 16s.; 12v. @ 14s.; ? cot. @ 6s.

---

[4] Although we have been largely concerned with tracing adjustments and variations after the Black Death, it should be borne in mind that perhaps the most striking feature of this troubled period was the substantial continuity of traditional tenurial arrangements.   See the *ad censa* data for the 1340's and 1350's in Appendix II of this chapter. The long-run picture can be seen by comparing App. II with the full schedule of earlier *ad censa* arrangements given in Table L, *supra*, Chapter VIII. It is only a corollary of the continued villeinage rentals *ad opera* that the number of works performed was maintained remarkably over the 1350's (see this Chapter,

Appendix VI).   At the same time, there were clear evidences of stringencies in the labour market: the *opera* sales fell in the 1350's (Chapter VIII, App. I); hired labour doubled in price (Chapter VII, Table I), while the total wage bill was kept around its former level, or even reduced, as the lord hired less labour (e.g. this chapter, Table LXIII).

[5] There are only a few rolls to supply some of the interesting details of adjustment in the actual year of the Black Death: e.g. the payment of over £6 at Elton for extra wage labour to replace the deficiencies in customary work, or the increase of *gersumæ* from around 3 to over £9 at Warboys.   From

bility of a scientific estimation. Even more, however, the fertile powers of expediency manifested by the manorial administration in finding new tenants, and the trend to commutation of works over previous decades (as in that movement from 28½ virgates *ad opus* in 1324 to 22 by 1343, at Upwood), call for cautious interpolation from the bald account roll data.[6]

Statistics of this relatively quick re-occupation of tenements after the Black Death give a deceptive impression of the real economic disturbances over those troubled years. As would be expected from the disruption of demesne cultivation, the total corn production was cut usually by a half, as in Wistow, and the livery to the cellarer fell to as much as one-fifth (e.g. Slepe and Holy-well, and Ch. VI, Section III) of the normal level over previous decades. But more surprising was the fall in money profits, despite the conversion of villein holdings to rents. Most of the cellarer's rents in kind, other than corn and fowl, together with the formerly commuted rents, were apparently settled for a lump sum payment in the first years after 1348-1349. This came to only £9.12s. for Wistow in 1351, and 36s.8d. in 1352, £4 in Upwood in 1357, £4.10s. in Abbots Ripton in 1364, £6 from Holywell in 1356 and £9.10d. in 1364 — while the value of the non-corn farm had previously been commuted at some-thing from sixteen to eighteen pounds for each of these manors. As the lists of manorial profits from the account rolls cover only very few years for this period, and certain allowances must be made for irregularity and disruption in the system of collecting revenues, a more thorough picture of economic returns on the manor may be obtained from those charters of the central abbey administration dealing with debt payments, which have fortunately been preserved.

Eight of these extant charters give the arrears, and (or) payment being made on arrears, over the dozen years after the Black Death. The largest portion of one manuscript actually reveals, in the detailed sources of many debts on the manors, a whole range of tenement rents, mill farms, customary rents, *gersumæ* — in short, it touches upon nearly every revenue source. The remaining rolls give debts for the years 1351, 1352, 1359, and more extensive information on debts and their rate of retirement for 1358, 1360, 1361, 1362. The 'debt' figures for 1351, 1352, and 1359 have been tabulated together, in order to show the debt structure immediately after the Black Death and then a decade later. It should be borne in mind here that the reeve had usually been able to balance his accounts over previous decades.[7] The

six virgates, two maltmen holdings, and four cotlands, that fell into his hands at Warboys in the year of the plague, Abbot Walter sold the standing corn for £7.20d. (*Add. Ch.* 39804).

[6] See Appendix II, this chapter, for statistics relative to the previous paragraphs.

[7] Even with the heavy taxation of the late 13th century the manor rarely went into debt by more than 4 or £5 (Ch. VIII, Table LVI), and the reeve was usually able to wipe out debts fairly quickly without fundamental changes in the demesne

structure. The same may be said for the effects of bad harvests and pestilence on some manorial accounts in the early 14th century. The level of the reeves' debts for the manors of Ramsey was much higher after 1348 than before, in contrast to that evidence found for the See of Winchester (A. E. Levett, *The Black Death*, etc., Ch. II). Miss Levett's concentration upon a short period (1348-50) has precluded an analysis of the re-organization of manorial economic life, and consequently, of the comparative changes in total manorial

rest of the information from these charters on arrears is put in a table arranged
to illustrate the solvency conditions on the manors around 1360.

A systematic amortization of manorial debts was not something new to
the mid-fourteenth century. Some rationalization involving the preservation
of manorial capital would always be necessary for the maintenance of profits.
In 1311, for example, the following note was appended to the regular account
roll items of Weston manor: "Arrears £7. For which the lord abbot allows
to the reeve the payment of one mark at the time of the Nativity of the
Blessed Virgin, one mark at Pentecost, ten shillings at the Gules of August and
ten shillings by Michaelmas. And likewise during the following years,
three and one-half marks are to be paid at the same time in full payment of
the £7." While no method emerges from the dozen or so remarks upon

TABLE LVIII

DEBT STRUCTURE ON RAMSEY MANORS AFTER THE BLACK DEATH[8]

Manor	1351	1352	1359
Holywell	£4.1s.7d.	£4.1s.3d.	£7.13s.2d.
Barton	£10.4s.8d.	£7.1s.0d.	£3.16s.5d.
Shillington	£3.14s.7d.	0	£34.1s.8d.
Hemmingford	£14.17s.0d.	£6.1s.7d.	?
Elsworth	£12.7s.3d.	£22.3s.11d.	£23.0s.8d.
Houghton	£9.7s.3d.	£24.1s.11d.	£31.11s.3d.
Abbots Ripton	£5.12s.8d.	0	£1.11s.9d.
Weston	£6.4s.11d.	£11.17s.3d.	£34.0s.8d.
Slepe	£23.6s.11d.	£4.17s.3d.	£22.2s.0d.
Wistow	0	15s.5d.	£1.6s.1d.
Burwell	£3.7s.2d.	£1.5s.2d.	£13.9s.4d.
Warboys	£3.14s.0d.	£12.3s.9d.	£36.8s.1d.
Elton	£2.18s.3d.	£6.13s.7d.	£9.19s.10d.
Broughton	£12.4s.11d.	£1.3s.9d.	£3.0s.8d.
Graveley	£7.7s.1d.	£5.2s.4d.	£12.1s.4d.
Upwood	£14.17s.2d.	£16.0s.11d.	£10.17s.0d.
Therfield	£4.17s.4d.	0	£12.14s.10d.
Brancaster	£3.16s.8d.	£9.8s.8d.	?
Cranfield	£1.19s.11d.	£6.13s.0d.	£1.3s.8d.

revenues and profits. The importance of many factors that had augmented the lord's manorial revenues immediately after 1348, like the *gersumæ*, was very temporary, perhaps largely an eating up of manorial liquid and movable capital accumulated over the previous generations.

[8] The data for this, and the following two tables, have been derived from *Add. Charters* 34640-1, 34484-9.

TABLE LIX

CONDITIONS OF SOLVENCY ON RAMSEY MANORS *ca.*1360

Manor	1358		1360	
	Debt	Payment	Debt	Payment
Cranfield	£22.8s.2d.	£7	£18.10s.2d.	£12
Barton	£38.13s.6d.	£16.10s.	£29.19s.8d.	£14.18s.
Shillington	£30.11s.9d.	£8	£44.5s.10d.	£23.5s.0d.
Therfield	£12.14s.10d.	0	£19.13s.0d.	0
Slepe	£15.5s.11d.	£3	£158.8s.3d.	£79.9s.7d.
Holywell	£8.5s.6d.	£3	£17.2s.8d.	£12.10s.0d.
Houghton	£19.4s.2d.	£3.10s.	£84.9s.11d.	£33.12s.1d.
Warboys	£21.2s.9d.	£11	£74.7s.6d.	£30.16s.0d.
Wistow	£5.11s.3d.	£3	£14.15s.7d.	£9.1s.3d.
Upwood	£7.5s.1d.	0	£25.0s.2d.	£18.14s.0d.
Abbots Ripton	£8.9s.8d.	£4	£8.2s.1d.	paid
Weston	£14.7s.4d.	0	£15.17s.9d.	0
Elton	£11.12s.3d.	0	£49.3s.0d.	£22.4s.9d.
Burwell	£12.14s.9d.	0	£63.11s.8d.	£10.2s.6d.
Elsworth	£36.15s.8d.	£18.10s.	£23.6s.7d.	£23.6s.7d.
Ringstead	13s.4d.	0	£3.14s.4d.	£3
Wimbotsham	14s.4d.	0	£4.10s.10d.	paid
Graveley	£9.9s.4d.	£11.18s.4d.	£3.11s.11d.	£1
Knapwell	£2.1s.11d.	0	0	0

Note: Since the debts and payments on Slepe, Houghton, Warboys, and Elton carry
back for many years, the 1358 tabulation presented above has tried to get the
more current balance of these manors, by giving the amounts which were apparently
applicable to the *previous year* only.   For the remaining years, however, all debts
and payments are summated for all manors.   The impressive list of six or eight
collectors and officials liquidating their debts at the same time on some of the
more deeply insolvent manors, must have tended to offset the rationalizing effects
of incremental payments.   But there is no consistent evidence that the reeve or
beadle were replaced because of the inordinate debt accumulation during the time
of their administration.

liquidation of debts in the 1351 roll, by 1360 the scribe notes in some cases
(Warboys, Houghton, Burwell) that '20s. were paid, and so for each year', and
the majority of debt payments in 1358, 1360, 1361, 1362, are transferred by
increments of 20s. or some multiple of this amount.   Due to the reception of
arrears from several former officials in the same year, this ordered solvency
does not appear in the tables below.   But, in any case, manorial solvency would
have to be attacked by more drastic measures.

The first table shows eleven cases of substantial debt a decade after the
plague first struck, and three cases of successful amortization.   Many of the

debts, in Houghton, Warboys, and Upwood, for example, can be traced back over several of the intervening years. So the 1359 data do not represent merely a tardy rent collection for that year. In addition, as Tables LIX and LX illustrate, other manors were going more drastically into debt around 1360, so there was no simple question of a backlog from the 1348-50 fluctuation.[9]

TABLE LX		
MANORIAL DEBTS IN THE 1360's[10]		
Manor	1361	1362
Cranfield....................	£11.4s.7d.	£1.4s.4d.
Barton.....................	£5.10s.4d.	£9.6s.4d.
Shillington.................	£21.0s.9d.	£29.2s.6d.
Therfield...................	£15.8s.7d.	£2.13s.6d.
Slepe......................	£26.3s.Cd.	£38.2s.6d.
Holywell...................	£16.4s.10d.	£15.12s.6d.
Houghton..................	£14.13s.4d.	£41.8s.4d.
Warboys...................	£17.8s.10d.	£15.19s.6d.
Weston....................	£46.3s.11d.	Condoned
Elton......................	£12.5s.11d.	£25.10s.9d.
Elsworth...................	£7.4s.8d.	?

The thinner stream of profits, coupled with this persistent manorial insolvency over two decades in the face of higher prices, points to a fundamental malaise in manorial production. There appears to be little doubt of an under-employment of capital and labour on Ramsey manors. As to capital, considerable amounts of demesne arable were put immediately *in manu domini,* and remained in that category longer than tenements from the villeinage. This is not surprising, since parcels of demesne had usually been farmed to wealthier peasants, — the pre-1348 account rolls refer to these as 'customary tenants' — and being held along with their family tenement, the former would tend to be vacated first, when the villein's family was decimated. Those manors in which farming of the demesne had become very prominent during the 1340's

[9] When a large debt suddenly disappears from the roll (e.g. 1361-2, Weston, Therfield, Upwood), it seems legitimate to suspect that the debt has been condoned, or simply not relisted in the accounts for that year. Some of these condonations can be found in the account rolls; e.g. the reeve of Elton (1360-61) was absolved from a debt of £53.4s.2d. — a debt which was largely made up of total failures in cheese liveries over the previous one-half dozen years. But in general the account roll evidence on condonation or amortization of debts is inadequate.

[10] There is still evidence of considerable debts on some manors in 1367 (e.g. Slepe, £19.5s; Warboys, £18.16s.4d.; Holywell, £16; Therfield, £16.18s.1d.).

were heavily affected by the Black Death. At Slepe, for example, 161 acres of the demesne were farmed in 1347; rents could only be collected from 58 acres in 1351, 137½ acres had been successfully farmed again by 1366, but throughout the rest of the century, the 1347 level was never regained.[11] It is true that some of these demesne lands that had previously been farmed were cultivated, if possible, during their 'vacancy'.[12] But when the profits were reported from such lands *ad wainagium*, they were small in comparison with the rent value of demesne acres.[13]

More important would be the nature of efforts made since 1349 to cultivate demesne lands which had never been let to farm. The various stringencies of capital and labour then took their toll. For some manors,[14] such as Wistow, the amount of seed was maintained, but probably because of the lack of cultivation returns dropped sharply; Elton, Slepe, and Abbots Ripton show an unusually low yield for barley, beans and peas over 1349-50. For other manors, such as Upwood and Broughton, the same effects on gross production followed from what appears to have simply been a decline in the amounts sown per acre — probably from deficiencies in cultivation.

In the meantime the decline of villein works due to renting of former *ad opera* tenements would in all cases be greater than proportionate farming of the demesne immediately after the Black Death. The correlative intensification of labour demands forced a gradual doubling of the money wage for the *famuli* over the 1350's[15] in the face of both Ordinance and Statute, thereby adding further to the costs of cultivation. The high mortality rate and the recurrence of the plague must have dispirited the villeins, and they would often be suffering from an insufficiency of labour on their own holdings. It may be indicative of labour shortage that the account rolls concede a margin of tenements, albeit small, that were not taken up for two decades after 1349, in the manors of Houghton, Abbots Ripton and Holywell. Certainly the labour force available for boon works seems to have shrunk drastically. Since there were gathered for such work tenants from croft, cotland, or virgate, whether *ad opera* or *ad censa*, along with much landless labour of the village employed by the virgater to make up his three or four men quota,

---

[11] See also Broughton, Upwood, Houghton in Appendix III, this chapter, for further statistics relative to the farming of demesne parcels in the 14th century.

[12] It was traditionally the reeve's duty to manage what profits he could from vacant lands which fell into the lord's hands; see Chatteris, 1273, (W. O. AULT, *Court Rolls of the Abbey of Ramsey and the Honour of Clare*, p. 267).

[13] The terms *Wainagium* or *Proficium* are used indiscriminately for these profits listed under the *exitus maneriorum*. Some examples from Slepe, when the virgate was *ad censum* for 24s. might be a typical entry for any time in the late 14th century: (1390) (*proficium*) 1 v. — 10s.; 1 v. — 6s.; 1 v.— 10s.; 1 v.—4s.

[14] See Ch. VI for this paragraph, as for previous remarks in this chapter concerning the livery of corn. It was usual for the amounts sown to fall, despite the paucity of farming from the demesne, until a couple of decades after 1348. The decline in amounts sown are roughly: Upwood 55%, Abb. Ripton 55%, Broughton 20%, Weston 30%.

[15] See Ch. VII, Table XLV. It should also be noted that the Court Rolls reveal fines for such wholesale non-performance of certain work over the two decades after the Black Death, that it may be logical to consider the lord's acceptance of these fines as another form of commutation.

the total number of these boon labourers must have been a significant approximation to the total village labour force.

There were two large contributions from this type of labour in the Weston
manorial group over 1297-8: 4 freemen, 365 'customaries', and 18 'families' at
the first; 298 customaries and 18 families at the second.   One boon period
brought four freemen, 324 customaries, and 20 families in 1311 to the same
manors.   But the only large boon congregation listed for these manors in the
second half of the century, over 1368-9, brought but 76 customaries and an
unidentified number of families.   On Slepe manor, which mustered 28 ploughs
and 116 men at the boon ploughing of 1324, one was able to count only 18
ploughs and 18 families in 1366.[16]

One logical corrective to this impasse might have been sought in a
wholesale conversion to pastoral farming, which would occupy vacant lands
and at the same time require less labour.   From the point of view of the
manorial budget, there is evidence in the statistics of several manors, that the
reeve was able to increase the herds of cattle and swine; but the stubborn
problem remains that a heavy capital investment was necessary in order to
make a telling and sudden conversion of the manorial system, and the reeve
had a constant burden of debt about his neck to restrain such imaginative
entrepreneurial ventures on the manorial level.   The fact that herds of cattle
had generally declined in size by the 1360's, partly at least from more numerous
sales, may point to the pull of debts from the arable millstone.   The vaccaries
were in many cases kept in production of milk and cheese during the 1350's
and 1360's at a profit of 2s.6d. or 3s. per cow, over the summer months.   But
by the 1370's the milch herd was being left to pasture with the calves, at
least in the fens of Houghton, Broughton, Slepe, Holywell, and Upwood.
Although the sales of stock increased considerably on some manors after the
mid-century — perhaps owing to the decline in food rents — in the total
revenues of the account roll they remained a petty item.

In the larger economy of abbey profits there was a huge increase in the
size of flocks of sheep over the decade after 1349, probably subsidized by
purchases of the central treasury.   Wool sales did not enter the manorial
account to ease the revenue problems of the reeve, however, nor are there any
specific notices that arable was being converted to pasture.   And from the
point of view of abbey revenues, the increased profit from fleeces (200 @ 6d.
as a manorial average) was about one-quarter or one-third the losses in corn
livery (125 q. @ 3s. as a round figure).   In any case, sheep farming was a
precarious and costly business at Ramsey.   The flocks were decimated by a
plague during the 1360's, and when rebuilding was left to the manors, it was
only slowly that some flocks came up to their earlier numbers.   A combination
of extreme climatic aberrations[17] together with dwindling expenditure on

---

[16] See App. IV, for further data on customary
workers.

[17] The recently discovered Fakynham Ms
(Brit. Mus.), now commonly attributed
to Babwell Priory, throws further precisions

upon the meteorological disturbances in
East Anglia during these troubled decades.
Ramsey manors would come within the
ambit of these elements; and a synoptic
account of the major incidents recorded by

drainage, probably reduced the available fen pastures. Later in the century the valuable rents from Holywell Fen were often condoned because of flood havoc.[18] Profits from pastoral farming never seemed to tempt the fourteenth-century administrators at Ramsey to a manorial revolution.[19]

II

Around 1370,[20] the chronic conditions of insolvency on Ramsey manors were finally attacked more realistically by a considerable re-organization of the manorial administration. The heavy food livery quotas to the cellarer were abolished after a history of nearly three hundred years. Into their place came an annual livery to the Ramsey bakehouse which seemed to vary pragmatically thereafter with the level of demesne production, and perhaps with price movements. The cellarer received in exchange a number of annual cash farms, £60 from Cranfield, £48 from Barton, £80 from Shillington (and Pegsdon), together with reduced cash farms from the former conventual manors which now averaged about £4 from each estate for the commutation of bacon and fowl dues.

At the same time villeins were encouraged to take up some of the vacant holdings by offers of longer leases. The life lease had been sparingly used a generation earlier: one small lot and a sheep-fold were rented at Holywell in

this document is given here. Fr. Conrad Walmsley, O.F.M., kindly lent his transcription of this Ms.
1349 plague arrived at Cambridge friary over Eastertide and lasted all summer.
1360 the plague was in London, first infants and then men and women were afflicted.
1361 the plague raged in the south of England, though less seriously than the former attack. A big storm in February, blowing down the church steeple and trees etc.
1363 extreme frost from December to mid-Lent.
1364 floods in villages near the sea ... terram penetraverunt ad magnam profunditatem ... se occultaverunt et blada destruxerunt et feras et cuniculos oves et lepores interfecerunt.
1369 pestilence great among young and old.
1370 isto anno fuit magna caristia bladi per totam angliam et maxime in estate ita quod quarterum frumenti valuit XX s., et in quibusdam partibus II marcas.
1373-4 famine again.
1374 large floods through many parts of this area; some villages and houses inundated; *proviens et pecora in pascuum* drowned; then intense frost until Christmas, penury of fresh water so that a 'pipe' of it sold for 12d.
[18] Losses to the sales of fen grasses in Holywell accounts were: 1371 — £3.7s.4d.; 1401 —

28s.9d.; 1404 — £17.10s.3d.; 1405 — £8.; 1418 — £10.19s.5d.
[19] The sale of 'herbage and fen grasses' to the customaries reached a new high on Ramsey manors during the second half of the 14th century. At the same time, the renting of demesne arable (App. III) was often paralleled by renting of pasture: e.g. at Holywell there was 10a. at Prestholm, 28a. at Estlong, 26 a. at Merlake, and 21½ a. at Redalfurlong rented in 1364 — much the same as the pre-1348 rent of pasture. By 1383 the pasture rents at Holywell had increased by nearly 50 a. to a total of 132 a. 3r. The pasture was usually worth about three times as much as the arable, i.e. about 3s. per acre.
[20] It is interesting to compare the rates of major adjustment at various places throughout the country after the Black Death. While some manors were farmed immediately after 1348 (e.g. the estates of Merton College, cited in Oman, *The Great Revolt of 1381*, Oxford, 1906, p. 6, n. 2), it seems to have been more usual for such major adjustment (i.e. the farming of the demesnes in all the following examples) to have commenced from around the 1370's (e.g. G. A. HOLMES, *The English Nobility in the Reign of Edward III*, p. 150, for examples from the Clare manors, and other references to Canterbury estates, Leicestershire manors, and the Ogbourne bailiwick).

1348 for life, a one-half virgate tenement was let at Slepe in 1351 on the same term. But twenty years later the practice was becoming more frequently and universally adopted on Ramsey manors. In 1367, five 'furrows' of demesne were farmed at Broughton for twenty years, in 1371, one virgate was let at Upwood for life. Abbots Ripton rented a 'land' in 1367 for ten years, and a meadow in 1368 for life. Holywell leased a field from the demesne for life in 1371, and Houghton a field in 1368 for twenty years. Wistow rented a thirty-three acre field from the demesne in 1362 for forty years, and a small field in 1363 for twenty years. Weston manor granted four acres for life in 1368.

Probably as a consequence of this policy, there came a decline in those discounts or 'allowances' that were permitted to the reeve every year because of decayed rents, vacant holdings and unfarmed parcels of demesne. The Houghton account never suffered so much from these losses, perhaps because of the *arentata*, but there exists a good series of accounts for this manor, and the range of variation here tabulated may be taken as typical of that occurring at most Ramsey manors.

TABLE LXI

RENT ALLOWANCES ON HOUGHTON MANOR

Year	Amount	Year	Amount
1369	21s. 8d.	1388	3s. 4d.
1371	9s. 8d.	1389	3s. 4d.
1372	6s. 4d.	1393	3s. 4d.
1379	3s. 4d.	1394	3s. 4d.
1383	3s. 4d.	1396	3s. 4d.
1387	3s. 4d.	1404	30s. 2d.

A new generation coming of age after the plagues, and ameliorations in meteorological conditions, may have given further encouragement to a more complete occupation of land at this time. Some manors registered rapid increases in the fragmentation of demesne. There were about six new bits and pieces let at Broughton, and near a dozen in both Holywell and Upwood over the 1370's. The entry fine no longer offered much of a tax upon tenancies. The administrators of some manors may have tried to capitalize upon the numerous transfers immediately after the Black Death, but thereafter the *gersumæ* remained mere token sums, as the following table illustrates:

TABLE LXII

GERSUMÆ

Slepe		Holywell		Abbots Ripton	
Year	Amount	Year	Amount	Year	Amount
1347	44s. 6d.	1347	4s. ?	1342	109s. 10d.
1351	166s. 6d.	1356	19s. 8d.	1364	51s. 9d.
1366	2s. 6d.	1371	8s. 4d.	1388	5s. 11d.
1381	2s.	1383	3s.		
1387	1s.				

Around 1380, this predilection for farming parcels of the demesne gave way to a renewed interest in demesne production on most of the Huntingdon manors of Ramsey. The failure to farm lands would not seem to be a sufficient or at least a successful reason, for this new course, since upon those manors more affected by vacancies, such as Slepe, the slack was not taken up from demesne lands over the ensuing decades. It may be more logical to suggest that the sound instinct of the convent, which had prohibited commutation of corn liveries from the early twelfth century, refused now to jeopardize its bread by a dependence upon market prices for corn, when demesne productivity could take a more encouraging turn. In any case, the amount of seed was increased on some manors until it approximated those quantities sown during the prosperous years of the early fourteenth century. In order to facilitate this intensified cultivation, for such it was, with no lands being taken out of 'farm',[21] two or three tenements were recalled from the *ad censum* on such manors,[22] and less works were sold. The renewal of *opera* sales had begun immediately after the Black Death despite the evident lack of hands on the demesne, probably from the same motive as the increasing commutation of works by the *censa* and *arentata*, that is, to keep the villeinage in production. But over the last two decades of the century, only one-half of the works that had been sold in 1357 at Upwood, for example, were now commuted, and a decrease in these sales was equally traceable for other manors.[23] A period of fairly high yields accompanied this renewed interest in production; and liveries were generally high over the 1380's and 1390's. For the manors of Upwood,

[21] See App. III, this chapter. Abbots Ripton may have been the only manor to recall parcels of demesne for cultivation at this period; several fields from Slepe may have been pastured or let for nothing to the priory of St. Ives, but they were not put *ad wainagium*.

[22] See App. II, this chapter.

[23] App. I, Ch. VIII, see Wistow, Holywell, Houghton, Elton, Broughton, Abbots Ripton.

Slepe, Holywell, and Weston, these liveries frequently touched a level during the 1380's, that they had attained in the second quarter of the century.[24]

While the relatively minor increase in works and services employed on the demesne land may have been a reason for the very few disorders that Dispenser was called upon to correct, as he rode back by Ramsey to quell the extensive peasants' revolt in East Anglia, the swollen profits from demesne production neither tended to subsidize the gross income of the villagers, nor to be paralleled by a similar buoyancy in general manorial conditions. It was no longer the manorial economy of the thirteenth century, when prosperity had benefited villein and lord alike, either by increased employment of the villagers to aid the lord's augmented production plan, or by the cession of immediate market profits to the villeins under the seigneurial control of *gersumæ* and adjustable money rents.

The new spirit of demesne management at this time is best revealed in the concern for annual production 'profits' at the expense of both capital maintenance and villein profits. Gross production was brought under a strict cash calculus by a *valor* system which was added to the traditional account roll. Usually, and because these matters were being taken more and more out of the hands of the reeve, only the total valuation figure is given on the rolls, but Slepe manorial accounts for 1381-2 include the index system employed: wheat at 4 shillings per quarter, malt at three shillings per quarter, peas at 3 shillings per quarter, oats at 2 shillings per quarter, wool at sixpence per fleece, and porkers at two shillings, sixpence each.[25] At the same time economies were introduced in manorial expenditures with a special view to compressing overhead costs. The purchase and sale of cattle, sheep, and sometimes hogs, became a market policy involving heavy capital disbursements, rather than

---

[24] Ch. VI, Table XXXVIII. However, the best years at Abbots Ripton, Slepe, Holywell, Upwood and Wistow never saw much more than half of the old *quota* delivered.

[25] As has been noted before in this study (Ch. III) a *valor* system was at least as old as the 12th century at Ramsey; and some valuation was probably applied to the crop estimates of the *progressus* and the livestock data of the account roll over later centuries (e.g. R. A. L. SMITH *Canterbury Cathedral Priory*, pp. 19-20). But only from the 1380's does the *valor* appear in immediate conjunction with the manorial account.
This *valor* was more in the nature of a productivity assessment than an estimate of clear profits. For example, all the payments from the manor of Upwood in 1386 (taking malt @ 3s., fleeces @ 6d., and *den' lib'*) comes to £67.17s.10d., but the *valor* was £123.6s.9d., a sum much closer to a gross output valuation. A few remarks accompanying other *valor* sums at Upwood offer further clarification: (1385) Clarus valor huic maner' de hoc cum diversis victualibus lib' in hospit' dom'. Or for

1384: "And this is the clear value of this manor for this year, having deducted all receipts and perquisites of corn provided from Graveley as indicated on the dorse, and with (i.e., including) wheat remaining in sheaves and malt in the granary and various foodstuffs delivered to the guest-house of the lord, as is indicated on the dorse."
When the demesne was farmed the *valor* assessment followed different lines, of course. In the *valor* table of Ellington given *infra* (App. V), for example, the farm of £40 plus the various extras determines the annual figure; or in Bythorn, in 1387-8 the *valor* was given as £32.17s.11d., a figure which tallies exactly with the total of demesne farm (£30) plus leet profits (17s.11d.), with *gersumæ* (40s.), the arrears being excluded. Unfortunately the *valor* seems to have been still largely a matter between the bailiff and his superiors rather than a tool of local administration (there exists but the one central roll, however, that of 1415-1416, *Add. Ch.* 34353), and the *valor* item sometimes appears in an infrequent fashion, if at all, on account rolls.

a dependence upon manorial breeding and build-up; and a heavier turnover of livestock at favourable prices occurred, rather than simply the former petty sales of the old and the infirm.   Expenditure upon implements and buildings followed a similar pattern: there tended to be fewer regular expenses, then periodic heavy investment upon demesne equipment.   Or in some cases, capital investment was not made, as with the mills of Broughton and Ellington, which fell down in the 1380's, and were not repaired for generations.   A factor more directly related to the livelihood of villagers was the fixing of wages from around 1360, and the fact that demesne management was further able to circumvent labour shortages by the stabilization, or even reduction, of the wage bill, at the period of more intense demesne production.

TABLE LXIII

WAGE BILLS ON SOME RAMSEY MANORS

Upwood		Slepe		Abbots Ripton	
Year	Amount	Year	Amount	Year	Amount
1324	36s.10d.	1324	52s.2d.	1324	43s.
1343	44s.9d.	1345	72s.1d.	1342	51s.10d.
1357	49s.6d.	1351	61s.8d.	1364	64s.4d.
1371	81s.4d.	1381	78s.9d.	1375	76s.2d.
1385	75s.8d.	1387	66s.1d.	1385	63s.10d.
1386	75s.8d.	1390	67s.4d.	1388	63s.10d.
1392	75s.8d.				

Broughton			
Year	Amount	Year	Amount
1326	37s.6d.	1378	62s.1d.
1342	46s.	1380	56s.1d.
1344	57s.2d.	1386	63s.
1346	44s.8d.	1392	57s.6d.

To direct this retreat from the old *Grundherrschaft*, a number of bailiffs appeared for the Huntingdon manors during the reign of King Richard II. This bailiff was a highly paid freeman who supplemented or subordinated the reeve.   With the withering of champion husbandry, the reeve became less important and was gradually replaced by the bailiff, at the head of the account roll from this period. These changes underlined the degree to which the previous demesne organization had depended upon a vital villein economy. But devolution of manorial control to villeins offered few opportunities when the labour market was stringent; and property demand was insufficient to make it possible to cushion revenues by entry fines and other villein taxes. In the meantime, the abbey itself was withdrawing further from the traditional paternal interest in manorial revenues and resources as integral parts of the abbey economy: the obedientiaries, even the cellarer, are no more than other rent collectors, in the administrative documents from this time; the system of passing on responsibility for stock maintenance, even of sheep, to market sale and purchase on the manorial level, threw a further exigency upon demesne profits. This commercial note in the bailiff's administration, and the increasing independence of the rent collector (usually the beadle) from the reeve, gradually transformed the accounts.[26]

While the cutback in utilization of wage labour, combined with the fixing of wages from around 1360, froze any advantages the villagers might have had from labour shortage, the picture of villein profits from the land was equally depressing. No doubt the Black Death placed the wage earner in a stronger position, and the peasant with substantial land and capital would be able to improve his condition, from the increasing returns of the late fourteenth century. But the rigidity of rents stultified all other encouragements to the occupation of land. Probably the most striking witness to the real depth of that difference between the manorial economic conditions after the Black Death and earlier conditions, was the failure of all the usual incentives to entice full employment of land even over the more prosperous period of the late fourteenth century: the *gersumæ* remained negligible; the life leases were still offered, such as the two tenements in Houghton during 1379, or over thirty acres of demesne, a cottage and messuage in Abbots Ripton over 1388-9; for some leases a large rebate was given upon taking up the holding, and the *census* frequently failed to gain the pre-1348 level.[27] But still some tenements remained unoccupied during the most prosperous years of the 1380's and 1390's.[28]

Was there simply no longer enough labour to work the land? Labour services were performed in surprisingly regular quantities over the latter half of the fourteenth century,[29] but it must be recognized that labour performance on the demesne would be the least sensitive index to shortage on the labour market. Literally all the adjustments permissable to the villein tenement

---

[26] From this period various entries appear to 'allow' considerable cash for purchase of sheep, corn, etc., apparently often without reference to the reeve. And in the debt items of the account, the beadle assumes as much prominence as the reeve, in contrast with the post-1348 debts, when the former held a relatively insignificant position.

[27] See the examples from Houghton, above,

n.3; at the same manor one demesne field which should have been rented for 30s., continued to receive but 26s.8d. over the rest of the century; another field was giving 20s., which should have farmed for 24s.

[28] See App. II, especially Slepe, Houghton.

[29] Cf. Appendix VI, this chapter.

were safety devices to insulate the main group of tenements *ad opera*; so that adjustments were possible through the sale of works, the leases *ad censa* or *arentata*, before a tightening in labour conditions might be reflected in the amount of *opera* performed. But, in addition, the fact that the sale of *opera* continued over this period, and that wage incentives were not employed, would argue against the importance of labour shortage as the crux of the problem. It is difficult to escape the conclusion that the lack of profit incentive offered to the customary tenant was a more determining factor in the manorial economy of the time than the lord's control over wages, commutation, or the level of rents.

In this respect, it is doubtful whether the traditional level of property rents themselves left much margin for villein profits, even with 'allowances' and negligible entry fines. The first determinant of rents for villein holdings was still the value of works, and over the fourteenth century commutation prices remained constant. In addition, the value of commuted services remained the 'standard' rent over the late fourteenth century; and despite the numbers, and the degree, of reductions in the *ad censa* or *arentata*, such reductions still were considered as exceptional during this century. On some manors (e.g. Slepe, Upwood) the *censum* was not lowered consistently after 1348; only a small percentage (about 10% at Upwood) of the demesne acres were reduced in farm price *ca.* 1350, and these were gradually raised again over the ensuing decades. Other rents were 'recovered' where possible (e.g. the *arentata* at Houghton, *supra* n. 3) in the 1370's and 1380's. In similar fashion, those lands which were taken from the demesne by the villagers during the late fourteenth century, were not an expression of strong competitive demand. These farmed parcels would seem to have been managed on a minimum profit margin, for with the ensuing decline in agrarian returns such holdings were rapidly abandoned on the demesne, before a major re-organization took place for other tenemental conditions. And the numerous villein holdings which were falling into the lord's hands after 1400 were often in a dilapidated condition.[30]

The economic recovery of the 1370's and 1380's was followed by a drastic depression which seemed to commence in the 1390's, according to the evidence of several manorial *valors* and the mill farms.[31] This decline in the productivity assessment, and the rapid increase in the number of small parcels of farmed demesne which could not pay rents or were owing large deficits from this time, suggests again that a series of poor harvests were fundamental to the decline. Adjustments began to be made along the lines of the programme adopted after 1348. There was a strong swing to the *arentata* over the *censa*, especially at Houghton, although this trend was first noticeable for the smaller tenancies on other manors before 1400 (e.g. the cotlands and crofts at Wistow and Upwood).

[30] See Ch. X, for detail on these last two points.
[31] See Houghton and Wistow, App. V, this chapter; and Holywell, Houghton, and Warboys, App. VII this Chapter. The important developments in manorial debts, as revealed in the account rolls, are studied in detail in Chapter X.

   Although there does not seem to have been a sudden crisis, as in 1348, and the impact of the new economic conditions forced only gradual adjustments for a decade or two, the demesne economy of Ramsey manors was much less resilient in 1400 than fifty years earlier.   From about 1400 the trend became apparent on all manors, and the adjustments over the next two decades assumed far more drastic proportions than those following upon the Black Death.   It occasioned the end of demesne cultivation by a farming of the demesnes at Elton, Houghton, Slepe, Holywell, and Lawshall over 1400-1410. On the remaining 'home' manors the bailiff continued to work the demesne, sporadically at least, over succeeding decades.   Whether the demesne was farmed or not, the sale of *opera* disappeared from the account rolls, and there was a re-organization of the *censa*.   By what was now called the 'new', or sometimes the 'larger' *censum*, the difference between the *censum* and the *arentatum* was often wiped out.[32]   Henceforth the rent roll becomes almost the sole means of acquaintance with the economic life of Ramsey manors.   The account rolls leave little doubt about the impelling necessity for this rental policy.   That the new conditions did not merely reflect a loss of interest in traditional demesne production by the abbey may perhaps best be seen in the fact that services were commuted on some manors after 1400 upon the express condition that they be revocable after a decade or two.   But as time wore on it became clear that the old demesne economy had disappeared for good. Chapter Ten has isolated something of the nature of this fifteenth-century transformation on Ramsey estates.

---

[2] These adjustments varied from manor to manor; at Holywell, where the *opera* were practically dissolved, the virgate rent increased from 15s. to 17s. or 18s.; at Slepe, where the virgater still had to plough 4 acres, to pile hay for 1 day, to give 1 day at the autumn boon, and to pay the taxes of sheriff's aid and hedsilver (*Ministers' Accounts*, 884/22), the rent fell from 24 to 22s. per virgate.

APPENDIX I

SOME *AD CENSUM* AND *ARENTATUM* RATES FROM THE MID-14th CENTURY

Year	Ad censum	Arentatum
	Slepe	
1319	18½ v. @ 15s.	0
1345	10 v. @ 24s.; 6v. @ 15s.	0
1347	19½ v. @ 24s.	0
1351	16 v. @ 24s.	0
1366	16½ v. @ 24s.; 3½ v. @ 15s.	1 v.–20s.; ½ v.–11s.2d.; 1 v.–13s.4d.
1381	9 v. @ 24s.; 5½ v. @ 15s.	1 v.–20s.; ½ v.–11s.2d.;?
1387	6½ v. @ 24s.; 10 v. @ 15s.	1 v.–20s.; ½ v.–11s.2d.; 1 v.–24s.; ½ v. & 1 cot.–20s.; ½ v.–14s.
1390	7½ v. @ 24s.; 8½ v. @ 15s.	1 v.–20s.; 1v.–24s.; ½ v. & 1 cot. –20s.; ½ v.–13s.
	Abbots Ripton	
1324	3 v. @ 15s,	0
1342	4 v. @ 20s.	0
1364	10 v. @ 15s.	½ v.–10s.
1369	9½ v. @ 15s.	2½ v. @ 20s.
1375	9½ v. @ 15s.	2 v. @ 20s.; ½ v.–11s.; 1¼ v.–24s.; 1 v.–14s.; ½ v.–9s.
1388	6¼ v. @ 15s.	2 v. @ 20s.; 1 v.–14s.; ¼ v.–5s.; (3)½ v. @ 10s.; ½ v.–9s.; 1 v.–22s.; 1¼ v.–24s.
1458	0	1½ v.–35s.; 1½ v.–20s.; 2 v.–28s.; 1 v.–20s.; 2 v.–24s.; 1½ v.–24s.; 2 v. @ 18s.; 1 v.–18s.8d.; 2 v.–13s. 4d.; 1½ v.–23s.4d.; 1½ v.–26s.; 1 v.–16s.; 1½ v.–24s.; 1 v.–23s.4d.; 1 v.–16s.; ½ v.–7s.8d.; ½ v.–8s.; ½ & ⅛ v.–11s.8d.; 1½ v.–11s.6d.; ½ v.–8s.; 1¾ v.–26s.; 1 v.–20s.; 2 v.–32s.; 1 v.–13s.4d.; ½ v.–7s.; 1 v. & 2 a.–10s.; ½ v.–9s.; ½ v.–5s.; ¼ v.–5s.; ½ v.–6s.8d.

APPENDIX II

THE DISPOSITION OF VILLEINAGE TENEMENTS ON RAMSEY MANORS

Note: *Ad op.* = *ad opus*; *Ad c.* = *ad censum*; *A.* = *arentata*;
M.D. = *in manu domini*; Off. = held by manorial officials for services. Tenements *ad c.* before 1350 are listed in Table L (in Chapter VIII). The information for this table is derived from membranes appended to the account rolls. The dash in these tables indicates that the entry is not available; the question mark indicates that an entry has not been given for this classification but some property remains to be accounted for.

Slepe

Year	Virgates					Cotlands			
	Ad op.	*Ad c.*	*A.*	*M.D.*	Off.	*Ad op.*	*Ad c.*	*A.*	Off.
1345	34	16	0	0	20	—	—	—	—
1347	31½	19½	0	0	2	—	—	—	—
1351	26	16	0	8	2	14	1	0	0
1366	27½	20	2½	0	2	12	3	0	0
1381	20	14½	3½	12	2	10	4	1	1
1387	16	16¼	3½	13¼	3	12	4	1	1
1390	14	16	3	12	2	12	3	1	1

Holywell

Year	Virg.			Cot.				Crofts		
	Ad op.	*Ad c.*	Off.	*Ad op.*	*Ad c.*	Off.		*Ad c.*	*A.*	*M.D.*
1343	—	5	—	—	6	—		0	0	0
1356	12	5	0	6	6	3		8	2	3
1364	11½	5	½	6	6	3		8	5	0
1371	15	2	0	10	2	3		8	4	1
1383	14	3	0	10	1	4		7	5	1
1396	13½	3½	0	11	1	3	*A.*	7	5	1
1399	13½	3	½	12	2	0	1	8	5	0
1401	14½	2½	0	13	1	0	0	8	5	0
1402	14	3	0	12	3	0	0	8	5	0
1404	14	3	0	12	2	?	?	6	5	(2)
1405	14	3	0	12	2	?	?	6	5	(2)
1409	10	7	0	12	2	?	?	6	5	(2)
1412	0	17	0	0	15	?	?	6	6	(1)
1450	0	17	0	0	15	0	0	6	6	1

APPENDIX II (*Cont'd.*)

THE DISPOSITION OF VILLEINAGE TENEMENTS ON RAMSEY MANORS (*Cont'd.*)

Houghton

Year	Virg.					Cot.					Crofts		
	Ad op.	Ad c.	A.	Off.	M.D.	Ad op	Ad c	A.	Off.	M.D.	Ad c.	A.	M.D.
1336	36½	20	0	—	—	17	—	—	—	1	8	—	—
1338	29½	27	0	—	—	—	—	—	—	—	12	—	—
1364	24	7½	17½	1	7	8	2	10	1	1	—	—	—
1369	26	?	?	?	?	9	—	—	—	—	—	—	—
1371	25	8	22	1	2	7	5	8	—	1	10	15	1
1372	25	7	23	1	2	6	6	8	1	1	10	16	—
1379	25	5½	25½	1½	½	11	2	9	—	—	6	12	8
1383	24½	5	25½	1½	—	10	2	10	—	—	6	15	5
1387	26	5	24½	1½	1	9	2	11	—	—	3	23	—
1388	24	0	—	—	—	9	—	—	—	—	—	—	—
1389	24	0	—	—	—	8	4½	—	—	—	—	—	—
1393	20½	0	—	—	—	6	—	—	—	—	—	—	—
1394	21	1½	33	1½	1	7	1	14	—	—	5	21	—
1396	22	1	33	1½	—	6	2	14	—	—	4	19	3
1399	18	1	34	½	4½	8	1	13	1	—	1	22	4
1403	0	18½	38	½	1	—	7	15	—	—	—	26	—
1418	0	15	28¼	—	14¾	—	6	14	—	2	—	24	2

Upwood

Year	Virg.					Cot.				
	Ad op.	Ad c.	A.	M.D.	Off.	Ad op.	Ad c.	A.	Off.	M.D.
1324	28½	4½	0	—	—	19	2	—	—	—
1343	20½	4	0	—	—	15	5	—	—	—
1347	22	2½	0	—	—	15	3	—	—	—
1357	15	5½	3½	1	2½	10	6	—	1	—
1371	13¾	4	8¾	—	2	7	8	8	½	—
1386	14	3½	8½	—	2½	10	—	—	½	—
1392	13¾	4	7¾	½	2½	5	8	10	½	—
1400	14½	2¼	10¼	—	1½	4	6	11½	—	2
1401	12½	2	11	—	1½	?	?	11½	—	2
1402	11½	2½	12	—	1½	?	?	?	—	2
1403	11½	2½	12	—	1½	?	?	?	—	?
1404	10½	2½	12½	—	2	?	?	?	—	—
1405	9½	3	12½	—	2	?	?	—	—	3
1406	8½	3	13	—	2	2	5	10½	—	6
1411	6	1½	15½	4	1½	1	5	13½	—	4
1412	5½	1	17¾	2¾	1½	1	4	15½	—	3

Appendix II (*Cont'd.*)

THE DISPOSITION OF VILLEINAGE TENEMENTS ON RAMSEY MANORS (*Cont'd.*)

Warboys

Year	Virg.					Maltmen			
	Ad op.	*Ad c.*	*M.D.*	Off.	*A.*	*Ad op.*		*Ad c.*	Off.
1343	—	0	—	—	0	—		0	—
1354	25¾	8½	—	2	1	6		—	2
1359	26¼	6¾	1¾	1½	—	5		1	2
1360	26¼	7½	1¼	1	—	5		1	2
1362	25	6½	3¼	1½	—	5		1	2
1363	23½	5¾	3½	1½	2	4	*A.*	2	2
1366	24¾	3¼	1¼	1½	6½	6		1	1
1371	22¾	2	3¼	¾	7½	3¼	3	¼	1
1373	22¼	2½	2	¾	8¼	3¼	3	¼	1
1374	22	2½	2	1¼	8½	2½	4	½	1
1375	21½	2½	2	1¼	9	2½	4	½	1
1377	20½	2½	1	1¼	11	2½	4	½	1
1378	21½	2	½	1¼	11	2½	4	½	1
1379	21½	2	½	1¼	11	2½	4	½	1

Warboys (*Cont'd.*)

Year	Akermen					Mondaymen				Dickmen		
	Ad op.			*Ad c.*	*M.D.*	*Ad op.*	*Ad c.*	*M.D.*	*A.*		*Ad op.*	*M.D.*
1343	—			0	—	—	2	—	—		—	—
1354	3			3	—	27	2	3	—		11	—
1359	2			1	3	24	3	3	3		10	1
1360	2			1	3	24	3	3	3	Off.	10	1
1362	2		*A.*	1	3	24	3	3	3		10	1
1363	2			1	3	20	7	3	2	1	10	1
1366	1	Off.	2	—	3	23	—	2	7	1	10	1
1371	3		3	—	—	19	—	3	11	—	10	1
1373	1	2	3	—	—	17	—	3	13	—	10	1
1374	1	2	3	—	—	17	—	3	13	—	10	1
1375	1	2	3	—	—	17	—	3	13	—	10	1
1377	1	2	3	—	—	17	—	2	14	—	10	1
1378	1	2	3	—	—	17	—	2	14	—	10	1
1379	1	2	3	—	—	17	—	2	14	—	10	1

Appendix II (*Cont'd.*)

THE DISPOSITION OF VILLEINAGE TENEMENTS ON RAMSEY MANORS (*Cont'd.*)

Elton

Year	Virg.					Cot.	
	Ad op.	Ad c.	A.	Off.	M.D.	Ad op.	M.D.
1358	2	14	10¾	1	10¾	11½	11
1360	2	14	13¾	1	16¾	11½	11
1376	7½	6	18¾	1	11¾	13½	9
1380	7½	5	30¼	1	1¼	13½	9
1392	0	0	34¾	1	9¼	12½	10

Weston

Year	Virg.		½ Virg.			Cot.
	Ad op.	M.D.	Ad op.	A.	M.D.	Ad op.
1368	3	1	32	—	—	5
1369	3	1	32	2	2	5

Brington

Year	½ Virg.	
	Ad op.	Off.
1368	22	2
1369	22	2

Abbots Ripton

Year	Virg.					Cot.		
	Ad op.	Ad c.	A.	Off.	M.D.	Ad op.	A.	M.D.
1342	—	¾	0	—	—	—	0	—
1364	20½	10	½	5¾	4¼	4	—	4
1369	—	9¼	2½	—	—	—	2	—
1375	24½	9¼	5¼	3	—	4	3	1
1381	23¼	8¼	5¾	4½	—	4	3	1
1385	24	7¾	5¾	4½	—	4	4	—
1388	23¾	6¼	8	4	—	4	4	—
1390	22½	7	7	4½	—	4	4	—
1395	21¾	6¾	9½	3½	—	4	4	—
1396	21¼	6¼	9¾	—	—	4	4	—
1458	—	—	39⅝	—	—	—	8	—

Appendix II (*Cont'd.*)

THE DISPOSITION OF VILLEINAGE TENEMENTS ON RAMSEY MANORS (*Cont'd.*)

Wistow

Year	Virg.					Cot.				
	Ad op.	*Ad c.*	*A.*	Off.	*M.D.*	*Ad op.*	*Ad c.*	*A.*	*M.D.*	
1335	23	5½	—	—	—	—	3	—	—	
1346	24½	4	—	—	—	—	4	—	—	
1351	21½	3	—	—	—	2	—	—	—	Hide-
1352	21½	6½	—	—	—	3	8½	—	—	men
1369	19	7¼	—	—	—	1	—	—	—	*Ad op.*
1388	18⅛	6⅛	4¾	3½	—	1	5	7	—	5
1389	19	5¾	4¾	3	—	1	5	5½	½	5
1393	18¼	4½	4¾	3½	1½	1	5	7	—	5
1394	18¼	4¾	5	3½	1	1	5	7	—	5

Broughton

Year	Virg.				Cot.
	Ad op.	*Ad c.*	*A.*	Off.	*Ad op.*
1346	—	2	—	—	—
1347	—	1¾	—	—	—
1378	20¾	7	½	3¼	3
1380	22¼	5½	½	3¼	3
1383	22	6½	½	3	3
1392	19½	9	½	3	3

Appendix III

PARCELS OF DEMESNE FARMED : TOTALS (Arable only)

ter. = terra; sell. = furrow.

Year	Parcels	Year	Parcels
	Abbots Ripton		**Weston**
1307	*ter.* (£5)	1324	40a.
1314	*ter.* (£5)	1368	175a. 3r. 5p.
1324	*ter.* (£5)+*ter.* (26s. 8d) (30a ?)		
1358	*ter.* (30a ?); 48½ a. 16p., *ter.*		
1388	60a. 1r.		
	Slepe		**Holywell**
1345	75a.	1247	12a.
1347	161a.	1364	74a. 2r.
1351	86a.	1371	79a. 1r.
1366	137½a.	1383	109a. 1r.
1387	87½a.	1399	109a. 1r.
1390	115a.	1401	109a. 1r.
		1402	109a. 1r.
		1404	114a. 1r.
	Broughton		**Upwood**
1344	11a.	1343	7a.
1346	87a. 1r.	1347	61a. ½r.
1378	71a., 9 *sell.*, *ter.*	1357	44a.
1380	95a., 5 *sell.*, *ter.*	1385*	185a.
1392	112a., 15 *sell.*, 1 mess., 1 p., 1 *ter.*	1406*	167a. 3½r. 2p.
		1420	31a. 3r. 2p.

* There is an unspecified amount of meadow, probably about 30a., included in the farmed demesne for this period.

APPENDIX III *(Cont'd.)*

PARCELS OF DEMESNE FARMED : TOTALS (Arable only) *(Cont'd.)*

Year	Parcels
	Warboys
1342	39½a.½r.
1359	60½a.½r.
1373	133a.1½r., 2 furrows, 1 foreland.
1377	151a., 2 furrows, 1 foreland.
1379	152a.1½r.1p., 2 furrows, 1 foreland.
1404	119a.2r.1p., 3 butts, 3 furrows.
	Houghton
1338	0
1379	55½a.2½r.10p., 3 butts.
1387	54a.(+ ?)2½r., 4 butts.
1407	27a.1r., *terra*, 4 butts.
	Wistow
1346	53a.
1379	116a.½r.
1388	124a.1½r.
1423	139a.3r. ?

APPENDIX III (*Cont'd.*)

PARCELS OF DEMESNE FARMED : INDIVIDUAL HOLDINGS

Each unit represents a separate tenancy.

Year	Parcels
	Broughton
1342	0
1344	11a.
1346	11a. + 24a. + 27½a. + 24a.3r.
1378	*ter.* + 11a. + 24a. + 26a. + 24a. + 4 *sell.* + 2a. + 3a. + 3a. + 5 *sell.* + 4a.
1380	*ter.* + 24a. + 27a. + 24a. + 1a. + 2a. + 3a. + 5 *sell.* + 4a. + 1a. + 1a. + 1a. + 1a. + 1a. + 1a.
1392	*ter.* + 11a. + 27a. + 24a. + 1a. + 3a. + 3a. + 5 *sell.* + 4a. + 1a. + 2a. + 1a. + 1a. + 1a. + 1a. + 30a. + 1 messuage + 2a. + 1p. + 10 *sell.*
1449	messuage + 32a.
	Holywell
1249	12a.
1364	11a. + 2a. + 2a. + 7a. + 9a.1r. + 10a.3r. + 9a.1r. + 12a.1r. + 11a.
1371	11a. + 2a. + 1½a. + 10a. + 9a.1r. + 10a.3r. + 9a.3r. + 12a.1r. + 2a. + 4a. + 3a.3r.
1383	11a. + 2a. + 1½a. + 10a. + 9a.1r. + 10a.3r. + 3a. + 9a. + 3r. + 12a.1r. + 2a. + 4a. + 3a.3r. + 19a. + 4a. + 7a.
1410	103a.3½p.
1435	123a. demesne arable, 26a.3p. meadow to ' customaries '

Note: The demesne parcels were usually farmed for about 12 or 14d. per acre. But even from the 1340's there were considerable fields farmed for as little as 6d. per acre; and from this, together with the spread of minute parcelling, it is difficult to derive a satisfactory tabulation of such rents. The same problems occur for the tabulation of pasture rents.

Appendix IV

CUSTOMARY BOON WORKERS ON THE DEMESNE

Note: The enumeration of these workers occurs very infrequently in Ramsey manorial rolls. Elton records afford the best series, although for the second boon work, which nevertheless always took place, the workers were less often enumerated.

Elton

Year	No. of Boon	Free Tenants	Customary Tenants	Others
1298	1	10	300	13 servants, 2 millers, 2 fullers
	2	11	222	17 servants
	3	0	60	0
1312	1	12	248	17 servants
1314	1	8	250	and 'servants'
1325	1	8	261	servants, except miller
1346	1	0	0	158 workmen
1351	1	0	0	90 "
	2	0	0	90 "
1360	1	0	0	104 workmen and families
	2	0	0	97 " " "
1380	1	0	0	135 " " "
	2	0	0	113 workmen and 20 families
1383	1	0	0	118
	2	0	0	109
1387	1	0	0	114
	2	0	0	99
1392	1	0	0	123
	2	16	0	110

Holywell Boon Ploughing

1307	112 customaries
1383	90 "

Appendix V

THE MANORIAL VALORS FROM THE LATE FOURTEENTH CENTURY

Year	Valors	Year	Valors
Houghton		**Broughton**	
1379-80	£105.10s.	1386-7	£60.5s.3d.
1388-9	£88.5s.4d.	1392-3	£64.10s.
1389-90	£90.16s.9d.	1415-16	£46.10s.
1394-5	£73.12s.10d.	**Ellington (farmed)**	
1396-7	£53.3s.		
1399-1400	£54.11s.10d.		
1408-9	£58.9s.5d.	1397-8	£45.6s.3d.
		1399-1400	£51.11s.8d.
Abbots Ripton		1411-12	£42.6s.4d.
		1415-16	£40.
1385-6	£46.7s.11d.	**Holywell**	
1388-9	£69.18s.1d.		
1396-7	£68.12s.8d.		
1415-16	£50.6s.	1399-1400	£71.11s.
		1415-16	£51.13s.9d.
Wistow		**Upwood**	
1379-80	£90.7s.6d.		
1393-4	£38.8s.6d.	1384	£65.8s.5d.
1394-5	£67.15s.7d.	1385	£103.6s.9d.
1415-16	£40.3s.	1415	£45.4s.0d.

Appendix VI

WORK PERFORMED

Year	Winter Work	Summer Work	Autumn Work	Extra Autumn Work	Total
			Abbots Ripton		
1324	4,070	1,784	2,160	444	8,458
1335	3,765	1,696	1,422	359	7,242
1364	2,038	1,065	962	274	4,339
1375	2,294	1,210	1,245	281	5,030
1385	2,375	1,111	1,023	352	4,861
1388	2,305	1,148	1,234	198	4,558
1390	2,145 ?	1,189	1,195	137	4,666
1396	2,100	935	951	271	4,257
			Warboys		
1342	5,019	2,210	704	545	8,478
1344	4,733	2,558	1,400	589	9,280
1347	5,243	2,079	1,305	551	9,178
1348	5,085	2,268	1,073	596	9,022
1354	3,759	1,642	939	929	7,269
1359	1,931	1,517	945	429	4,822
1362	3,649	1,469	954	414	6,486
1363	3,678	1,588	859	378	6,503
1366	3,450	1,669	898	408	6,425
1371	2,910	1,407	740	349	5,406
1373	2,901	1,173	765	339	5,178
1375	2,859	1,079	754	324	5,016
1377	2,321	1,336	720	312	4,689
1378	2,710	1,211	772	324	5,017
1393	2,670	1,046	692	306	4,714
1404	2,098	865	563	246	3,772
1413	0	198	278	19	495
			Holywell		
1356	1,320	360	784	192	2,656
1364	1,247	366	805	215	2,633
1371	1,860	400	824	335	3,419
1383	1,705	418	743	306	3,172
1399	1,793	390	882	287	3,352
1401	1,821	615	984	126	3,546
1402	1,680	600	824	214	3,318
1404	1,720	520	944	240	3,424
1405	1,840	546	904	26	3,316
1409	1,408	0	0	0	1,408

Appendix VI (*Cont'd.*)

WORK PERFORMED (*Cont'd.*)

Year	Winter Work	Summer Work	Autumn Work	Extra Autumn Work	Total
Broughton					
1342	3,098	457	807	324	4,686
1378	2,541	326	700	261	3,828
1380	2,695	418	720	279	4,112
1386	2,753	547	735	285	4,320
1392	2,396	369	635	246	3,646
Wistow					
1335	2,637	886	1,086	251	4,860
1350	2,096	753	943	204	3,996
1351	2,427	562	1,028	215	4,232
1368	2,106	483	848	189	3,626
1379	1,771	650	828	177	3,426
1388	2,011	461	810	181	3,463
1389	1,983	603	892	190	3,668
1393	2,006	464	798	183	3,451
1394	1,589	519	815	182	3,105

Year	Winter Work	Summer Work	Autumn Work	Extra Autumn Work			Total
Houghton							
1336	958	1,778	2,069	923	326	2,020	6,074
1364	376	2,311	1,280	312	753	348	5,380
1369	374	2,823	425	522	828	260	5,232
1371	410	2,583	616	503	708	374	5,194
1372	405	2,469	524	318	663	448	4,827
1383	435	2,535	543	324	942	354	5,133
1387	425	2,841	368	339	883	427	5,283
1388	421	2,459	526	315	826	174	4,721
1389	415	2,349	599	448	923	112	4,846
1393	326	2,135	367	264	666	282	3,940
1394	359	2,123	451	273	696	294	4,196
1396	319	2,255	511	282	704	356	4,427

Appendix VII

FARM PRICES OF MANORIAL MILLS

Year	Price	Year	Price
Broughton		Wistow	
1307	66s.8d.	1307	73s.4d.
1311	66s.8d.	1311	73s.4d.
1312	70s.	1324	80s.
1314	73s.4d.	1335	73s.4d.
1319	66s.8d.	1346	73s.4d.
1326	73s.4d.	1351	46s.8d.
1342	63s.4d.	1368	42s.
1344	53s.4d.	1379	46s.8d.
1345	53s.4d.	1388	20s.
1346	53s.4d.	1389	20s.
1378 (to 1450?)	broken	1393	33s.4d.
		1394	40s.
Houghton, Warboys and Hemmingford		1407	35s.8d.
		1419	13s.
1446	£17.16s.8d.	1445	22s.
1448	£17.16s.8d.	1446	22s.
1452	£16.6s.8d.		
1453	£16.6s.8d.	Warboys	
1454	£16.6s.8d.		
1455	£10.1s.6d.	1303	66s.8d.
1456	£16.6s.8d.	1306	66s.8d.
1468	£20.0s.0d.	1318	66s.8d.
		1325	66s.8d.
Abbots Ripton		1330	66s.8d.
		1336	66s.8d.
1307	73s.4d.	1343	66s.8d.
1314	73s.4d.	1344	66s.8d.
1315	73s.4d.	1347	66s.8d.
1324	80s.	1353	47s.8d.
1342	76s.8d.	1359	46s.8d.
		1371	53s.4d.
Houghton		1378	53s.4d.
		1404	40s.
1379	£6.13s.4d.	1413	40s.
1383	£6.13s.4d.	1442	broken
1387	£6.13s.4d.	1447	26s.8d.
1388	£6.13s.4d.	1448	26s.8d.
1389	£6.13s.4d.	1454	26s.8d.
1399	£6.13s.4d.	1460	26s.8d.
1405 *	£7.6s.8d.		
1407	£6.13s.4d.	Holywell	
1408	£6.13s.4d.		
1418	£6.13s.4d.	1307	50s.
		1354	53s.4d.
		1396	40s.
		1399	20s.
		1402	20s.
		1404	20s.

* The fishery profits, worth a mark, are included from this date despite the fall in the total.

CHAPTER X

A FIFTEENTH-CENTURY DEPRESSION AND THE END
OF THE DEMESNE ECONOMY

THAT gradual attenuation of administrative information from the early
fifteenth century, which culminated in the terse entries of the Augmentation Roll, leaves much to be desired for a study of the final stage in the
economic history of the Ramsey estates.   Above all, the information on the
management of the demesne becomes decidedly abstract, even where this
property was not being farmed.   The records reveal little of that tenacious
demesne re-organization which had typified the post-Black Death era.   However, at the beginning of the fifteenth century at least, the villeins were still
immersed as much as ever in the economic life of the manor.   Until the
long-term leases of the late fifteenth century would sever their economic ties
with the lord, the responsibilities of these villeins would give a considerable
continuity to the traditional account rolls.   So, at least in terms of villein
rents and manorial debts, the account rolls of the first half of the fifteenth
century still provide an index to economic conditions on the Ramsey estates.
Consequently, it will be proper to deal first with something of the evolution
of the customary tenancies.

I

The unique preservation of names of Burwell tenants (see Table LXIV,
below) from some account rolls of the early fourteenth century illustrates the
disposition of villein holdings at this period.   From what we do know of other
Ramsey estates this table would appear to be typical in showing only a minor
tendency to the concentration of holdings in fewer hands since the time of the
extents.

But from the mid-fourteenth century the structure of villein holdings
changed considerably.   For example (Table LXV, below), a considerable
increase in the number of tenancies appeared with the parcelling out of the
Holywell pastures after the mid-century.   Most of the new tenants were
probably villagers, like their counterparts on the Elton roll who were said to be
'from the towne'.[1]   They were presumably the artisans and other landless
men in the village, who were now able to buy a few head of livestock and to rent
some pasture on the less competitive land market, with their income from the
higher wage returns.   The very minute parcels of demesne arable farmed over
the last half of the fourteenth century on all Ramsey manors[2] seem to be part

---

[1] P.R.O. *Sc.* 6, 874/13, 1368-9: twelve men
rented one or two acre bits of pasture;
about thirty men, some the same as those
renting pasture, rented demesne in acre
and one-half acre parcels at 12d. per acre.
The arable was mentioned as sown with

dredge by these men.   This appears to be
the first extant manorial document of
Ramsey which was written in English.
[2] See the typical examples from Broughton
and Houghton *supra*, in Chapter IX,
Appendix II (individual holdings).

of the same phenomenon, that is, characterized by the addition of many new names to the roll of traditional customary tenants.   As far as the demesne arable was concerned, it would be the non-availability of labour which permitted this new level of land distribution in contrast with that period before the Great Pestilence, when, with plenty of labour available, it was the leading customaries and their companions who had been able more and more, in particular over the 1340's, to rent the demesne in large parcels.

TABLE LXIV

EARLY FOURTEENTH-CENTURY TENANTS AND TENANCIES AT BURWELL[3]

(49 names) 1307

Godfrey Edward (reeve) 24a. + 20a. + 15a. + 1 cr.
Thomas Edryth (beadle) 15a. + 8a. + 1 cr.
Alice in Woodland 24a.
Radulph Kantelyn 20a.
Thomas Ungent 20a. + 24a. + 1 cr.
Godfrey de Reche 20a.
John (Inlop) 20a.
John Le Were 20a.
Basil Hering 20a.
William Le Wynner 15a. + 8a.
William Le Milwyn, Sen. 15a. + cr.
Christina de Macham 15a.
Godfrey de Holm 15a.
Thomas Carlewayn 15a. + cr.
Margaret de Macham 15a. + cr.
Robert Ardayne 8a.
Richard Edward 8a.
John Sene 8a.
Henry Le Wyse 24a. + 1 cr.
John Kantelyn 1 cr.
Lawrence Le Wynner 1 cr.
John Ardayne 1 cr. + 8a.
Daniel Le Orymere 24a. + 1 cr.
? Hamond 15a. + 1 cr.

Michael Godfrey 1 cr.
Radulphus Miller 1 cr.
Mabel Helewys 20a. + 1 cr.
William le Milwyn, Jun. 15a. + 1 cr.
Basil Waleys 1 cr.
John Machner 1 cr.
John Morite 1 cr.
John Pope 1 cr.
Robert Martmot 1 cr.
John Lawrence 1 cr.
Gilbert Lawrence 1 cr.
John Edward 1 cr.
William Ardayne 1 cr.
Hugh Edward 24a.
Agnes, wife of Henry 24a.
John Milward 15a.
Henry Kantelyn 15a.
Alicia Le Wyse 15a.
Agnes Le Bere 15a.
Thomas Le Milner 15a. + cr.
Matilda Morite 15a.
Robert de Macham 15a.
Alberic Le Maleys 15a.
Ormond Fedde 8a.
John Le Waleys 8a.

These conditions changed abruptly from early in the fifteenth century, with a decline in the parcelling of the demesne and in the renting of small bits from the villeinage most noticeable, followed by a more numerous[4] exodus of

[3] The tables have been presented solely with the object of offering an illustration of land distribution, not as genealogical sources. The spelling of proper names seemed to vary considerably from time to time until the late fourteenth century. The Burwell villein lists for 1307 and 1324 may be found appended to the P.R.O. account rolls of Holywell for the same years.

[4] There was a considerable 'flight' of villagers

Table LXV

HOLYWELL TENANTS AND TENANCIES IN 1371

(84 names)

William Palmer 1v.	Thomas Barnwell 1a. meadow.
Andrew Goodman 1v.	Henry Grenty and others 6a. meadow.
Richard Grey 1v.	William Botiller and others 2a. meadow.
William Scott ½v.	John Waley and others 2a. meadow.
Michael Scott 1v., 1 cot.	William Machling 2a. meadow.
Richard Drayn 1 v.	Simon Thatcher 1a. meadow.
Thomas Hunne 1v.	John Niel 1a. meadow.
John Hamond ½v.	William Raveley 1a. meadow.
Walter Denmeys 1v.	Thomas Hogge 1a. meadow.
Michael Machelon 1v., ¼v., meadow.	William Digge 1a. meadow.
John Denmeys 1v.	John Wrighth 2a. meadow.
John Appelon 1v., 1½a. (with others)	William Lawton and others 2a. meadow.
Robery Mowe ½v.	Simon Hart 1a. meadow.
Richard Thatcher ½v.	John Hyne 1a.
Adam Godfrey 1v.	Simon Attechurch 1a. meadow, 1a.
John Nicholas 1v., meadow (with others)	Richard Daloc 1a. meadow.
John Merton 1v.	John Artford 4a. meadow, 1p.
Robert Houghton ½v., ½ cot.	John Clerk 1a. meadow.
Robert Attewell ⅛v., 1 cot.	John Reynold 1a. meadow.
Agnes Hunne ½v.	John Henyman 1a. meadow.
Thomas Carter 2 cot.	Simon Hauch 3a. meadow.
Nicholas Sheperd 1 cot., 3a. (with others)	William Leighton and others 2a. meadow.
John Hemmington 1 cot., 1 'cottar'.	Hugh Cabe 1a. meadow.
John Sande 1 cot.	Andrew Pye 1a. meadow.
John Skinner 1 cot.	William Parson 1p. meadow.
John Attewell ½ cot.	Thomas Sewayn 3a. meadow.
Richard, son of Roger 1 cot., 2 'cottars'.	Robert Cook 2a. meadow.
William Rene 1 cot.	William Wokester 1½a. meadow.
John Edward 1 cot.	John Coler and John ? 3a.
Nicholas Scharp 1 cot.	Thomas Caldent and John Fyn sen.
Richard Flacwere 1 cot.	1½a. meadow.
Roger Milde 1 cot.	Edward Hogge de Hurst ½a. meadow.
Robert Sarer 2 'cottars', 2a. (with others)	Roger Cowe 1a. meadow.
	Edward Gross 1a.
Thomas Godrich 2 'cottars'.	Richard Gernon ½a. meadow.
William Cotete, sen. 2 'cottars'.	John Laucher and others 2a. meadow.
John Baron 1 'cottar', 2a. meadow, 1a.	John Throw de Hurst 1½a. meadow.
William Baron 1 'cottar'.	John Apwold de Grange 1a. meadow.
Robert Fannell 1 'cottar'.	Thomas Bowie and others 1a. meadow.
John Effort 3a. meadow.	William Rene ½a. meadow.
John Tretford 7a. meadow.	John Pope 1a.
William Wardell 2a. meadow.	Simon Brunne 7a. 1½r. 1p. meadow.
John Wakenham 2a. meadow.	Hugh Chrae 1p.

in some parts of the east midland region from the time of the Black Death. See e.g. MAITLAND, 'History of a Cambridgeshire Manor', *E.H.R.*, IX (1894), 436 ff. But the account rolls of Ramsey manors give little evidence of this phenomenon; perhaps the renting of demesne parcels over the 1370's and 1380's was a sufficient attraction to hold most of the Ramsey *nativi*.

the *nativi* from the villages.   The good account roll series for this period available for Houghton, reveals a trend which seemed to be common to all Ramsey manors, even those like Ellington which were farmed to the *villata*. The chevage entry first appears on the roll of the beadle for Houghton in 1399, when for this fine for permission to leave the lord's manor 5s.4d. was being received from an unknown number of men; in 1404-5, 4s.6d. was received for four men; by 1407 chevage was being paid by seven men, by eight men in 1408, and a dozen by 1418.   Over the next generation the manor lost contact with many of the *émigrés*: at Houghton in 1448, three men paid chevage, two were reported dead, and the whereabouts of five was unknown.   Of the fifteen names of those owing chevage in 1455, three were reported dead, the whereabouts of five was unknown, one was in London, and the remaining men paid only 2s.6d.   By 1460 nothing was being received from the same group of *nativi*, though none had returned.   On an average this source indicates that about a dozen families would seem to have disappeared for good from each of the home manors by this period.[5]

This dissipation of the manorial labour group was not stimulated by any economic motive on the part of the lord.   The chevage payment was very small.   Robert Miles of Upwood paid twelve capons as a licence for marrying and going to live in King's Ripton in 1427.   Thereafter he was to pay two capons per year.   Even when the *nativus* did not go to another manor belonging to the abbey, the *chevagium* remained small.   William, the son of Nicholas Allyn, tenant at Upwood manor, was granted permission to marry in 1440 and to stay at Wisbech, for fourpence per annum.[6]   Despite the large numbers who were failing to report for the yearly manorial view around 1450, the chevage requirement was generally less at this date than a generation earlier.

The available documents do not give much evidence of manumission at this time; and the freed men, if they remained on Ramsey holdings, were a very small proportion of the total tenants by the sixteenth century.[7]   Still there was a movement towards freedom around 1400.   A note in the Upwood account roll of 1412-13 shows the payments necessary for this judicial process: "Received from John Pyre of Setheford £10 in full payment for manumission; and £20 from John, son of Alexander Baldwin of Brancaster, in full payment for manumission; and 100s. from John, son of Thomas Accomer, in part

---

[5] Two men were away from Upwood in 1406, and 12 by 1445, of whom 9 could not be found; 3 men were away from Wistow in 1403, 4 in 1420, and 12 in 1445-6. In general the movements were greatest between 1420 and the mid-century. Mediæval villages had begun to disappear in some parts of the Midlands by the mid-century (see W. G. HOSKINS, *Essays in Leicestershire History*, Ch. III). It is important to note that many of the *nativi* movements *ca.*1400 were among Ramsey manors, or to adjacent estates. But fifty years later the *nativi* were commonly moving distances of forty or fifty miles.

[6] The payment of 2 or 3 chickens for chevage was apparently an ancient customary charge (see examples from Ramsey rolls in W. O. AULT, *Court Rolls of the Abbey of Ramsey*, pp. 276-8, where 7 men paid 2 *gallini* each over a number of years to stay outside the manor).   But the chevage payments were probably much higher at more prosperous agricultural periods, and especially when the *nativus* was going outside the lord's fee: for example, the *nativi* from several Ramsey manors were paying 20s. plus 2 capons, to stay outside the lord's fee in 1309-10 (*Add. Ch.* 39693).

[7] The free tenancies were usually paying less than 5% of the rents from Ramsey manorial tenements in the Augmentation accounts.

payment of £20 for manumission." The high charge for manumission probably precluded a full-scale resort to this escape for the villein. But the account rolls or court rolls of the period fail to convey any economic motive on the part of the villein tenant[8] for the change in social and legal status.

Although the chevage would usually be paid by a landless man leaving the manor to settle elsewhere, the *nativi* group included members of the landed villein families as well. Frequent marriages between the daughters of prominent villeins and freemen, offered another means by which the former class could dwindle at this time. For marrying a fellow villein on the manor the merchet was quite small, like the two shillings paid by William Herying in 1406 for the marriage of his daughter Alice at Upwood, or the six capons paid in 1436 by Richard Payne for the marriage of his daughter Alice to William Howe, a *nativus* of Upwood. But Nicholas Martyn paid one mark for the marriage of his daughter Margaret to John Ellington, a freeman, in 1406; or Richard Herying paid ten shillings in 1415 for permission to marry his daughter Agnes to John Forgon, a freeman.

With families leaving the village, and with more parcels of demesne and smallholds falling vacant, it became increasingly difficult to keep the land occupied and to avoid dilapidation. There developed a heavy exchange in tenements, often at a rent discount, or with an entry fine condoned for repairs to the property.[9] A remarkable 'court book' for Ramsey estates which covers manorial land settlement for nearly every year in the first half of the fifteenth century, provides a useful supplementary picture of the customary tenurial structure.[10] It may be noted that the increasing number of *arentata* leases from the end of the fourteenth century is usually associated with the concentration of holdings.[11] Through the Court Book we may trace new additions, and the following reconstruction from the manor of Upwood illustrates the contrast developing against the late fourteenth-century dispersion of manorial tenements and parcels:

[8] There is some evidence, however, that the free labourer could demand a higher wage; see Ch. VII, Section II.

[9] It is difficult to calculate the exact degree to which entry fines were condoned for dilapidation, since very often there is only the entry 'condoned by the seneschal'. There were 21 fines condoned outright, out of some 186 entries for Wistow, in the Ramsey Court Book of the early fifteenth century. But of the 165 fines paid, about 80 were for 1 to 3 chickens, one fine was for 1 mark, about 8 for one-half mark, and the remaining were one to three shillings. The size of the entry fines seems to be important,

since there are such entries as the following for William Benet at Wistow in 1450: the 13s.4d. fine is condoned for repairs; he pays 2 capons (for 1 plot, 1¾ virgates, and an acre lot).

[10] Much of the evidence for the last few paragraphs, as indeed for this whole section, has been supplemented or derived from these court roll excerpts. See further Appendix I, *infra*, on this document.

[11] Composite customary holdings were first evident in other parts of the east midlands too, from around 1390. See F. M. PAGE, *The Estates of Crowland Abbey*, p. 123.

TABLE LXVI

TENANTS AT UPWOOD
IN THE EARLY FIFTEENTH CENTURY

Note: o — *ad opera*; c — *ad censum*; A — *arentata*

Tenant	Account Roll 1402	Court Book
William Hering (Sen.).	1 v. (o), ½v. (A), 2 a. (A).	½ v. (A).
William Hering (Jun.) ..	1 v. (o).	
Philip Bigge (Jun.).....	¼ v. (o).	
Edward Halkot........	1 v. (o), ½ a. (A).	
John Hunne..........	½ v. (o), ¼ a. (A).	
Richard Gowlere.......	1 v. (o), ¼ v. (A).	messuage, ¾ ter' (A).
Thomas Penny........	1 v. (o), 1 v. (A).	
John Couler..........	½ v. (o), ¼ v. (A).	
William Edward.......	1 v. (o).	meadow, 1 plot, 1 v. (A).
William Payn.........	1 v. (o), ½ v. (A), ¼ v. (A).	
John Rolyn (Jun.)......	1 v. (o), ¼ v. (c).	
William Symond.......	½ v. (o).	
William Alcok........	1 v. (o), 1 a. (A).	
John Rolyn (Sen.).....	1 v. (o), ½ v. (c).	
Robery Milys........	1 v. (o), 1 v. (A).	½ v. (o), 1 v. (A), 1a. (A), 1 v. (A), ½ v. (A), 2 forlands, 2 pigstyes.
John Hikkesson.......	1 v. (o), ½ v. (c), ¼ v. (A).	+ ter' (A).
Thomas Warboys......	½ v. (o), ½ v. (c), ½ v. (A), 1 a. (c).	
John Colopyn.........	½ v. (c), ½ v. (A), 1 a. (c).	+ ½ v. (A).
William Camblyn......	½ v. (c), ¾ v. (A).	+ 1 v. (A), ¼ ter' (A), house.
Thomas Newman......	1 v. (A).	+ ½ v. (c), plot.

TABLE LXVI (*Cont'd.*)

TENANTS AT UPWOOD
IN THE EARLY FIFTEENTH CENTURY (*Cont'd.*)

Tenant	Account Roll 1402	Court Book
Edward Howe..........	½ v. (A).	
John Alby.............	¾ v. (A), 1 a. (A).	
Robert Wylde.........	½ v. (A).	+ ¼ ter' (o).
William Baker........	½ v. (o), ¼ v. (A),	+ ½ v. (o),
	2 a. (A), 1 a. (c).	2 a., ½ a. (A).
John Allyn............	¼ v. (A).	+ ½ v. (o),
		½ v. (A),
		plot (A), 1 cot.
		(A),
		3 houses (A).
John Cook............	¼ v. (A).	
William Symond.......	¼ v. (A).	
Richard Thacher.......	¼ v. (A).	
John Bigge...........	½ v. (A), 2 a. (A).	
John Wise............	½ v. (o).	
William Flemyng.......	2 a. (o), 2 a. (c).	
William Hunne........	2 a. (c).	
William Allyn.........	2 a. (c).	+ 10 a. (A),
		field (A),
		½ v. (A), ½ v. (o).
Nicolas Aston.........	1 a. (A).	+ ¼ ter' (A),
		2a. (A).
Thomas Rolf..........	2 a. (A).	+ 2 a. cottage (A).
John Loneday.........	2 a. (A).	1 plot,
		1 v. (A),
		½ v. (A).
Richard Pony.........	2 a. (A).	
William Attewell.......	1 a. (o).	
Nicholas Hendesson....	½ a. (A).	+ ter' (o),
		½ v. (A),
		1 plot (A).
John Unen............	½ a. (A).	
William Bracon........	2 a. (A).	ter' (A).
John Sywell..........	½ a. (A).	

One of the most useful indices for the measurement of property demand, and of agrarian returns, would seem to be the discount allowed on tenement rents.   The discount took many forms.   A frequent method was the reduction of the property rent in the first year of the lease 'for repairs' or 'recovery'. The farms of the demesne or mill were usually reduced in this fashion for at least the first half of the fifteenth century.   Other allowances were probably made when the beadle or bailiff was collecting the rent, although such data cannot be accurately measured.   The best ordered estimate of the land market can be made from the 'deficits allowed' classification, which appeared in the *expensæ* part of the account roll.   These were the discounts formally allowed at the commencement of the financial year due to deterioration in property values, and (or) to encourage the renting of vacant holdings.   The list of these discounts gradually lengthened, especially after the first quarter of the fifteenth century.   The 'deficits allowed' at Hemmingford in 1442 are a typical mid-century list:[12]

Holdings	Discount	Holdings	Discount
½ v. (2), 1a..........	10s.	½ v................	5s.8d.
½ v. *..............	4s.	½ v................	14d.
1 *ter*..............	3s.8d.	½ v................	5s.8d.
1 cr., 1 v............	8s.	½ v................	5s.8d.
1 v.................	16d.	½ v................	5s.8d.
2 v., 1 messuage......	24s.2d.	1 dovecote..........	8s.
½ v. *..............	6s.	15a.3r..............	10s.
4a..................	2s.6d.	1 monday acre........	5s.
½ v................	5s.6d.		
			£5.12s.

* A lessee could still not be found for these holdings.   The half-virgate was 'normally' rented for about 10s. on this manor.

The tabulation of some totals for these 'deficits allowed' shows the movements of property demand over a number of years.   The following illustrations point to greater allowances about the mid-15th century, thence tapering off.   However, the less-detailed rolls from the late fifteenth century make it impossible to discover whether the drop in 'deficits' was due to a new form of renting, that is, a change in the rent level and term of the lease, or to an actual strengthening in property demand.

[12] Another method of visualizing the decline in rents is, of course, the contrast between late fourteenth and mid-fifteenth-century rents, although the many combinations of tenancies make comparisons difficult.   An example may be taken from the tenements of Abbots Ripton in 1390 and 1458; see Ch. IX, App. I.

Table LXVII

DEFICITS ALLOWED

Houghton

1387	3s. 4d.	1453	£5. 13s. 6d.
1396	3s. 4d.	1454	£7. 2s. 6d.
1404	30s. 2d.	1455	£2. 11s. 0d.
1407	47s. 7d.	1456	£3. 9s. 0d.
1418	16s. 8d.	1460	£8. 19s. 3d.
1446	£6. 17s. 2d.	1462	£7. 18s. 3d.
1448	£8. 7s. 0d.	1475	£4. 6s. 0d.
1452	£6. 5s. 5d.		

Broughton

1386	9s.	1475	£2. 8s. 4d.
1392	9s.	1476	£1. 7s. 4d.
1450	£10. 10s. 9d.	1477	18s. 0d.
1451	£10. 7s. 3d.	1484	£1. 8s. 8d.
1452	£10. 2s. 9d.	1517	4s. 8d.
1458	£10. 5s. 0d.	1525	0

Another manifestation of the concentration of manorial property in the hands of fewer villeins may be seen in the system of farming the demesne, which now replaced the minute parcelling of the fourteenth century. It would be incorrect to assume that one or two villeins could 'farm the manor' in the traditional sense.[13] The old system of farming to the *villata* continued at the manors of Hemmingford, Ellington, and Bythorn. This full manorial farm is easily distinguishable by the size of the farm (£42., £40., £30., for these manors), and of course, by the terms of the contract, which included everything but judicial profits. It is interesting to note that, when the *villata* farmed a manor, the reeve, and, presumably, the old villeinage organization, continued with the same prominence that had obtained in the thirteenth century. The reeves apparently remained in charge of Bythorn and Hemmingford until around 1440. They were able to keep up the farm payments fairly well until the 1440's, but at what cost to the villeins it is impossible to say. Certainly, as Table LXX illustrates below, the debt accumulation on these manors from the 1440's was as depressive as the average.

[13] See Chapters III and IV, above, *passim.*

TABLE LXVIII

RAMSEY ABBEY BAKERY ACCOUNTS (Receipts)

(*Add. Ch.* 34714)

Produce	Source	1422-3		Source	1423-4	
		q.	b.		q.	b.
Wheat	in stock	105	7	in stock	42	
	from manors	32	7	from manors	38	6
	bought	443	5	bought	918	7
Malt	in stock	148		in stock	40	
	Warboys	28	7	Warboys	210	1
	Upwood	160		Upwood	81	
	Broughton	80		Broughton	102	
	A. Ripton	146		A. Ripton	44	3
	Houghton	125	1	Houghton	5	1
	Wistow	85	1	Wistow	101	1
	bought	520	1	Knapwell	129	7
				bought	579	
Oats	in stock	26	5		?	?
	Walsoken	385			?	

But the farming of the demesnes to the leading villeins which began around 1400, was a much more modest contract. These arrangements were a natural evolution from fourteenth-century parcelling of the demesne, and in some cases involved no more than one field with the manorial building. For example, around 1410, John Poulter and John Benet farmed 80 acres of the demesne and 23½ acres of meadow at Holywell for a life period, at only 60s. *per annum*. Yet these men were listed as the *farmers* of the demesne. The fen pastures, which were worth over thirty pounds at Holywell, and the remaining arable, continued to be rented to various customaries. The bailiff got rid of all the sheep, and most of the hogs and other stock, when this 'demesne' of Holywell was farmed. It was more usual, however, for the farmer to hold some stock with the lease of the demesne in the first half of the fifteenth century. At Elton, for example, where the arable demesne was farmed for £8 around 1400, the traditional numbers of horses and oxen, and a reserve of corn, went with the demesne lands. Apparently the plough animals were kept up on most manors until the mid-fifteenth century.[14] The sheep flocks, which had been sharply increased[15] to offset the decline in arable profits from the 1390's, were either all sold[16] or farmed in very reduced numbers, from fifteen or twenty years later.[17] The plough teams and the corn reserve were probably maintained to enable a reversion to direct cultivation of the demesne,[18] and to help ensure a corn livery to the abbey by the farmer. The accounts from the abbey bakery for 1422-24 show that eight manors were still delivering corn at this date, although purchases supplied about fifty per cent of the needs (see Table LXVIII, above). Since there is no indication of corn livery from the account rolls, it must be assumed that these amounts were paid by the farmers as rents in kind. Wistow delivered several hundred quarters of corn to the abbey in 1466, but there is no other evidence of these payments from the mid-century.

The Ramsey Court Book shows that it was usual for mills and the largest tenement leases, to be let for a period of 7 to 12 years, while other tenements were always let for life. The demesne seems to have been regularly let for life from the very early fifteenth century. From the late fifteenth century the demesne began to be farmed for much longer periods,[19] although it was a much-abbreviated demesne unit, rather than the larger manorial revenues included in traditional farms. Around the mid-fifteenth century the 'demesne' of Broughton was being farmed for £6.13s.10d., that of Warboys for £7.8s.2d., or that of Wistow for 60s. The Ramsey manors, as these demesne farms were then termed, were still being farmed for such small amounts in 1539.[20] In short, the demesne had been so reduced in value by the sale of stock, and the commutation of *opera*, and probably in area by other leases, that the formal 'farm' of the curial house and property was now only ten to twenty per cent of total manorial revenues from the fifteenth century. The leading customaries on Ramsey estates never succeeded as a co-operative group, or in severalty, to the large land and stock leases of the thirteenth and fourteenth century *villata*. The old demesne economy could be salvaged neither by the village group nor by the feudal lord. From early in the fifteenth century, until those manorial leases by which Richard Cromwell dispersed Ramsey lands to entrepreneurs after the Dissolution,[21] a new order gradually prevailed.

[14] See Chapter V, especially Houghton, Wistow, Elton.
[15] See Chapter V, especially Slepe, Warboys, Abbots Ripton.
[16] As at Holywell and Wistow.
[17] See Chapter V, Houghton and Elton.
[18] As has already been mentioned at the close of Chapter IX, a number of *ad censum* arrangements were made after 1400 with the express condition that the lord could put these lands back to *opera* in 10 or 20 years.
[19] The 'demesne' of Abbots Ripton was farmed in 1532 for 40 years at £8.6s.8d. These long terms appear for most leases in the early 16th century (*Add. Ch.* 33971-33983): a pasture was leased for three lives, one close for 41 years, another for 60 years, etc.
[20] Since the early 15th-century farms were often varied by additions of the mill, bits of pasture, etc., it does not seem possible to compare these figures, even where available, with the undefined farms of the *Augmentation Roll*.
[21] There is considerable material among the *Additional Charters* on the farming of Ramsey manors throughout the rest of the sixteenth century.

II

This fifteenth-century re-organization of the manorial economy was accompanied by the deepest and most prolonged depression in manorial revenues that the Ramsey documents have revealed for any period in the abbey history. The trend may be traced in both the abbey accounts and the manorial rolls. Neither series of documents is completely satisfactory: it would be more exact to have the picture of total receipts at the abbey rather than that of the main obedientiary revenues only, since the latter were largely fixed returns, paid out of manorial profits before other rental liveries. But the complete central account view is unobtainable.

The manorial account rolls for this period are likewise incomplete, since there was usually a threefold administration of expenses through the hands of bailiffs, seneschals, and beadles. Although it seems sufficiently clear that the revenues handled by the beadle were entirely included in the account rolls, there remains an uncertainty about the movements of other revenues in the extensive but too briefly summarized 'debt paragraph', which became an ever growing accretion to the account roll after 1400. When debts were repaid they usually were given to the bailiff or seneschal. Many of these payments were allocated to these officials for expenses of the manor, which was usually in the hands of the bailiff and farmer, or bailiff and beadle, according to the manorial accounts at this period. But sometimes there is absolutely no information on the disposition of funds from repaid debts. Perhaps they were paid into the abbey treasury, or again they may have been tacitly allowed for expenses. The few rolls pertaining to the bailiff alone that exist in addition to a manorial account roll for some years, throw no further light on the problem. In any case, the general trend and movement of revenue magnitudes is sufficiently clear for this period. The debt totals have been tabulated along with liveries of cash profits. Since these figures are 'final' debt totals for that year, that is, they come *after* repayments to the bailiff not given in the regular account roll structure, they provide a further index of decline in profits. It must be emphasized, however, that the table of debts is not a direct correlative of revenue returns (cash liveries). The debts were often paid off in block amounts, though accumulated over many years, and in such instances give an exceptional 'lift' to net revenue totals;[22] or, on the other hand, debts might be condoned *en masse*,[23] thereby affecting drastically the 'trend' shown by the debt column, without registering an increase in the revenue column.

The long-run trend in payments to the abbey treasury and the increase in debt, show that on all manors, whether the demesne was farmed immediately or not, there was a gradual worsening of conditions from the last decade

---

[22] For example, the huge increase in cash liveries at Houghton over 1452-3 (*infra*, Table LXX) was due to a payment of £21.3s.10d. for arrears. Generally such increases in livery over the 1440's and 1450's seem to be due to repayments of arrears.

[23] The debt total was kept down regularly by the cancellation of certains sums, because the debtor 'was dead and left nothing in goods'. From the 1450's, however, debts seem to have been cancelled from the account roll in a more wholesale fashion, although the reason is not evident.

of the fourteenth century. As far as evidence is available, most of the farmed manors were de-valued after 1420.[24] The rapid increase in the *arentata* and the re-organization of the *censa* have already been mentioned. An inexplicable gap occurs in the series of accounts for all manors between 1420-1440,[25] but from the listing of manorial officials owing debts, it is clear that conditions worsened with increasing intensity over this period, and the debt accumulated by 1450 or 1460 was often phenomenal (see Table LXX, especially Houghton, Hemmingford).[26]

Since the customary tenants were immediately responsible for the maintenance of agrarian revenues, either as officials or farmers of the demesne, they received the full force of the depression. The holders of villein tenements were regularly pardoned debts at the foot of the account roll, usually by the phrase 'because there is no way in which it can be raised'.[27] But the debts of officials and farmers were catalogued with a monotonous annual repetition for fifty years. The farmers of the demesne, like the previously mentioned John Poulter at Holywell, were soon heavily in debt. As an example from Slepe will illustrate, the reeves, beadles and even farmers, once the leading men of the vill, were often reduced to bankruptcy with the collapse of their 'manorial economy':[28]

[24] This was only £2 or £3 at Ellington and Hemmingford. As noted above, the reduction or cancellation of the entry fine was still the more common discount, and this was recorded in a haphazard fashion.

[25] A visitation at this time notes that accounts were not being properly kept at the abbey, but there is no comparable gap in the court rolls and obedientiary accounts.

[26] The food farms collapsed at Canterbury Cathedral Priory over the second quarter of the fifteenth century (R. A. L. SMITH, p. 201); and a depression was general throughout the country at this time. See M. M. POSTAN, 'The Fifteenth Century', *Ec. H. R.*, IX (1938-9), 160-168. Ramsey Abbey received a royal grant of privileges in 1442 because of 'insufficiency of revenues' (*Chronicon*, p. 324, n. 3). The gradual disappearance of manorial stock over this period might be a sign of capital dissipation to offset depressed revenues. One popular emergency cash sale over the late fourteenth and fifteenth centuries was found in the manorial woods. See e.g. M. MORGAN, *The English Lands of the Abbey of Bec*, p. 125; *Plumpton Correspondence*, Camden, ed. Thomas Stapleton, (1839), p. 199; *Paston Letters*, ed. J. Gairdner, III (1904), p. 46. The sale of *gross' bosc'* became common on Ramsey manors after the Black Death, and may have wiped out much of the woodlots. Over the late 14th century, wood to the value of £157.15s.6d. was sold from the Warboys woodland of 'Needingham' (*Add. Ch.* 39922). The general account of the former Ramsey properties in 1540 (*Add. Ch.* 34657) gives £22.0s.1d. from wood sold at Warboys, £4.2s. at Ellington, £31 at

Abbots Ripton, £13.6s.8d. at Cranfield, £16.7s.7d. at Shillington, £16.9s.3d. at Chatteris.

[27] E.g. at Abbots Ripton in 1395 a number of debts (including £10.18s.10d. of the former reeve John Bank) were condoned because 'they do not know where they are able to raise them' (*ubi possunt levari*). Or at Weston in 1394 a debt of 39s.8d. owed by the tenants for 'a certain old *redditus* is pardoned because it cannot be raised nor could it be paid over the last four years'. At Holywell in 1418 the bailiff condoned £4.6s.7d. owed by William Attehill from 1408 'for William has died', and also £10.19s.5d. for rent of fen 'for no profit was received from it this year'.

[28] For more complete samples of debt burdens upon manorial officials, and the maintenance of these debts over long periods, see Appendix J for this chapter. The *mendicus* in Ramsey documents would seem to be an official or tenant with no free capital for the liquidation of his debts, rather than one who is completely destitute. Apparently chattels were seized for the payment of debts only when a tenant had died or fled from the manor. From the evidence thus far available, it has not been possible to assume that real poverty and hunger were suffered in proportion to the depression of the manorial economy in the early fifteenth century. The villein could move easily to other manors where tenements were available at discount; and the convent, as will be seen below, was insulated to a considerable degree by the system of fixed rents.

TABLE LXIX

A DEBT SUMMARY AT SLEPE (1418-19)

(*mendicus*)	William Pilgrim, formerly beadle 25s.
(*mortuus*)	William Brown, formerly beadle 20s.
(*fugitivus*)	John Filborne, formerly reeve £7.
(*mortuus*)	Richard Canne, formerly reeve 15s.
(*mortuus*)	John Nutheslow, formerly beadle £15.18s.
(*mortuus*)	John Brown, formerly beadle £6.4s.4d.
	Thomas Porter, from lands in the lord's hands 20s.
(*mortuus*)	William Cotter, formerly beadle 40s.5d.
	Thomas Pope 7s.
(*mendicus*)	John Goodrich, formerly beadle 49s.10d.
	John Hogg, formerly beadle 30s.
(*mendicus*)	Robert Ellington, formerly farmer of Slepe £59.8s.6d.
	John Hogg and John Bailly 10s.
	William Harris, beadle for this year £10.

Between 1460 and 1470 the huge debts were wiped off the account rolls, probably by a general condonation. Debts began to accumulate immediately on some manors,[29] though generally the accounts of the 1470's balanced better.[30] At this period the manorial account roll series fall off. But from the fact that the demesnes began to be farmed for very long periods in the last quarter of the century, and since the same policy prevailed over the generation before the dissolution of Ramsey Abbey, agrarian conditions would appear to have remained stagnant.[31] The issue of new and higher farms in 1540 was a sign of the new stirring.[32]

[29] The occasional more complete account rolls from this period, like that of Brington, and Bythorn for 1477-8, still show the inability of many tenants to meet the annual charge set for their tenement.

[30] There are many instances of economic recovery throughout the nation at this time: e.g. R. A. L. SMITH, *Canterbury Cathedral Priory*, p. 203; B. A. GOODWIN, *The Abbey of St. Edmondsbury* (Oxford, 1931), Ch. IV.

[31] Ramsey was able to invest in some property in the third quarter of the fifteenth century, as is clear from the payment of £200 for property at Great Stukeley in 1453 (*Add. Ch.* 34004). But the anniversary account left by Abbot Stowe from his purchases in 1468 came to only 13s. *per annum* (*Add. Ch.* 33680, 34646-34651). As noted above there

is nothing in the account rolls to indicate a real recovery in the value of arable over this period. Conditions at the fen properties seem to have been no better. On July 8, 1482, for instance (*Calendar of Patent Rolls*, 1476-85, p. 315), Ramsey obtained a licence to acquire in mortmain, after due inquisition, manors, lands, rents, and services not held in chief, to the value of £20. yearly as a great part of their possessions among the marshes in the counties of Cambridge, Huntingdon, and Norfolk, have been destroyed by water in the past 60 years, and certain grants by letters patent of H. IV, V, and VI, are void by virtue of an act of resumption in the late parliament at Westminster.
It is not clear whether statutory regulations in the early sixteenth century (see A.

This century of depressed manorial revenues affected abbey revenues according to the degree of insulation from agrarian vicissitudes.[33] The cellarer's revenues were largely cash farms, considerably less than the annual profit level expected from these lands, and having first claim on manorial revenues. Accordingly, most of the cellarer's revenues remained stable over the century, except for that small dependence on grange profits (*infra*, Table LXXI). Where the abbey administrator depended more immediately upon the cycles of manorial returns, like the illustration from a rent collector whose debts are tabulated below (Table LXXII), there was a direct reflection of that cycle which has been traced above for the manorial accounts.

SAVINE, *English Monasteries on the Eve of the Dissolution*, Oxford, 1909, p. 120) may have prevented Ramsey from actively re-organizing her manorial revenues.

[32] The 'new' mill farms from nearly every manor had considerably increased according to an account of 1540 (*Add. Ch.* 34657).

[33] There are some good remarks from the administrative records of Westminster Abbey obedientiaries to illustrate how farming was clearly understood to be a protection from revenue losses at this period. See H. F. WESTLAKE, *Westminster Abbey* (London, 1923), I, Ch. 10, and II, Ch. 25.

TABLE LXX

MANORIAL ACCOUNT BALANCES
IN THE FIFTEENTH CENTURY

Year	Cash Liveries	Debts
	Ellington	
1399	£51. 8s. 6d.	3s. 4d.
1407	£41.14s. 4d.	£ 8. 5s. 6d.
1411	£42.12s. 4d.	£ 7. 8s.10d.
1415	£42.19s. 2d.	£ 9.16s. 5d.
1416	£42. 5s. 6d.	£13. 0s. 5d.
1444	£16.11s. 4d.	£55.11s. 6d.
1445	£32.11s. 7d.	£34.10s. 4d.
1450	£20.13s. 4d.	£35. 1s. 2d.
1451	£12. 0s. 0d.	£33. 2s. 2d.
1452	£22. 3s. 4d.	£30. 8s. 0d.
1454	£18. 0s. 0d.	£50.15s. 6d.
1455	£30. 0s. 0d.	£43.10s. 2d.
1468	£20. 0s. 0d.	£ 6. 8s. 9d.
1473	£12.13s. 4d.	£24.14s.10d.
1474	£24.10s. 0d.	£ 6. 6s. 3d.
1477	£29. 3s. 8d.	£ 2.11s. 3d.
1480	£23. 0s. 0d.	0
	Hemmingford Abbots	
1373	£51. 0s. 4d.	£ 8.17s. 5d.
1385	£64.16s. 0d.	£ 1.14s. 1d.
1401 ?	£53.14s. 6d.	£ 1.17s. 0d.
1442	£14. 3s. 4d.	£62.15s. 3d.
1448	£11.10s. 0d.	£71. 2s.10d.
1454	£28.12s. 8d.	£102. 4s. 4d.
1455	£22. 0s. 0d.	£100.13s. 2d.
1468	£22. 0s. 0d.	£10. 3s. 5d.
1472	£43.10s.11d.	£13.10s. 8d.
1473	£43.10s.11d.	£13.10s. 8d.
1474	£23. 0s. 0d.	0
1475	£23.10s. 2d.	0
1477	£30. 9s. 0d.	£10.12s. 1d.

TABLE LXX (Cont'd.)

MANORIAL ACCOUNT BALANCES
IN THE FIFTEENTH CENTURY (Cont'd.)

Year	Cash Liveries	Debts
	Upwood	
1371	£25. 5s. 10d.	£ 7. (?) 9d.
1406	£15. 7s. 4d.	£17. 7s. 7d.
1408	£28.14s. 4d.	£18.12s. 4d.
1446	£17. 6s. 1d.	£54. 6s. 7d.
1447	£14. 5s. 1d.	£53. 6s. 7d.
1448	£15. 3s. 2d.	£53.14s. 1d.
1452	£10.14s. 9d.	£55. 3s. 3d.
1480	£23.11s. 4d.	£24. 3s. 5d.
	Warboys *	
1377	£19.16s. 9d.	0
1378	£19. 1s. 4d.	0
1379	£31.10s. 6d.	£12.18s. 6d.
1393	£27.11s.10d.	£26. 4s. 8d.
1404	£32. 2s. 1d.	£18.15s. 3d.
1413	£ 3.18s. 0d.	£39.14s. 3d.
1442	£39.11s. 1d.	£70. 8s. 8d.
1443	£30.10s. 0d.	£71.10s. 0d.
1445	£49. 3s. 0d.	£58. 2s. 3d.
1446	£50.18s.10d.	£59. 7s. 4d.
1447	£31. 9s. 6d.	£42.16s. 6d.
1448	£27.12s. 4d.	£49.12s. 5d.
1454	£36. 0s. 0d.	£87. 5s. 4d.
1460	£35.11s. 8d.	?
1475	£29. 0s. 0d.	£33.19s. 11d.

* It must be recalled that Warboys and other home manors were still delivering corn rents until the 2nd quarter of the 15th century; therefore cash
liveries were less important at the earlier period, and are not strictly comparable with
the later date.

TABLE LXX (*Cont'd.*)

MANORIAL ACCOUNT BALANCES
IN THE FIFTEENTH CENTURY (*Cont'd.*)

Year	Cash Liveries	Debts
	Bythorn	
1387	£33.10s. 5d.	6s. 9d.
1451	£12.16s. 8d.	£17. 1s. 0d.
	Houghton	
1372	£32. 1s. 0d.	£ 4. 1s. 7d.
1379	£35. 6s. 6d.	£12.11s. 7d.
1383	£37.18s. 8d.	£ 5. 5s. 2d.
1387	£26.16s. 2d.	£ 2. 2s. 7d.
1388	£30.16s.10d.	£ 4. 8s. 1d.
1389	£29 11s.10d.	£10. 9s. 6d.
1393	£22. 9s. 7d.	£22.12s. 6d.
1394	£28.10s. 0d.	£22.13s. 7d.
1396	£26. 6s. 3d.	£29. 5s. 7d.
1399	£23.10s.11d.	£31.16s. 1d.
1404	£54.19s. 2d.	£29.11s. 2d.
1405	£40.19s. 5d.	£55.12s. 9d.
1407	£30. 9s.10d.	£52. 7s. 3d.
1408	£49. 5s. 0d.	£48. 2s. 5d.
1418	?	£53. 9s. 9d.
1446	£43.11s. 0d.	£161.17s. 0d.
1448	£23. 0s. 0d.	£161. 1s. 7d.
1452	£40.17s. 2d.	£170. 0s. 9d.
1453	£28.16s. 8d.	£170.15s. 2d.
1454	£18.13s. 4d.	£175. 1s. 8d.
1455	£18. 6s. 8d.	£196. 0s. 7d.
1456	£22. 0s. 0d.	£261. 0s. 0d.
1462	£34. 5s. 4d.	£255.18s. 2d.
1475	£34. 0s. 0d.	£11. 0s. 3d.

TABLE LXX (*Cont'd.*)

MANORIAL ACCOUNT BALANCES
IN THE FIFTEENTH CENTURY (*Cont'd.*)

Year	Cash Liveries	Debts
Broughton		
1380	£ 9. 7s. 5d.	10s.
1386	£ 8.12s. 8d.	£ 2. 2s. 6d.
1392	£ 7. 6s. 0d.	£ 2. 0s. 0d.
1450	£11.10s. 0d.	£46. 6s. 2d.
1451?	£ 7. 0s. 0d.	£47. 8s. 3d.
1452	£ 3.10s. 4d.	£57. 2s. 9d.
1459	£14.16s. 8d.	£43.19s.11d.
Holywell		
1383	£33. 5s. 4d.	£ 2. 0s. 0d.
1399	£29. 2s. 5d.	£ 4.19s.11d.
1401	£31. 3s. 5d.	£ 1. 0s. 0d.
1402	£29.10s. 0d.	£ 9.14s. 5d.
1404	£11. 8s. 3d.	£ 9.14s. 5d.
1405	£16.14s. 8d.	£18.18s. 5d.
1409	£29.19s. 1d.	£33. 9s. 7d.
1412	£37.17s. 4d.	£47. 4s.10d.
1416	£66. 2s. 7d.	£31.16s. 1d.
1418	£32. 0s. 0d.	£23. 3s. 0d.
1442	£34. 0s. 0d.	£58.13s. 3d.
1450	£41.14s. 8d.	£53.11s.10d.

TABLE LXXI

CELLARER'S RECEIPTS

	1405	1416	1424	1453
Abbot's Treasury.	£46.9s.10d.	£40.4s.8d.	£24.11s.8d.	£37.13s.4d.
Cranfield........	£60.0s.0d.	£60.0s.0d.	£60.0s.0d.	£60.0s.0d.
Barton.........	£48.0s.0d.	£49.0s.0d.	£48.0s.0d.	£48.0s.0d.
Shillington......	£80.0s.0d.	£80.0s.0d.	£80.0s.0d.	£80.0s.0d.
Livestock (tax)..	£49.15s.8d.	£41.7s.11d.	£39.16s.7d.	£38.11s.1d.
Ramsey (rents)..	£15.1s.0d.	£15.6s.3d.	£15.7s.7d.	£19.9s.2d.
Fisheries........	£31.14s.10d.	£27.18s.6d.	£28.3s.6d.	£29.6s.10d.
Ramsey (fines, etc.)	£4.1s.2d.	£7.18s.4d.	£4.10s.10d.	£2.13s.2d.
Over...........	£81.3s.1d.	£76.0s.2d.	£77.1s.3d.	£60.16s.3d.
Niddingworth....	£17.5s.2d.	£16.16s.2d.	£17.14s.7d.	£14.10s.7d.
Granges........	£17.0s.10d.	£11.0s.8d.	£2.2s.0d.	£2.8s.0d.
Hemington......	£15.7s.11d.	£12.9s.3d.	£12.5s.11d.	£12.4s.7d.
Welles..........	£13.4s.11d.	£13.11s.7d.	£13.5s.11d.	£13.12s.11d.
Etc., etc.				
Total.......	£628.7s.2d.	£554.8s.0d.	£553.16s.8d.	£475.8s.4d.

	1489	1518	1521	1537
Abbot's Treasury.	£38.3s.4d.	£23.5s.0d.	£24.17s.8d.	£33.4s.0d.
Cranfield........	£60.0s.0d.	£60.0s.0d.	£60.0s.0d.	£60.0s.0d.
Barton.........	£48.0s.0d.	£48.0s.0d.	£48.0s.0d.	£48.0s.0d.
Shillington......	£80.0s.0d.	£80.0s.0d.	£80.0s.0d.	£80.0s.0d.
Livestock (tax)...	£38.11s.11d.	£38.11s.11d.	£38.11s.11d.	0 ?
Ramsey (rents)..	£18.11s.7d.	£18.3s.8d.	£11.3s.8d.	£18.3s.8d.
Fisheries........	£32.2s.10d.	£33.15s.9d.	£33.15s.9d.	£33.17s.2d.
Ramsey (fines, etc.)	£1.5s.9d.	£4.7s.0d.	£1.10s.2d.	7s.4d.
Over...........	£61.7s.3d.	£60.14s.4d.	£64.10s.2d.	£62.0s.3d.
Niddingworth....	£14.8s.8d.	£14.8s.0d.	£14.7s.11d.	£15.18s.0d.
Granges........	£2.4s.9d.	£2.2s.8d.	£3.0s.4d.	£4.5s.4d.
Hemington......	£11.18s.7d.	£11.18s.7d.	£11.18s.7d.	£11.18s.7d.
Welles.	£14.5s.11d.	£11.0s.0d.	£11.0s.0d.	£12.0s.0d.
Etc., etc.				
Total.......	£467.10s.10d.	£498.17s.1d.	£515.7s.4d.	£425.0s.5d.

TABLE LXXII

A RENT COLLECTOR'S (TREASURER?*) DEFICITS

Year	Amount	Year	Amount
1436	£28. 8s. 11d.	1460	£10. 8s. 10d.
1443	£41. 4s. 7d.	1472	£81. 16s. 10d.
1457	0		

* *Add. Ch.* 34762; there seems to be no reason for calling this a Treasurer's Roll, as has been done in the B.M. catalogue. This collector usually obtained about £70 or £80 from several manors.

The demesne economy manifested through the history of Ramsey Abbey estates from the twelfth to the fifteenth centuries was a system of surprising flexibility. The demesne might be farmed, let in custody to freemen or *villata*, worked by the villeins, or partially parcelled to them. The villein tenements might be held for services, farmed, or let for partially commuted services. As the dependence upon commutation of services and the parcelling of demesne became a more regular feature from the thirteenth century, solvency in the demesne economy turned more and more upon prosperity of the village community. When the villein was not only unable to retain parcels of the demesne but fell into a chronic state of indebtedness for his home tenement from the end of the fourteenth century that neither discounts on rent or relaxations of services could counteract, the demesne economy too was at an end. The old mediæval village lost its function as the traditional economic unit, and indeed disappeared altogether in some regions,[34] when the villein found his greatest opportunity in migration from the ancestral holding or in the concentration of many ancient tenements.

[34] See Maurice BERESFORD, *The Lost Villages of England* (London, 1954), especially Chapters 5 and 6.

APPENDICES

Appendix A

RAMSEY MANORIAL EXTENTS

Except for a few isolated instances, like that extent of Barnwell at the time of the thirteenth-century purchase of this manor by the abbey (*Carts.*, I, pp. 48-54), nearly all the inquisitions made for Ramsey estates seem to have been initiated by maladministration, or at least as a reaction to some tampering with the traditional organization of the demesne economy. The result has been very fortunate in as much as the materials of these documents throw unusual light upon changes in the manorial structure: the large group of extents in the time of Henry II (*Carts.*, III, pp. 241-314), are clearly concerned with changes over the turbulent generation from the time of Henry I; the other concentration of extents, for the mid-thirteenth century (*Carts.*, I, pp. 281-498; II, 3-48), also show concern for the loss of services, in some cases over a period of two generations (*supra*, Ch. IV, Section I). On the other hand, the abbey was much less interested in the immediate administration of its manors in the twelfth century as against the thirteenth, and with the dependence upon unwritten custom stronger at the earlier period, the thirteenth-century extents provide a far greater coverage of detail. The frequent reference made from manorial courts to a 'register' at the abbey for the solution of tenurial problems from the late thirteenth century, may indicate another practical use for such very detailed inquisitions by this period. However, there does not appear to be a basic difference between the structure of the inquisitions for the two centuries concerned. Certainly for these Ramsey materials at least, the twelfth-century extents cannot be considered as evaluations proper, in contradistinction to the thirteenth-century inquisitions.[1] As is suggested in Chapter III, the extent of a manor that is usually farmed may be more concerned with an assessment value of the stock and perhaps of the *opera* and total farm price, but the *valor* proper is a document of quite distinct species, though complementary to the extent. The more elaborate detail upon customary services, etc., in the thirteenth-century extent, seems to be solely the result of the greater need felt for the written precedents at this period; the general structure of the extent or inquisition — the demesne stock, freeholds, money rents, villein tenements and services, etc. — appears with due regularity in both centuries.[2]

The twelfth-century extents can be roughly dated from their references to kings, and abbots. The basic notion of these extents is a comparison between tenurial conditions 'now' (*nunc*), with 'the time of King Henry' (*in tempore Regis Henrici*). It is quite clear that the King Henry in question

---

[1] As was suggested by Reginald Lennard, 'What is a Manorial Extent', *E.H.R.*, XLIV (1929), 256-263.
[2] It is interesting to note that the extents *ca.* 1195, and those of the early thirteenth century, are about half-way between the 1160 and the 1250 extent on this matter of detail.

is Henry I.[3] *Nunc* would seem to be a generation later since the tenants are nearly all sons of those holding at the time of King Henry, although there are rare exceptions who 'hold now as they held in the time of King Henry'. Moreover, since there are some references to grants by Abbot William[4] (1161-79), even though very few in proportion to his ultimate alienations, the inquisitions must have been made at least after 1160. It must be assumed, therefore, that the earlier period of reference was towards the close of Henry's reign, *circa* 1135. As sources of information, the references to tenant, services, and demesne stock for the two periods is sufficiently distinct to consider this as a double set of extents (1135 and 1160) in the tabulations below. Another set of extents, now scattered throughout the series in Volume III of the Cartularies, were made later in the twelfth century, and were not compared with the 'time of King Henry'. Since they certainly came after the time of Abbot William, and probably late in the office of the next abbot from the number of references to his name (Robert Trianel, 1180-1200), they have been dated *ca.*1195. A number of twelfth-century extents are obviously incomplete,[5] and there have been grave errors in transcription by the early fourteenth-century scribe,[6] so that the number of manors for which a comparative enumeration of tenants between the twelfth and thirteenth century can be derived, has been considerably curtailed. For the thirteenth-century extents themselves, the year and even the month and day of the inquisition have usually been given in the preamble. Where a date has had to be derived, the main reason for the suggested period is given in footnotes to the following table. This table provides a list of manors with the dates for which there is some description in the extents.

ca.1135		
Elton		Wistow
Brancaster		Broughton
Ringstead & Holme		Stukeley
Upwood		Hemmingford Abbots

[3] References to the abbacy of Walter (1133-61) are the simplest way to establish this point. See *Carts.*, III, p. 259: Post mortem Henrici Regis, Radulphus de Asekirche accepit ab Abbate Waltero unam virgatam, ...; p. 270: Willelmus autem, de Clara Valle, ex donatione Walteri Abbatis, post mortem Regis præfati, habet unam virgatam, ... These statements are preceded by the usual reference to 'the time of King Henry'. For the Cranfield extent (p. 301), there is also a reference to a present tenant having been given his land by Abbot Reginald (1114-30). Another reference to gifts by Abbot Walter after the death of 'King Henry' may be seen for Ellington on p. 305; and 'King Henry' can be clearly seen to be Henry I from a sequence of references to kings and abbots on pages 289-290.

[4] *Carts.*, III, pp. 258, 262, 272.

[5] Slepe and Barton. These have been classified with the earliest extents on the basis of their general structure. The fragment from Elsworth (pp. 299-300), however, is from the late twelfth century for both Robert *filius* Thurkill and Thomas *filius* Militis were mentioned as holding land in the more complete extent of that time. It has been impossible to date the fragment from Knapwell, on pages 300-301.
Reginald Lennard has brought out how Lawshall was included in the Holywell charter in 'An unidentified Twelfth-Century Customal of Lawshall', *E.H.R.*, LI (1936), 104-109.

ca.1135 (Cont'd.)	
Graveley Houghton & Wyton Holywell Lawshall Cranfield Ellington Shillington & Pegsdon Burwell	Brington Weston Bythorn Wimbotsham Hilgay & Snorehill Girton Slepe

ca.1160	
Elton Brancaster Ringstead & Holme Upwood Wistow Broughton Stukeley Hemmingford Abbots Graveley Houghton & Wyton Holywell Lawshall	Cranfield Ellington Shillington & Pegsdon Burwell Brington Weston Bythorn Wimbotsham Hilgay & Snorehill Girton Barton (?) Slepe

ca.1195	
Hemmingford Grey Knapwell Graveley Elsworth Warboys	Walsoken Ramsey (1201) Welles (1201)

ca.1250	
Slepe — 1251 Woodhurst — 1252 Holywell — 1252 Warboys — 1251 Abbots Ripton — 1252 Broughton — 1252 Upwood — 1252	Wistow — 1252 Elton — ca.1250 ? Hemmingford A. — ca.1250 [7] King's Ripton — ca.1250 ? Ellington — ca.1250 Burwell — ca.1210 [8] Girton — 1239

[7] The history of a tenement given on p. 381 clearly shows that this extent falls in the third generation after the time of Abbot William.

[8] No mention is made in the extent of Burwell of the lawsuit concerning services due from Alexander son of Nicholas (Carts., II, p. 371) in 1228, so that this extent may be after that date. On the other hand, if the Nicholas son of Orgadus holding this land in the twelfth-century extent of Burwell (Carts., III, p. 309. The tenuit of the Rolls Series edition here should clearly be tenet) was the father of Alexander, this extent would be unlikely to be much after 1228, or even as late as 1228. From the fact that grants by Abbot William seem to have been but one generation away (see references to these on pages 26, 27, and 35), we are inclined to date this document around 1210.

ca.1250 (Cont'd.)	
Shillington & Pegsdon — 1255 Cranfield — 1244 Ringstead — 1240 [9] Holme — 1240 Brancaster — 1240 Chatteris — 1240	Stukeley — ca.1250 [10] Barton — ca.1250 Houghton — ca.1250 ? [11] Weston — ca.1230 [12] Brington — ca.1230 Bythorn — ca.1230

ca.1275	
Therfield — 1271 Barnwell	Whiston Doddington

[9] The extents of Ringstead, Holme, Brancaster, and Chatteris, seem to refer back to the time of Abbot Hugh (1216-1231), and were during the lifetime of some persons mentioned in the court rolls of 1239 and 1240 (*Carts.*, I, pp. 411-412, and 423-429), so they were probably related to legal suits of that period.

[10] The descent of a tenement (p. 396), suggests that this extent was in the third generation after the third quarter of the twelfth century.

[11] While a survey of the land of Roger de Nortone, purchased by the abbey in 1307, is appended to this extent, the Houghton inquest is of a much earlier date. The amount of *censum* to be paid per virgate is similar to the amounts indicated for the mid-thirteenth-century extents, and much less than the amounts that were paid in the account rolls from the late thirteenth century; in addition, the number of virgates *ad censum* in this extent is much less than the numbers given in the early fourteenth-century account rolls for this manor.

[12] Richard Porter holds grants from both Abbot Robert Trianel (1180-1200) and Abbot Hugh in this Weston extent (*Carts.*, II, 36 ff.), so the extent is probably within the first quarter of the thirteenth century. Since Bythorn and Brington were always administered with Weston, it is probable that their inquests were of the same time. However, at Brington (II, pp. 42-3), Robert Porter is spoken of as dead. So these extents should likely be dated towards the close of Abbot Hugh's reign, i.e. *circa* 1230.

APPENDIX B

THE DATING OF SOME RAMSEY FOOD RENT DOCUMENTS

As has been discussed in Chapter III of this study, some of the most important materials for the economic history of Ramsey Abbey estates are those records dealing with combined food and money rents, that is, the so-called farms (*feorms*; *firmæ*). While there is abundant information scattered throughout the charters and account rolls for nearly three centuries on the payment of these farms, the only comprehensive document[1] describing both the constitution and the functioning of such farms is not dated in the Ramsey Cartularies. Since this document, or statute as we may call it in keeping with the title of the charter, appears to throw vital light on the difficult problem of administration and valuation of manorial farms at a very early period, it will be useful to present here in some detail the main reasons for the suggested date of its compilation.

The statute is found among a series of twelfth-century documents in the third volume of the Cartularies, apparently the group described by the late thirteenth or early fourteenth-century collector of the Cartularies in his table of contents as alia scripta de maneriis pertinentibus ad officium celerarii, et de statuto facto per Aldewynum Abbatem.[2] No great importance can be given to this placing of the statute, however, since the charters of the Ramsey Cartularies do not follow a regular chronological pattern. As noted in Appendix K below, groups of documents pertaining to one period do tend to be found together, but not infrequently the pattern is broken by a half-hearted effort to collect the records according to some common title. The chief difficulty with the dating of this statue (called here for convenience statute A), lies in the fact that another statute (B) claiming confirmation by Abbot Aldwin and others[3] appears among the charters, but B differs in many significant details from statute A. Since Abbot Aldwin founded the system of conventual food farms, or at least this farm system as known to later chroniclers of the abbey, it would seem simply that statute B was the foundation document and that A must belong to some later arrangement. But upon closer examination of A it becomes clear that this document differs in quantities and valuations of produce from all later mediæval food farm descriptions, and furthermore, the latter all follow the standard set by B. We are left then with the possibility that A must be an earlier statute than B and perhaps the contemporary statute of Abbot Aldwin.

---

[1] *Carts.*, III, pp. 230-234. This charter is entitled, Hoc est statutum victui, et vestitui et ceteris usibus Monachorum Ramesensium, et eorum Servientium, et Hospitum suorum.

[2] *Carts.*, I, p. 21.

[3] *Carts.*, III, p. 163: Hoc est statutum quod statuit piæ memoriæ, dominus Alduuinus, Rameseiæ Abbas, victui monachorum suorum, et hospitibus regulariter supervenientibus; quod post eum Gilbertus Capellanus, ex parte Regis Henrici, confirmavit. Et post eum Johannes Capellanus; post quem Reginaldus Abbas idem concessit. Item post eum Albericus de Veer, ex parte ejusdem Regis Henrici, annuit.

The relation between these documents may now be illustrated in more detail. Statute B gives the amounts to be paid for the farms but does not describe the use or meaning of these, nor does it list the manors under the obligation. But statute B does refer to a preliminary document for this information: In primis statuit, et ad celerarium, pro victu prædictorum monachorum et hospitum, assignavit diversa maneria, quæ vocantur firmae monachorum, *sicut superius plenius annotantur*.[4] Statute A is the only extant Ramsey document fulfilling these requisites of a more complete edition since it prescribes in complete detail the basic notion of the monastic farm, that is the weekly food requisites of the monks, their servants, and guests, how these food quotas are called farms and allocated to certain manors, how the burden is distributed on the specified manors during the year, and how it must be subscribed by a 'farmer'. But when it comes to listing the actual food and money rents, the documents are no longer complementary. Indeed, even the terminology differs:

Statute A		Statute B	
pork	*lardus*	pork	*baconus*
cheese	by the *pensa*	cheese	by the *pondera* and *cumulus*
corn	by the *treia*	corn	by the *sextaria*
honey	by the *sextaria*	honey	by the *bolla*
butter	by the *treia*	butter	by the *discus* and *tina*
tally	*dica*	tally	*talea*
people's bread	*panis villarum*	people's bread	*vokepani*

The editors of the *Medieval Latin Word-List* have been able to find both these sets of terms in the twelfth century, so they do not supply us with sufficient foundation for a chronological distinction. However, we find no further common use of *lardus*, *treia*, *dica* and *panis villarum*, whereas other charters and account rolls from the thirteenth century on use the terms of statute B, especially the *bacon*, *discus*, *talea*, and *vokepanni*.

The similarity between statute B and farm rents for the next two centuries is most accurately revealed by a comparison of actual farm quotas. For the full farm statute B gives the produce amounts, and, except for the corn, their commutable values. In all subsequent records for the thirteenth and fourteenth centuries, the same amounts and values are to be subscribed.[5] Since statute B does refer to confirmations not only for the time of Abbot Aldwin but even after Abbot Reginald, we may conclude that it is a twelfth century

---

[4] *Carts.*, III, p. 163.

[5] That is, such charters as no. DLXXXVI (*Carts.*, III, p. 160-2), *Additional Charter* 39707, or thirteenth and fourteenth-century account rolls, follow the pattern of statute

B. A list of the liveries owed from statutes A and B has been added at the end of this appendix; the items there given for statute B may be compared with Table XXXIX, *supra*.

Statute A	Add. Ch. 39707	Carts., III, p. 160
Full Farms	*Full Farms*	*Full Farms*
Therfield	Burwell	Burwell
Burwell	Elton	Elton
Elton	Elsworth &	Elsworth &
Elsworth	Knapwell	Graveley (one & one-half farms)
Warboys	Warboys	Warboys
Weston, Brington & Bythorn	Weston, Brington & Bythorn	Weston, Brington, & Bythorn
Slepe	Slepe	Slepe & Holywell (one & one-half farms)
Houghton	Houghton	Houghton
	Ripton (Abbots)	Abbots Ripton
One-half Farms	*One-half Farms*	*Three-quarter Farms*
Cranfield	Graveley	Therfield
Upwood	Holywell	Wistow
Graveley		Upwood
Broughton	*Three-quarter Farms*	
Ripton (Abbots)	Therfield	
Holywell	Wistow	
Wistow	Upwood	
Knapwell		
Hemmingford (Abbots)		
Ellington		

FARM PAYMENTS TO THE CELLARER

Statute A[6]		Statute B	
Livery	Value	Livery	Value
12 quarters flour.......or	60s.	12 quarters flour........	
		12 rings *melehouse*......	
2,000 loaves........or	13s. 4d.	2,000 loaves............	
48 *mittæ* malt......or	32s.	50 *mittæ* malt..........	
24 *mittæ* meal......or	24s.	25 *mittæ* meal..........	
24 *prebendæ*.......or	16s.	28 *prebendæ*...........	
10 *pensæ* cheese....or	30s.	10 *pondera* cheese.....or	£ 4.
10 *pensæ* lardi.....or	50s.	10 *pondera* bacon......or	£ 5.
2 *treiæ* beans.......or	16d.	8 *ringa* beans..........	
ad compadium......	£4.	*in denariis*............or	£ 4.
two *sextaria* honey..or	5s. 4d.	8 *bollæ* honey........or	8s.
120 hens...........or	20d.	138 hens...............	
2,000 eggs..........or	4s.	2,300 eggs.............	
14 geese...........or	7d.	14 geese...............	
2 *treiæ* butter......or	6s. 8d.	3 *disci* butter.........or	6d.
fresh cheese........or	12d.	fresh cheese...........or	12s.
10 best *frescings*....or	9s.	20 *frescings*..........or	66s. 8d.
		2 *tina* butter..........	
14 lambs...........or	14d.	15 lambs.............or	4s. 10d.
		½ carcass............or	2s.
		1,000 eels............or	6s. 8d.
		4 *verveces*..........or	6s. 8d.
		in bracino, etc........	8d.
		in sartino, etc.........	
firmarius.........	4s. 11d.	1 acre *ad mandatum*....	10d.
Total (value).......	£17.	Total (estimated value).....*ca.*	£37. 15s. 6d.

document probably re-issued after the troubled adjustments over the middle of the century, and that this quota was to remain for over two centuries.

Perhaps the most important confirmation of this relation can be gained from a list of the manors owing farms to the cellarer. Statute B does not list the manors, nor mention any subdivision of farms except the 'full farm'. But for all other charters on the subject the manors owing food farms and their method of subdivision differs from statute A (see the above table, page 311).

The livery from Holywell, Graveley, or Knapwell, might be sent with one or another of several full farms, but as the second and third columns above illustrate, all the records except statute A show the same organization both as to the manors and the quota required. Various thirteenth and fourteenth-century inquisitions listing the manors 'of the convent' against those 'pertaining to the abbot' provide ample corroboration of the fact that the arrangement of statute A stands outside this period.

It remains to suggest the date of statute A. This document may be immediately ruled out as a mediæval arrangement later than B, that is, subsequent to the re-organization after the Black Death. As noted in Chapter IX, in this re-organization the old farm system was completely changed when the food rents were compounded for large money rents, and this change was to remain until the Dissolution. Statute A must be before B therefore, and since it refers to no earlier confirmations and is definitive in its description, it would appear to be the original document of Abbot Aldwin. Several factors corroborate this dating. For example, we know from charters of the time of Abbot Reginald that Cranfield and Ellington, which were never to appear again as conventual food farms, owed food rents to the monks at this early period. As noted in Chapter III, the commutation values for produce in statute A are much below such values for the late twelfth century and there-after. Furthermore, statute A employs the generic term *monachorum* when referring to the recipients of the food rents, rather than the more precise *conventus* that was always employed after the division between convent and abbot had been fully realized. Statute B referred to the *firmæ monachorum* when mention was made of Abbot Aldwin's charter,[7] but the actual payments being made in the time of statute B are called *firmæ conventus* (see the table opposite for the structure of these Statutes).

[6] (*Note for the opposite table.*)
Most of the small items appearing here only under statute B, like the one-half carcass, the 10d. *in sartino*, the acre *ad mandatum*, etc., were also owed under statute A but did not come under the 'farm' payment of £17. The small items were to be payed at special feasts, and have not been itemized clearly under statute A. It might also be noted that the only place, beyond statute A, where I have been able to find the *treia* measure for corn, refers to the time of Abbot Aldwin (*Carts.*, III, p. 289).

[7] *Carts.*, III, p. 165.

APPENDIX C

THE SIZE AND NUMBER OF TWELFTH-CENTURY PLOUGHTEAMS

The twelfth-century extents for Ramsey manors usually listed the numbers of ploughs — the terms *aratrum* or *carruca* being employed indifferently for this designation —, followed by an enumeration of the draught animals used per plough.[1] Sometimes the size and composition of the ploughteam was not given and in such cases these figures have been interpolated from the numbers of ploughs and the gross plough stock data, for the following table. Other horses mentioned among the demesne livestock, such as the *occator* — probably a general purpose animal for harrowing and more speedy service — have not been included in the compilation of this table. It may be remarked that the ploughhorse was given the same value as the ox; and there is evidence only at Houghton and Wyton for a reduction in the size of the team from greater use of the horse, in the later extents.

Manor	Number of Ploughs	Composition of team		Size of Team	Total Plough Animals	
		Horse	Ox		Horse	Ox
Elton (H.I.)........	5	0	8	8	0	40
Elton (H.II.)......	4	2	6	8	8	24
Broughton.........	4	2	8	10	8	32
Wistow............	3	2	6	8	6	18
Upwood...........	4	?	?	7	6	22
Houghton & Wyton (H.I.)...	3	0	8	8	0	24
Houghton & Wyton (H.II)...	3	?	?	7	6	16
Ellington.........	2	0	8	8	0	16
Weston...........	3	0	8	8	0	24
Bythorn..........	2	0	8	8	0	16
Girton............	2	0	8	8	0	16
Pegsdon..........	2	4	2	6	8	4
Shillington.......	3	0	8	8	0	24
Hemmingford G...	2	2	6	8	4	12
Knapwell........	2	2	6	8	4	12
Graveley.........	2	2	6	8	4	12
Elsworth.........	2	?	?	8	5	12
Warboys.........	3	2	6	8	6	18
Brancaster.......	3	3	4	7	9	12
Ringstead........	3	3	4	7	9	12
Barton...........	2	0	8	8	0	16
Stukeley.........	3	0	10	10	0	30
Lawshall.........	2	2	6	8	4	12
Wimbotsham......	2	2	6	8	4	12
Hilgay...........	2	2	6	8	4	12
Hemmingford A...	3	4	4	8	12	12

[1] E.g. Broughton (*Carts.*, III, p. 273): Hæc sunt instauramenta apud Brochtone. Quatuor aratra, quæque de octo bobus et duobus equis. Et novies viginti oves. Et duæ vaccæ, et duæ vituli, et unus taurus. In this table H. I indicates the time of Henry I, H. II that of Henry II.

Appendix D

THE THIRTEENTH-CENTURY CUSTODY OF A RAMSEY MANOR

William, by the grace of God Abbot of Ramsey, sends greetings to his freemen and villeins of Gravenhurst. Be it known to you that we have instituted Robert de Vandry and Roger Smith, villeins of ours at Gravenhurst, as our bailiff and attorney for the custody of our, and our convent's manor of Gravenhurst, together with the mill, woods, and all its appurtenances. Accordingly, the said Robert and Roger will render their account which pertains to us for the said manor, to the pittancer, whoever he may be, and to our convent. In the first year after the making of this agreement, nine pounds of silver at the Annunciation of the Blessed Virgin in the beginning of our sixteenth year, and at the Nativity of the Blessed Virgin nine pounds. And each year thereafter, as long as the convent shall so desire, at the Annunciation of the Blessed Virgin ten pounds, and at the feast of St. Benedict in the summer ten pounds. And the aforesaid Robert and Roger must keep the manor with its buildings, woods, mill, gardens, walls, etc. . . . for the time of their custody with improvements and as it was received by them. And nothing of the wood etc., etc., nor will they take any of the reliefs etc, etc. And they will disclose their expenses to our pittancer for the above land in the last quarter of the year, whenever he shall happen to come there.

> And in testimony we affix our seal,
> Given at Ramsey on the feast of the Apostles
> Simon and Jude, Anno domini MCCLXXXII.

(Cambridge University Library, Ms. Hh. vi. 11, fol. 66ᵛ)

Appendix E

INDENTED SCHEDULE: ELTON 1350

"This indenture witnesses that on the Sunday next after the feast of St. Michael the Archangel in the twenty-fourth year of the reign of King Edward the third from the Conquest, John Goslyn, reeve of the lord abbot of Rames(ey), retired from his manor in Elton, to whom there succeeded immediately in the same office John Colyn of Elton and by the hands of the said John (Goslyn) there were delivered all the things underwritten, namely in the granary 13 rings of barley and 3 bushels of another year; in the hall 1 basin with ewer, 2 tables with 1 pair of trestles, and four forms and 1 other table; in the buttery 2 casks, 3 vats and 1 *knapne* and 3 small vats, 1 *raser*; in the kitchen 3 brazen pots and 2 pitchers, 3 pans and 1 small pan and 1 pan of iron; in the larder 3 flitches (of bacon) and one quarter of beef; in the dairy 4 *cheafates*, 2 *knopnes*, 1 *panken* and six tables upon which to put cheese; in the house 2 geese and 1 gander and six geese of the first year, 9 ducks and 14 ducks of the first year, 2 cocks and 7 hens and 2 chickens; likewise in the chapel 1 missal and 1 chalice and all the vestments pertaining to a priest celebrating mass; in the stable 4 cart-horses, 5 stots, 11 *cumlyngges* of which 3 are male, and harness for 4 cart-horses and 8 stots, and four cords for binding carts, and 1 half cord, and 2 forks fitted with iron (prongs) for corn and 4 forks fitted with iron (prongs) for dung; 2 spades and 2 flails, 2 baskets and 1 bushel (measure) bound with iron, 2 riddles and 1 *zeve*, and 3 hives of bees and 5 pairs of wheels with iron (tyres) and 1 pair without iron (tyres) and the iron (tyres) from 2 pairs of wheels, and six bodies of carts for corn and six for dung and 4 ox-ploughs and 1 horseplough and 16 oxen and 5 *steres*, 21 cows and 3 heifers, and 6 young bullocks of the second year; in the sheepfold 260 sheep, 80 pigs and 3 sacks and 2 fens and a *inynunynclot*."

(P.R.O. *Sc.* 6, 874, no. 10; this translation has been adopted from S. C. Radcliff, *Elton Manorial Records*, p. 386.)

Appendix F

EXCERPTS FROM THE INQUEST ON THE INTERFERENCE TO FEN DRAINAGE FROM A DAM AT OUTWELL
(*Carts.*, III, pp. 143 ff.)

. . ., dicunt super sacramentum suum, quod unum fossatum quod vocatur Suthdik', incipit apud Cruland', et extendit se usque Tyd' in eodem comitatu. In quo aquæ dulces descendentes de partibus mariscorum, et de partibus superioribus, solebant evacuari usque in mare, per exaltationem crepidinis ejusdem fossati de duobus pedibus tantum.

Et jam, per superonerationem prædicatarum aquarum dulcium descendentium de prædictis mariscis a partibus superioribus, prædictum fossatum, licet exaltatum sit de quindecim pedibus ex utraque parte, vix sufficit ad aquas prædictas evacuandas, et hoc occasione obstructionis prædictæ. Et ante obstructionem prædictam, quotiens opus fuerit ad prædictum fossatum mundari et exaltari, contingeret (quod) quælibet acra terræ partium illarum sufficeret agestari ad unum obolum. Et modo, per superonerationem aquarum prædictarum, quælibet acra agistatur ad quattuor denarios.

Et quod occasione obstructionis prædictæ, quadraginta mille acra moræ et marisci in Holandefen sunt submersæ et superundatæ.

Dicunt etiam, quod abbatia de Cruland' fundata fuit a progenitoribus Regum Angliæ. Ad quam abbatiam duo mille acræ terræ, prati, moræ, et marisci, sunt pertinentes. Similiter ea occasione ita sunt submersæ et superundatæ, quod possessiones Abbatis et conventus abbatiæ illius non sufficiunt ad sustentationem eorumdem, nisi numerus monachorum ejusdem abbatiæ diminuatur.

Et quod dominus Rex, tempore vacationis ejusdem abbatiæ, perdit proficuum, quod ei inde pertinet in hac parte.

Dicunt insuper, quod causa obstructionis prædictæ, terræ, prata, moræ, marisci, et tota pastura de Depingefen, Brunfen, et Spaldyngfen, quæ continent septuaginta mille acras, et similiter moræ et marisci usque ad moras de Kesteven submersæ sunt et superundatæ.

Ita quod domini et communarii omnium villarum circumquaque adjacentium, proficua eis pertinentia, per obstructionem prædictam amittunt.

. . . .

Prætextu cujus obstructionis prata, pasturæ, marisci, turbariæ de Thorneiefen, et similiter prata, pasturæ, marisci, turbariæ, et magna pars terrarum arabilium omnium villarum inter villam de Fendraiton et prædictam villam de Benewik', usque juxta Outwelle in comitatu Cantebrigiæ, et quæ sunt ibidem contigua, videlicet longitudinis triginta leucarum, et amplius, et latitudinis aliquo loco decem leucarum, aliquo loco plus, aliquo loco minus, sunt communiter, quolibet anno, submersa et superundata.

. . . .

Dicunt etiam, quod omnia: terræ, prata, pasturæ, marisci, turbariæ, a villa de Sancto Neoto in comitatu Huntingdoniæ, aquæ quæ vocatur Ouse, contigua et adjacentia, longitudinis triginta leucarum, et latitudinis aliquo loco decem leucarum, aliquo loco plus, aliquo loco minus, usque ad villam de Benewyk', ubi aquæ de Ouse et Nene concurrunt adinvicem,

Et similiter terræ, prata, pasturæ, et marisci omnium villatarum, inter villam de Ayllington in eodem comitatu usque ad quemdam locum qui vocatur Muscote in marisco, videlicet, per spatium sexdecim leucarum, tempore cretinæ aquarum submerguntur et superundantur, eo quod aquæ illæ evacuari non possunt, sicut antiquitus evacuari solebant.

Ita quod domini mariscorum et tenementorum illorum, et similiter communarii in eisdem, proficuum, quod eis inde attinet, penitus inde amittunt,

Ad damnum domini Regis et hominum partium illarum sexcentarum macarum per annum.

Appendix G

A LETTER OF ABBOT SIMON EYE TO THE KING CONCERNING THE POVERTY OF THE ABBEY, SEPTEMBER, 1319 (*Carts.*, II, 201). (The two introductory, and the concluding paragraphs, are not here included).

Ea propter, Serenissime Domine, licet, retroactis temporibus, plus solito per diversas exactiones decimarum, procurationum cardinalium, et aliarum, quæ præsentibus non oportet inserere, cum volentibus eas advertere satis se ostendant, fuerimus, et adhuc simus oppressi, propter quod vivere non valentes de propriis proventibus, multo tempore transacto pecunia caruimus, et caremus in presenti, et ad mutuum aeris alieni accipiendum coacti diversis creditoribus onerose nimis simus obligati, tamen advertentes discrimina guerrarum, quæ patimini nobiscum, quia etsi non in corpore, in anima tamen patientes credebamus de bonis et fructibus, quæ Deus in anno præsenti nobis ministraret, vobis succurrisse de aliqua parte mutui, quod petistis, ipsa bona et fructus venditioni exponendo.

Et ecce, Reverende Domine, occulto quo nescimus Dei judicio faciente, et malitia hominum cooperante, qui antiquos meatus aquarum in partibus nostris obturarunt, prata, pascua, mariscos nostros, *aquæ hoc anno adeo inundaverunt*, quod, ad instar diluvii dudum precata (*sane* peccata) priorum hominum ulciscentis, ita graviter sævit in partibus nostris, ut omnia commoda, quæ ex eis provenire debuerunt, sint consumpta, ac *deinde subita pestilentia in animalia nostra irruente*, in tanta multitudine mortua sunt, quod aer ex fetore cadaverum infectus sit, et de pestilentia hominum postmodum verisimiliter timeatur.

Adeo namque sævit ista pestis in partibus nostris, et adhuc sævire non desistit, *quod unde terras nostras colere possimus non habemus*. Regiam idcirco excellentiam vestram pronis mentibus humiliter exoramus, quatenus, periculis et dispendiis nostris hujusmodi regia benignitate compatientes, ex eo quod pecuniam juxta tenorem brevis vestri ad Scaccarium vestrum non transmittimus, impotentia nos artante, erga nos in aliquo, si placet, non turbetur quia ad omnia subsidia quæ poterit paternitas nostra, et ad ea, quæ nobis grata esse poterunt, parati semper erimus, meliori fortuna nobis arridente, et concedente Domino, ut speramus.

Appendix H

CORRODIES

The complaint of Abbot Simon Eye against the imposition of another corrody in 1331 (*Carts.*, III, p. 102): . . . Excellentiæ vestræ significamus, quod idem pater vester (Ed. II) nobis sæpius scripsit pro diversis clericis et laicis, videlicet — pro domino Arnaldo de Tyle, clerico, qui percepit pensionem decem marcarum, quousque fuisset sibi provisum per nos de beneficio ecclesiastico; pro domino Johanne de Ferybi, percipiente pensionem sex marcarum; pro magistro Henrico de Cantuaria, percipiente annuitatem sex marcarum; pro magistro Johanne de Bramptone, percipiente annuitatem centum solidorum, quos Arnaldus Brocaz prius percepit, ad procurationem domini Petri de Gavestone, et eidem magistro Johanni in vita sua resignavit, qui etiam dominus Petrus multa de oneribus supradictis per multas minas extorsit; similiter pro Roberto de Manifield', qui percepit sustentationem suam, sicut unus de liberis servientibus nostris; vobis constare faciens per eosdem, quod non fuit intentionis suæ, quod post mortem illorum, vel dicti Hervecti, qui magis ad instantiam dominæ nostræ, matris vestræ, sustentationem suam habuit, de aliis succedentibus prædicta domus nostra imposterum fuisset onerata.

Ac vos, Domine Serenissime, non diu est, prædictam domum nostram onerastis de Johanne de Sauterion, qui percipit sustentationem suam ad mandatum vestrum in dicta domo, sicut unus de liberis servientibus nostris; et de David de Gromfeld', quem mandastis nobis ad standum in servitio nostro, quamdiu nobis bene et fideliter deservierit. *Propter quæ onera gravia et importabilia, sæpedicta domus nostra, et celeraria nostra in tantum exhausta est, quod non sufficit ad victum monachorum,* jugiter Deo servientium in eadem, secundum intentionem et ordinationem fundatoris nostri, Comitis Aylywyni. *Immo oportet nos minuere numerum monachorum, et subtrahere elemosinas per dictum fundatorem nostrum ab antiquo statutas;* . . .

APPENDIX I

THE RAMSEY COURT BOOK

The traditional catalogue title of Harleian Manuscript 445 as simply 'a list of *gersumæ*' has been taken from the summary of its contents given on the first folio in a seventeenth-century hand and has probably distracted students of Ramsey history from the more substantial contents of this volume. This manuscript actually provides a set of entries from Ramsey manorial courts which would seem to place the document with that class identified as Court Books.[1] The excerpts pertain to all (29) the most important of the Ramsey manors, and cover the years 1399-1403, 1406-1468. There are 256 folios, written in a legible, contemporary hand.

Unlike the Court Books mentioned by Miss Levett,[2] however, this Ramsey document does not appear to have been constructed from traditional court roll entries. Judicial decisions of a penal character involving fines and the routine business normally grouped under the heading of view of frankpledge have not been recorded. Indeed, this Court Book is almost entirely composed of entries that were never to be found in the court rolls for Ramsey manors unless there was some question of a legal offence connected with the transfer of property. The Ramsey Court Book lists the farm of mills and small parcels of the demesne, and there are a considerable number of merchet and chevage payments. But the vast majority of the entries deal with the movements of villein tenements through the manorial courts. Since this Court Book was not, as Miss Levett has suggested for the Court Books of St. Albans, a substitute for court rolls, some other explanation must be sought for its composition.

While it is quite possible that a few folios have been lost from the beginning of the manuscript, from its present condition it would seem that this collection was begun roughly about the same time as the new policy of letting out numerous demesne parcels and former tenements *ad opera* in the 1390's. The reasons for this are not far to seek. With the sharply intensified movement of villagers from their native manors, the concentration of more holdings in fewer hands, and the disintegration of ancient manorial units, manorial custom and local inquest would no longer be sufficient to record the conditions of tenure. In short, the Ramsey Court Book is a record evoked by that very crucial period of change over the early fifteenth century that has rightly been called by a recent writer 'a no-man's-land of English historical research'.[3]

Since many of the Ramsey manors were sufficiently contiguous to form one large block of land it is hoped that these entries will provide sufficient materials for a social and economic study of that mobile peasantry of the early

---

[1] A. E. LEVETT, *Studies in Manorial History*, (Oxford, 1938), pp. 79-96.
[2] *Ibid.*, pp. 93-4.
[3] Maurice BERESFORD, *The Lost Villages of England* (London, 1954), p. 166.

fifteenth century. There are many difficulties, such as the precise representative nature of the excerpts, and an obvious interchange of tenants with non-Ramsey manors. Furthermore, minute comparisons will have to be made with extant fifteenth century account and court rolls. The present writer is now editing this manuscript as a first step towards the utilization of its contents. A sample page (fol. 5) has been given here in order to illustrate the contents of this volume:

Elton — ad curiam ibidem tentam septimo die augusti anno supradicto Henricus Balle cepit de domino unum messuagium edificatum et dimidiam virgatam terræ servilis que Johannes Purcas prius tenuit, tenenda eidem Henrico in bondagium ad voluntatem domini secundum consuetudinem manerii ad terminum vite sue, reddendo et faciendo domino annuatim omnia servitia et consuetudines debita et consueta in omnibus sicut predictus Johannes Purcas inde facere consuevit. Et dat domino de gersuma II capones.

Holywell — ad curiam ibidem tentam undecimo die augusti anno supradicto Willelmus Prykke cepit de domino molendinum suum ventriticum ibidem, tenendum eidem Willelmo a festo Nativitatis domini ultimo preterito usque ad finem et terminum septem annorum ex tunc proxime sequentium et plenarie completorum, reddendo inde domino annuatim viginti solidos tertio anno termino prime solutionis incipiente ad dictum festum Annunciationis ultimo predicto. Et predictus Willelmus dictum molendinum sustentabit reparabit et manutenebit per totum terminum suum predictum sumptibus suis propriis in omnibus præter grossum meremium habendum de domino cum cariagio et præter sex bordas de estricho quas dominus abbas similiter inveniet pro reparatione et emendatione pistorii dicti molendini.

Ramsey — anno domini Thome Abbatis Ramseye tertio tempore Fratris Thome de Pilton, subcelerarii Ramseye, Johannes Bonde XIIII die mensis Septembris cepit de domino unum messuagium cum pertinentiis in Ramseye jacens in le Wyghte quod Johannes Schywode prius tenuit, tenendum eidem Johanni Bonde a festo Sancti Michælis proxime futuro usque ad finem et terminum quadraginta annorum ex tunc proxime sequentium et plenarie completorum, reddendo inde annuatim domino abbati et successoribus suis decem solidos termino Annunciationis et Nativitatis Beate Marie equis portionibus. Et predictus Johannes Bonde omnia edificia et domos super dictum messuagium constructa tam in carpentaria quam in coopertoria ac omnibus aliis necessariis per totum terminum suum predictum sumptibus suis propriis in omnibus præter meremium habendum de domino quotienscumque neccesse fuerit, bene et competenter reparabit sustentabit et manutenebit, etc. Idem Johannes Bonde die et anno supradictis cepit de domino quondam peciam prati dominice vocati Lytilldyke quod Lawrence Mildecombe prius tenuit, tenendam eidem Johanni Bonde ad terminum quadraginta annorum ut supra, reddendo inde domino annuatim tres solidos terminis supradictis. Et non licebit dicto Johanni Bonde tenementum predictum infra terminum suum predictum relinquere nec alicui dimittere sine licentia domini inde petita et optenta.   Et si predictus redditus ad aliquem terminum ut promittitur per VI septimas in parte vel in toto aretatus esse contigerit etc., aut si idem Johannes conventiones supradictas non observaverit etc., quod ex tunc licebit domino abbati et ministris ac attornatis suis omnia tenementa predicta cum omnibus et singulis pertinentiis reintrare reseisire et ut in pristino statu suo retinere sine contradictione aliqualibet.   Et dat domino de gersuma IIs.

Appendix J

THE STRUCTURE OF MANORIAL DEBTS

Holywell

	1406	1409	1412	1416	1418	1449	1451
William Prikke, miller	40s.	60s.	60s.	60s.	60s.		
John Hemington, beadle	41s.	£ 7.16s.10d.	0	0	0		
Men of Broughton, for fen	£ 6.10s.	£ 7. 1s.	£ 7. 1s.	£ 7. 1s.	£ 7. 1s.		
John Hogge, for fen	£ 8. 7s. 5d.	£ 8. 17s. 8d.	£ 3. 5s.	£ 3. 5s.	£ 3. 5s.		
Robert Rochesden, for fen		£ 4. 6s. 8d.	£ 4. 6s. 8d.	£ 4. 6s. 8d.	£ 4. 6s. 8d.		
William Carter, for fen		£ 8. 0s. 1d.	0	0	0		
Roger Edward, beadle			£ 1.13s. 8d.	£ 1.13s. 8d.	£ 1.13s. 8d.		
John Poulter, fen			£11.16s. 9d.	£10. 1s.10d.	0		
John Palmer, beadle			£ 6. 1s. 5d.	£ 6. 0s. 0d.	£ 4. 4s. 0d.		
John Poulter, farmer				£ 3. 0s. 0d.	0		
Fen					£ 1. 6s. 8d.		
William Bright, fen collector (1441)						76s. 9d.	76s. 9d.
John Bright, fen collector (1447)						42s. 5d.	42s. 5d.

John Nicholas, fen collector (1445)	£7 . 3s . 4d.	£7 . 3s . 4d.
John Clarke	15s.	15s. 9d.
Villata subsidy	£5.	£5.
John Edward (11 years at ½ mark)	73s. 4d.	73s. 4d.
John Sandys (chevage at 6d. a year)	2s. 6d.	2s. 6d.
John Censland	£5. 11s. 8d.	71s. 8d.
John Dobberey and William Stoubrugge	10s.	10s.
John Aspelond, beadle formerly	20s.	0
Roger Customers, beadle (this year)	£24.15s. 3d.	£27. 4s. 3d.
Simon Gallyng	3d.	68s. 11d.
John Coppelan		23s. 4d.

Houghton

	1396	1399	1404	1408
Alan Ode, beadle	£7 . 4s. 4d.	£7 . 4s. 4d.	0	0
Robert Nichol, reeve	£5. 16s. 8d.	£5.16s. 8d.	0	0
William Aldelyn, reeve	69s. 8d.	64s. 8d.	64s. 8d.	64s. 8d.
John Andrewson, beadle	£7. 14s. 3d.	£13.10s.	0	0
John Atte Style	12s. 1d.	0	0	0
William Ode, beadle		£2. 0s. 4d.	£1. 0s. 4d.	7s. ½d.
William Ode and Robert Upton			£4. 2s.10d.	
Godfrey Smyth, farmer			£21.13s. 4d.	£25.15s. 2d.

APPENDIX J (*Cont'd.*)

THE STRUCTURE OF MANORIAL DEBTS (*Cont'd.*)

Houghton (*Cont'd.*)

	1408
William Smyth, for mill in 1405 & 1407	26s. 8d.
William Alt	3s. 4d.
John Pope and Robert Roger, beadles	£ 6. 0s. 9d.
John Bethans	9s.
William Smyth	£ 5. 0s.
John Andrew and Peter Andrew, beadles	£ 1. 0s. 10d.
John Catworth (shepherd, losses in 1405)	26s.
John Plumb and John Andrew, beadles (1407)	£ 1. 7s. 2d.
Thomas Styward, for mill	£ 3. 6s. 8d.
Robert Waryn, bailiff	23d.

	1446	1448	1454	1455	1456	1462
William Lowe (mill, 1444)	£22. 4s. 4d.	£22. 4s. 4d.	£22. 4s. 4d.	£22. 4s. 4d.	£22. 4s. 4d.	£22. 4s. 4d.
John Scheplode and John Myles	£25. 6s. 8d.	£25. 6s. 8d.	£14. 0s. 14d.	£14. 0s. 14d.	£14. 0s. 14d.	£14. 0s. 14d.
John Scheplode, collector	£43. 0s. 3d.	£43. 0s. 3d.	£43. 0s. 3d.	£43. 0s. 3d.	£43. 0s. 3d.	£43. 0s. 3d.
Richard Attekyn	33s. 4d.	0	0	0	0	0
William Wythe, beadle	£ 7. 0s. 7d.	£ 6.13s. 4d.	£ 6.13s. 4d.	£ 6.13s. 4d.	£ 6.13s. 4d.	£ 6.13s. 4d.
John Miller, Warboys mill	53s. 4d.	£ 5.	£ 5.	£ 5.	£ 5.	£ 5.
Robert Onty, farmer	£31.17s. 2d.	£28. 4s.11d.	£30.15s.11d.	£34. 2s. 8d.	0	0
John Eliot, chevage	2s.	3s.	0	0	0	0

			1450	1451	1452	1458
Subsidy of *villata*	66s. 8d.	66s. 8d.	0	0	0	0
John Fuller, leet, etc.	72s. 8d.	0	0	0	0	0
Thomas Eliot & Wm. Myles	40s.	40s.	0	0	0	0
John Fuller, collector	£19.	£25. 2s. 4d.	£24.19s. 7d.	£24.19s. 7d.	£24.19s. 7d.	£24.19s. 7d.
dozen small items			same	same	same	same
farm of mill			£12.	£27.19s. 7d.	£43.12s. 6d.	£16.12s. 7d.
beadle's roll			£5.11s. 1d.	£7. 5s. 6d.	£26.13s. 1d.	£24. 0s. 7d.
John Sheplode				£8.11s.10d.	£8.11s.10d.	£8.11s.10d.
Th. Greene and John Brown, farm					£64.12s. 6d.	£64.12s. 6d.
Robert Smyth, farmer of manor						£45.
Broughton						
William Attegate			10s.	13s. 4d.	16s. 8d.	36s. 8d.
Henry Russell			2s.	2s. 8d.	3s. 4d.	7s. 4d.
Richard Birt (farm of 1432)			£10.19s. 5d.	£10.19s. 5d.	£10.19s. 5d.	£10.19s. 5d.
John Bonde, collector (1441)			£8.16s. 8d.	£8.16s. 8d.	£8.16s. 8d.	£8.16s. 8d.
Richard Cabe, collector (1444)			20s. 1d.	20s. 1d.	20s. 1d.	20s. 1d.
Thomas Smyth (leet, etc., 1444)			13s. 4d.	13s. 4d.	13s. 4d.	13s. 4d.
Thomas Russell, former farmer			33s. 4d.	33s. 4d.	33s. 4d.	33s. 4d.

APPENDIX J (Cont'd.)

THE STRUCTURE OF MANORIAL DEBTS (Cont'd.)

Broughton (Cont'd.)

	1450	1451	1452	1458
Thomas Pultor, collector	16s. 6d.	16s. 6d.	£ 9 . 5s.11d.	£ 4.15s. 4d.
Robert Russell, farmer	46s. 9d.	47s. 5d.	47s. 5d.	£ 4.11s. 5d.
William Russell, farmer	36s. 8d.	11s. 9d.	40s. 5d.	£ 4. 0s. 4d.
John Rocton, sales (1449)	40s.	40s.	40s.	0
John Pool, beadle	£13. 8s. 3d.	£17. 7s.16d.	£17. 7s. 9d.	£ 4. 7s. 4d.
redditus		5s. 4d.	0	5s. 4d.
fines				6s. 8d.
rent				7s.

APPENDIX K

A NOTE ON RAMSEY ABBEY DOCUMENTS

The extant twelfth-century documents for Ramsey estates are available for the student in a more satisfactory editorial arrangement than later charters. This is partly due to the fact that the contents of the *Chronicon*, which carries up to about 1160, had been organized in a chronological sequence. Twelfth-century charters in the remaining three volumes of the Rolls Series for Ramsey are found in a half-dozen groups, but they are still better organized than their thirteenth-century counterparts. Perhaps the fourteenth-century compiler of the *Cartularium* depended upon the *Chronicon* for his handling of twelfth-century materials, for from an inventory (found in *Carts.*, I, 63-74) probably made prior to the compilation of the *Cartularium*, there was clearly an inability to identify documents to be dated before the thirteenth century.

This inventory underlined the need for some organized collection of Ramsey charters since it shows that in the early fourteenth-century muniment room the documents were packed into various linen bags (*bagæ*) and baskets (*frælla*) and quite often theological works, account rolls, deeds, and transcriptions from the classics were piled together indiscriminately. The list of charters given on pages 80-112 of volume one in the *Cartularium* tallies fairly closely with the contents of the *Cartularium* itself and was probably employed for its construction. This list also shows clearly the practical reasons for the compilation of charters. The instances where seals are missing or broken are indicated. It is noted (no. 65) that a *protectio* of Henry II is of little value *quia ad tempus*. Charters that have specified some particular privileges, such as the abbot's right to the front of the stalls in St. Ives during the fair (no. 129), have this factor pointed out. A corrody of the time of Abbot Ranulph (no. 207) is noted to be of little value, no doubt owing to the demise of the receiver. An ancient cyrograph about some land in Over (no. 258) is said to be of little value *quia ad terminum vitæ*. About an agreement between the prioress of Harwood and the vicar of Braunfield over meadow at Abingdon there is the remark *nihil ad nos*.

Unfortunately the *Cartularium* was compiled only with a view to this practical objective of preserving property titles. No effort was made to continue the *Chronicon*, and we know surprisingly little about the 'deeds' of important abbots throughout the thirteenth and fourteenth centuries. The editors of the *Chronicon* and *Cartularium* in the Rolls Series were apparently conscious of these gaps in Ramsey history and attempted to fill them by appending biographical details and letters to the *Chronicon* as well as inserting in the *Cartularium* charters from the Patent Rolls concerning the appointment of abbots (III, pp. 189-207), and from Ms. Cotton, Galba E. X. (see III, p. 218, n. 1) twelfth-century extents, food rents, etc. (III, pp. 218-328). Quite possibly mediæval collections other than the *Cartularium* were to serve as histories of the abbey, but the disappearance of some important Ramsey collections in recent years, in particular the register reported at Stow Hall, Norfolk, by the Historical Manuscripts Commission, 3rd Report, has hindered the task of tracing these for the present.

Since a list of Ramsey manuscripts is not readily available in printed catalogues it has been thought advisable to append a list of the main documents employed for the above study. The account rolls are listed in general chronological sequence; the chronological scope of these documents may best be seen in the tables of chapters five and six. It may be added that quotations from Ramsey documents throughout the foregoing study have been for illustrative purpose only, not with the intention of editing these materials. Hence the Rolls Series edition has been followed where possible although the collation of charters, particularly in the *Cartularium*, is far from complete in many instances. It has not seemed necessary to list the printed secondary sources to which reference has been made throughout this study since these have now become established as standard material for the agrarian history of mediæval England.

SOURCES

I

MANUSCRIPT SOURCES

OXFORD, BODLEIAN LIBRARY

    Rawlinson Ms B. 333.
    Western Mss (XV), 3041.

LONDON, BRITISH MUSEUM

    ACCOUNT ROLLS:

        Broughton — *Add. Ch.* 34903, 39669, 39462, 39851-2, 34917, 34798-34832, 39528-39562.

        Upwood   — *Add. Ch.* 34879-34892, 39669, 34851-34878, 34516, 39741-39744, 34747.

        Warboys — *Add. Ch.* 34903-34904, 39669, 39767, 39795, 39889, 39797-39851.

        Wistow   — *Add. Ch.* 34879-34880, 39669, 39736, 34912, 34914, 39895, 39906, 39908-39916.

    ADDITIONAL CHARTERS:

        General   — 33651, 34758, 39707, 34341, 34713, 34709, 34912, 39671-39672, 39736, 34672, 34004, 33680, 34646, 34651, 34657, 39922-39923, 34332, 33653, 34517, 34352-34353, 34643-34644, 34666, 39681, 39709-39717, 39692-39693, 39719-39720, 34722.

        Obedientiary — cellarer: 34710-34711, 39707, 34607-34617, 39683-39689.

                chamberlain: 34638, 34530-34606, 34893.

                others: 34640-34642,   34484-34489,   34732-34757, 34618, 34620-34637, 34658, 34762-34766, 34698-34708, 34731.

    COURT ROLLS:

        Broughton — 34303-34311, 39456-39500, 39754, 34335, 34894, 39597, 34913-34916, 34342, 34768, 34803, 39758, 39759, 34363, 39762, 34899, 34808.

        Upwood   — 34911, 34769, 34798-34836, 34917, 39851, 39852, 34321, 39582, 39854, 34915, 39597.

        Warboys — 39754-39766, 39769-39780, 34335, 39597, 34894-34899, 39850, 34774, 34901, 34342, 34324, 34910, 34777, 34918, 34363, 34919, 34470.

        Wistow   — 39850-39872, 34335, 34911-34928, 34910, 34809-34810, 34804-34806, 34801, 34799, 34342, 34777, 34896, 39755, 39465, 39758, 39760, 39763, 39757, 39562.

OTHER COLLECTIONS: Cottonian Charter XIII, 25.
Cottonian Ms Galba E. X.
Cottonian Ms Vespas. A. XVIII.
Fakynham Ms, Add. Ms 47214.
Harleian Mss 445, 5071.

CAMBRIDGE, UNIVERSITY LIBRARY

Ramsey Ms Hh. vi. 11.
Red Book of Thorney, Add. Mss 3020-3021.
Registrum de Bury, Mm. iv. 19.

LONDON, PUBLIC RECORD OFFICE

ACCOUNT ROLLS (Sc 6):

Abbots Ripton	— 882/5-882/24.
Broughton	— 875/6-875/12.
Ellington	— 875/22-875/28, 876/1-876/30.
Elton	— 874/11-874/27.
Hemmingford	— 876/26-876/30, 877/1-877/14.
Holywell	— 877/15-877/30, 878/1-878/13.
Houghton	— 878/14-878/23, 879/1-879/26, 880/1-880/13.
King's Ripton	— 882/25-882/29.
Lawshall	— 1001/1-1001/17.
Little Stukeley	— 885/8-885/9.
Slepe	— 884/1-884/26, 885/1-885/6.
Therfield	— 872/17-872/20, 873/1-873/2.
Upwood	— 885/11-885/16.
Weston et al.	— 873/6-873/22, 885/19-885/27, 875/5, 875/16-875/21.
General	— 880/14-880/31, 1280/8, 1261/26, 1259/1-1259/9, 1240/2, 1108/27, 1109/1, 874/13.
Rentals and Surveys	— Sc 11/ Rolls 301-328. Sc 12/ Roll 314; Sc 12, 18/26. Sc 2, Port. 179, no. 26; Sc 2, Port. 8, nos. 3A, 51-58.

II

UNPUBLISHED SECONDARY SOURCES

Beveridge Committee, Statistics of Prices and Wages, The Institute of Historical Research, London.

Halcrow, E. M., Administration and Agrarian Policy of the Manors of Durham Cathedral Priory, B. Litt. Thesis, Oxford, 1949.

Holmes, G. A., The English Nobility in the Reign of Edward III, Ph. D. Dissertation, Cambridge, 1952.

Thirsk, Dr. Joan, Lincolnshire Farming Regions.

NOTE : Since this book has gone to press, the study of Mr. Holmes has been published under the title *The Estates of the Higher Nobility in Fourteenth-Century England* ; that of Dr. Thirsk under the title *English Peasant Farming*.

INDEX